D1187721

THE FAMILY IDIOT

Volume Four

Translated by Carol Cosman

Jean-Paul Sartre

THE FAMILY IDIOT
Gustave Flaubert

1821–1857

The University of Chicago Press • Chicago and London

Originally published in Paris as part three, books one and two, of *L'Idiot de la famille: Gustave Flaubert de 1821 à 1857,* © Editions Gallimard, 1971.

11605839

Learning Resources
Centre

The University of Chicago Press, Chicago 60637
The University of Chicago Press, Ltd., London

© 1991 by The University of Chicago
All rights reserved. Published 1991
Printed in the United States of America
00 99 98 97 96 95 94 93 92 91 5 4 3 2 1

Library of Congress Cataloging in Publication Data

Sartre, Jean Paul, 1905–80
  The family idiot.

  Translation of: L'Idiot de la famille.
  Includes bibliographical references.
  1. Flaubert, Gustave, 1821–1880.   2. Novelists,
French—19th century—Biography.   I. Title.
PQ2247.S313   843'.8[B]   81-1694
ISBN 0-226-73509-5 (v. 1)   AACR2
      0-226-73510-9 (v. 2)
      0-226-73516-8 (v. 3)
      0-226-73518-4 (v. 4)

CONTENTS

TRANSLATOR'S NOTE

I would like to give special thanks to James R. Lawler for his help in preparing this volume for publication.

CAROL COSMAN

Elbehnon, or the Last Spiral

BOOK ONE

The "Fall" Seen as the Immediate, Negative,
and Tactical Response to an Emergency

Publisher's Note
In the title of part three, the Gallimard edition uniformly shows the spelling "Elbenhon," which appears to be a misspelling of "Elbehnon," the name given by Flaubert's companion Knight of Nothingness, Stéphane Mallarmé, in the subtitle of his strange metaphysical prose-poem of 1869, "Igitur ou la Folie d'Elbehnon." Several etymologies, none conclusive, have been proposed for this name, which Mallarmé invented in order to evoke a derealized region of the mind. In this translation, we have chosen to use Mallarmé's spelling.

The Event

One evening in January 1844, Achille and Gustave were returning from Deauville, where they had been to see the site of the new country house. It was pitch dark; Gustave was driving the cabriolet himself. Suddenly, in the vicinity of Pont-l'Evêque, as a wagon passed to the right of the carriage, Gustave dropped the reins and fell at his brother's feet as if struck by lightning. Seeing him motionless as a corpse, Achille thought he was dead or dying. In the distance, the lights of a house were visible. The elder son carried his brother to the house and gave him emergency treatment. Gustave remained for a few minutes in this cataleptic state; he had, however, retained full consciousness. When he opened his eyes, he may have had convulsions, but we have no firm evidence. In any case, his brother took him to Rouen that same night.

Before going further, we must determine the *date* of this attack. In a letter from Caroline written *17 January 1844* and addressed to rue de l'Est, we read: "Your letter reached us only at five last evening and we were afraid that you had been ill, so if we had not received news of you, you might well have had a visit from someone from the family." Since the Flauberts were worried on the 17th, Gustave must have departed at least three days before, hence, close to the date he had set in December. On the other hand, he writes to Ernest toward the end of January or the beginning of February: "I nearly popped off in the hands of my family (where I had gone to spend two or three days recovering from the awful scenes I had witnessed at Hamard's)."

Most commentators consider that the letter to Chevalier alludes to the *first* crisis, that is, to the one at Pont-l'Evêque. According to this supposition, Gustave would have left for Paris, nervous but unscathed, around 15 January. At Caroline's entreaty, he would have

3

paid a visit to Hamard, who had just lost his mother, *after* 17 January.[1] Shaken by the "awful scenes," he would have returned to his family around the 20th to calm down a little before getting back to his studies.

The incident at Pont-l'Evêque would have happened during the two days that followed his arrival at Rouen, since he writes that he had "come to spend *two or three days*." We could then safely locate the event between 20 and 25 of January—closer to the 20th if Gustave left Paris without warning, in a sort of retreat; closer to the 25th if he had first wanted to inform his parents—by a note which is now lost.[2]

This commonly accepted thesis is countered by Jean Bruneau, who contends that the crisis of Pont-l'Evêque had taken place *before* the 15th, during Flaubert's first visit to Rouen. It "could not have inordinately worried the two doctors Flaubert," since they allowed him to leave again for Paris. The attack that felled him, which in his letter to Ernest he calls "a miniature apoplexy," would thus be a *second* crisis, more serious than the first, and would probably have occurred in the town itself, perhaps at the Hôtel-Dieu. In other words, the letter to Chevalier describing his "congestion" and that of 2 September '53 in which he recounts to Louise his accident at Pont-l'Evêque would not concern the same event. We would have to accept the following chronology: during the New Year's vacation, a first "apoplexy"; then, from around the 15th to the 20th, Paris; after that, between the 20th and the 25th—approximately—a second attack, of which we know only what Flaubert tells Ernest, that is, almost nothing: indeed, he mentions neither the circumstances, nor the moment, nor the place, nor the singular form of this new accident.

That Gustave *discovered* his illness at Pont-l'Evêque when he suffered the first seizures, no one doubts. The question—an important one, as we shall see—is to determine whether this discovery took place *before* his return to Paris or *during* his second visit to Rouen. We lack precise information on this point. However, unless Bruneau has evidence that he did not provide in his book, his hypothesis of *two* crises seems inadequately supported.

What argues in its favor is that Flaubert "had an epileptic fit" when returning from Deauville, where he had gone with Achille to examine the work the chief surgeon was having done on the recently acquired

1. Caroline's letter informs us that at this date, Madame Hamard lay dying.

2. This would not be the only one. For example, the letter that Caroline says she received on the 17th at five o'clock in the evening—which might allow a better understanding of Gustave's mental state at this date—has been lost or destroyed.

land. Wouldn't Gustave have wanted to see this "country house," which "was preventing" him "from working," and to see it *right away*? He arrives on New Year's Day. What is the family discussing? The country house. That is enough for him to fix a date with Achille: they will go to inspect the work in three days, or at latest by the end of the week. Therefore, according to Bruneau, probability requires that this unfortunate journey should take place in the first half of January, and as near as possible to New Year's Day. Caroline's letter alone would suggest it; it betrays the family's anxiety: "If you were not to go . . ." This is not her usual way: obviously something has happened. Having searched carefully, I see nothing else to support this conjecture except perhaps the fact that Gustave in '52, recounting the first accident, mentions simply "the house where my brother cared for me"; whereas in the letter of '44 to Ernest he writes that he was given three simultaneous bleedings.

What are we to make of these hypotheses? That they have very little foundation. We know that, on 20 December, Flaubert was delighting in the thought of the country house that his father was going to have built. Let us note in passing that in the two letters where he speaks of it he does not even say that he wishes to see the work in progress. Had it even begun? On 20 December, it seems they were still discussing the architect's plans. There is no evidence that Gustave wanted to go to Deauville, or that there was anything to see there. There is no evidence, either, that he did not go there twice: first before the 15th, and again on his return from Paris. It could even be that around the 20th, Achille-Cléophas, worried by his son's extreme nervousness, had the idea that a journey by cabriolet followed by a brief visit to the seashore would help calm him down. Thus, the attack could very well have taken place after the 15th, in the course of either a first or a second return from Deauville to Rouen.

There remains Caroline's anxiety. But no one doubts that during the New Year's vacation Flaubert appeared tormented, or that certain troubles of previous years recurred during his period at home. Besides, the postscript is curious: "Papa read your letter and said nothing to me about your arm, but here is my prescription: rest and grease." Flaubert was complaining of an arm: had he bruised a muscle? His father takes the letter from Caroline's hands, reads it in silence, and gives it back without a word; so the problem Gustave mentioned was a minor one. In any case, this is not the attitude of a doctor who feared the return of a "miniature apoplexy." Besides, is it conceivable that the two doctors Flaubert would have allowed

Gustave to return if Achille had "thought for ten minutes that he was dead"? Maxime tells us that Achille, at Pont-l-Evêque,[3] "hoped, though he didn't really believe it, that the crisis would not be repeated," and that the father "was in despair." Certainly he is a doubtful witness and begins by mistaking the date and the place. But he had seen Flaubert during the winter of '44 and took this information from him. If the two doctors had allowed him to depart after the attack, Gustave's resentment would have prompted him to point out this huge professional error to Maxime, who would have taken pleasure in reporting it to us: Du Camp's testimony, in fact, aims at denigrating Achille-Cléophas by presenting him as a disciple of Broussais, "who doesn't know how to do anything but bleed people."

And then, if Gustave *had already* suffered his crisis by 17 January, his father's diagnosis would already have been made: cerebral congestion. In this case, the family's anxiety—as it becomes apparent through Caroline's letter—seems rather feeble: if he was in danger of a relapse, if to survive he urgently needed bleeding, it would not have sufficed to send someone to Paris; they should not have let him out of their sight. The words "we were afraid that you had been ill . . . , you might well have had a visit from someone from the family" are justified only in a case of *moderate urgency*. If Flaubert was really subject to bouts of apoplexy, this "someone from the family," at the end of a long journey, was in serious danger of finding a decomposing corpse at rue de l'Est. The sentence becomes clear, on the other hand, if we suppose that Gustave left his family without notable incident but in an alarming mental state. When he arrives at the Hôtel-Dieu, he has just spent a day at Vernon with the Schlésinger family; he is certainly relaxed, happy. But the next day, a change of scene: in Paris, Rouen was hope, happy expectation, escape; now the expectation remains but offers up its true meaning: it is the Parisian prison that he awaits, the dreadful repetition of the already done, the already seen. He wouldn't dream of resisting, but in the inflexible temporalization that leads him toward a future so near and so detested he sees the symbol of his entire life, drawn by that other-future, the *profession*. From one day to the next he grows more nervous, more irritable; he is sometimes depressed, sometimes overexcited, always anxious. We shall say that the disorders are nonsignifying because they are symptomatic of neither an identifiable illness, nor an enterprise, nor a hidden intention: they simply indicate that Flaubert lives with increasing exaspera-

---

3. He writes "Pont-Audemer."

tion a contradiction that can be neither borne nor transcended. If these disorders expressed anything, it would be the structural disarray of an unhappy young man who does not know what to do, who doesn't even take it into his head to devise a solution, who is at once convinced of the fate that awaits him and unable to believe in it; in sum, the disorders present themselves exactly for what they are: meaningless agitations that take the place of an impossible and even inconceivable behavior in a tormenting but unrealizable situation. Overexcitement feeds on itself: he sleeps badly, no doubt, scarcely eats, drinks too much. He flies into a rage over nothing. Maxime claimed that these disturbances were a consequence of his illness—rather quickly assimilated to epilepsy. "At the least incident disturbing the extreme quiet of his existence, he would go off his head. I have seen him shouting and running around his apartment because he couldn't find his penknife." But we have enough familiarity with his youthful works and the correspondence to know that these disorders long preceded the illness: Gustave's impulse to shout, to bellow, to smash everything, his sudden desire to throw himself on passersby and massacre them did not begin just yesterday. It seems certain that these "itchings"—as he himself calls them—or these panics probably grew in frequency and intensity at the beginning of January, to the point that the family finally took notice. For Achille-Cléophas, the tremors have *one* very precise meaning: they remind him of the "illness" which, from '39 to '42, compelled him to keep Gustave near him. Isn't his son cured, then? He lets him depart, nonetheless, but in this hypothesis his behavior is perfectly comprehensible; his paternal obstinacy aside, he does not want to "settle" his son into his illness by taking its vague symptoms too seriously: nothing could be worse for Gustave, he thinks, than to be authorized to interrupt his studies and once more sequester himself in his room. The father promises himself to watch over his son from a distance; after all, isn't Dr. Cloquet keeping an eye on him? For the moment, the paterfamilias intends to make no change of plans. Gustave must have left in a state of extreme despondency; for this reason his mother and sister are worried by his silence; and if it had lasted, one of them would have come to settle in at rue de l'Est; this is the meaning of "someone from the family." A woman to watch over him, to look after his needs while awaiting the father's decisions, and, *especially*, to "boost his morale." What the Flauberts dread, on 17 January, is not the return of a definite attack but the physical effects of solitude and anguish.

In the letter to Ernest of January-February 1844, we find a confirmation of our conjectures. This time *an* attack has taken place, and he says so. Is it the first? The second? What is certain is that the description he gives of it can be applied precisely to the attack at Pont-l'Evêque. For ten minutes Achille thought I was dead, he would write in '52; and in '44: "I almost popped off in the hands of my family." Then I was bled, he tells Louise. And to Ernest he speaks of a triple bleeding. In both letters he says that he "opened his eyes again." Both mention the bad case of nerves that follow the "resurrection," etc. It is not conclusive, of course, that both letters are describing the same attack; the first attacks, in any case, must have closely resembled each other. But if the accident he reports to Chevalier is not the first, why doesn't he tell him that an earlier one preceded it? To be sure, he is not always sincere with his old friend. But what need does he have to conceal this particular truth from Ernest? Subsequently, between February and June, he readily speaks to him of his attacks, in the plural: "My last major attack," etc. Why not mention the original one? The lie would not jibe with a certain attitude Gustave took toward his ailment, an attitude we shall discuss shortly; it would also be absurd because unmotivated. Forgetfulness? Negligence? Quite the contrary: although he nowhere says, "This was the first time it happened to me," everything suggests that it was. Gustave is still astonished; he tells of his adventure with the importance of someone who has had a brush with death. But the most significant thing is that he unreservedly adopts his father's diagnosis, although within eight days he will radically challenge it.[4] For him to believe he was the victim of a cerebral congestion, he must have been taken by surprise: this can be explained only by his stupefaction at an unfamiliar event, that is, an event which is unrecognizable, unique. In fact, he will very quickly understand, as we shall soon see. And if by the end of January he had undergone *two* experiences of the same kind, separated by an interval of a fortnight, if before the second attack he had been able to spend two weeks thinking about the first and doing some soul-searching, we can be certain that he would have seen the second in the light of the first and interpreted it quite otherwise.

To conclude: although firm proof remains impossible for lack of documentation, the strongest probabilities are that one evening at Pont-l'Evêque, between 20 and 25 January, Gustave fell victim to an affliction he had never before experienced. This shall be our working

4. 9 February 1844, to the same Ernest: "[I am following] a stupid regimen." We shall return to this point.

hypothesis. If the attack at Pont-l'Evêque had indeed taken place *before* 15 January, and if the two doctors Flaubert had treated it lightly, they would have found themselves in contradiction with the patient himself. For them, in effect, the second manifestation of illness would have been decisive. But for Gustave, the only one that counted was the first, which he still regarded ten years later as the chief event of his life. It was at Pont-l'Evêque, according to him, that his youth was "concluded," it was there that one man died and another was born. In the "attacks" that followed he never saw anything but weakened repetitions of this archetypal fulguration. Is such a misunderstanding likely? Is it believable that Achille-Cléophas regarded merely as a negligible incident what his son experienced as the "fatal moment" determining an entire existence? Of course, the good surgeon hardly knew his son. But in this case it was not a question of fathoming a heart: somatic disorders were manifest, and, for Gustave to have kept this terrifying memory of it, their intensity must have been extreme: he fell down, he says, in floods of fire, as if struck by lightning. To the credit of Achille and Achille-Cléophas, we refuse to believe that they could have been mistaken. For if there were *two* accidents—the first at Pont-l'Evêque before the 15th, the second after the 20th—and if they were similar, the *repetition* would most certainly have prompted them to change their diagnosis. It was after the attack at Pont-l-Evêque that they were able to settle on cerebral congestion. But a "miniature apoplexy" does not repeat itself after eight or ten days without being fatal. If the attack recurs, and if the patient survives it, other interpretations must be considered. This is precisely what Achille-Cléophas did in February: before the cyclical return of the problems, he abandoned apoplexies and congestions for the diagnosis of a "nervous illness" and, perhaps more precisely, epilepsy. He must be given credit for this correct aboutface: since it was made between the end of January and the beginning of February, he would have been capable of making it two weeks earlier. In short, it was perfectly excusable, if the first appearance of illness is situated around the 20th or the 25th, to reach the conclusion of congestion, and then, with its recurrence, of a nervous disorder; on the other hand, if the accident at Pont-l'Evêque had taken place before the 15th, it would have been absurd for him to begin by diagnosing a nervous illness and later, when it recurred, to decide that it was a cerebral congestion. And that is precisely what we cannot accuse Achille-Cléophas of doing: one more reason for situating at Pont-l'Evêque Gustave's first pathological experience and for dating it at the end of January 1844.

Toward the middle of the month, then, the young man once more finds himself in his Paris apartment, deeply shaken but still unscathed. For the neurosis to become structured, he needed to discover, during the trajectory of the return, the true meaning of passive activity: he does what repels him because he cannot find in himself the will not to do so. No sooner does he return to Paris than his despondence is transformed into a stupor: he *should not* be there, it is absurd since he cannot bear being there; and yet he is there; he came *willingly*, so he *must* be there. No contingency here: the necessary is indeed the impossible—and the reverse is also true. Merely being present between these walls seems at once an objective truth and a nightmare. The denial is total but passive, and conscious of being so; obedience—passive also but subsumed by the appearance of activity—seems convincing to him, like an underlying determination of his life: this is what will determine his future. Thus posed, the contradiction can find a precise solution within him: his passivity must be charged with depriving him of the means to obey. This scheme is obscurely linked to this temptation to collapse, which will give that abstract, rigorous form its content. Nothing is said, however, nothing is known; and yet nothing is hidden, no choice is made: it is a matter of setting up an arrangement that may facilitate a future choice. At the heart of clear consciousness, by contrast, is resentment on the one hand (he did not find the strength to write immediately to his family that he had arrived—*as if* he wanted to enjoy their anxiety and prolong it awhile, *as if* he wanted to compel them to say to themselves: we were wrong to let him go),[5] and, on the other hand, a passionate desire suddenly to find himself at the Hôtel-Dieu again, in his room, and to stay there forever. But this desire is not only disputed by rancor; it can end only in dream: it poses itself as unrealizable since there is no conceivable means of satisfying it. Gustave said so in his letter of 20 December, and he certainly said the same thing to his father: on 15 January he will start preparing for his February exam. This is what was repeated at their farewells: "Good-bye, see you soon, we shall expect you on 1 March." The young man knows he will have no excuse to renege on his commitments. But of course—illness. Yet he is not ill, just desperate. Simulation would be revolt and would testify to a cynicism of which this inveterate boaster of vice is quite incapable.

---

5. But his submission prevents him from making the pleasure last: after one day or, at the most, two, he sends a note to Caroline.

Besides, as he knows from experience, it would be merely an expedient. For those few days, between the four walls of his room in Paris, Gustave felt as Baudelaire would feel later, "brushed by the wing of imbecility": the inconceivable realizes and imposes itself but can be neither lived nor thought; one can only fall into the daze or escape into the imaginary. He does not touch his law books: this time he does not even find the strength to push obedience to the point of active complicity. He waits—for *nothing;* he vegetates, oversensitive, a stranger to himself, in the midst of a crisis of depersonalization.

This was the moment Caroline chose to advise him to pay a visit to Hamard: "The news of Madame Hamard's illness made me sorry for her son; in less than two years he will have lost everything he loved, poor Hamard; go see him, for he likes you and has often spoken to me about you."[6] The tone is new; a few years earlier, Gustave, Hamard's friend and Caroline's brother, was their only link. Now it is Caroline who acts as intermediary, informing Flaubert of Hamard's feelings and dictating how he should behave toward his comrade. From the beginning of June '43, Hamard, who shuttles between Rouen and Paris, is charged with transmitting Caroline's letters to Gustave. He sees the girl frequently and regularly. It is true, they will not announce their engagement until November '44, but in this new year there is already something between them that is more than friendship. Gustave, who will feign astonishment when he announces the "big news" to Ernest the following autumn, does not know, perhaps, precisely that they are in love: he cannot be unaware that they now have a personal relationship and that he has no place in it. We are already familiar with his jealous rages, and, as I have shown above in my analysis of one of his letters, he will make a clean break with his sister—without telling her—the day the two young people make known their engagement. It is therefore perfectly clear from this time that he harbored a vigorous personal resentment of Caroline. Of course, he could not help being jealous, but there is more: the little sister was his vassal; she lived in his dependence and was the object—he thought—of his inexhaustible generosity. Here another man unexpectedly turns up: there is no question of sharing her; Gustave must be everything to her, or she must be nothing to him. A vassal's betrayal is more criminal than that of a friend: it is the denial of *homage.* And above all it casts doubt on the Lord: he perceives that his

6. Letter of 17 January 1844.

11

"man" was his objective truth; without fealty, no longer Lord, just a poor wretch. Vassal to his father and to Alfred, rejected by both, Gustave was sovereign only to Caroline. By breaking her bonds, she leaves him *destitute* and causes him to fall back into a dark, hopeless vassalage; she ravages his memory by sullying the remembrance of their common childhood; beside her he was *himself,* a subject, an agent of history: she has returned him to his other-being, to his relative-being. In short, in this moment of his life when the failures are accumulating, he experiences his sister's love affair as a new failure, more profound, perhaps, than all the others. We shall have no difficulty imagining his mood when he reads the letter in which she enjoins him, kindly but peremptorily, to go to her lover's home. He goes, nonetheless. Out of a masochism born of resentment; it is as if he were saying to his sister: I shall go, nervous and morose as I am; I shall do what you wish; but you will see what a state this visit will put me in.

He has another motive as well. According to him, Hamard is "pitifully stupid." Once, however, when he was telling Gustave about his brother's death throes, he was fascinating. As we have seen, Flaubert observed then: "I didn't like it at all; that man humiliated me. He was full of feeling and I was empty . . . I recall how I hated myself and thought myself loathsome for a moment." This time it will be even worse. No sooner emerged from his first bereavement, Hamard sees his mother die and is about to find himself utterly alone. We know the effect these repeated shocks would produce in this unfortunate man: after Caroline's death, he went quite mad. Beginning in '44, at the bedside of his dying or already dead mother, suffering makes him fall into mental disarray. Gustave suspects it: half-mad himself, he goes to the home of a madman; unfeeling and wretched, he goes to contemplate a despair incommensurate with his own. Not that Hamard's unhappiness is deeper: it is *other.* Gustave's, most of the time, is lived intensely and for short periods: he calls it *ennui,* and at times must *summon* it by gestures in order to establish it inside him. The *other* has entered Hamard by breaking in: it imposes itself and sponges on him. Here again, Flaubert thinks, is the dichotomy of empty and full. In fact, he is mistaken. Mourning is an unlivable emptiness, and yet it must be lived, no matter how; it is a discourse that cannot cease to address the other; remaining a dialogue, it experiences itself as monologue. Lacking an answer, in these real moments when the living person, amputated, feels the mutilation internalized, there is some phantom of dark comedy that holds in derision the worst suffering. Then comes mental disarray, prompted by the unrealizable fracture of a reciprocal relation whose reciprocity the entire act of mourning maintains in a vacuum. In order to realize an impossible plenitude, one resorts to the craziest gestures or loses oneself in meaningless convulsions. Flaubert is unaware of all that: empty, and ashamed of being empty, he is about to contemplate a horrible void, which he takes for plentiude. He has understood for himself that our misfortune is to be *lacunary;* he has generalized in vain—he is unaware that this lacuna is characteristic of our conditon and is to be found in all our feelings.[7]

Of course, the reality surpasses his hopes. Hamard is dazed, convulsive; he probably falls upon Gustave and clings to him; he may even be delirious. Flaubert abhors him and finds *himself* abhorrent. He is cold, stiff, exasperated: he doesn't "go along" with it, and yet this appearance of plenitude fascinates him. He would like to establish it inside himself, this beautiful suffering, this opaque block of unhappiness, in order to fill his emptiness at last, to *realize* Hell even as he scorns the man writhing before his eyes. It seems to him, in short—this is what disconcerts him—that Hamard does not deserve his suffering and that he, Gustave, who alone is worthy of it, is condemned not to feel it. At the same time, terror overtakes him: this fascination, already a temptation, may tomorrow be an attempt. He vaguely understands his pithiatism, as we have seen; he is afraid of autosuggestion, of letting himself go in an act of irreparable, fatal violence initiated by envy and self-loathing. Yes, he is transfixed by *his doom:* he wants to die and to survive, to play at once the role of mother and son, because he is sure that he can weep for only one death with that marvelous intensity—his own. He can no longer cut himself off from Hamard; apparently he returns several days in a row to the house of death, for he speaks to Ernest of *some* scenes that took place there. This will not be surprising if we recall that beginning in April '38, he evoked—out of a generalized prudence—the "natural feeling that impels man to become impassioned by what is hideous and

7. It goes without saying that I do not mean to deny the *truth* of such suffering. I am saying only that this biologically *rational* fact, the death of the other, is lived *in irrationality* because it is unrealizable and that, for this reason, all our acts are transformed into gestures. To cite only one example, to carry out the last wishes of a dying man can lead to real and difficult endeavors. But they are derealized from the outset because they are born of the futile decision to keep him alive, to institute him as living by claiming that he is at the source of acts which are in fact born of our personal options. The carrying out is *in principle* incommensurate with the *intention* one claims to realize; the results will be always *other* than what the dead man had foreseen, and we cannot help being aware of it.

13

bitterly grotesque." What is hideous, here, is agony and death; what is grotesque is that despair which has mistaken the sufferer and gives itself undeserved to Hamard, defrauding Gustave. Two words make Flaubert's real feelings manifest: "horrible scenes." He is rarely so pathetic where a death is concerned. These scenes, he says, so shook him that he needed to "recover" from them. Yet the word "horrible" betrays him: it implies a certain blame, a repugnance, which is not contained in "terrible." Hamard's *terrible* suffering *horrifies* Gustave. Precisely because it attracts him, it repels him. He must flee, flee these nightmarish days that he lives now at his friend's and now immured in his own room, trembling with fear. Here he has found the pretext for rejoining his family. But it is already too late. For what he flees is himself, the option that imposes itself on his shattered nerves. In vain: the choice is made. Barely two or three days after the return to Rouen, he will execute the sentence he has passed on himself. So it must *also* be understood that his haste is motivated by a presentiment: if the worst must happen, let it strike in the midst of his family. First of all because the "survival" will be less painful, and second because it will make his family eyewitnesses to the disaster they have provoked. We might say that he both retreats from this disaster and pursues it. Come tonight to Samarkand. This is what gives all its meaning to that sentence in the letter to Ernest: "I almost popped off *in the hands of my family.*"

Before interpreting the attack at Pont-l'Evêque, we must ask what role it played in that curious neurosis from which Gustave was to suffer for nearly ten years. Was it a warning signal, a symptom, the first appearance of an illness that would run its course, intensifying to a *maximum* point, after which it would begin to abate? Would this first disorder, original and definite, be followed by others, equally definite but of a different nature, which cannot be identified with it because, although they might have been the effect and expression of the same morbid entity, they manifested it at different moments in its evolution? In short, was it the initial stage of a complex and unforeseeable development, or did it embody the entire illness in a flash of lightning? Would this illness grow, overwhelming other aspects of his being, or, to the contrary, would it mark time, be lost in repetitions, in replays? Would there be, at least for a few months, a progression of psychopathic inventiveness, or was the neurotic structure completed at Pont-l'Evêque once and for all? In order to answer these questions, it will suffice to examine the subsequent attacks.

14

On those that took place from January to June we have little information: Gustave tells us only that they were numerous at first and subsequently became less frequent. On 7 June he writes to Ernest: "As for your servant, he is doing all right without precisely doing well. Not a day passes without my seeing something now and then like bundles of hair or fireworks passing before my eyes. This lasts for quite a long time. Still, my last big attack was milder than the others." In short, the frequency and intensity are diminishing; several years later, Flaubert will write to Louise that his "attacks" are repeated about every four months.

Maxime was not an eyewitness to the attack at Pont-l'Evêque. But he witnessed several of those which followed, and we have no reason to doubt his testimony.

> He grew very pale . . . This state . . . sometimes went on for several minutes . . . He still hoped it was just a scare . . . Then he walked, he ran toward his bed, lay down, as dismal as if he were lying down alive in a coffin . . . He would cry: "Drop the reins; here comes the wagoner, I hear the bells! Ah! I see the lantern of the inn!" Then he would groan . . . and the convulsion would lift his body . . . a paroxysm in which his whole being would shake, [followed] invariably by a deep sleep and a fatigue that lasted several days.

This description calls forth several comments. First of all, the basic character of these attacks is that they are explicitly constituted as references to the first attack. In a way, they resurrect it. But these stereotypical repetitions of the archetypal event are also weakened reproductions. The attack at Pont-l'Evêque had jumped Gustave like a thief: now the young man has a *warning*. An unutterable malaise and the impression of seeing "fireworks" serve as alarms. He waits, *conscious* of the danger that threatens him, and instead of falling as if struck by lightning he has time to go and lie down on his couch. From this point on, the primal scene is relived *in the imaginary* on the basis of a few indices, always the same, provided by memory. "I see the wagoner, the lights," etc. In a sense, it is *played* and, above all, *spoken:* the psychopathic aggression that Flaubert suffered he reconstitutes here as a *role*. The content is, moreover, debased: Flaubert often spoke of the millions of images and ideas that rushed through his consciousness when he fell at his brother's feet; they were "all the ignited rockets of a fireworks display." This incommunicable richness of perception—illusory but experienced—contrasts with the poverty of discourse, and consequently of thoughts, in the referential attacks. The wagoner's noisy cart, the distant lights, etc., make up the meager bunch of auditory and visual images or, rather, the assortment of *words* that monopolize his consciousness. It is like a conjuring trick: the patient *invokes* and *convokes* the false death that felled him one night. But it doesn't come: Achille believed for ten minutes that he was dead; Maxime doesn't believe it for a moment. Cataleptic immobility is replaced by convulsions; these disordered movements, it seems, are born of the futile quest for a former state and the impossibility of reproducing it. Did the "fireworks" of thoughts light up at that moment in Flaubert's head? It is unlikely. He repeated, of course, that he never lost consciousness on those occasions. But the "catalepsy" at Pont-l'Evêque was favorable to "mentism" [the flight of ideas]. During convulsions, the jerks of the body suffice to occupy the consciousness; it is hard to imagine that they accelerate thought and foster ideas. *Physically* exhausted, the patient falls into a heavy sleep, and this is how it ends until the next time.

These referential attacks occur frequently in certain patients. Janet cites, among others, the case of a young girl who *reproduced* the terrible night she had kept vigil over her dead mother with her dead-drunk father close by. Autonomous systems, constituted *on one occasion*, reappear in progressively weakened form and are finally reduced to a symbolic skeleton, a few stereotypical movements. In Flaubert's case, a single moment seems to have assured the passage from a normal to a pathological state. The morbid creation and the *fiat* (the neurotic consent to the neurosis) are merged into a single moment on a moonless night in January 1844. After that night, the neurosis in Gustave invented nothing more; it seemed out of breath. As a result, no other disorder appended itself to the first ones; the illness did not develop, it had no history, it was maintained in the circular time of repetition: it was an *involution* rather than an evolution. Flaubert feels this; he feels that his illness *consumes him.* In a word, the only moment that counts is that of the archetypal event: in it, the neurosis is chosen, structured, realized; in the depths, a choice has taken place, four years in the making, which has willed itself to be irreversible or, rather, was none other than a consented irreversibility. Afterward, for nearly ten years, disorders will occur that no longer have the same meaning, precisely because their purpose is merely to reproduce the original choice, maintain it across the temporal flow. The convulsive attacks are suffered yet playacted ceremonies intended to commemorate the irreversible, to confirm the patient in his neurotic option. We shall certainly have to explain the meaning of this eternal return. And, in a sense, the original crisis *aims* to reproduce itself symbolically. Be that as it may, the original crisis is what creates the irreversibility and will consequently be the essential subject of our study: we shall attempt to use it in order to illuminate the entire "illness."

Gustave's Diagnosis

Despite Dumesnil's very convincing demonstration, the nature of the problems that began to afflict Flaubert in 1844 are still under discussion: Were they hysterical or was Flaubert an epileptic? Today it is acknowledged that certain forms of epilepsy originate in hysteria. So, to stay closer to the facts, we shall be frankly nominalist. The point is not to search for a concept that subsumes Flaubert's attacks but to ask ourselves whether or not they have *meaning*. The most prevalent thesis—and, curiously, one held by Dumesnil himself, who believed that they were of a hysterical nature—is that they were *accidental*. If that were so, they would originally have been nonsignifying—like a head cold or a purulent pleurisy—and Gustave himself would have given them meaning a posteriori by using these chance misfortunes as the means to reorient his life. In the preceding pages we have tried to establish the opposite thesis: the illness was organized as a function of an original intention; its sudden and terrible structuring at Pont-l'Evêque was not an accidental fact but a necessity *endowed with meaning*. Before establishing this underlying meaning by a detailed examination and interpretation of the circumstances, we should support our assumption by interrogating the principal witness, Flaubert himself. What does he think of his "attack"? How does he see it? How does he endure its "return" in the course of the years and months that follow? Does he see it as something final? Does he understand the archetypal event and the referential attacks as an absurd and mechanical whole merely involving his organism, or as a *comprehensible* totality?

It will be said, perhaps, that the patient, as judge of his own cause, is by definition a false witness, that his discourse must be regarded as one symptom among others and not as a valid interpretation. And this is true in certain cases, but not in Flaubert's. From the beginning of this study, we have understood him from the inside, in complicity

Flaubert did have strange, weary awakenings whose pathological nature was perhaps *thenceforth* manifest to him. But I am especially struck by the movement of his thought: he rummages in the past as if, after the first stupor, he *recognized* the event despite its irreducible novelty. As if astonishment gave way to some kind of fatalistic certainty, as if the "What's happening to me?" were quickly followed by a "This had to happen to me," or, rather, "This has happened to me before." Indeed, the disaster at Pont-l'Evêque would have been neither more acceptable nor more intelligible if he could have proved that obscure, nocturnal disasters had occurred previously. He would merely have pushed back in time the origin of the illness. Isn't this his real concern? But he is mistaken in the object of his search: when he reflects on the archetypal event, it strikes him as being vaguely familiar, and so he wants to find an antecedent to it; but it is not the *repetition* that provokes this recognition; rather, this wholly new present, unexpected as it may be, presents itself mysteriously as a conclusion. "Conclusion" is the word he will soon use to designate the crisis. At the moment of crisis he grasps this characteristic of lived experience, but he does so immediately and without yet possessing the means to name it. He is bewildered: he tries to discover what *preceded* it when his real concern is to determine what *paved the way* for it. The error was inevitable: we have seen him live this path to the abyss without ever making its meaning clearly explicit. But if he says he was "persuaded" that the first disturbances were nocturnal, we must also see the symbolic aspect of this certainty: the darkness here represents the unconscious, the night of nonknowledge; it also refers to the *black night* of January '44. These early attacks, which, because of their lesser intensity, seem to represent the *terminus a quo* of a hidden progression of which the crisis at Pont-l'Evêque was to be the final destination, seemed to Gustave to have been lived without his living them, separated from the self by a dark shadow. Isn't this just how our passive agent, always maneuvering himself as if he were manipulated by Another, behaved toward the *preparation* of the cataclysm? Didn't he live this slow setting in place *from afar,* and in a blindness pierced by flashes of light? And didn't that blindness itself, rather effectively symbolized by sleep, contain a certain consciousness—nonthetic at the least—of itself?

In other words, beginning in February, Gustave is torn by a contradiction he wants to resolve. What is new, for this imaginary young man, is the irreparable *realized,* the *suffered* shift from ruminations and gestures to a real determination of his person which he must live and

21

which forbids any retreat; what is *recognized* is the prophecy of *Novembre*, probably in a new form, in certain instantaneous perceptions and in the "monologue" of July–August '43. The obscurity comes from the fact that Gustave at the time believed he was isolating himself in his imagination: he saw himself—although telling the truth—in the guise of the *fictive* hero of *Novembre*; or else he played the role of the "journalist of Nevers." In short, before measuring the frightening power of his body—his autosuggestibility— he sensed only that these circus tricks had a dreadful counterpart, and that the practice of the unreal was conditioning him in his reality. Yet he pondered his anorexia, he discovered his pithiatism from the time of *Novembre*, he meditated on that vow to collapse that he dreaded making. Be that as it may, everything was ludic then; just as he felt himself slipping toward an appalling conclusion, he seemed to be living a fantasmagoria and could at any moment wake up, pick up his marbles, and go home. Gustave is a man of belief. And belief remains on the border between certainty and the game of faith: it is nourished by itself and thus remains imaginary unless the body undertakes to assume it. Flaubert lived what was also the progressive organization of his fatalities as though it were a range of *possibles*. The lightning flash is the catastrophic appearance of the *real*. Someone was dreaming: I am condemned to death; he awakens in a stupor: he is condemned *for real*, it is the very morning of his execution. Gustave is like this condemned man, with the minor difference that he has the inexpressible feeling that this nightmare is not only the effect of the sentence but also, in part, its cause. If he had not dreamed that he was in prison, he might not have found himself in a real cell. This is the shock: reality takes hold in him, he feels its weight for the first time in his life; belief becomes evidence—and at the same instant he recognizes in it his oriented reveries. In this first moment, however, incapable of comprehending the *finality of the unreal*—precisely because this finality is its singular law—he wants to link the suffered reality of his crisis to anterior realities: the slumbers of July will do well enough. But this very deviation in his inquiry helps put him back on the right track, for what is this unlived archetype, then? A crisis or a dream of crisis? In the absence of any valid proof, there is nothing to distinguish this imagined accident from an imaginary event. In seeking the truth of his past, Flaubert perceives that he has left the domain of certainty based on evidence only to fall back again into the domain of faith.

However that may be, his diagnosis has been made: there is no congestion; it is his nerves that are affected. The letter to Ernest of 7 June, without specifying the illness he is suffering from, mentions nervous symptoms: fireworks in front of his eyes, etc. He speaks of "his last major attack," which would make no sense if he still shared his father's opinion. That same day, to Louis de Cormenin: "As for me, I have my nerves, which leave me little peace." In January '45, in any case, one year after the accident, he is certain of its cause, as he makes clear to Vasse: "The cure is so slow in coming, in these wretched nervous diseases, that it is nearly imperceptible." That he should have this assurance—he says the word in passing, almost nonchalantly, as if Vasse were well informed—the case would have to have been publicly acknowledged. In other words, the paterfamilias must have been convinced in the meantime and changed his diagnosis. It is striking, however, that he had not modified the treatment: in June '44, Gustave still has his seton; the leeches were put on him the day before, he is stuffed with valerian, indigo, castor oil. The prohibitions persist: no wine, coffee, or tobacco. Why treat a neuropath like an apoplectic? It could be said that Flaubert pride compelled Achille-Cléophas to explain his son's deficiencies by an excess of health: "Excess of plethora, too much strength, too much vigor!" he would say.[2] Gustave retorts that he is following a stupid regimen, and we fully grasp what he means. Indeed, Maxime notes that "the extreme bleeding augmented a nervous predominance that was already only too dreadful." This reflection was evidently whispered to him by his friend. Several years later—we shall return to this—Gustave attributes his illness to a constitutional weakness of his nervous system. Maxime tells us that he "never heard him state the true name of his illness. He would say: 'my nervous attacks' and that is all." Maxime is convinced that Gustave is epileptic, knows it, and wants to hide it—or hide it from those around him. But since Du Camp is mistaken, this refusal to *name* a complex process, like all neuroses escaping abstract classification, suggests intelligent prudence and patient determination: Flaubert wants to understand, to probe; if he were to place his disorders under a rubric, he would enter into a conceptualism that would curb his investigations.

We should observe here a curious aspect of Gustave's illness that will allow us to penetrate his "insight" more effectively. Immediately following the crisis at Pont-l'Evêque, he writes that "at the slightest sensation [his] nerves vibrate like the strings of a violin." In short, beyond the attacks themselves, he suffers from a permanent hyper-

---

2. Did he still consider these excessive powers the *forces vitales?*

activity that never leaves him for long. He is "in a rotten state." But what is immediately striking is that he takes care to distinguish his nervousness from his morale: "Morale is good because I don't know what it is to be troubled." On 9 February he insists: "If you are asked how I am doing, say: very badly, he is following a stupid regimen; as for the illness, he doesn't give a damn about it." Maxime claims that he would have said at the time, when he was reading works of neurology: "I am lost." We may well wonder if he is reporting Flaubert's exact words. In the first letter to Ernest, Flaubert declares, "I already have the ailments of old age," and, in the second, "I am a dead man." But these are familiar themes with Gustave: how could he not be old at twenty-two when he has been old from the age of fourteen? And then, of course, he is dead—we shall see that in each of his attacks he claims to die. But the context shows us that the young man's explicit intention is more superficial and less tragic: good food, wine, a pipe are forbidden him, he is a dead man. It is not his body that is killing him, it is the regimen he must follow. And he alludes to his sufferings in a similar fashion: "I have suffered horribly since you saw me";[3] what provoked them was his setback in August, his torments in the autumn of '43, his hypernervousness in the winter of '44, and, above all, his present regimen, which proscribes everything he likes. On 7 June '44 he writes: "pipe deprivation, *horrible suffering* to which the early Christians were not condemned."[4] He complains of his seton as well, of the hand his father scalded, in short, of the care he is given. Of his illness, never. This angry young man has no shadow of anger at the stupid and undeserved accident that just flattened him. Could it be that he sees it as something more and other than a stroke of bad luck? What has become of the shame that was still eating at him in December '43?

He was afraid that some sort of vow was pushing him toward a collapse. And here he is, actually fallen: his nerves have snapped, he must spend long months recuperating. Will he ever be able to catch up with his studies? From February on, he knows that he is abandoning them *sine die, unable* to continue—acknowledging himself to be incapable. He used to say he was *above* the law, he has fallen *below it;* the others—Ernest, Alfred, Maxime, Vasse—are all going to continue their work or their travels while he cloisters himself; there he is, in the fascinating and dreaded position of the journalist of Nevers: he suf-

3. *Correspondance*, 1:149.
4. Ibid.

fers the compassion of his peers and even that of his inferiors. Is he ashamed? Not for a moment. Later, his mother and his niece would think it necessary to throw a veil over his illness. Gustave himself does not think of doing so. Maxime says he "didn't like speaking of it, but in confidence he spoke of it unreservedly." From February '44, he begins to express himself freely in his letters to Ernest, to Vasse, to Louis de Cormenin. Better still, he charges Chevalier with spreading the news: "Present my respects, or rather utter some obscenities for me to my lords Dumont and Conti; if you are asked how I am doing, say: very badly . . . ," and so forth. It would be going too far to say he demands publicity, but in any event he is not afraid of it. He cannot be unaware, in fact, that the Rouen bourgeoisie and his friends in Paris are informed of his adversity, that news of it is being repeated in all the circles he has frequented. Six months earlier, humiliated by a minor failure, he summoned Attila with his prayers to destroy Rouen, Paris, all of France, all the possible witnesses to his mishap. Now, he knows that the second son of the Flauberts is the subject of gossip—that he is regarded as an eccentric character, struck by a suspicious affliction—and he does not seem moved by it. He writes, resigned: "That's life!"; he drinks medicinal orange blossom tea and says with a little smile: "It is inferior to the Sauternes." In the following years he will not depart from this attitude: to Louise, to Bouilhet, he will tell everything, obviously. But after the publication of *Madame Bovary*, he takes a fancy for an unknown correspondent, Mademoiselle Leroyer de Chantepie, and for no apparent reason—unless it is sympathy—he confides in her point blank that he suffered from nervous disorders for ten years. The least we can say is that for the first time in his life he takes things *with simplicity*.

Of course, pride remains; it has merely been displaced. He conceals his irritations from no one but maintains publicly that he is not affected by them: "I do not know what it is to be troubled." He has always cultivated a certain affectation of stoicism, as witness the letter he wrote in January '42 to Dugazon—it was a way of valorizing his passivity. Now he insists on it: I *suffer* the illness but I do not worry about it. How can he boast of this serenity to Ernest, who has at hand all his letters from '39 to '43, full of rages, cries, anguish? It is because he truly is serene. After all, a year later he will say to Alfred, reversing the terms: "I have indeed a deep serenity, but everything troubles me on the surface."[5] Is it possible to have nerves "that vibrate like

5. Late April '45.

25

the strings of a violin" and yet preserve, beneath all the permanent agitations of the body, true tranquillity of soul? Undoubtedly. And Gustave explains himself on the subject two weeks later, in a letter dated 13 May '45: "For myself," he says to Alfred, "I am really rather well since consenting to be always ill." These words are revelatory: taken superficially, they suggest that Gustave merely wants to mention his proud, lucid, and reflective resignation to his degrading infirmity. In January '45 he wrote to Vasse: "My illness will always have had the advantage of leaving me to occupy myself as I like, which is a great point in life; I cannot see anything in the world that is preferable to a good room, well heated, with the books you love and all the leisure you desire."

Examined more closely, however, the sentence from the letter to Alfred seems denser and more mysterious: disorders, to be sure, are the price that must be paid. But *what if his consent were the illness itself?* It would then be the source of the underlying serenity. In any event, Gustave could not have written these ambiguous lines without knowing those strange states in which *doing* and *suffering* are indistinguishable, in which it is unclear where *endurance* ends and *compliance* begins.

Moreover, shame is not all that has disappeared: paradoxically, his anguish is no longer manifest at the very moment when the situation seems to justify it. If we accept the classic scheme—for example, Maxime's diagnosis—we see that an unforeseen, unforeseeable, unknown affliction has pounced on him; it inhabits him and leads an alien life inside him, and he suffers its repercussions as the products of an exterior and invisible reality. He is battling in the dark with a night-blind enemy who strikes out at him unexpectedly. Isn't it appropriate to be afraid? He has repeated attacks. How do we know that the next one will not kill him (he thought he was dying at Pont-l'Evêque) or that he will not lose his mind ("you feel you are going mad")? At the time of *Novembre,* when he had a presentiment that some terrible force was going to hurl him into a subhuman condition, anguish grew with the risks. Now the fall has taken place: he must live out its consequences to the end; he is not yet a subhuman, but what guarantee does he have that he will not be one tomorrow? Death and madness are probabilities all the more menacing as the doctors Flaubert were at first mistaken and their new diagnosis remains uncertain. Gustave would be repeating to himself in horror those words he once said—if he really said them—to Maxime: "I am lost!" But he seems never to have feared that his illness would grow worse; it is as if, from the first attack and ever after, the illness had reached its limit and was frozen there, as if the fall had been definitively arrested the very moment it had begun, as if, at Pont-l'Evêque, "opening his eyes again" after the bleeding, Gustave had understood that the worst was *already* behind him. To be sure, Maxime declared that "this illness broke his life in two." In a sense that is true, but we shall see further on how it must be understood. No doubt his attacks "saddened" him; each one must have been a torment to be lived through from beginning to end. But when Maxime informs us that they "determined, in him, veritable bouts of misanthropy," we have to laugh; by his own admission, Gustave was a misanthrope from the time he entered the *collège*, and, as we have seen, we must go back still further to explain his passionate hatred of the human race. Perhaps he is more expansive on this subject to Maxime—who is already beginning to irritate him. But his misanthropy is neither stronger nor weaker than at the time of *Novembre* or *Quidquid volueris*. It may be, indeed, that he "had had a seizure in the meadows of Doltville once, and that he subsequently stayed there several months without wishing to leave": who would want to make a spectacle of himself? But did this nervous affliction merely *result* in "augmenting his natural savagery," or, on the contrary, was it designed to serve it? Flaubert's letters by no means corroborate Maxime's testimony on this point. The "downcast" young man nonetheless writes on 13 August '45: "I never spent better years than the two that just passed because they were the freest, the least constricted."[6] And, speaking of his illness, he defines it in the same letter as "a sacrifice to freedom"; he adds: "It is long, quite long, *not for me* but for my family." A month later, of course, he describes himself as "ill, irritated, prey a thousand times a day to moments of atrocious anguish." But at the same time he affirms his serenity: "I continue my slow work . . . I was not like that formerly. This change came about naturally. My will also had something to do with it. It will lead me further, I hope." The deaths of his father and his sister disturb him for a moment, but he writes the day after Caroline's burial: "I was dry as the stone of a tomb but horribly irritated . . . I am crushed, stupefied: I will certainly need to resume my quiet life for I am suffocating with boredom and irritation. When shall I rediscover my poor life of tranquil art and prolonged meditation?"[7] The deep bond with Caroline was broken by her marriage: what Flaubert deplores is the disturbance. Two weeks

6. *Correspondance*, 1:187.
7. Ibid., p. 198.

later he writes: "You might regard me as heartless if I told you that it is not the present state that I consider the most pitiful of all. While I had nothing to complain about, I found much more reason to complain."[8] Thus, despite the deaths, he maintains that the years following his crisis are happier, or less unhappy, than the years preceding it. And he adds, as if he had only been waiting for this double bereavement: "I am going to get back to work at last! At last! I desire, and, I hope, to be slogging away immoderately and at length."[9] Indeed, several days later he says: "I am beginning to ease into the habit of work . . . I read and write regularly eight to ten hours a day."[10] In short, apart from a few brief recurrences, we no longer find any trace of his past anguish: he awaits the next attack and yet unreservedly enjoys the respite it allows him, as if the attack were the means and his tranquillity of soul the essential end. In order to be so reassured, he must feel he is at once victim and sacrificer; the latter alone can say, in effect: so far and no farther. He lives in such familiarity with his illness, he yields to it so profoundly, that he finally understands it and becomes vaguely aware that he is mastering it.

He goes even farther, to the point of sensing that a basic connection links his nervous affliction to the existence of the paterfamilias. Shortly after his father's death, he makes this extraordinary confession: "Fifteen days ago, everything [that is, the burial of Achille-Cléophas] was over . . . I am crushed, overwhelmed on all sides . . . Caroline gave birth to a little girl. But [she has bouts] of pernicious fever . . . We had a big battle over Achille's affairs . . . As for me, I am in charge of things . . . In all of this, my nerves were so horribly shaken that I no longer feel them. Perhaps I am cured; perhaps it has affected me the way burning would remove a wart."[11] And there is no doubt that he then has a long period of remission, for in August '46 he speaks of "the nervous illness that lasted two years." Two years: from January '44 (Pont-l'Evêque) to the death of his father (January '46). Seven months later, he considered himself permanently cured, having suffered only slight difficulties in the meantime. In fact, things are not so simple: the fits will return but less powerfully and much less frequently. In December '47 he writes to Louise: "I am waiting from day to day for a rather serious attack, for it has now been four months

8. Ibid., p. 201–2.
9. Ibid., p. 203.
10. Ibid., p. 204.
11. To Ernest, late January '46, *Correspondance*, Supplement, 1:54–55.

since I've had one; for a year now this has been the usual interval."[12] He must therefore have had only three attacks in '47 and probably quite a few more than that in '46 between August and the end of the year. The improvement cannot be doubted. Flaubert made only a slight error: the death of Achille-Cléophas did not cure him, it made him decide to cure himself. He adds, indeed: "For the rest, I don't give a damn, as Phidias would say. With the force of time everything grows exhausted, illnesses like the rest, and I will exhaust this one with the force of patience, without remedy or anything; I feel it and I am almost certain of it."[13] This theme is new for him: he seems to believe he can exercise a subterranean control over his illness. "I will exhaust it . . . I *feel it*." To Louise he merely speaks of "patience," but from this period on he must have had something quite different in mind. On 18 May 1857, he writes to Mademoiselle Leroyer de Chantepie:

> You ask me how I cured myself of the nervous hallucinations I used to suffer from. By two means: first, by studying them scientifically, that is, by trying to account for them in my own mind, and second, by *will power*. I have often felt madness coming on . . . But I clung to my reason. It dominated everything, though beseiged and battered. And at other times I tried, through imagination, to give myself these horrible sufferings factitiously . . . A great pride sustained me, and I vanquished the illness by grappling with it.[14]

Thus Flaubert is aware of his basic intention: after the chief surgeon's demise, he no longer sees his neurosis merely as a survival. It has played its role: now it must be liquidated. And that, of course, not by a voluntary *fiat*—since it is itself *as other*—but by exercises, ruses, and detours; in particular, by a curious counterpithiatism (reproducing in the imaginary the actually experienced sufferings in order to unmask their unreality *a posteriori* or to constitute them as unreal). Is it true that he cured himself "alone and without remedies"? We shall see; what must be noted here is that this conviction—illusory or not—rests on the comprehension of the nervous illness as an intentional process which, to the extent it escapes direct and conscious control, has fixed its term, its own limits, and, simultaneously, its aim.

---

12. To Louise. *Correspondance,* 1:75.
13. Ibid.
14. *Correspondance,* 4:180–81; Flaubert's emphasis.

When he speaks of it to Louise, delivered of certain inhibitions by
his bereavement, he presents the rupture of Pont-l'Evêque as the logical result, the symbolic expression, of his life, and as a strange ascesis
that freed him of his passions:

> Before knowing you, I was calm, I had become so. I was entering
> a manly period of moral health. My youth had passed. The ner-
> vous illness which lasted for two years was the conclusion, the
> closing, the logical result. In order to have had what I had, it was
> necessary that something must first have happened rather trag-
> ically in my brain box. But everything was reestablished. I had
> seen clearly into things, and into myself, which is more rare. I
> went forward with the rectitude of a particular system made for a
> special case. I had understood everything in myself, separated,
> classified, so that I had never been more at peace, whereas every-
> one else thought this was a time when I was to be pitied.[15]

He understood above all, he says in the same letter—and we shall see
that it was something he had previously developed at the end of the
first *Education*—that "*I was not made for enjoyment*. This sentence must
not be taken in the ordinary sense but grasped in its metaphysical
intensity."[16]

Thus, between '44 and '46 he "went forward with the rectitude of a
particular system made for a special case." This is the very definition
of neurosis: the self-defense mechanisms have refined a rigorous
strategy that is none other than the illness itself. The Flaubert son has
organized himself deep down to suffer as little as possible. In this
neurotic planning, the encounter with Louise was not foreseen:
Gustave is troubled for a moment but returns, like a robot, to his un-
swervingly rectilinear progression. The crisis of January '44 is, in his
eyes, the beginning of an ascesis: "My active, passionate life . . .
ended at twenty-two. At that time *I suddenly made great progress*, and
something else came about."

And let us not believe he imagines he has *profited* from an accident
in order to reclassify everything, to see clearly into himself and recognize "that he is not made for enjoyment." On this point, he is precise:
"I have had two quite distinct existences. External events symbolized
the end of the first and the birth of the second; all that is
mathematical."[17]

15. To Louise, 9 August 1846, *Correspondance*, 1:230.
16. *Correspondance*, 1:231.
17. To Louise, 27 August 1846, *Correspondance*, 1:277.

1. The illness is a conclusion and closure. Youth culminates even as it vanishes. There is totalization by a false death he always dreamed of: "All that [his former loves, Madame Schlésinger, Eulalie] is over and done with; I scarcely have any memory of it; it even seems to have happened in another man's life. The man who lives now and who is me only contemplates the other, who is dead. I have had two quite distinct existences." In short, the attack, a mathematical result, *death by thought*, is expressly seized upon by Gustave as the moment when a life is totalized and realizes the destiny it bore within itself.

2. It is true that he calls the first attacks of his illness *external events*. But he immediately adds that they *symbolize* the end of his first existence. External, yes: they are not the product of his will; he *suffers* them like cholera. But they are situated at the boundary that separates the internalization of exteriority and the externalization of the interior: as such, they constitute the symbolic *representation* of what truly happens inside Flaubert. For him this means that the external process (death and transfiguration *experienced* at Pont-l'Evêque as an accident of exteriority) is the *image*, the *figuration* of a process much deeper and more directed which is produced within himself. The crisis is defined at once as a strict necessity—it is the result of a slow totalization—and as a superficial event that *manifests* an intentional meaning rather than being itself that meaning. "Previous" to this external accident, "something rather tragic" happened inside. It is evident that the "brain box" does not represent the physiological organ but subjectivity.[18] Thus the crisis is the summation, the image, and the external manifestation of a tragedy, that is, of a conflict that can be resolved only by the annihilation of the conflicting terms. For this reason, we can understand why Flaubert no longer fears anything: *before* the night of Pont-l'Evêque, the chips were down. The attack is merely a *realization*, irreversibility experienced at last—nothing more. It adds nothing, it concludes; therefore, contrary to what he could fear in January '44, no *novelty* is presaged by it. In other words, Flaubert's life until the age of twenty-two appears to him as a directed process of which he is victim and agent, which leads him at last to the final tragedy, for he has not ceased to prepare simultaneously for his death and his resurrection or, if you prefer, for his madness and the establishment of a particular system made for a special case. He says to Louise: I went mad, I succumbed *in order* to take my illness in hand and *in*

18. But conversely, for Flaubert the materialist, subjectivity is the result of cerebral processes.

order to make it my salvation by sequestration, the renunciation of real pleasures, and the definitive choice of the imaginary.

Yet, does he know how this destiny was prepared within him? Has he given up seeking the antecedents of his attacks in his excessively heavy slumbers of '43? Did he try, after his stupor in January '44, to recompose the slow, organizing process that led him to his first accident? Beginning in '46, his letters contain frequent attempts at interpretation. On the surface, his explanations are not always very coherent; underneath, we shall discover their deep unity.

a) The simplest reason for his ills, the one he most often cites, is that prolonged suffering consumed him, disordering his nervous system.

"Think how much I must have suffered to arrive, despite the robust health evident in my appearance, at a nervous illness that lasted two years."[19]

"I fell ill from studying law and being bored."[20]

". . . at twenty-one I nearly died from a nervous illness brought on by a series of irritations and troubles, by dint of sleeplessness and anger."[21]

These passages clearly show that Flaubert saw the study of law as the source of all his problems. He *suffered* from it to the point of ruining his health: he was working in a state of perpetual irritation, lying awake entire nights; and above all he was bored. This boredom, akin to mental disorder, he described in *Novembre,* and we know that it expresses not only—nor especially—his disgust with the stupid work imposed on him, but primarily his anguish at being "too small for himself," at being unable, for want of genius, to change being that way, and at feeling every moment the bite of the future, of the *bourgeois* fatalities that await him.

b) But he occasionally gives his troubles a very different explanation: "Madness and luxury are two things I have so plumbed, areas I have navigated so well by force of will, that I shall never (I hope) be either a madman or a de Sade. But I have suffered for it, indeed. A

19. To Louise, *Correspondance,* 1:309.
20. Ibid., 2:461.
21. To Mademoiselle Leroyer de Chantepie, 30 March 1857, *Correspondance,* 4:169. It will be noted that he is still presenting his fall of '44 as a death escaped by a hairsbreadth. "Popping off in the hands of my family" becomes "almost dying of a nervous illness." But can one die from this illness? Isn't there a contradiction between the way he now presents it and the old theme of the fatal outcome? In fact, he returns to the conclusion of *Novembre,* "dying by thought." As we shall see, he wants to keep all the scenarios together.

nervous illness was the foam of these little intellectual jests. Every attack was like a kind of hemorrhage of the nervous system. It was a seminal spillage of the imagistic faculty of the brain, a hundred thousand images leaping at once, like fireworks."[22] In the same letter he tells us what he means by probing the depths of madness: human misery—as exhibited in hospitals, insane asylums, brothels—has "something so crude about it that it stimulates the mind to cannibalistic appetites. It leaps up to devour them, to assimilate them. With what reveries I often remained in a whore's bed, looking at the frayings of her couch. What ferocious dramas I constructed at the Morgue, which I used to have a passion for visiting, etc. I believe, moreover, that in this respect I have a particular faculty of perception; as regards the unwholesome, I speak from experience."

It will be observed, curiously, that what he offers Louise as the reason for his illness he presents to Mademoiselle Leroyer de Chantepie as a means of curing himself of it. Indeed, he will write to her in '57: "You ask me how I cured myself of [my] nervous hallucinations? By two means: first, by studying them scientifically . . . Second, *by will power* . . . I tried, through imagination, to give myself these horrible sufferings factitiously. I played with madness and the fantastic like Mithridates playing with poisons." The two texts are contradictory only in appearance: true, he writes to Louise that he surrendered to these masturbatory and unrealizing incantations *before* his attacks, which are their "foam," but he adds that by his imaginary soundings he was *vaccinated* against madness. He is *unwholesome* by constitution and also because as a child not six years old he had already acquired ghastly memories: the cadavers of the Hôtel-Dieu, the madwomen at the Rouen asylum.[23] He recognizes in himself a pathological taste for the horrible and the base, which in his eyes have more "moral density." Wasn't there something here that inclined him toward madness? Thanks to his *experiments in seeing,* he threw himself into an insane but unreal universe. In other words, he satisfied his sadistic and necrophiliac desires without risk. Although his organism was exhausted in this almost unbearable tension, and finally his nerves were shattered, these were the least of his ills; attacks, hypernervousness, but not delirium. The delirium was *before;* he made it happen *by will power;* as a result, he knows its deepest wellsprings, he no longer takes the risk of *believing* in it. The hallucinations remain "nervous"

22. To Louise, 7–8 July 1853, *Correspondance,* 1:270.
23. He alludes to it in the letter of July 1853, cited above.

and cannot become "mental": he has penetrated too deeply into the mechanisms of the imagination to let himself be taken in by images. No doubt they acquire a kind of consistency by the fact that they command attention. But even then they cannot utterly fool a trained dreamer. This is what he explained to Louise a little earlier: "You speak to me of a category of hallucinations that you have had; watch out. First they are in the mind, then they appear before you. The fantastic invades you, and the hallucinations cause ghastly anguish. One feels one is going mad. One is, and one is conscious of it." [24]

The systematic cultivation of the "fantastic" can lead this far, no further: the unreal dominates, yet cannot entirely replace reality; one feels one is going mad. One is, and *one is conscious of it*. Consciousness—which Flaubert, even at his worst moments, affirms he never lost—is the "ghastly" feeling of being mad that always separates him, he believes, from a real madman. For Gustave implies, of course, that a madman is never conscious of his madness, a mistake that comes not from him but from the stammerings of the psychiatry of the time. In any event, this somewhat blustering interpretation of his illness implies a certain theory of the imagination—his own—according to which the image is not a lack, the indicator of an absence, but a plenitude that distinguishes itself from the real by its perfection and its infinite lightness.

Before '44, then, there were mental exercises that had the double effect of vaccinating Gustave [25] and ruining his nervous system—or rather of rendering him hypersensitive and of constituting in him the "habit" of spontaneously producing images. Vaccinated, immunized; in other words: for a time I was in greater danger of mental accident than other men; but by the systematic organization of conscious delirium, I produced in myself miniature psychoses that immunized me against madness by familiarizing me with it. So why should we not believe him when he tells Mademoiselle Leroyer de Chantepie that he cured himself by recreating "those horrible sufferings" at will? Convinced that by his previous asceses he had reduced the peril that lay in wait for him *in that lesser illness,* nervous problems, why wouldn't he have tried voluntarily to imitate his own major attacks, beginning in '45, in order to replace them gradually with imaginary and con-

24. To Louise, *Correspondance,* 2:51.
25. Curiously, he takes up the phrase apropos of Hamard, who was deeply shaken by Caroline's death and shut himself up in a dream world: "I did not innoculate him with my intellectual vaccine." In other words: he began dreaming too late, he will go completely mad.

trolled attacks? By feigning to obey, he could have tried to take himself in hand. And perhaps deep inside, fascinated by his condition as he had been earlier by that of the journalist from Nevers, he wished to enjoy without danger those terrible, dizzying moments when he felt "his soul and his body separate." It is therefore perfectly possible that Gustave, alone in his room, or—who knows?—even in public, might have produced, between two referential attacks, attacks that were similar in every respect, yet were simulated.

Nevertheless, the two interpretations he gives of his illness seem hardly reconcilable: Was it the horror of choosing a profession, the anguish of being a great man manqué, his exasperation with the Code, that shattered his nerves? Or did the imaginary child play too long with his imagination?

In the first case, the source of the disorders is the Other: Flaubert exhausts himself out of obedience, performing work that is imposed on him and does not suit him. In the second, it is the young man himself who provokes these disorders by his "intellectual jests." Yet if we examine both hypotheses in the light of their contexts, we shall see that, though they do not coincide, they complete each other.

Let us begin with the first interpretation: "I fell ill from studying law and being bored." And let us try to situate it. This sentence is taken from a letter in which Flaubert inveighs against Musset and, through him, against the whole of Romanticism: no, pain is not the source of inspiration. The better to convince Louise, he begins by establishing that hypersensitivity is a weakness and that poetry has nothing to do with nervous susceptibilities. "Let me explain," he says. "If I'd had a more solid brain, I would not have fallen ill from studying law and being bored. I would have profited from it instead of taking ill. The irritation, instead of staying in my head, ran into my limbs and stiffened them in convulsions. This was a *deviation*." [26] Irritation, if it stays in the head, is conscious pain and lived as such. Like most of his contemporaries, Flaubert must have thought that emotions and feelings were specific affections and that their seat was in the brain. The irritation he speaks of is determined by a totalizing perception of the situation (I am a mediocrity, I will be bourgeois, etc.) and this includes a reflexive dimension, [27] which allows one to keep it at a distance and make systematic use of it. This is the moment to recall the "great sorrows" he speaks of in *Novembre*, which are the

26. *Correspondance*, 2:461; Flaubert's emphasis.
27. Gustave says elsewhere, in a letter that we shall take up again later, in which he describes his attack: "I was conscious, or else there would have been no pain."

35

heights from which everything seems tedious and futile. A magnificent "position": perched above human passions, Flaubert can speak of our follies with detachment, as an artist. In the previously cited passage, "to profit from it" doesn't mean, "I should have passed my exams and become a good jurist," but quite the opposite: "I should have taken my pain not as a source of inspiration but as an instrument for distancing."[28] Felt as a determination of consciousness, pain serves: it allows an aesthetic "pause." Of course, Flaubert does not claim that pain is solely the negation of lived experience; he knows from experience that this "cerebral" sensation is accompanied by a succession of physical disorders. In "strong" people, that sensation ought to produce the disorders without letting itself be absorbed by them. On the other hand, if the irritation descends into the limbs—if it becomes incarnate in the organism, if it lets itself *be expressed* by purely physiological upheavals—it can no longer be the means of "putting [anguish] in parentheses," but falls to the level of pure lived experience. The distance from the world is annulled, since an object in-the-midst-of-the world, the body, is charged with materializing that absence, that flight, with making it into worldly determinations, such as a fit of weeping, or colic. Put another way, all pain is convulsive, but it *begins* by being hatred of the world, hatred of the self, flight from the world into the self and from self into the world, withdrawal from being-there, from facticity. But when the convulsions, increased tenfold, absorb the faculties of the soul, facticity triumphs, it drinks transcendence the way blotting paper drinks ink, while claiming to incarnate it; the world closes around the being that claimed to be escaping from it.

Flaubert develops this idea by means of another example:

> We often find children who are made ill by music; they have great aptitude, retain melodies at the first hearing, exult in playing the piano, their heart beating; they grow thin, pale, fall ill, and their poor nerves, like a dog's, are wrenched in suffering at the sound of the notes. These are certainly not the Mozarts of the future. *Vocation* has been displaced; the idea has passed into the flesh, where it remains sterile, and the flesh rots: the result is neither genius nor health.[29]

---

28. We see the subtle difference in points of view. For Musset, "nothing makes us so great as great pain." At the time he wrote *Novembre*, Flaubert was, by and large, of this opinion. But now that he has died and been resurrected, he gives pain a dehumanizing function. It must be experienced as a human death and surpassed toward ataraxia.

29. *Correspondance*, 2:461.

Here we have the meaning of deviation: *the idea has passed into the flesh.* The idea is transcendence, the relation of a being to that absence, a musical totality to be created. Once it has passed into the body, it will no longer find a way out. In truth, every note heard remains a summons, but it is no longer a question of *vocation;* it is the sign of silent disorders by which the organism strives to *realize* what on principle escapes it: the creative relation to future nonbeing. The idea made flesh remains sterile, the negation of the real in the name of an unreal totalization is lived by the body as agony.

This text calls for several remarks: it is one of the rare moments in which Flaubert expresses himself with clarity about his nervous illness. At the source of his troubles he resolutely puts deviation, that is, *displaced vocation.* This is a return to his bitter and fundamental certainty: "I am a great man *manqué.*" But he does not limit himself to that: he expounds his views on what created this explosive mixture of genius and sterility; in an oversensitive body, nervous troubles suppress the transcendence of the idea but are themselves endowed with meaning since they attempt to incarnate that very idea in immanence. Thus Flaubert's illness, an idea that moved into his body, is also the vain effort of his body to transform itself into an idea, its convulsive attempt to realize an unrealizable situation (namely, transcendence as relation to nonbeing) and to totalize the world by a *suffered* annihilation. From now on it is clear that Gustave does not regard his illness as accidental or nonsignifying in relation to the whole of his life: quite the contrary, the illness seems to him like his life becoming manifest to the self as predestination. Even before falling ill, Flaubert belonged to the category of inadequately gifted children, he suffered from a displaced vocation; what is involved, he tells us, is the solidity of his brain. He does not mean the chemical constitution of cells; he indicts the relation of the cerebro-spinal system to the neuro-vegetative system. The role of the former, according to Gustave, is to transmit *signals* to the latter. Instead, it has allowed the idea to run through it, and the neuro-vegetative system has taken over, stupidly. At first, of course, the metamorphosis is not total: the idea is only in part absorbed by the body; the young man thus defines his childhood as preneurotic terrain. His excessive sensitivity, from his earliest beginnings, robbed him of a portion of his means. Mozart was an artist because in him the imaginary was pure: he did not suffer *in his art;* he captured the relation of the incomplete (the real) to the complete (totality as nonbeing) and conceived musical *images* as the representation of the unreal by reality; in his case there was a vocation, a *summons to activity;* the unreal solicited him to produce centers of un-realization in the real by a conscious effort. In Gustave, as in the melo-maniacal children, the imaginary is impure, it is *experienced* as a physiological malaise; instead of seeking to fix this absence, this non-being, by elaborating an analogue, the subject lets his body turn itself into a denunciation of incompleteness, miming and suffering the im-possibility and necessity of totalization by means of nervous dis-orders. Transcendence is *then lived* on the terrain of the immanent as an inert "structural defect" of immanence itself. When the idea passes into flesh, the body becomes speech, but its message is indecipher-able since *designation* is degraded as *disease.* There is symbolization without symbolism, without code. The decay of the organism, the negation of health, obscurely symbolizes the annihilation of the real by genius—or, if you will, by praxis. Thus that original given—a de-viation or displacement of vocation—is *already pathological:* it proph-esies a mortal illness which is nothing less than the radicalization of the symbol of an immanence exasperated at being able neither to *artic-ulate* transcendence nor to cease mimicking it. The nervous attacks, for Flaubert, have no accidental cause: in them the idea-become-flesh reaches its limit; the flesh is *expressive* suffering but physical suffering. It experiences simultaneously the necessity and the impossibility of meaning; in it, transcendence is degraded as outbursts of feeling, and convulsion is nothing but the tearing away from the self played by facticity—and thereby denied. As we see, this first *explanation* of the crises is rather more complex than it first appeared. When Flaubert writes in '57 that his illness was "brought about by a series of irrita-tions and troubles, by sleepless nights and anger," he is oversimplify-ing out of resentment; but he knows very well that his exasperation, his distastes, his irritations torment him in the general framework of his pithiatism. He has not, in his own eyes, simply been worn out by repugnant forced labor; quite to the contrary, he has borne his destiny within himself since childhood, when the excessive docility of his body doomed him to failure: it is his overly suggestible nature that has deprived him of genius by substituting *somatization.*

And what is found beneath the second interpretation is again pithiatism. There, as well, "the idea has moved into the flesh"; in its stupid spontaneity the body takes charge of the troubles with which the young man was pleased to be afflicted. Still imaginary, those troubles *impose themselves.* This time it is not a matter of convulsions but of the "nervous hallucinations" that accompany them. A passage from a letter to Louise is significant: "As for my health, which worries you, rest assured once and for all that whatever happens to me and whatever I am suffering from, it is good in the sense that it will go far (I have my reasons for believing it to be so). But I will live as I live, always suffering from nerves—that port of entry between the soul and the body through which I may have tried to transport too many things."[30] In this first paragraph, the accent is on the will: he *wanted* his body to realize too many of his reveries. Negative reveries; the examples he cites (voluntary fasting at fifteen, chastity at twenty) concern solely his determination to deny his needs. But no sooner has he spoken of will than he changes his mind:

> My *nature*, as you say, does not suffer from the regimen I follow because I long ago taught it to leave me in peace. One becomes accustomed to everything, to everything, I repeat . . . and the strange thing about it all is that neither bias nor obstinacy is involved. I don't know why that is the case; apparently it had to be that way.

This correction is important: it underscores the ambiguity of his thought: he *wanted*, he *taught his nature*, he has *become accustomed* to his way of life. On the other hand, he subtracts the chief qualities from that will: neither fasting nor chastity without some voluntarism. But he has invested it, he says, with neither bias nor obstinacy; it happened by itself. The "I don't know why" and the "apparently it had to be that way" refer us to the underlying organization of lived experience. Flaubert's will is a superficial inclination, which would be of no consequence if the body did not spontaneously take it in hand. He is sick, he says, from having made *too many* things pass through his nerves; but immediately he corrects himself: in fact, the nerves have transmitted too many things to the organism on their own. Because what happened necessarily had to happen, Flaubert divines a secret intention behind his body's strange plasticity. Not only does he recognize his autosuggestibility, but he also surmises that it is constituted, oriented, toward an end. When absorbed in his "unwholesome" reveries, all he had to do was push his preoccupation with the imaginary to the limits: he already knew that he could count on his body to realize an intermediary step between the simple certainty that it was merely a matter of images on the one hand and hallucinatory belief on the other. You make yourself mad, or you make yourself epileptic

30. 11–12 December 1847, *Correspondance*, 2:71–72.

(meaning: you are playing a role); you concentrate on sadistic images, and suddenly something is given which is not so much the realization of the unreal as the reality of its presence, its power of *appearance*. As a result, the fireworks, the fleeting succession of images, the hallucinations "before your eyes" have something rather crude and undifferentiated about them: these "floods of fire" no longer resemble states of cultivated delirium. For the body, docilely, stupidly, has set about producing the fantastic on its own; it is a "hemorrhage of the imagistic faculty of the brain."

Deviation as "hemorrhage," then, is explained mainly by *somatization:* this is Flaubert's basic opinion. Suffering does not remain in the cranial box; it slips into the limbs, is taken over by the body, and becomes convulsive, just as directed deliriums are soon followed by simpler but involuntary hallucinations. This is what autosuggestion means to Flaubert. What one began by wanting one suddenly takes on as something suffered. And what one suffers is not entirely what one wanted—it is both its reproduction and its negation. The translucidity of the image is transformed into an uncontrollable opacity; one recognizes without recognition. What the two interpretations have in common is their insistence on Flaubert's pithiatic constitution: both interpretations see it as the source of his illness, which can be defined as the substitution of an atrophied quasi-reality for the unreal. Gustave hardly differentiates between the two: the first emphasizes passive activity, the basis of autosuggestibility, and presents it as a character trait, as an *exis;* it is more *explanatory* than the other and tries to understand the illness through its causes, beginning with pithiatism considered as a factual given. On the other hand, the second interpretation, more *interpretive,* throws into relief the teleological aspect of the process, presenting simultaneously the suppression of need as willed and as "coming about of itself" because it "has to be that way." Flaubert expressly relates his disorders to pithiatism by showing us an intentionally structured somatization in him which simultaneously replaces the will and denies the will as an autonomous power of practical decision. In both conceptions the young man shows that he is fully aware of the psychosomatic character of his illness; he can speak of it in two languages without fear of contradicting himself because he regards causality and finality as two inseparable and complementary ways of expressing the ambiguity of his personal experience.

There is no doubt that he sees his illness as a symbolic totalization of the years of suffering and mental exercises that preceded its appearance. From the time of the first attack, his youth descended into his body; it showed itself for what it was while being absorbed into his body, and his body reconstituted his youth, unrecognizable and recognized, in the form of nervous disorders; his body has freed Flaubert from the unbearable passions that ravaged his youth by taking charge of them, *representing* them as convulsions. In Gustave's eyes a somatic symbolism is established, in which the least differentiated alludes to the most differentiated, which has disappeared, in which contractions and spasms are charged with reducing the discomforts of subjectivity to pure physiology. The "closing" of youth is its burial in the organism and its resurrection in the form of illness *endowed with meaning*. Flaubert never ceased to consider his neurosis the most highly significant fact of his life. Far from seeing this "death and transfiguration" as accidental, he does not distinguish it from his own person. It is *he*, inasmuch as he has become what he was. He never thought, as Dumesnil believes, that he had adjusted or would adjust to his affliction; quite to the contrary, he thought his affliction was in itself an adaptation. In short, he regarded it as a *response*, a solution. Later, his Bovary would have an explicit somatization-response. Abandoned by Rodolphe, she falls ill, a terrible bout of fever seems to threaten her life; and then, after a few weeks, she finds herself cured of fever and love at the same time. Or, if you will, love *becomes* fever in order to be eliminated through physical disorders.

Despite this very profound understanding, this intimate familiarity, this firm conviction that his bodily troubles are unified by a meaning, Flaubert's statements remain obscure and imprecise. Either he cannot find the right terms in which to render his intuition, or the intuition itself remains embryonic, or he wants to conceal from us part of what he intuits. Be that as it may, this "conscious grasp" is an integral part of the neurosis itself. The neurosis conditions and defines the extent and limits of that grasp, designating itself as having to be lived thus and not otherwise. This justifies our investigating it, in an attempt to elucidate its *meaning* without abandoning the point of view of interiority.

SEVENTEEN

Neurosis as Response

We have established that the morbid invention—or, if you prefer, the neurotic option—is situated in January '44 at Pont-l'Evêque, and that the subsequent attacks have a referential character. We shall need, of course, to inquire into the reason for these lesser repetitions, but in the main our investigation concerns the *living* moment of the illness, the first attack: we must investigate its meaning and its function, that is, attempt a description of its intentional structure. We shall see that, through a regressive investigation, increasingly deeper *levels of intention* can be found, each of which, while preserving a certain regional autonomy, symbolizes the level below it and dialectically conditions the level above. Thus the meaning we shall bring to light is bound to escape a conceptual determination: it can be grasped in its complexity only as the totalization and living unity of the contradictory and complementary intentions of the neurosis. Which does not mean that it cannot be thought: we simply have to look for what constitutes the object of a notional approach. And by notion I mean that global but structured comprehension of a human reality that enables temporalization to enter—as directed becoming—into the synthetic apperception it seeks of its object and simultaneously of itself.

A. Belief as Passive Resolution

When Flaubert leaves for Rouen, he is mentally blocked, distraught; he is a man-problem who by his flight internalizes an emergency, an unsurpassable contradiction, which he is compelled to surpass by the very fact that he ek-sists. We have found this contradiction in him from the time of *Novembre;* now it has hardened: his passive obedience robs him of any possibility of refusing the activity his father imposes on him, but this increasingly difficult passivity, and his basic distaste for the future being prepared for him, succeed in making it impossible. Impossible to obey, impossible to refuse obedience. There is no solution, he knows, but he also knows that *there will be one.* His flight resolves nothing; it is a magical behavior: turning one's back on danger so that it will be annihilated. Flaubert's retreat is an attempt to provoke magically that annihilation of Paris he demanded in vain of a new Attila; but at the same time he senses that he is running toward *something.* Nothing is said: there is no doubt that in the course of the journey he is absorbed by physiological disturbances—trembling, cold sweats, etc.—which distract his thoughts. The carriage bears him toward his destiny. This is the *lived meaning* of every turn of the wheel, of the horses' every step. He persists in saying to himself that he is going to spend "two or three days" with the family in order to get over his emotions: this means that he will be *taken at his word,* that he will *take himself at his word,* and that he will be sent back, gently, implacably, with his own full consent, to the Parisian prison. The imaginary escape would be only an inconsequential escapade if he did not have the obscure conviction that he is *awaited* there by a terrible and ineluctable event: a fall is etching itself on the horizon.

This presentiment is merely the internalization of the only objective solution to the problem. Since refusal to act is impossible and necessary, he *must* impose passive obedience on himself as a strict impossibility of obeying; Flaubert must *suffer* it in spite of his zeal, in spite of his rush to do his father's bidding; he must *discover* it in himself not as a minor handicap (fatigue, laziness, allergy to the Code, etc.) but as a radical incapacity. It is no longer a question of enduring transitory and reparable failures but of revealing to others and to himself that he is a *man-failure.* By this "must" I do not claim to define an internal imperative but simply the objective set of conditions that make a solution possible. These conditions are abstract; from this starting point, the solution is not yet defined in its singularity; yet these conditions constitute the rigorous framework in which it must be found: fall beneath man and let the catastrophe land *unexpectedly* on his shoulders.

The impending fall cannot be the object of a rational decision, and simulation—deliberate revolt—is forbidden Flaubert. By what means will he determine to *suffer* what he *does?* We already know the answer: by *belief.* As we have seen, Gustave's relation to truth is embryonic. He has effectively defined his mental disposition in his *Notes et souvenirs:* "I believe in nothing and am disposed to believe in everything except the sermons of moralists." The permanent doubt he evinces in the first part of the sentence comes from his incapacity to affirm. The inclination to believe in everything that he mentions in the second part is born, conversely, from the impossibility of denial: he can shout out his disgust, curse to the skies, but not *refuse* out of a clear and precise judgment. In this sense, his "belief in nothing" is not distinguishable from his belief in everything, that "naïveté" which, according to Caroline Commanville, he never lost. And this naïveté is merely another name for his pithiatism. In a way, his convictions are exposed as being *merely* beliefs, but since he is unaware of the original savor of the true—*verum index sui*—as it imposes itself on free choice, those beliefs will have little difficulty standing in for the certainties he lacks. An idea fascinates him *in another*, it establishes itself inside him, and as he is unable to renew the operations that made it a truth for the other, he *believes* in it, that is, he *lives it pathically* and makes it an indispensable structure of lived experience rather than a determination of objective knowledge. In short, the idea "moves into the body," which is charged with replacing the irresistible and sweet power of evidence[1] with the weight and seriousness of its materiality. An idea that is degraded as a physical need yet not affirmed as truth—such is naked belief. But if it must be seen as the beginning of somatization, conversely, all of Flaubert's pithiatic somatizations begin as mere beliefs.

On this level, *choice*, which reveals freedom through the unveiling of its rigorous conditioning by the field of possibles, is from the start inaccessible to him; hence the unrealizable and necessary project turns back on itself as *believed* destiny. And destiny, of course, involves a choice, but for Gustave that choice, for lack of being disclosable in the dialectic of negation and affirmation, is constituted as the announcement of a fatality and as the subjective *expectation* of what awaits him in the objective future. In Flaubert, the idea of the fall, at

1. Evidence is a moment of praxis: its complementary and inseparable characteristics are the free surpassing of the object toward a defined end, and the undeniable presence of this object "in flesh and bone," in the movement that attempts to make it the means to that end, as the unsurpassable condition of the entire enterprise. It discovers itself as having to be transformed within the practical field, but also as itself defining the conditions and limits of that transformation. Evidence is the real discovering itself as the regulation of possibles; it is contingency constituting itself, in its very contingency, as necessity in the light of freedom. This dialectical connection of the possible with the impossible, of the contingent becoming necessary, and, speaking like Hegel, of necessity unveiling its contingency, even if it is encountered on the level of mental operations (discourse, symbols, mathematics, etc.), has its source in the relation of the body (practical matter) to the world, in other words, facticity, as instrumentalization of the organism. On principle, therefore, the moment of evidence cannot belong to Flaubert's experience.

first simple fascination, begins to *take shape* when he lives it in *fear*. For fear, here, is not a refusal but an *already resigned* repulsion. In a practical agent, fear relates to the field of possibles by defining a possible to be avoided. But the passive agent has no such active relation to his possibilities: because he is not guiding an enterprise, he cannot distinguish the possible from the real. Thus, when we sleep, torn away from action by neurological disconnections, the dimension of *possibility* disappears with our practical capacity, and everything we conceive during our waking hours in the form of conjecture, of things more or less likely to happen and lived as anxiety, we find again in sleep *through belief* in the form of suffered realization. Awake, a psychiatrist waiting for the visit of a dangerous patient may think: "And what if he has a knife?" This questioning is certainly born of fear, but it is merely a way of envisaging all the possibles—even the least probable—with the practical and conscious intention of being prepared for them. If I dream of a madman, I cannot even *pose* the question: if the idea of a knife is born, it is in the form of a "real" determination; I can only put a knife in his hands, or, if you will, as I am in a state of *pure belief*, the hypothesis—the highest form of experimental thought, the indispensable structure of all practice and of the simplest work—is degraded as fatality. The project as transcendence cannot disappear—since it is existence itself; but it flows back on the present as purely suffered future: it cannot be otherwise, for in sleep we have lost the capacity to *make* that future which is made and suffered in the waking state. Here, then, embodied by somatic disorders, it is *constituted* by emotional discharges and derives its substance from these upheavals alone; even as I suffer it, however, and feel I am condemned to it, it remains in my eyes an object of belief—while dreaming, we frequently tell ourselves we are dreaming. But this nonthetic consciousness of dreaming does not free us from the *world without possibilities* into which we are plunged by *faith:* it is simply an efflorescence appropriate to any image and incapable of replacing a liberating act; when I tell myself while dreaming that I am dreaming, I am not reflecting on my dream, I am dreaming that I am reflecting. In the waking state, it is the appearance of the knife that provokes my panic; asleep, it is my panic[2] that is responsible for *embodying*, unmediated, the idea of knife. Or, if you will, the oneiric equivalent of a real threat is the provisional impossibility in which I find myself—for lack of a reducing agent—not to believe in it as soon as I conceive it.

2. Provoked, obviously, by a latent set of dialectically linked desires and fears.

Pushed to the extreme, this is young Flaubert's state toward 20 January '44. And of course, he has reducing agents available to him: minor enterprises (he reserved his place, packed his bags, locked up his apartment, etc.), *real* environment. As we have seen, however, the unreal and magical meaning of his escapade is enough to transform his acts into gestures: besides, he suffers this flight rather than deciding on it; and surely he has real traveling companions, sees real trees out the window, etc. But to the extent that, as a passive agent, he realizes the possible through belief, he cannot avoid *somewhat derealizing the real*. This means that his relation to the tree that appears and disappears along the route, behind the carriage, remains essentially a peaceful coexistence. The tree glides by, a useless apparition as it is not inserted into any praxis.[3] And since Gustave, as in dreams, seems

3. Of course, this pure coexistence can appear also in the relation of a practical agent to certain sectors of the real. But in this case it comes from the fact that he experiences and reveals reality (as instrumentality and as adversity) beginning with a certain enterprise that leaves outside it—as unusable—the sectors in question. Every action neglects—as a function of its own end—certain intramundane objects, which, for this reason, remain *for the agent* halfway between the real and the unreal since they are perceived as objective determinations, yet are not affirmed, denied, experienced, surpassed. Taken in the immediate, they are *apparitions*. On the other hand, the practical field itself, singularized by the particular action, delivers itself in its radical reality and, by the same token, realizes the agent (meaning it can dissolve in this agent whatever remains of the imaginary and put the imagination in the service of realization). To this extent the neglected apparitions are indirectly affected by an index of reality: they are linked to facts actually revealed by the enterprise because, despite everything, they belong to the unity of the field of possibles; beyond my present concerns, they outline possibilities and responsibilities provisionally nonsignifying but nonetheless referring to the concrete set of my activities—past, present, and future, real and virtual—insofar as they are manifest as the undefined but rigorously limited variations of *one* praxis, mine, beginning with *this* anchorage, here and now.

In other words, the project creates possibles by revealing the real; but unutilized possibles delegate the structure of possibility to praxis itself by signaling to it that other means await it if it chooses other ends. In this way, the objects that are passed over in silence and limit themselves to designating me in my freedom are revealed in their truth: integrated into the practical field, thus indirectly linked to the means that I at present employ, though neither real nor unreal *for me*, they permanently become *realizables*. This is demonstrated rather well by the type of attention described by Revauld d'Allonnes under the name of "reflection with auxiliary fascination." Take, for example, a man who is seeking the solution to a practical or scientific problem and trying in his own mind, to enunciate all its terms, who at the same time has his eyes turned toward a small clock on his desk. Can we say that he is *looking at* it? No, the look is practice, it deciphers, analyzes, classifies with an always defined intention. Does he see it? Yes and no: to be truly seen it would have to detach itself as a form on a background; so we return to the selective gaze. Yet the clock *fascinates*: it imposes itself as pure apparition which, *as such*, aids the reflexive effort; arresting the eyes without soliciting the gaze, it is a *means of not looking elsewhere*. But, at the same time, the researcher cannot make it become anything but a *realizable*—its coefficient of adversity—that is to say, a possibility, proper to praxis, of changing options. Indeed, at times the attention is

to have lost his power to make things possible, the real environment, a pure present, is restricted to nourishing his belief and symbolically prophesying his destiny, the captive future that awaits him; it will never offer him fresh possibilities.

And how should we understand this presentiment, this organizing scheme of future somatization? Is it born of fear or desire? I would say both: the fall beneath the human is in truth an end, but a horrible end, and the horror that Flaubert feels, at once in the face of this fall and in the face of the silent, inner conspiracies that seem to prepare him for it, helps convince him that he will be the victim of his fatalities and not responsible for them. But to understand his pithiatism better, we must recall that the relation between teleological intention and the end that defines it, in a practical agent, is characterized as *transcendence*: it is the fundamental being-outside-the-self, which derives its qualification from a future that it will realize even as it is engulfed by it. At the same time, this relation is *distancing*: the end is *postponement*, it is put off, and this postponement is constitutive of the intention: it is the position of nonbeing to be realized as the *mediated* term of an oriented temporalization. If—as happens to passive agents in extreme cases—the ability to conceive of possibles as possible is suppressed, the teleological intention remains—for it is awakened by need, desire or fear—but it is *deconstructed:* the end is no longer *mediated* or called into question in terms of possibilities ("Is it worth it?") or even made explicit as the term of a temporalization; consequently, the distancing does not take place, it no longer bursts out of the intention to stand outside it and define itself by unveiling the present. Quite to the contrary, the end remains inside the intention, implicit, mingled with it, nameless, as its *present* characteristic. Impossible, however, that it should lose its determination as future objective. In short, the future is captive of the present: implicit, atrophied, the basis of all transcendence falls back into immanence: it is its *internal limit*—as death is the internal limit of life. This is what Anouilh's Antigone says—which is certainly not passive but simply negative, and by which the author would have us understand that the radi-

---

clearly broken, and, unable to find the word, the idea he has been pursuing, the man *realizes* the small clock: it emerges from limbo with its own nature, its resistances; for example, it *denies him the time* because it has stopped, and the realizable passes into the real when its owner, abandoning his reflections for a moment, decides to rewind it. As we have seen, however, Flaubert *incubates a belief* the way one incubates a sickness: marginal apparitions, even if they mark out his journey, are not *realizables* in his eyes: he is not launched on any practical enterprise, he flees reality, and so these phantoms cannot even reveal to him his permanent power of changing activity.

calism of youth is the very expression of its powerlessness: "I want everything, right away." Thus in the passive agent the immediate and unmediated realization of the end becomes the essential determination of teleological intention. Furthermore, since *doing* is absent or hardly sensed as a possibility in others, it is *being* that it aspires to. In this sense, the passive agent identifies *in his being* with the aspired end. That is to say, he believes he suffers it as he suffers his being and his life. Here, as in the dream, there is an immediate and fictive realization of the future, although this future even in captivity, preserves an allusive reference to future temporalization. Which means that the end presents itself to belief as something being realized and, at the same time, as something already realized. For someone constitutionally passive, his incapacity to make an end possible renders belief as the turning back on itself of a desire that cannot be deployed and therefore does not perceive itself as desire but as oracular foreknowledge. Conversely, belief has a teleological structure since it is the somatization of the aspired end and the body's co-option of choice *without responsibility*. In this sense, pithiatism *can only believe*, but its beliefs are always manipulated.

When Gustave spoke of those young melomaniacs who "will not be the Mozarts of the future," he clearly saw the source of his illness. But the example—by design, no doubt—was badly chosen. It is *his projects* which, losing their transcendence, "move down into the body" and are lived in immanence as the *expectation* of an event, when in reality they are laying the groundwork for this event by becoming belief. Even in the passive agent, however, teleological intention is not transformed into belief by itself and at every turn; it can preserve its form as project or be deviated, exhaust itself in emotional disorders, disappear. For a belief to appear and be developed in the circumstances defined by one's protohistory, it must manifest itself on the basis of an original belief, which it will merely actualize in a particular form. And this primal belief, the setting, matrix, and basis of all others, is in sum the singular event, dated, unforgettable, by which the subject has been *constituted a believer*. This event, which has put him into relationship with an object that is in essence ungraspable,[4] can only be the eruption in him of a certain discourse of the Other, insofar as that prestigious Other represents a sacred authority. This moment of discourse affects him with belief insofar as an au-

---

4. One believes what one does not see.

thoritative discourse designating the unrealizable bears in itself the demand that it be believed. The affirmation is *from the Other,* the active and judicial synthesis is executed by the other—the passive agent receives it as a petrified judgment. And since on principle it concerns a radical absence, this dead-synthesis by its nature forbids him any mental operation that might verify it. Thus, the first inducer of belief, in one's protohistory, the first discourse that will constitute the child as believer is that which is itself aimed at him insofar as he is an object for his parents. Belief is the impossible internalization of this discourse. At issue, of course, is not merely an organization by the other of articulated language but a determination which depends on a general semantics. Maternal attentions are *also* signs; belief appears on the very level on which one discovers oneself by discovering others; in other words, the constitution of the ego engenders in each of us a primary belief, the source of all others. And, undoubtedly, in the practical agent this original belief is limited, contained, and sometimes partially dissolved by activity. But in someone constituted as a passive agent by the circumstances of his protohistory, the original belief—whatever it may be—invading the entire subjectivity, reproducing itself in diverse forms, becomes the *means* of living and of adapting to external conditions in the absence of the ability to conceive of possibles, that is, of the subject's practical relation to the environment.

These remarks apply directly to Gustave. Indeed, his old belief in the paternal curse has not disappeared; it has never ceased to condition him. By the beginning of 1844, he has carried it inside him for nearly fifteen years, and it has structured his imagination and his affective life: whereas you have displeased or disappointed me, whereas I have taken your measure and discovered your vicious nullity, I condemn you to death, or—according to Gustave's whim—I turn my back on you and withdraw my protection from you. In any event, the younger Flaubert son is a mistake, a monster, a bad deal of the cards, a defeat for the progenitor. It might be prudent to liquidate him on the spot: immediate death is the logical consequence of his infamy. But if they leave him his life, it amounts to the same thing: left with the sole resource of passive activity, Gustave will roll down the slope and be crushed at the bottom; his destiny will be merely the suffered temporalization of the original failure; the chink that makes him useless will grow wider; a defective machine, he will break down a little more each day until the final dislocation. There is no doubt that his new belief is a reactivation of that original faith. What difference is there between the two? The first was lived soberly yet, in a way, comfortably: the relation to the world was mediated by the relation to the father, and while Gustave was living in his family, he benefited from a long respite—though in a desperation that was more supposed than felt. The fall, in any case, began slowly, curbed by that compensatory counterbelief: he would tear himself away from Hell through fame. But at the end of '39 and until the beginning of '42, two principal changes affect him: his literary failures disillusion him; he will not be the doomed genius bearing witness for all men to their common damnation. At the same time, the father reveals his true intentions: he does not wish to kill his cursed son, or even to doom him to ignominiousness; the sentence becomes attenuated with time: condemned to simple bourgeois mediocrity, Gustave will be an average man, he will follow a career, sadly. And this commutation of punishment is found to be even more unbearable than the primal sanction: better to recover his former condition of dreaming and passive monster than to suffer the new and become an activist prisoner. How can he avoid it without directing an appeal to the old severity of the symbolic Father to support his opposition to Achille-Cléophas's caprice? Gustave becomes obliterated: in him, the paterfamilias will annul the decision of the head surgeon. Doctor Flaubert must be made to stand trial against himself, and the old sentence must be promptly executed by rendering the other inapplicable. As a result, the primal belief takes on a virulence it never had. It becomes *an emergency:* the destiny that he has been living every day and that extended over his entire life is gathered here into the immediate future: when Flaubert enters the Hôtel-Dieu around 20 January, he believes he is running toward that encounter with himself and is going to find himself finally face to face with the idiot or the cadaver that is his truth. The fall awaits him: it is his anomaly making itself lived as a catastrophe. And since, from 1842 on, work strikes him as playacting, since he *is playing the role* of law student, the abrupt reappearance of his passivity, beyond the fantasies of death or insanity that haunt him, seems to him a return to the real.

B. The Circumstances of the Fall

Gustave "feels odd." The *setting in place* has begun: somatization sustains and overflows belief, estrangement extends to conscious corporeal modifications. In the first days at the Hôtel-Dieu it is not yet a serious matter, save that an unprecedented nervousness, joined to intimate perceptions of bindings and loosenings, signs of a restructuring that is suffered and achieved blindly, in stupors perhaps, confirm him in the feeling that at any moment he could lose control. And this feeling in its turn contributes to precipitate the moment when Gustave will suffer in shock and horror the dazzling manifestation of his incapacities. Is this to say that the attack—or radical somatization—must proceed from this slow preparation as its logical conclusion and its completion, without the convergence of external circumstances? To answer this question, let us accompany the two brothers on the road from Deauville to Pont-l'Evêque, and let us try to describe the *situation* in which the younger brother finds himself when the crisis occurs.

Gustave is returning to Rouen, he is holding the reins, night is falling, Achille is beside him—such are the circumstances to be examined. The first is essential: Gustave fell *on the way back.* He had taken refuge in the Hôtel-Dieu, and to calm him, no doubt, they sent him to Deauville with big brother Achille at his side, who was probably charged with exercising a discreet medical surveillance. Deauville, the end point of his evasion: beyond lies the sea, he must embark for America, as Chateaubriand did, as Henry will do at the end of the first *Education,*[5] or else return. Thus far and no further: he must have dreamed of the New World at the water's edge. At the same time, during the twenty-four or forty-eight hours he spends outside of Rouen, he has known a period of equilibrium. The Hôtel-Dieu is an ambiguous refuge: in it he has rediscovered the paterfamilias's ironic solicitude or sermons, but then something was broken in his relationship with Caroline. Deauville offers him an unexpected opportunity: the family without the family. Outside of Achille, none of its members is present, but the land that belongs to them is there, designating them as a society of co-owners. This is what Gustave, the misanthrope, likes best: things indicating the man and touching him with their inertia; he is surrounded by his family's absence, which is so present for him: petrified and mute, the Flauberts inhabit every clod of earth. As for himself, this property designates him as an *heir.* Not that he is sure of inheriting this particular piece of property. But in whatever way the goods are divided, certain of them will have to come to him; the land at Deauville is the symbol of this transmission. He has been thinking about it for a long time, as we know. What fascinates him right now is the process of appropriation by inheritance. So much so that the

5. As did Monsieur Paul and Ernest.

"ground" provisionally delivers him from the obligation of taking on a profession by indicating another future to him, a purely familial one: building is about to begin, there are plans, Gustave has been consulted. True, the chalet won't be much more than a summer cottage; yet the site, the groundwork, reveal to him at once his family's future—growing rich, prospering—and the family as his real future as property owner. Things aren't that simple, he knows: before getting there, he will pass through the eye of a needle. Paris awaits him, and the law. But in this moment of equilibrium, so rare for him, he discovers—once again—the way a yearly income conforms to his passive activity, and, feeding his illusions without much difficulty—the earth is there, in front of his eyes—he believes he is touching his future truth.

Now it is getting late, he must go home. This means turning his back on his glimpsed reality, rediscovering his *living* family, and above all returning to Paris. Rouen is merely a step along the road that leads to the capital: let us not forget that he has come for "two or three days." He still has a respite of twenty-four hours, no more. When he climbs into the cabriolet, *he is going to Paris;* he cannot doubt it: the return to the Rouen will be lived as a calvary. Seen from the rue de l'Est, the family was a refuge; when he leaves Deauville, it looks like the passageway to slavery. They are going to show him the door, send him back to his studies, he detests them; with every turn of the wheel he feels the burgeoning of fear and disgust, he senses physically the necessity and impossibility of this return.

Let us refrain, however, from seeing these dispositions as simply a transient determination of his subjectivity, for they have not been called forth this moment by a creation *ex nihilo.* In the objective fact of driving a cabriolet and returning to prison, there is nothing that can *in itself* incline any random—that is, abstract—subject to bring on an attack of nerves. But the subject here is singularized by twenty-two years of life. In other words, the situation as it is lived is already structured by the totality of the past. In particular, by the half-symbolic way that Gustave has always *experienced* journeys by coach. In this regard, a letter written four years before the fall, on 21 April 1840, is highly significant. He had spent the Easter vacation at Andelys, and he addressed himself to Ernest, three days after his return:

> I was sitting on the outside of the coach, silently, my head in the wind, rocked by the pitching of the gallop; I felt the road flee under me and with it all my young years; I thought of all my other journeys to Andelys; I was plunged up to the neck in all these

memories . . . As I was approaching Rouen, I felt positive life and the present were seizing me, and with them everyday work, trivial life . . . the cursed hours . . . What must be done is not to think of the past . . . but to look to the future, to crane one's neck to see the horizon, to hurl oneself forward, head lowered, and to advance quickly, without listening to the plaintive voice of tender memories that would call you back to them in the valley of eternal anguish. You must not look at the gulf, for in its depth there is an inexpressible charm that lures us.[6]

Everything is there: the transposition of expanse into duration, the road that "flees" assimilated to the "young years" that flow by, motivating by its flight a search for lost time; the need to totalize, which makes of this particular journey a singularization of "*all* the journeys to Andelys" that are present in this one as its resonant depth, in the way a whole resides in each of its parts; the repugnance for Rouen, for the cursed hours, and suddenly the temptation—to look into the dizzying gulf, to experience its lure, to drop into it—to fight it without much conviction by a recourse to the future and by the ethical decision to advance quickly, by tearing oneself away from memories and mastering their anguish. We would find analogous remarks and descriptions by leafing through Flaubert's letters of 1849–51 or his *Voyage en Orient*: a displacement by horse or by carriage, provided it is of some consequence, prompts him to actualize his entire life: the journey becomes, properly speaking, its analogue, and through it Flaubert tastes the savor of *time suffered*: "motionless and silent" he is borne along; his point of departure and his point of arrival recede, one back to his birth, the other into the future to his death. In leaving Deauville, there is no doubt that his gloomy mood and his anguish had inclined him to totalize: what else had he been doing since the month of January? But the totalization is accomplished according to that deeply rooted plan which structured the "situation" of April 1840. It is pathogenic in that he cannot live it without its presenting to him the contradictory unity of all his intentions, of the impossible and the necessary, of praxis and inertia. The gulf is there, as in the return from Andelys, but the almost agreeable attraction it then exercised on him has changed into vertigo.

If he *were suffering*, as he *suffered* his life until 1842, well and good. But he was the one who was driving. Was Achille tired? Had they decided to take turns driving, or did the demon of masochism prompt

6. *Correspondance*, 1:68.

Gustave to take the reins? The fact is that he was not content just to be transported, an inert, protesting bundle; he demanded or at least accepted an active complicity: he wanted to assume responsibility for this abhorred return. Ordinarily, he loves to drive as he loves to swim: it is a game, a sport, he expends his energies for the gratuitous pleasure of expending them. But in this gloomy night the pleasure was lost almost immediately: it did not take him long to *realize* the serious, practical, ineluctable end of this journey, to see it as the very image of his life and of that activity so contrary to his "nature," which, born of passivity itself, leads him toward his destiny *with his consent*. Guiding the horse in the dark night, he constitutes himself as a practical agent in horror: he seems to be taking his own life in hand, not as he would wish it to be but as it is imposed on him. By this linkage he *restores* the integral nature of his Parisian existence, he finds himself again in that set moment—past, future, a hundred times begun anew—in which passive obedience—to which he could accommodate himself—by becoming radicalized, is transformed into activity. To take the reins, to work at the Code, it's all the same. The first of these actions is not only the symbol of the other, it leads logically to it, it is the necessary priming. One easily imagines the result: insofar as he instrumentalizes his body in a voluntary enterprise, he delegates passive resistance to that obscure and visceral part of the organism that does not obey him at all, that does not obey his obedience. As a result, Gustave's activity is in part unrealized: he takes a role, he *makes himself* effective and decisive, he plays at driving, all the while knowing that the drama will have unbearable and real consequences. Masochism and resentment are the factors that incline him to carry on an absurd activity to the very end, to punish the other in the self, while remaining irreproachably faithful, Achille will be able to testify to that by denying the revolt of the *soma* in the name of paternal Authority. And by seeing it—applying the grids of classical thought, as Achille-Cléophas would do: reason, passions—as merely the reactions of a vicious beast that will surely be brought under control in the end, even though *belief*, solidified, prophesies the worst, the imminence of the fall.

If Gustave looked that belief in the face, he would recognize it: it has inhabited and possessed him now for two years. If he were paying attention to the physical symptoms that announce his breakdown, perhaps it would not be too late to calm them. It might suffice simply to pass the reins to his brother or to stop at the side of the road. But this is precisely what he won't do: if he must be felled in full obedience, his right hand must not know what his left hand is doing;

in relation to the threatening somatization, he must be in a *state of distraction*. Even the distraction would not be possible if it had to be the object of a decision: in truth, it is simply the product of that real and symbolic action in which he is absorbed and which requires all his attention: driving in the dark. The lanterns barely show the way, he must look in front of him; hardly begun, Gustave's enterprise, image of the activities imposed on him, tears him from his depths, forces him to remain on the surface of himself, to keep scrutinizing the external gloom while in the internal gloom *something* is happening—which he is unaware of to the extent that his *role* of practical agent is played out against his constituted passivity, and as its blind negation. He is exaggerating, someone will say, he is working to rules. Of course, but, as we have seen, he cannot *act* without exaggerating, without *taking refuge in alacrity*. Everyone asks for oblivion in work; but for practical agents, action encloses them, they become the means to their end. Flaubert's case is more complex: his activities, contradicting his constituted passivity, far from *bringing* him oblivion, *require it*: always on the point of abandoning his enterprise, he never takes full advantage of the acquired momentum; he must rivet his attention on the instrumental object by a kind of continued creation, on pain of it breaking. As a result, he exaggerates; he *playacts* attention, and consequently he playacts oblivion. This does not mean that being oblivious to his belief and to the alarm bells ringing everywhere in his organs is a lie or a simulation; what it does mean is that at the heart of the real and of the calculated adaptation of options to possible objectives, attention and its complement, distraction, are a dimension of unreality. He playacts being oblivious to the mute prophecies of his body in order to drive, and must playact driving in order to be oblivious to them. On this level he can believe he is sincere, since action for Flaubert requires his being ludic; but because he must playact in any event—with bad faith and good conscience—there is every reason to believe that the role of driver bears another teleological intention: that of obscuring, through activism, his marginal consciousness of the rising perils in order to permit him to suffer the catastrophe *in all innocence*—to persuade him, in other words, that he *did not see it coming*.

On this point alone Gustave seems suspect: it is clear, indeed, that his troubling symptoms stem from his belief, from his autosuggestibility, the site of the encounter and coproduction of his passive activity and of the active passivity of his body. But the general characteristic of his behavior being what we have called "gliding," we cannot dismiss the suspicion that his pretension to dominate revolt is doubled by a more secret intent: to profit from it. Indeed, as we have seen, the tactic he adopts as distraught masterer—mastering the horse that pulls the cabriolet, mastering his nerves—is the worst conceivable course: if there were still hope, he should have turned back to himself, taken himself in hand, calmed himself down, in short, replaced unreflected action with reflection. That is what he has done a hundred times before; we are not unaware of it, he cannot be unaware of it. In this sense, whatever his intentions when he took the reins, we can be certain that he threw himself into the activity not *in spite* of the growing danger but *because* of it. A single ambiguity: Does he insist on driving in order to *let the peril grow* or in order to *make it grow?* Is he absorbed in his role of practical agent with the sole intention of *not intervening*, of not disturbing by reflection the process that is preparing itself inside him? Or, feeling that his activism evokes and reenforces his belief in the worst, does he make his obedience the means of precipitating the catastrophe? In my opinion, the two intentions coexist, but the second is deeper and more secret than the first. Thus, in going from the clearer to the more complex, we shall be able to disclose several intentional levels at the root of his activity: (1) to obey his father, whatever the cost; (2) in frenzy to make himself the artisan of his bourgeois destiny in complicity with those who have assigned it to him; (3) to master the obscure revolt that is rumbling inside him, as he is unable to assume it in negative action; (4) to take refuge in the role of agent, which absorbs him, so as to forget the resistance that is organizing itself and leave the field free to belief—in short, to run to his death in all innocence; (5) to exasperate this passive resistance to the same degree that the role of agent—in this case, driving the vehicle—symbolizes the general activity that is imposed on him and that he cannot tolerate; (6) more profoundly still, to restore, with the favor of propitious circumstances, the situation as a whole in which he has been struggling with himself since adolescence, to condense it into a moment so short that he can live it all, and to do this in such a way as to evoke in himself a global response to his problems; in short, to conjure *through absolute and partially playacted submission* the two contradictory wills of the Other—that of the bourgeois Achille-Cléophas who assigns him a bourgeois destiny, and that of the symbolic Father who condemned him to nothingness—and to let them (or make them) devour each other.

From this starting point, there is no objective circumstance he does not interpret as his *designation*. The night is as black as the inside of an oven, he is going forward blindly. The totalization through movement (borne along, he drives) takes on a particular significance from the simple fact that it *adopts the night as its material;* this journey in the gloom, lived as an entire existence, becomes the symbol of a *nocturnal* life. Of course, for other men—for Novalis—the night can serve as material support to other obsessions, to other themes: it is enough that the totalizing unity be executed out of other intentions. By itself, it *wants* to say nothing, but if one wants to *make it speak,* it responds through its own structures, through its relations with the practical agent (modification of the field of possibles, etc.), to a plurality of incompatible interrogations—which, moreover, it always goes beyond simply by its being-there, impenetrable, irreducible, surrounding its "responses" with a halo of confused, inert questions, as if the matter questioned were in turn interrogating the man. But this plurality of possible interpretations, although numerically indeterminate, has its internal limits: one cannot make it talk as one wants it to; it will never say what the day says, and if the inquirer tries to unify it by diurnal schemes, it will deflect his questions.[7] But when the concerns of the questioner bear some relation to the structures of the object, the object will allow itself to constitute the questioner's point of view as an incomplete, inert, and somehow indecipherable response-interrogation because the other objective characteristics—which would be manifest from a different viewpoint—remain in an implicit state as the contents, both opaque and fleeting, of that singular totalization. This is precisely what happens to Flaubert. There can be some affinity between his internal determination and the environment. And the questioned objectivity reflects to him, deflected, impenetrable, the *representation* of his subjectivity. Between the outer darkness and the inner darkness there

7. Today, various currents of thought (God proved by his absence, Evil conceived as the ethical positive beyond all negation) have inclined certain poets to speak in solar terms, not to pronounce his name without qualifying it by adjectives that evoke light. But I have shown elsewhere that this procedure—which is, moreover, perfectly legitimate—aims only to *shock* the reader by the coupling of contradictory words in order to suggest, beyond impossible synthesis, the unrealizable surpassing of all contradiction (in a certain place, Evil is none other than absolute Good, absence is the highest manifestation of existence, etc.). It is a question, therefore, of simple determinations of language: words that burn each other are yoked together, and it is their conflagration that *signifies,* beyond all signification. But these verbal syntheses—which find their source in the fact that nomination is not only the intentional aim of the thing but also the negation of the thing aimed at—have nothing in common with lived syntheses that have as matter the thing itself—diurnal-being, nocturnal-being—insofar as the human agent is *in situation* in relation to it. Verbal syntheses, much more varied, find their only limits in the structures of language; lined syntheses find their limits in the thing itself.

is a reciprocity of symbolization. The opaque gloom sets an *undifferentiated future* against the miserable but sunlit future Achille-Cléophas imposes on him.

For Gustave, his activity as driver represents submission, forced labor accepted, the bourgeois future. But the night *resists:* one must drive carefully; out of this indecipherable opacity *anything at all* can happen. One must *be prepared* for the accident. And, certainly, prepared to *avoid it.* Being expected, the accident is inscribed in the impenetrable density of being. Not as a *possibility*—the faculty of conceiving possibility has been broken in Gustave since childhood—nor exactly as a fatality, but rather as an already constituted reality, which at the last moment will or will not decide to take them by the throat. That other, almost immediate future, which envelops Flaubert and merges behind him with his most recent past, is being, to the extent that it presents itself to Gustave as the radical negation of man. The darkness proclaims the absurdity of every enterprise, the crushing of projects by the nonhuman order of causes and effects; it reflects to him the dumb desire of his constituted passivity by revealing that *praxis* is theoretically impossible, that there are only agitations and gestures. The inverted practical field of passive activity designates Flaubert as a dead-man-to-be, his wretched zeal is disqualified by the darkness, it is an epiphenomenon, an illusion that will be destroyed when the darkness, united with itself, will finally crush him. Thus the meaning of the practical field is abolition. But at first this is merely a tension, merely a set of potentialities that designate Gustave as a doomed man, denied by the world. The macrocosm in its inhumanity reflects to the microcosm the desire for death; Flaubert has constituted it as a pitilessly destructive universe by surpassing it toward his own end, which is nothingness. Here, at last, is infinite substance: it is the night of nonknowledge surrounding by its inhumanity the little futures, slender and clear, that our species has constructed for itself, and stealing its ends, which it has buried in its opacity. In this sense, the young man once more perceives in it the blurring of being and nothingness: it prophesies death—immediate or not, in any case certain—it turns itself into its image (Isn't this the fusion with everything through the bursting of individual difference that he dreamed of in *Novembre* and will dream of even in the final version of *Saint Antoine?*). And here is the all: opaque materiality, the Parmenidian Unity revealing itself by the engulfing of appearances and, as a result, showing what it keeps hidden: an obscure invitation to self-destruction of the finite mode. Thus, the internal *belief* in the fall finds its objective reflection in the threatening proposition of the nocturnal substance. Not entirely, however, for the night within is a pithiatic meditation on the *collapse*, whereas the night outside is an offer of *death*. But we shall soon see that this discrepancy between Gustave's underlying aim and the image etched on the black pane, far from impeding the process that is organizing itself, is apt to accelerate it: if madness looks at itself in the mirror and sees death, it will be less afraid of itself.

Finally, let us mention that essential factor of the situation which binds the elements together and brings out their meaning: the presence of Achille. In general it disturbs Gustave, it exasperates him; even when they seem to understand each other, the younger brother cannot prevent himself from seeing his elder as the one primarily responsible for his frustration, and Achille speaks to him, as can be seen in *La Peste à Florence,* with a benevolent condescension (Is this true, or does Gustave represent it this way?) that enrages him. This relationship to his brother is, on this level of abstraction, intentional but not teleological. Certainly Achille acts as a catalyst; he modifies his brother's relations with the environment, but this modification is a result, not a goal to be attained. When the usurper appears, the unloved boy thinks he will lose his head, everything becomes *more difficult* for him, that's all. This remains true on the night of Pont-l'Evêque, but other intentions—teleological ones—graft themselves onto the first.

It will be observed that for several days, without deciding either the date or the form the event will take, Gustave is preparing to *suffer* an irreversible collapse. And this still oneiric option *requires* that an accident be produced *before witnesses*. I do not mean that Flaubert had cynically decided to collapse in public: he does not even know, or want to know, what is in preparation. The public nature of his future disaster is an implicit structure of his option. Let us imagine that he falls apart in his room, when everyone is sleeping: all that trouble for nothing. He could always recover, hush up his collapse; and even if he should speak of it, the news, being *reported*, would lose its virulence. To what extent would they believe him? He needs an affidavit: someone must be able to bear witness under oath that the illness felled him in full activity, when he was hastening to return to his studies, to Paris. In principle, the crisis is addressed *to the father*, since it must be an important moment in their deaf-mute dialogue; the *designated* witness is Achille-Cléophas. In point of fact, his presence would inhibit the disorders, which might not even occur or might be

59

transformed into simple nervousness. For Gustave, the medical director has remained the "demon" whose surgical gaze pierces the most
secret lies, or rather reduces pithiatic belief to a mere lie. A frank
skepticism, born of frequent visits with patients, of the empirical
knowledge of their pathetic ruses, and of the will to thwart them, to
take their subjective estimate of their illness as little as possible into
consideration, to stick to objective symptoms—in short, the whole
mental organization of this practitioner might have prevented him
from taking seriously the event that must shatter his son's life—
Gustave has had this sad experience only too often. It was in his presence that Flaubert resisted in his imitation of the journalist of Nevers:
God knows what comparison might be established in the mind of the
philosophical practitioner between these somewhat forced dramas
and the convulsions that really will seize his son. Let us make sure we
understand each other: Gustave is not pretending, he *believes*. But
pithiatic belief has its limits, it includes the nonthetic consciousness
of being an ersatz form of an impossible, inconceivable certainty that
is yet sensed in others: the dry and rigorous facts that inhabit Doctor
Flaubert and can be read in his eyes are the external but powerful reducing agents of autosuggestion. Despite a certain show of familiarity, Gustave is paralyzed by timidity in his father's presence: he
irritates him with his crude clownings—he knows that they exasperate him (Caroline has not hidden it from him), and that he cannot
help indulging in them to the point where they become intolerable.
But this itself is a way of escaping, of not revealing himself, of hiding
from himself the fact that a relationship between father and son is unrealizable. The young man will not show his *belief* to the philosophical
practitioner *at any price*. For years he has been hiding from his father
that inner unreality which reveals what he is through what he is not,
the fascinating and evanescent unhappiness that constantly occupies
him, in short, his suggestibility. The "object relation"—to speak like
an analyst—that links son to father is basically pathogenic; it is the
chief source of his neurosis. Superficially, however, it contributes
little to its development, paradoxical as that might seem.

Achille is the opposite: secretly despised, he is no impediment.
And then, of course, he hardly knows Gustave: separated from him
by nine years, by his studies, his marriage, his patients, he has had
neither the leisure to study him nor, most likely, any concern to
understand him. But it is he, in this dark night, who represents Authority: the father has delegated his powers to him. Authority degraded, unintimidating, this simple fellow will register the attack and

institute it; the paterfamilias sees, alas, through his eyes: the deposition will have the force of law. Of course, Flaubert does not *formulate* these considerations; after all, *he* did not ask for Achille's company; he *suffers* it, like everything his father imposes on him, and he has no thought of *exploiting* the situation. Quite the contrary, it is the situation, through its objective structures, that becomes a *temptation:* Achille, by what he represents in the eyes of his younger brother— meaning, in large part, by what he is—appears to him a permanent and external solicitation to collapse. This is what fascinates Gustave: without a word, without reflective explanation, the temptation is mingled with the tall, placid mass of the older brother, half-consumed by shadows, with his immobility, his silence. Inasmuch as this abusive brother has himself driven by his younger brother, Gustave's portion is work, infamous activity, while the other takes it easy. The meaning of this nonreciprocity is complex: it indicates that the older brother has long since finished his studies while Gustave is still at forced labor; but it also indicates that Achille is the elect and that the other, working to take him to the family hearth, exaggerates the injustice that has produced his unhappiness, accepts it with submission, and, still worse, takes responsibility for it by making himself, through this servile task, the *inessential means* of which the usurper is the end. Yet, it will be said, he has chosen to drive. An additional reason: it is in his own heart that he discovers a transport of servility. This discovery nourishes his belief, enriches it with a masochistic impulse: to push base acquiescence to the extreme, to fall here and now at Achille's feet as though prostrating himself, to roll into the nonhuman before the eyes of the more brilliant of the Flaubert sons, and by this irreversible collapse to recognize humbly that the usurper was indeed the sole worthy heir, the only one capable of pursuing the father's work. Thus, this silent companion provokes two contrary inclinations in Gustave that mutually reinforce each other: Achille is the only worthy witness to his degradation, but he is also the rival before whom the young man is most ashamed to collapse. This is of little importance: the fall itself horrifies him, therefore it must be hyperbolic; which means that the horror, heightened by the masochistic postulation, is transformed into a ghastly attraction to the worst. This is indeed the worst: to realize and proclaim his radical inferiority before the enemy brother to whom he believed himself so superior, to recognize that the father's choice was just, to confirm it by revealing himself as a subman and, finally, to put himself into Achille's hands, to be dependent on his goodwill, on his medical knowledge, on his diagnostic and therapeutic abilities—in a word, on everything that was denied in him a priori or would in any case be considered secondary. These were the years when Flaubert, without saying much about it— except in his stories—regarded physicians as charlatans; what a dizzying temptation to make himself absolutely dependent on them, to compel them to show their imposture by not curing him or, still worse, to compel them to give him the lie, crush the contempt he bears them, show that contempt was merely a disguise for this poor devil's envy *by curing him.* If he falls, Art is smashed to bits, the universe of science and of practice closes around him. The washout believed he could compensate for his shortcomings by imagination. And behold; in him, imagination confesses that it was only a symptom of failure, that is, of his illness. As for Achille, he never imagines anything; in him, inventive ability serves only diagnostic purposes. At his feet, the dreamer, victim of fancy, will confess that he made poor use of his creative power: he should have subjected it to practice as a mere auxiliary of some real enterprise. Here we see a most atrocious nightmare taking shape, and one that Gustave recognizes: Garcia, *swooning,* calls to François for help: my brother, save me from death or imbecility, you will be my Lord. And everything will fall back in Order.

I have tried to describe the situation, namely, the internalization of objective structures by means of a certain constitution, which is objectively disclosable but is first *lived* as the permanent, anxious internalization of a certain *unsurpassable past*—or, at least, regarded as such. The objective whole (the detestable return from Deauville to Rouen through a black night, in a cabriolet he is driving, in the presence of his brother) is internalized by a simple totalization, which is the work not of reason but of anguish and unhappiness, and which expels chance, refusing to see the situation simply as the coexistence of fortuitous events (the night could be clear, the sky full of stars, Achille could ask to drive himself, etc.), and giving them, instead, the rigorous and necessary unity that belong only to works of art. And certainly the operation does not occur without dropping a few decimal points and without mistaking itself for something else, without passing itself off as the simple perception of the world as totality, produced for Gustave in that time, in that place, by a hideous Providence. In fact, the transformation of scattered contingency into a structured unity, each element of which is the necessary expression of the all, in which each part, far from coexisting passively with the others, is defined by all the others and would not exist without them, is the work of his perception, required by his belief. But what is this? It is to perceive. With more or less power, it is what every man does all the time. Indeed, what is a practical field but an agent's real environment revealing itself though projects conditioned by an anchorage (the accident of having been put into the world by a certain womb, at a certain place, at a certain moment, specific needs denatured as desires by a singular history, etc.) as a set of means and obstacles whose underlying unity corresponds to the particular style of an enterprise of living and reflects to the subject his objectivization—himself as going beyond his facticity and toward the world—in the form of destiny? In this sense, the practical field is a language: it is the agent announced to itself through exteriority. At the same time, it is a multiple tension, a totalitarian set of potentialities surrounding and conditioning the real and present praxis of the subject, all the more effectively endowing it with a meaning as it expresses, in its way—however superficially and partially—the basic reciprocity of the world and of the enterprise of living.[8] In these conditions, every event that *takes place,* even if it must soon break the structures of the field by revealing itself as the impossibility of continuing the enterprise of living, first presents itself as a singular way of speaking—understood through the totality of *everyday* language as differential appearance, as totalizing and totalized expression of the totalization in progress—and as the *actualization* of a potentiality conforming to the potential unity of the experienced world. The eruption of the unpredictable is thus an unexpected expectation; the contingent, material, irreducible fact throws my life in my face and announces my destiny to me. Even if it breaks me, I begin by recognizing myself in it: the appearance, in the moment it is produced, is already designated by the discourse that things contain for me; I comprehend it immediately because this discourse is permanent and prophetic. The difference is that, for the most part, it is a matter of discovering on the outside the possible action of the body—instrument of instrumentalization—on the unified field of the environment, which allows us to interpret the relation of the agent to the world as a dialogue in which the two interlocutors are signifying-signified. Instead of this,

8. A product of the world, my fundamental enterprise expresses it in its totality through my anchorage: totalization in the course of my ends and my means, the world announces me to myself as the practico-inert set of my realizations qualified synthetically from the horizon of the realizable, of the unrealizable, and of the inevitable.

Gustave produces that unification as passive agent so that an *inverted* practical field may be organized whose unity resides in the action that the world, through prophetic pronouncement—fascination and vertigo—must exercise on his body. Flaubert has *nothing to say* to the macrocosm; quite to the contrary, he makes the unified environment into a *signifying subject* of which he is the *signified object:* the night speaks to him and teaches him what he will be, what he is. All the changes that affect the reversed practical field, far from presenting themselves to him as the *means* to attain a transcendent end (or as difficulties to be resolved), manifest him in his own eyes as the means chosen by the field to achieve its own ends—in the present case by the night to recover its purity by eliminating the intruder.

All these conditions—some of which necessarily derived from his project (he was returning from Deauville, he asked or agreed to drive), while others were more or less fortuitous—had to be conjoined for him to internalize them as the unique opportunity to *take an important step*. Is this to say that lacking any one of these conditions, the opportunity would never have been recovered? We can only affirm that at this time he was permanently disposed to unify his practical field in the form of an invitation to collapse, to turn it into a language addressed solely to him. Most probably he would have found another assemblage of events, even diurnal, equally propitious to his fall—or perhaps a little less, certainly not more. Otherwise the neurosis would have taken a different course, would have manifested itself differently, while remaining the same; the underlying results would not have been altered.

C. The Stimulus

It is important to note that this reciprocity of perspectives between the world and the man—the former announcing the latter's belief, which can be perceived only from the outside in its reexternalization—by itself manages merely to promote a *disposition*. The belief is reinforced from one moment to the next and becomes inclination, *penchant*. But for the fall to be realized, for it to become an irreversible event breaking Gustave's life in two, an additional determination is necessary, a kind of fiat. Yet this fiat is impossible, in the first place because the power of decision does not belong to passive agents, especially where a major option is concerned. And, second, because everything occurs in shadow, and the point for Gustave is to *suffer*, not to simulate. Must it be admitted, then, that a brutal impulse throws him off balance and casts him at Achille's feet? No; this crisis cannot be blind; it will be *conclusive* and will have to be thought of as the moment of totalization. What Gustave wanted to do in a literary way in *Smarh* and in *Novembre* he will realize here in his body: he achieves totality in and through his annihilation. It is therefore inconceivable that a nonsignifying fillip should be the cause of this destructive synthesis. Yet there must be a triggering mechanism; what is happening here is the result not of a long evolution—although in the past few years there has been a maturation of his belief—but of a lightning flash: the *moment before,* he was a student; the *moment after,* a patient. What could have provoked this metamorphosis? Gustave gives us the answer himself: at nine o'clock in the evening, leaving Pont-l'Evêque "at a time when it was so dark that you couldn't see the horse's ears," a wagon driver emerged from the darkness and his heavy cart passes on Gustave's right. No danger of an accident—just an apparition. Devastated, the young man crumbles. There we have the provocation and the response; how are they to be understood?

An explanation has been proposed that I do not totally reject: for those nerves "taut as the strings of a violin," the emotional shock must have been terrible; it was followed in the organism by undifferentiated symptoms which, being substituted for learned reactions, for the everyday construction of perceptions, overflowed the adult's ordinary circuit and returned to that of early childhood. By way of this panic, the motor scheme of the fall, long since established and consolidated by exercises, was substituted for adapted responses; it became the order of these disorders, assembled them, imposed a provisional unity on them, integrated them, and transformed the panic into an intentional response, giving a lived meaning to that which at first had none at all. I repeat: I do not totally reject this interpretation; indeed, long after the crisis the slackening of the nerves seems to have persisted, as if the disturbances provoked by the trauma and channeled for a moment by the behavior of collapse took over again when Gustave opened his eyes, extending themselves, freed of all intentional unity, as nonsignifying perturbations of the organism. This, at least, is what can be concluded from the letter to Ernest that we have already cited: some days after the crisis, all his nerves are vibrating like the strings of a violin; his knees, his shoulders, his stomach are trembling like a leaf. It could be said that his nervous system reacts to any external aggression—however minimal—by reproducing the panic of Pont-l'Evêque. A psychic trauma often prompts an oneiric delirium, which opens the way for hysterical accidents. Gustave, by his immediately hysterical reaction, could thus be said to have made economical use of his mental confusion, but could not have avoided the nervous irritation that accompanies it.

Such clarifications, however, are not very satisfying. They are inspired by a mechanistic psychology, and, furthermore, the essential thing is left in shadow: one would like to know, for example, *how* the motor scheme of collapse could have substituted itself for the organism's habitual responses. More seriously, this interpretation cannot be adopted without *distorting* the event it claims to explain. It is based on the hypothesis that Gustave first of all experienced an emotional shock, that surprise and fear provoked some nameless *organic deviation* in him, which the fall subsequently *informed*, transformed as named behavior. But Maxime and Gustave are in agreement on one point: there was no emotional shock. Since no emotional disorder preceded the fall, the fall could not have united and channeled scattered agitations that did not even exist. The cart passes by, that is the act of aggression; Gustave crumbles, that is the response. Not the slightest surprise: the swiftness, the precision of his behavior would suggest rather that he was expecting the very event that provoked it. It would be futile to object that passive fear, when pushed to extremes, induces fainting. It is true that Gustave, a passive agent, responds passively to the sudden transformation of his perceptual field, but, as we know, there was no fainting: Gustave remained conscious for the entire duration of the crisis. Furthermore, how do we know he had been afraid? He hears, he sees, and he takes a nosedive: he hasn't even had time to understand what is happening to him. Passive or not, fear implies a certain consciousness of impending danger: one does not faint from horror before "realizing" the horrible thing, at least in part; and not only does Gustave report that his fall followed the act of aggression without intermediary, but he emphasizes the "floods of fire," the "fireworks of images" that *instantaneously* crossed his mind. In other words, the passing of the cart launches an ideational process without connection to the apparent nature of the stimulus that produced it. The moment when Flaubert crashes to the floor of the cabriolet, *he is elsewhere,* and his thought is invaded by a fantasmagoria that distances him from present reality: he becomes *entirely imaginary.* We shall return to this point in due course. Here, I simply want to indicate that Gustave responds to the external excitation with a structured behavior in which fear has no place. The swiftness and the intentional unity of his reaction suggest that it is an *act of consent.*

But to what can he consent? In other words, what could he grasp of the event, and what did he see in it? He said later, *after* Achille had recounted in his presence the circumstances of his crisis: "A wagon driver passed on my right." But on this occasion, he made the discourse of the Other his own: the wagon is the objective reality, detached from any individual "practical field" and restored by discourse as a strict determination of abstract space-time. In other words, the fact loses all its dramatic qualifiers: it is the *possible means* for no one; to no one does it reveal its *coefficient of possible adversity*. This is approximately the way it appeared to Achille: a marginal and semi-neutral accident, an inconsequential meteor traversing the environment and sinking into the night. Only in retrospect does it take on its importance in the eyes of the young Doctor Flaubert: it played—perhaps—the role of an efficient cause; under this heading it is proper to mention it. But if we want to understand, we must undo Achille's work and put this meteoric event back into the practical field occupied by Gustave, who has neither the pleasure, the leisure, nor the presence of mind necessary to identify the wagon driver as such and to grasp him in his reality as an inoffensive meteor, appearing only to disappear. On the other hand, falling *instantaneously*—as if he were obeying an awaited signal—he grasped the driver and his cart as a real and total presence, richer and more intimate for him than a mere threatened collision (not a gesture to protect himself, though he knows how to drive, knows the route, and ought ordinarily to have estimated the risks so as to be prepared for them). He must have had the immediate and yet complete intuition of a "matter concerning him" if he instantaneously and effortlessly grasped this bright and noisy little lightning flash as *endowed with meaning*, when he was in no position to define it in its objective reality; he felt it and lived it as an internal modification of the inverted practical field.

Flaubert, as we have seen, gets an announcement of his death from the dark night, a confluence of being and nothingness. But as a passive agent, he will not kill himself: he expects the night to take charge of his death, to *realize* it spontaneously. This expectation is polyvalent: for the moment, the nocturnal impenetrability manifests the homogeneity of the substance and designates it simply as undesirable; as long as this equilibrium remains, nothing will really threaten it; but the latent promise of the inverted practical field is that something is going to be produced that will strike it down; and the thunderbolt can come from *anywhere* by virtue of that very homogeneity. The young man believes in it: he has already installed death in his body;

his organism, passive and resigned, is disposed to be felled by a knockout blow: all that's needed is a fiat coming *from the outside. Belief* appears here as an inclination to structure as mortal accident the first abrupt break in external equilibrium. Thus, the event at Pont-l'Evêque is not grasped for what it is in itself: Gustave does not understand that a wagon driver passed him on his right, but he apprehends this modification of the practical field through the general meaning that the homogeneous opacity of the environment has continued to reflect to him, and he immediately constitutes that opacity as murderous spontaneity. There is no need to observe, to make a decision: provided it is brutal and unforeseen, provided it appears as a local materialization of nocturnal hostility, provided it concerns Gustave and takes him by surprise, it can be anything at all, though that won't prevent it from being *recognized*. The wagon driver's passing fulfills all the requisite conditions: Gustave recognizes it on the spot. How exactly does he see it? As an order? As accidental death pouncing on him from outside? As a sign? As a signal? Something of all those things.

First of all, this unpredictable and long awaited event necessarily has an imperative structure. In the field of a practical agent, the event, whatever its utility or its coefficient of adversity, appears as given in fact, or, strictly speaking, it can be grasped through the whole of the enterprise—in which it is necessarily lodged—as indication, solicitation, invitation to invention. If utility outweighs adversity, it can even be offered as the inert equivalent of invention itself, the means arriving at the right moment, that is, a human production, a creation of the practical field as such.[9] In a passive agent, however, the relation to the event is reversed: since the power to decide is absent, the thing produced on the outside passes itself off as the *decision taken*, and this underlying anthropomorphism comes from the fact that the passive agent, in his social setting, has always grasped decisions as a determination which is *other* and produced by others. And this decision produced in *his* practical field necessarily concerns him. In other words, in the field of a passive agent, the event can receive from the signifying totality the structure of an imperative; it will be internalized as an order *bursting-inert from the world.* If a comparison is

9. It matters little, of course, if, at another level, reason attributes these means, which are furnished by the exterior, to the rigorous and nonteleological succession of phenomena. The rain, so long awaited—for such and such a reason—will be *first of all a gift* in the eyes of the practical, even reasonable, agent. Its hindrance, by contrast, is more easily reduced to a nonsignifying determination of matter: the general attitude of the practical agent is based on the surpassing of the given, whatever it is, that corresponds to the profound certainty that meaning comes to matter through man.

needed to make myself better understood, I shall recall the way in which an automobile driver (a practical agent but marginally passive on the level of safety instructions) *realizes* through certain behavior the imperative content of an event such as the sudden emergence of a road sign announcing a dangerous turn or the proximity of a school. Certainly, beyond the apparition there is a relation to the Other, to a society; but what is given *first* to the self-domesticated beast is the object-instruction. For the passive agent, the world is full of object-instructions that have not been forged by the society but reflect to him the *impact* of others on himself. What Flaubert has been waiting for, and what has just been produced, is fatal accident as an instruction to die. Indeed, the decision made outside him in "the matter concerning him" is the ancient sentence, the father's curse, which is about to be abruptly executed: no more respite; here and now, he must die. By this sentence, Gustave in a flash is returned to his finitude: condemned in advance, the monster was born to live twenty-one years of life, neither more nor less. This time the totalization is done by constraint: he is annihilated *on command*.

At the same moment, the event reveals its savage and irreducible materiality: those sinister noises to his right, those bells, those lights are a localized concretization of the darkness, the eternal night abruptly and in one fell swoop becoming temporal, the brutal actualization of a permanent potentiality—the cruel indifference of the universe—becoming *in its way* the executor of the paternal curse (as Gustave's body, in its way, executes his impossible desires), which amounts to stripping it of any human signification. But it is the victim, above all, who is fully *signified* by the violence of things: fortuitous birth, accidental death; what is Gustave but an absurd, fleeting dream of matter? The sign contradicts the imperative: Is it Abraham who commands him to die? Or, in putting an end to his agitations and recalling him to his condition of inanimate matter, doesn't the night remove him from the paternal imperatives? He makes no decision: he has always hoped for both outcomes. If the father is a murderer, so much the better: Achille-Cléophas's remorse will leave him no peace. And if the reason for his decease is merely the unpredictable encounter of two causal series, the dead young man will have given proof of his filial zeal to the end; death will overtake him in full obedience. In both cases he declines all responsibility.

Wrongly. That tumult to his right is crying out to him: "You are a dead man!" Doesn't that mean: "Your turn"? Isn't it a *signal*? An invitation? Or permission, given at last, to play his role? Beyond his desire to annihilate himself, might not this sign also be addressed to his temptation to collapse? "This is the moment; take advantage of what you think is falling into nothingness to throw yourself into illness, into insanity, in a word, into subhumanity." This is not a matter, let us repeat, of simulation. But death and madness are two irreversibles, and Gustave's underlying intention is to cut himself off from his future being by a moment of irreversibility. And what has happened? Gustave has been inhabited for some years now by the awful temptation to sink into the subhuman in order to escape his class-being: that is his underlying intention, which he has often disguised as a suicidal impulse. The fact is that he neither can nor wants to kill himself. But his real determination is unbearable to him: it indulges his masochism and his resentful sadism, it terrifies his pride. Upon returning from Deauville, the die is cast, he feels sure; anything rather than begin all over again. He believes that imbecility is gaining on him, but his terror is such that he will never dare *take an important step* without tricking himself, without masking the deeper work going on inside him with a *screen of belief*. The night provides that screen by designating him a future corpse: it denies him, claims to abolish him; from this moment on, he is prepared to die: he has disposed his body to mimic a resigned crumbling, which amounts to establishing inside him the conduct of collapse by persuading himself pithiatically that it is the conduct of death. We have often seen Gustave hestitate between necrosis and neurosis, and we have noted the ambiguity of the solution he adopts in *Novembre*: to die by thought. Thus, of the two irreversibles, the savage event that overtakes him at Pont-l'Evêque seems to impose *one* of them on him, death; but thanks to that superficial belief, his body, in its suspect docility, jumps at the chance to realize *the other*. *To be* a corpse is the perfect solution: he is freed from his manly obligations without falling into subhumanity. *To make oneself* into a corpse is to be afflicted with mental troubles and to renounce human dignity while still alive. Yet although he falls *in order to be abolished*, he must understand in some obscure way that one is not killed "by thought," and that his "I am dying" has this deeper meaning: "I am becoming publicly the monster that I was." Thus he *also* receives the nocturnal aggression as a *signal* addressed to his intention to collapse. Yet that signal would have been inoperative if Gustave had not received from the night a message of death and an order to die. With the apparition of the wagon driver, he saw his death coming at him as a process already begun, issuing already objective from the external darkness in order to become radically internalized: all he had to do was let himself go, in pseudo-ignorance of what would follow. We shall see that the crisis and the subsequent disorders will make themselves lived simultaneously according to these two systems of reference.

D. NEUROSIS AND NECROSIS

Let us examine from this double point of view Gustave's own interpretations of his crisis after it has taken place. We shall see that, for him, death and madness are two inseparable aspects of his affliction.

Gustave insists on the first aspect from January '44 on. He writes to Ernest: "I nearly popped off in the hands of my family." And if he then accepts his father's diagnosis, if he *believes* in it, it is because it sets things in order—"cerebral congestion, miniature apoplexy," meaning: death entered me, and, for some reason I am unaware of, it stopped in the nick of time. In short, it is a *true* beginning of the process of death. An *experience of dying*. He will frequently return to this experience; it even seems to him that he has lived it to the end: "It is my conviction that I have died several times." [10] It is survival that is accidental; for his part, Gustave did all he could. We can better understand the words he writes to Ernest: "I am a dead man." He harbors the conviction of being *beyond annihilation*. However, his hesitation is manifest: did he "nearly pop off," or was he really "dead and departed"? His body embraces a hysterical behavior of *false death:* in the letter of 2 September '53, he indicates the *imitative* aspect of his comportment. Apoplexy is no longer merely a metaphor: he fell "as though struck down by apoplexy." Which is to say that he lost motor control; he explains it to us: his eyes were closed, he could neither speak nor move—one would say, a generalized hysterical contraction. Not the least convulsion during the first ten minutes: the organism mimics the immobility of a corpse. What matters above all is that this paralysis is lived as a rupture of communication. The important thing for him—he reveals it to us when returning to this experience nearly ten years later—is that "for ten minutes his brother believed he was dead." As if, in a sense, that belief reinforced his own, as if the underlying intention was to convince the Other. Attended to, he opens his eyes; but as this chance treatment was unrelated to his illness, it is inconceivable that it cured him: let us say that it persuaded him to open his eyes. As though it were providing him with proof that *he went all the way to the end*, that he was saved *in extremis*. Did convul-

10. *Correspondance*, 3:270.

sions follow? He does not even speak of it and tells Ernest only that "cases of nerves" *accompanied* the congestion (nervous trembling, hyperaesthesia, visual but more differentiated hallucinations—flames, bundles of hair, etc.). Moreover, if convulsions had occurred *at Pont-l'Evêque*, Achille would not have diagnosed cerebral congestion. In other words, when Gustave fell, he was afflicted with a hysterical paralysis that mimics the cadaverous state and is lived as pithiatic belief: he is dead and does not want to let go of it, his body did what it could to give him satisfaction.

This is pretty good. But Garcia actually fainted. That loss of consciousness represented the most perfect imitation of a corpse. Thus, when Gustave a few years earlier prophetically imagined the fall at Pont-l'Evêque, he radicalized it: even if he should survive it (Garcia recovers his spirits), he wanted it to be accompanied by catalepsy. In January '44, nothing of the kind: not for an instant, he will tell us, does he cease to be conscious: "I was always conscious, even though I could no longer speak."[11] During the fall, he is "utterly transported in a flood of flames."[12] Then, "a hundred thousand images leaped up at once, like fireworks. In one second he felt a million thoughts, images, combinations of all kinds." Later he was to say: "Everything in Saint Theresa, in Hoffmann, and in Edgar Allen Poe I have felt, I have seen, hallucinators are quite comprehensible to me."[13] He is certainly exaggerating: several years before the crisis, he already makes mention of his imaginative power, "meaning, according to them, an exaltation of the brain akin to madness."[14] He was specific in the beginning of *Novembre:*

> Sometimes, when I am exhausted, devoured by limitless passions, full of the ardent lava flowing from my soul, loving with frenzied love a thousand nameless things, regretting magnificent dreams, tempted by all the voluptuous pleasures of thought, inhaling all poetries, all harmonies, and crushed beneath the weight of my heart and my pride, *I would fall annihilated into an abyss of agonies,* the blood would whip my face, my arteries deafened me, my chest would seem to split apart, *I no longer saw anything, I no longer felt anything,* I was drunk, I was mad, I imagined I was huge, I imagined I contained a supreme incarnation whose revelation

11. Ibid., 7–8 July '53.
12. Ibid.
13. *Correspondance,* 4:169, 30 March '57. He is evidently speaking of the attacks as a whole and not only of the first.
14. *Mémoires d'un fou.*

would enchant the world, and its anguish was the very life of the god I carried in my entrails.

Couldn't this be characterized as a dress rehearsal? Everything is there. In many another text he mentions those explosions of ineffable images, linked to some vague, broad theme of a generally affective order. Thus the "floods of fire" at Pont-l'Evêque find their precedents in these ecstasies and are rooted in Gustave's protohistory. What distinguishes them from the previous fantasmagorias? In a letter to Louise, Flaubert tells us: "First you have them in mind, and then they appear in front of your eyes." In other words, in January '44 the mental images are held to have become hallucinations. Is this entirely accurate? Note that he himself makes one qualification and insists on speaking of *nervous hallucinations,* as if he wanted to distinguish them from other hallucinatory facts in which the patient takes his visions for realities. These would be *external,* like afflictions of the optic nerve (no matter whether the stimulus is external or springs from nervous tension), and he *would not believe in them.*

Although Flaubert is fond of using the *word,* he is not describing the *thing.* Edgar Allen Poe and Hoffmann are not hallucinators. Saint Theresa's mystical experience is entirely interior: Gustave's experience can bear only a distant resemblance to it, through those alternations of barrenness, langor, and plenitude that we have often found in him. But the mystic feels the hallucinatory presence of the divine only after being stripped—or believing to have been stripped—of sensory perceptions, of the images that correspond to them, and of language. Above all, the experience of the mystic, whatever name it is given, has a *meaning,* it is produced within the framework of an instituted religion, whereas the "fireworks" of '44 are nowhere given as signifying facts. We shall never know their content in detail—for the simple reason that he does not breathe a word about it. Not that he wants to hide it, but how can one describe "a hundred thousand images leaping up at once," "a million thoughts, images and combinations"? In fact, we are dealing with a multiplicity of unconnected "rockets." Flaubert lives these apperceptions, which do not communicate among themselves and are incommunicable to others, as a dissociation of his person.

A fact can be "normal" or, at least, subpathological: at certain moments of mental fragility, a situation, a word striking the ear, any sort of *stimulus,* instead of provoking the appropriate reaction, will evoke an abundance of imagery without explicable connection to the proposal of the external world and without internal structure. The heard sentence resonates, absurd, uncomprehended, in the midst of a swarm of impressions, which at once claim relation to the sentence and distance us from it without explicitly referring us to our real concerns. Those moments are of brief duration: one readapts. The important thing is that they are sometimes experienced as an enrichment and an acceleration of the flight of ideas, whereas they actually correspond to an abrupt *deceleration* of ideational activity. The structures of comprehension are broken: analysis and synthesis, provisionally impossible, have given way to a syncretism of interpenetration. We encounter these symptoms in Gustave: his highly pronounced inclination for metaphor is exasperated, or rather, the two terms of the metaphorical construction lose their contours and merge; thought does not "emerge," it remains inherent in the images; and other images assert themselves as if they were ideas.[15] These afterimages persist in a color or a sonority imagined as their present but ungraspable meaning; the primary images pretend to be signifying, pass themselves off as the vivid and elliptical expression of an idea, but this is merely a delusion: they offer no readable meaning. The ensemble of these false illuminations and obscure lights remains vaguely governed by the great affective themes proper to Flaubert. But they no longer either articulate or symbolize those themes: they sometimes pass for dizzying but indecipherable abridgments (because they are, in truth, abridgments of *nothing*); sometimes they refer to it precisely. But in the absence of intellect, the reference is made without knowing and remains unperceived, such that the representation is isolated and posed for itself as merely the imaginary restitution of materiality; and sometimes, unable to affirm itself and *conceive its own possibility*, the theme becomes a naked and dizzying presence: it attracts *from below*, unformulated, and entreats Gustave, through an artistic concurrence, to hurl himself and merge into it.

The fireworks are *illusory*: the rockets are neither as numerous, nor as brilliant, nor as rapid—Flaubert's internal gaze has become too slow to follow them or count them. Without any doubt, these manifestations remain altogether in the framework of the imaginary: they *are not embodied*, they do not impose themselves as real determinations of the visual and auditory field; they do not become integrated with any structured whole. Hence, precisely, their evident diversity: a synthetic thought is quite as complex, but it integrates its elements

15. Indeed, he says: "a million images, *combinations, thoughts.*"

74

into the unity of a totalization in progress; here the elements are at liberty, and their multiplicity has no other reason than the paralysis of synthetic apperception and of the powers of selection. Gustave's imagination is not *richer:* at this moment he lets his imagination over-flow as if, incapable of subordinating it to creative invention, he were suffering it like an invasion of parasites; as if this flux of disconnected apparitions had only one role, to convince him that he is the victim of a dissociation from his person. He admits it himself in his letter of 18 May '57: "In my poor brain there was a whirlpool of ideas and images in which my consciousness, my Self, seemed to be sinking like a ship in a storm." This text shows convincingly that during Flaubert's at-tacks he was not in the least tempted to take these disordered appari-tions for external realities, but that he was afraid rather of "sinking into the whirlpool," of remaining forever the site of insane agitations, his *self* swallowed up. In a word—contrary to the conclusions of the mechanistic interpretation we have criticized above—Flaubert was not spared *mental confusion:* he did not go as far as "oneiric delirium," but he is certainly describing a state of confusion when he recounts his first fall—a state that seems to be reproduced during the following attacks, at least until July '44.

Here the relationship between neurosis and necrosis is clearly manifest. The whirlpool of images, far from contradicting the suicidal intention, is, on the contrary, its immediate product. The hysterical paralysis is an imitation of death, and the brutal disconnection of the nervous centers, by endowing his body with the passivity Gustave envies in reclining mortuary figures, simultaneously engulfs his mind: mental activity can be exercised only on the basis of an organic tension assured by a minimum of physical activity. This "death" plunges him into a state resembling sleep: before sinking into sleep, certain subjects suddenly feel their powerlessness; it seems to them that they have lost the use of their arms, their legs, and that they can no longer even move their little finger; they are invaded by hyp-nagogic images. They are awake, however, and know that these appa-ritions are insubstantial phantasms whose eruption and precision are in exact proportion to the paralysis that extends from their body to their thought. Thus it is with Gustave, except that this imagery, devel-oped in the setting of belief in the father, is lived by him as the first symptom of a psychosis. He does not believe in the present reality of the phantasms, he believes in their future reality: this means that their substance is temporal and that they will be maintained in him until the end; better, that they are going to multiply, swarm, invade him entirely. The words "It seemed to me that my consciousness . . . was sinking" could be said by any man passing from a waking state to sleep, and this is indeed what Gustave fears and prophesies; he awaits the minute when, by a modification of his belief, those sequences of images will become *dreams*. The properly pithiatic moment is the fall and the false catalepsy that followed it; insanity, the object of his underlying intention, profits from this experienced powerlessness to establish itself inside him. In a way, although it is more deeply awaited, it can be called parasitic; it manifests itself *in place of* the impossible annihilation.

Since we have been studying Gustave's relations to his "picture-making faculty," we have discovered in him that constant which I call "passive choice," characterized by the (futile) intention to suffer his imagination. In January '44, following the *false death*, the passive option is radicalized and the intention *to suffer* seems to have achieved its aim: the imaginary imposes itself in its savage purity, in its disorder. Gustave, lying on his back, inert in his brother's hands, realizes his old dream: to become entirely imaginary. Only two years earlier this unformulated wish corresponded to the mad desire to be *another*, Nero, Tamberlaine, that is, to live *in the imaginary* the singular experience of a great man now dead. That experience appeared to him then as the *unity of a role*; it implied art's compression of real life, which is always a little too encumbered, unnecessarily and idly complicated. *To become imaginary* could mean, in Gustave's eyes, only one thing: to fall headfirst into a role of power and glory as rigorous as if some dramatist had conceived it, to be the character's prey, to be capable only of incarnating that character, to grasp in himself each of his gestures and even his perceptions as *representations* of the vampire that was nourished by him, yet without actually identifying with this sumptuous occupant. And this last qualification implied, of course, that he wanted to remain sound of mind, but above all that he maintained in the face of all opposition the superiority of nonbeing, of the ineffective, and of sensuous pleasures not experienced over the base savor of being and the vulgarity of truly felt sensations.

Yet, in the night of Pont-l'Evêque, the *becoming-imaginary* is experienced *as a failure*: it is still a falling into the unreal. But unreality takes on a wholly different meaning: it manifests itself as decomposition, and the spasmodic bursting forth of these raw materials has as its primary result the suspension of all rational operations. To become unrealized for good is no longer to *play Nero*, it is to fall into insanity. The man prey to images is a subman: he will never become a notary, that is certain, but he no longer has any chance of becoming an artist. Those absurd phantasms do not cease because their nonbeing has been exposed at the very moment of their appearance; Gustave does not *believe* in this disparate swarm of vampires. What he does explicitly experience as a belief is the cruel sentence that binds him to images in perpetuity. Later, he repeatedly says that he is punished where he has sinned; because he teased the imaginary, it has ended by imposing itself as an alien force and has become radicalized. And the domination of man by a nonsignifying nonbeing is Evil. He *was waiting for* that still noble collapse in which external abjection—stupor, hyperaesthesia, nervous problems—would be the obverse of a monstrous and disordered exuberance of the interior life. This noble failure is the punishment of Prometheus. The moment it came, he *recognized* it. In terror but without shame: he is chastized for having played with fire; victim of his magnificent ambition, his nerves shatter because he tried to tear himself away from the baseness of the human race and raise himself, by taking himself out of nature, to the level of the superhuman. What happens when the wagon driver issues from the shadows is, from this point of view, an abrupt suspension of the higher faculties, a kind of *conscious fainting* that is accompanied by a scattering of images. Here belief intervenes: Gustave *identifies* with this scattering insofar as it is at once the dissociation from his person, the pronouncement of his new destiny, the radicalization of his failure, and, in the very core of this radicalization, the affirmation of a humble success: the great man *manqué* has managed, despite everything, to breach the wall of the real, to make himself entirely imaginary. So much the worse for him if the imaginary is not what he hoped.

But Gustave is not so simple: above all, he must be innocent. If the false death makes itself lived as psychosis, the psychosis, conversely, on this night and later, seems to him like a real death every time he speaks of it. "The fantastic invades you," he writes in '47, "and it is an atrocious anguish. You feel you are going mad. You are, and you are conscious of it. You feel your soul escaping, and all your physical powers cry after it and call it back. *Death must be something* like this when one is conscious of it."[16] And six years later: "A hundred thousand images leaping up at once . . . There was a tearing of the soul from the body, atrocious (it is my conviction that I have died several times), but what constitutes the personality, rational-being, went on to the end; without that the torment would have been nil, for I would

16. To Louise, July '47, *Correspondance*, 2:51. My italics.

have been purely passive, but I was always *conscious,* even though I could no longer speak. Then the soul was folded entirely back on itself, like a hedgehog trying to hurt itself with its own quills."[17] In the first text, the equivalence of the two interpretations is underscored: "You feel you are going mad . . . Death must be something like that." The second passage is a little different: Flaubert has just explained to Louise that he will never lose his mind because he has "plumbed the depths of madness." Read: in imagination. Thus the "psychosis" that he prophesied in January '44 passes to the rank of the imaginary.

It has left him with a nervous illness, however; his "picture-making faculty" suffers from a hemorrhage of images. But it is lived as death throes. And he adds: I have died several times. Meaning: in each attack. This divergence can be explained: in '47, Gustave has not properly recovered, he has relapses; he is still wondering whether he will sink into insanity. In '53, he has recovered—or just about[18]—and the pithiatic character of his psychic troubles is entirely manifest to him. All the more so as he takes pride in having cured himself. What remains is the memory of the intolerable torments he has undergone. It will be observed that, when writing about it, he uses the word "atrocious" twice in an interval of six years. So let us proceed to a new dimension of his attacks: the pain. Is it mental or physical? We cannot settle this question without examining closely those two texts in which neurosis is once more masked and passes, experientially, as necrosis. In the crisis, he tells us in '47, you feel you are going mad, you are, you are conscious of it: in short, he describes the moment when, he will say later, "his consciousness seemed to sink"; but consciousness immediately becomes a thinking substance: this glimmer on the way to *being extinguished* is changed into *soul,* and under that name it attempts to *escape* the body. In other words, his hysterical sleeping, that slipping away primed by the fall and never completed, suddenly poses as a *tearing away,* a physical dislocation in the process of being produced as a result of the abrupt appearance of a centrifugal force. Is it a simple, substantialist metaphor? Surely not, since he adds, "All your physical powers cry out after it and call it back," and concludes: death, *when it is conscious,* must be like that. The pain of consciousness is transformed into the consciousness of pain. But looking more closely, we find to our surprise that from another point of view this consciousness is doubled: it ought to be a consciousness-

17. To Louise, 7–8 July '53, *Correspondance,* 3:270.
18. "A nervous affliction that lasted ten years."

of-escaping—of being extinguished—but, since "you feel your soul escaping," it must be that an *other consciousness* feels the first consciousness leaving the body. And this *other* consciousness is *none other* than the body itself, since it "cries out after the soul" to recover it. The instant he feels he is going mad, Gustave turns himself into a purely physical organism in order to apprehend his madness *physically* as a receding of the soul; he takes refuge in an obscure and animal thought, the intuition of a body that is abandoned. Of course, this organic thought does not exist—at least in this form: it is Flaubert who produces it through an illusory dichotomy of his consciousness, the same consciousness that feels itself sinking, tries in vain *to be other* in order to recover itself and, as a consequence, poses at once as soul escaping and as body that feels itself dying. Or, if you prefer, Gustave manipulates himself to feel, with horror, his hysterical paralysis as the *effect* of his mental problems, although, as we have seen, it is the indispensable condition for them. By reason of this attitude, his terror of sinking into madness becomes a *physical torment*. How does this manifest itself? Even if there were no convulsions at Pont-l'Evêque, the subsequent referential attacks ended often, though not always, with violent jolts: Maxime, who reports it to us, was an eyewitness. It appears, therefore, that Gustave quickly reacted to the necrosis with convulsive spasms, which pulled him out of his pithiatic paralysis. Suffered spasms, of course, random muscular contractions, which left him battered for several days. The nervous influx, deflected, passed through old circuits; those agonizing jolts were physically felt, but their *meaning* was to materialize the moral torment.

In his letter of July '53, on the other hand, Gustave does not mention "physical forces." Quite to the contrary, apropos the "atrocious tearing away of the soul from the body" he declares: "I was never purely passive, and I was always conscious, even though I could no longer speak." The only *activity*, here, is that of consciousness: "even though I could no longer speak" refers us to the hysterical paralysis. In other words, even when he is reduced to impotence, even when his body passively suffers that "tearing away of the soul," there is still suffering: at Pont-l'Evêque, in the course of the *nonconvulsive* crisis that devastated him, Gustave experienced *atrocious* pain. That pain was *original*. The other pangs, the convulsive ones, merely follow the pattern of the first: they emanate from the original and reproduce that agony on another terrain. And Gustave clearly indicate in this text that this first torment is *moral*: "the rational-being went on to the end; without that, the torment would have been nil, for I would have been purely passive and I was always *conscious.*" In '57, he said: "My *self* was sinking . . . But I clung to my reason. It dominated everything, though besieged and battered." These two passages inform us: *to go on* to the end is to *hold on* to the end. *Besieged and battered,* what can reason be but the reaffirmation, vacillating but constant, that "those are images, I am me"? But the moment he affirms this proposition, Gustave, already lacking the talent for assertoric judgments, is robbed of the means to sustain it: gone simultaneously are the will and the mental functions of integration. Hence, reason is "battered": it cannot—at least at first—restore truth and dissipate error through mental operations; it is therefore only *postulated,* during the crisis; Flaubert relates to it as to something that has existed, that can always reappear on the ruin of his phantasms; he intentionally aims at it but does not encounter it. Proof that it exists is the summons of an already obscured memory. Somehow, "clinging to rational-being" is to *believe in it,* to believe that it can be reborn and, like the sun, dissipate the clouds—for rational-being, in Gustave, his belief in death, in madness, is combated by a counterbelief: it is on this level that torment appears, which is merely this contradiction *lived out.*

Is it *truly* atrocious? Certainly Gustave *is afraid* of sinking. But, after all, *he is the one* who has gradually become determined to initiate this wreckage. For him, this invasion of parasites is not like an unexpected danger, though it is made manifest by an external stimulus; disturbing as it is, it has some aura of familiarity. Not that that makes it any more reassuring, I admit. But Flaubert undergoes an induced anaesthesia: Is he still capable of *actually* suffering? Our dreamed-of terrors become part of our dreams; they are feelings rooted in the real but unrealized and lived *in the imaginary.* As the desire that is unreally—oneirically—gratified shows itself a bit too much for what it is, the proscriptions reappear and the dream becomes a nightmare. But has it not been structured spontaneously as an unreal gratification *before being experienced at the cost of a nightmare?* Isn't the nightmare often potentially contained and accepted as something that reestablishes equilibrium by demonstrating that the dreamer renounces his desires? An analyst reports the following dream: the subject finds himself with his father and a grenadier of the Grande Armée in the middle of a great plain covered with snow; *with horror* he sees the soldier taking aim at his father; he leaps onto the man and tries to grab his rifle—too late: the shot is fired, the old man falls, the subject experiences his *atrocious* impotence. Isn't it apparent that an obscure teleological intention has brought everything into combination? It is the son's ardent wish that his father will die, but he will be killed *by another*, whom the subject will sincerely but vainly attempt to thwart; yet that does not suffice to free the dreamer from all implication: he *must* experience his impotence *in horror*. Otherwise, as Gustave says of himself, "he would be purely passive." To be sure, the basis of that horror is real: it is the horror of the forbidden. But the horror is deviated, unrealized: it is no longer the horror of the self, it is the horror of the Other-who-accomplishes-the-desired-act. In a word, it is not only a consequence of the oneiric gratification but is seen to be assigned a function within the dream by the intention that produces the dream and structures it as totalization; it is a means of *attenuating it* (the self-disgust is lived as repugnance for the gesture of the other) and of putting it in the service of the oneiric enterprise. By this twisting of sentiment, the subject constitutes his fictive act as an *alien act;* the horror is lived as the futile denunciation of an objective event. It matters little that he wakes up trembling and bathed in sweat—this even testifies to his innocence and his filial love.

There is thus a finality to the atrociousness; in the nightmares and through this finality, anguish and fear, becoming the constituent parts of the dream, are changed—on the basis of real interdictions—into dreamed determinations of the affective life. So it is for Gustave at the onset of the first attack. Certainly he dreads collapsing; but doesn't he obscurely understand that he will never go *too far* in this direction? And doesn't he arrange to turn this trial insanity into a final agony—because death frightens him less than madness? His pride suffers, no doubt about it. But is he *in a state of pride,* this reclining funerary figure who undergoes a triple bleeding? On the other hand, the torment is *imposed* on him by the intention that structures his neurosis: if he had not suffered, as he himself says to Louise, it would have been because he was *purely passive.* But that passivity would not have differed from perfect detachment. As a result, his obedience would have been disqualified. His father compels him to act, he submits himself; the crisis robs him of the means to obey, he accepts it with the same tranquillity: either he is merely a malleable wax inertly subsisting to being molded in any shape (in which case, where is the merit?), or else his obedience is suspect. The only way of disavowing his crisis, of seeing it as a totality that is destroying him in spite of himself and will forever thwart all his deepest aspirations, is to *turn it into a nightmare.* To suffer is not enough; what is required is the disavowal of horror. It is integrated with the pre-oneiric whole and becomes itself pre-oneiric. It is neither entirely suffered nor entirely dreamed—its basis is a real fear. But he unrealizes it by pushing it to the limit: *atrocious*, it becomes a hypnagogic hallucination. Which signifies that it is a *constituent part* of the crisis and that, far from being its real effect, is *plays a role in it*. The whirlpool of phantasms is sustained and qualified—as unknown accident and disavowal—by a phantasmatic terror. The nightmarish atmosphere of the crisis is, like the "fireworks," an imaginary product of the fundamental intention, whose structure is teleological but which appeared as the disavowed determination of passive activity; and in the subsequent attack the convulsions will be aimed at realizing this intention as *physical pain* insofar as it is not really lived as moral suffering. Simple inertia does not suffice to make him the innocent victim of a blow of fate: so as not to be suspected—by Others, meaning, first of all, by himself—of complicity, he must *deny* the illness that devastates him. And for this denial to be ineffective, it must not be a practical negation but an unrealizing determination of the affective life. Nothing is easier for this passive agent in whom the faculty of *yes* and *no* is atrophied. And that "torment" has a dual function, for even as it makes him innocent it gives notice of the extreme gravity of the peril: *atrocious*, it becomes the presentiment of the worst.

Another look at the letter of '53 confirms our interpretation. Not only by that strange "I would have been purely passive"—which demands this complementary statement: "And that, at any price, I could not be; therefore I had to structure myself in such a way that I might suffer"—but also by the contradictory images that Flaubert employs. There is, on the one hand, that "tearing away of the soul from the body," expressly defined by Flaubert as a *death*, which seems to indicate that the vital principle *is departing* and that the organism is on the way to becoming a cadaver, and, on the other hand, that folding back of the soul on itself, "like a hedgehog trying to hurt itself with its own quills," which seems to signal a kind of *introversion* of lived experience. No doubt one could maintain that the soul tears away from the body *in immanence*, without leaving it, by abdicating its functions of surveillance and direction and abandoning itself to the disorders of an uncontrolled nervous system. But in this case what becomes of the assimilation of crimes to successive deaths? There is death if the "soul" departs. And, above all, *who* is suffering? In the first metaphor, it is the body (in '47, it cried out after the soul and called it back), or, strictly speaking, *the soul and the body together*. In the second, it is the soul alone. It is no longer a hemorrhage, an illness —*expanding*, but a folding back, an illness *retracting*. The quills of the hedgehog are no doubt the projections by which the soul penetrates into the nervous system. It turns them against itself: does this mean that it takes responsibility for breaking off communications? But with what psychic pain is it afflicted, then, beyond any real modification of the organism? Flaubert's obscure and contradictory description bears witness to a pathological experience that cannot be rendered by discourse. He needs these two opposite approaches in order to reveal, through their opposition and because of it, the unspeakable affective quality of lived experience—to be precise, that unlocalizable "atrociousness" that is profoundly but unreally experienced as the assurance that the hysterical *commitment* is indeed *suffered*. In general, however, it can be held that the image of the tearing away represents necrosis, whereas that of the hedgehog, through the implicit intention it presupposes (the soul turns *itself* in on the self, it *takes the initiative* in breaking communications with the exterior and even with the body, which, as a result, is paralyzed), evokes neurosis as pithiatic belief.

E. HYSTERICAL COMMITMENT

If we wish to penetrate further into Gustave's neurosis, a summary of the "event" at Pont-l'Evêque is now in order, and provisionally setting aside the two systems of references, we shall attempt to envisage it in its concrete reality. There was a *fall*, followed by temporary paralysis. It is this fall itself and *as such* that we must now describe. And we affirm that beyond or on this side of madness and death (to die, to go mad, is not necessarily to fall) it presents an immediate meaning that is all its own: to fall is, in the first place, to fall from honor, etc. I hasten to observe that here we have a "popular" metaphor: what I mean is that it has been internalized by Flaubert but is not properly his. Although high and low are principal determinations of his space, he has internalized a social scheme. What does belong to him is the underlying meaning he gives to the fall. As a common symbol, it marks primarily the passage from a higher echelon of the accepted hierarchy to a lower one. Gustave sees even more in it: to fall is to cede to gravity, therefore to return, at least for a moment, to original passivity. Indeed, a man who falls causes himself to be signified by the world as temporarily dehumanized: he is no more than an inert object on which great physical forces exert themselves, the first being gravity. As long as he has not touched the ground, it is of no use to him to be an organism, he is no more than a mass. Most of the time, accidental falls are due to a loss of equilibrium. For Flaubert in January '44, the fall—the return to the state of inorganic materiality—is the consequence of a muscular resolution, a sudden weakening of tone in the muscles that support upright posture.

I am pushing ahead a little, and it is not clear whether we are dealing in fact with a generalized loss of tone rather than a sudden tension of the opposing muscles. Was Gustave "betrayed" by his body, or did he fall at his brother's feet in imitation of the *suffered* collapse? In the latter hypothesis, we would find ourselves confronted by a behavior closer in appearance to simulation. It must not be forgotten, however, that in the former hypothesis the muscular resolution in this particular case can result only in a modification of the nervous influx. Thus, in any event, the origin of the phenomenon is central. Similarly, when he is down, the fact that he finds it impossible to move or even to open his eyes can be conceived equally as resulting from a contraction of the striated muscles or from a neural disconnection, such as we experience during sleep when we feel literally incapable of moving a finger. For my part, I lean toward this latter interpretation without entirely excluding the first: fascinated by the cold and polished metal of the night, Gustave may have gradually put himself into a neuro-vegetative state. As we have seen, the decisive factor was belief and not revolt or affirmation.

In any event, this problem is of only minor interest to us. If Gustave's behavior is the result of sudden muscular contractions (like the spasms in referential attacks), we can easily assure ourselves that although it *seems* to betray some simulation, there is none. Whatever our interpretation, the disorders at Pont-l'Evêque are organized under the direction of a vigorous, autonomous scheme, which we can call psychomotor because it has imposed itself on Flaubert's body and sensibility for many years. From the beginning of this study, we have had occasion to point out that the scheme of verticality conditioned the child, then the adolescent. He raises himself up or throws himself down. Behind the description of his ascents, we have often discovered actual falls. Furthermore, most of the time it is not true that he rises to the heavens unaided: he is lifted, and it is the Devil who kidnaps him, only to let him fall like Smarh into a nothingness where he will twist and turn endlessly. In short, negative verticality, passive descent, yielding to one's own weight is a dominant theme, and the pseudo-ascents, still passive, spontaneously turn into tumbles. The future tumble is inscribed in advance in these pseudo-ascents as their underlying meaning and their purpose, signaled from the moment of his takeoff by dizziness and fear. Smarh, clinging to Satan's coattails, is a mass that is terrified to be the object of universal gravity. Nothing like this would be imagined if an actual Assumption were in question.

In the preceding chapters, the theme of negative verticality appeared to us as an organization of the imaginary. And that must be so, for we have discerned it especially in Gustave's fictional works. However, we observed it just now, without any loss of its unreality, in its symbolic function—the fall of Smarh, or reversed ascent, or the false elevation of the schoolboy who ends by *drowning* at the edge of possible worlds—as well as in a more material though still symbolic aspect—the fainting of Garcia, or of the Bibliomane who displays his pain and his impotence by crashing to the ground. This fascination with absolute passivity did not come to Gustave from the outside: it is and always will remain the temptation of a passive activity that tries to resolve its underlying contradiction (the necessity of praxis and constituted passivity of lived experience) by forcing one of the terms, by seeking through it to realize the pathetic element as an absolute. Thus the reclining mortuary figures—whose status he envies—have fallen, overtaken by death, and their perishable flesh has been replaced by stone; this petrification, and not real death, is what the young author of *Novembre* covets. The fall and mineralization are one and the same.

Of course, these are dreams. But the dreams, so often repeated, bear witness to an exis of the imagination. Once solicited, the imagination will construct all the concrete images demanded of it within the framework of negative verticality conceived as a return to the mineral state. We all have our own guiding schemes, and we surpass them by the singular inventions they structure. But rarely has a writer set down rules so meager and constraining. The ironclad law that compels him to playact his being with the means at hand, to determine himself in the unreal lived according to negative verticality and passivity, can be taken as constitutive of his unreality.

All the evidence suggests that this structure of being overflows the fictions and is lived equally as a real impulse of his ordinary existence. Originally there was the stupor of a wretched boy fascinated by the world, but there were also those very real falls which, as a child, landed him on the floor, head first, when he was engrossed in his readings, as if, incapable of the marginal vigilance necessary to remain upright, he no longer reacted as an organism and was transformed into a purely mechanical system. The falls are not *only* imaginary, nor are those vague impulses to suicide that push him to throw himself out the window, to hurl himself from the height of a

sea wall into the black waves that "detonate like cannons." This suicidal scheme is so imperious in him that much later, in 1875, when he
recounts the life of Saint Julien *l'Hospitalier,* he writes: "He resolved to
die. And one day when he found himself at the rim of a fountain, as
he leaned over to gauge the depths of the water . . ." [19] One would
expect this turbulent captain, this violent and bloody hunter, to fall
on his sword. But the author, out of love, chooses for him that most
feminine of deaths: drowning. He leans, leans, and if it had not been
for an unforeseen event, which we shall discuss later, he would have
let himself fall head first, dragged down by his weight to be swallowed up in his own reflection.

These remarks indicate that during the crisis of Pont-l'Evêque, and
on that level, *morbid invention* counts for very little. True, he has
fallen; he has become an inert mass, his brother and neighbors had to
carry him like a sack of potatoes to the nearest house and lay him
down on the table where Achille was going to treat him. But he had
been carrying every aspect of this behavior inside him from his childhood: a dream of abdication, a desire to fall, to be one with earth or
water, with the original passivity of matter, with minerality; he knows
and acknowledges this primary theme, which is the organizing principle of his life, the immediate flavor of his consciousness, dreaded in
real existence and considerably exploited in the imaginary. Beginning
in 1838, his neurosis is organized—to the extent that it is organized at
all—around this temptation. I'm certain that Flaubert allowed himself
to fall like this continually: in Paris, he would fall onto his bed, his
eyes open, his boots on; he may even have given himself the pleasure
of falling to the floor, like Garcia. These were solitary celebrations,
offered to himself only briefly and behind closed doors. Yet they were
implicitly, at least by way of an *anticipatory experiment*, the radical
meaning of the attack that would knock him down at Pont-l'Evêque;
for this was surely an *abdication* embodied by a loss of equilibrium and
a fall into passivity. Even in the crudest way, the fall always signified
the denial of the human for Flaubert, a role too difficult to maintain as
long as the status of humanity seemed to him to coincide with an upright posture, the symbol of activity. But while this collapse offered a
total meaning—and, besides, was consolidated as exis and impulse
together—Gustave was conscious each time from the outset of being
able to recover himself. Once up again, dusted off, unseen, unappre-

19. G. Flaubert, Pléiade ed., 1:644. It will be observed that he has already sought
death "by saving . . . children from the depths. The abyss rejected him."

hended, he found human dignity once more. Indeed, if he authorized these descents into the inhuman, it was because he was sure of a return. When he threw himself onto his bed in the rue de l'Est, or when he set about aping the fits of the journalist from Nevers, all four paws in the air, he did not really feel he *was committed.*

For this reason, the accident at Pont-l'Evêque encourages nominalism. In itself it seems atypical: if we start with the universal, we shall understand nothing about it. By contrast, to anyone who has followed Gustave from early childhood, it is clear that the attack somehow reproduces a singular experience, repeated a hundred times, now sudden and suffered, now playacted, now imagined and attributed to a fictional character. At issue, here, is a protean behavior that mimics itself or lives itself or speaks itself, but gradually becomes a guiding scheme of Flaubertian spontaneity. The sole difference—but it is crucial—is that the January fall bears in it a deliberate intention of irreversibility. So the teleological intention is reversed: ordinarily, he *realizes* the fall (or is unrealized in it, if he takes it as a role) in order to enjoy passivity through it. But another barely decipherable, ambiguous intention is discernible in this abandon: the intention to constitute the fall as a revelation of his true nature, which according to him is absolute inertia. It is this implicit intention that becomes fundamental in the crisis. It is no longer a matter of enjoying a moment of his "nature," either in act or in illusion, but of obeying it; that nature *produces* the fall: it is Flaubert's *truth,* which external influences, ignorant or ill-intended, have vainly tried to mask for more than twenty years by imprinting on him, from the outside, motions that he could not *sustain* and that were perpetuated in him for a time by his very inertia. On a certain level of meaning, the fall appears, as we have seen, to be provoked by obedience pushed to the limit: Flaubert has been *too obedient,* which presupposes that he admits to himself a certain power of activity that is, however, restrained and characterized by singular ends, that has been broken by being forced, pushed artificially beyond its limits, and deviated by substituting for his own aims objectives that are alien to him. But, underneath, the challenge is much more radical: we are no longer dealing with an illness, an abnormal reaction, but with the abrupt appearance, a sudden, experienced illumination, of the absolute truth. On this level, Gustave enjoys his passivity bitterly and fully, in the midst of total wreckage, passivity being conceived here as a negative power—passive resistance or the force of inertia. Despite the ill-will of others and his own illusions—maintained through obedience—the truth is unmasked in a lightning flash and publicly denounces the bad shepherds. Triumphant passivity becomes a fall: and Gustave, who has so often played this role of inert mass, *recognizes himself* in this "thing" that *falls like a mass*, that reveals itself as mere weight, defined by its multiple relations to the great cosmic forces. Therefore, to the extent that the fall, as a unique possible response to the singular Destiny he has been assigned, has been in preparation for twenty years through various exercises, it reveals itself in a flash as a return to the truth. Shortly afterward, Gustave proudly states that one must live *according to one's nature*. He adds: circumstances allowed me to do it, but my will also had something to do with it. Which means: the attack was the rebellion of my true nature (I am not made to act, nor above all to enjoy), my merit is in having been able to understand that and in limiting myself henceforth to being only what I am.

Precisely for these reasons the crisis at Pont-l-Evêque, despite its public character, would be more symbolic than efficacious if taken in itself and enclosed in its instantaneousness. To fall, as we have said, is to fall from honor, etc.—so be it. But this is merely a humorous image; the real collapse accommodates itself splendidly to upright posture. One can, of course, measure rank by altitude. But there are other signs (badges, medals, uniforms, etc.) that allow dignitaries to be distinguished from the common people while remaining on an equal footing with the man in the street. Moreover, when Gustave takes a nosedive and crumbles at his brother's feet, two images interfere and become muddled: is he becoming infamous or is he encountering his essence? Neither: to fall is merely a symbol of infamy, decipherable for him alone; and although he is certainly a passive agent, inertia is not his status except metaphorically. I know quite well that he collapses with the conviction of destroying himself or finding that he has turned into an idiot. But what of it? He will pick himself up exhausted, anxious, his nerves in shreds, *sound of mind;* he will be shaky on his legs but will remain standing and, alone or supported by his brother, will go back to the cabriolet *walking on his own feet.* In short, if it were *merely itself*, the crisis would have to be regarded as a metaphoric, localized totalization by which Gustave has gathered his grievances, his disgusts, his anguish, his resentments in an instant by affecting qualities (mad, dead, inorganic) that he has never really possessed. As such, I have noted, the crisis would have been inefficacious: indeed, as we have seen, Gustave will be a notary or an attorney unless an event independent of his will deprives him of the possibility of obeying his father. And the accident at Pont-l'Evêque cannot suffice to remove him from practical life: if it were not to recur, the young man would remain a few months under observation at the Hôtel-Dieu, then again take the road to Paris. This is the meaning of Maxime's sentence: "[Achille] was hoping, without much assurance, that he had just been witness to an act that would not happen again." The older brother, who sees the attack *from the outside*, can still suppose that it is an isolated event. The violence and force of the manifestations, however, already trouble him: but he sees them as merely a sign of the possibility—strictly speaking, the probability—that they will be repeated, nothing more, for the brother does not know *what* is at issue. Gustave himself has a certain comprehension of lived experience on the level of non-thetic consciousness: a feeling of *déjà-vu*, of familiarity, gives him the obscure certainty that the crisis *will not go any further*, that he "will not pop off" in Achille's hands, or become senile. All this would be of no consequence if the fall itself did not present a counterpoint to his acknowledged inefficacy, a neurotic mortgage on the future, the commitment not to go instantly to the worst but to repeat itself indefinitely. Nothing is as clear as that, of course: let us say that it is lived as a *beginning*. Not at all as an immediate and decisive rupture but as the beginning of an illness *that becomes temporalized*. And what can it forecast, in that atrocious moment when Gustave is incapable of forming a single thought, except *itself*, its eternal return? This unformulated anticipation is in itself merely a certain temporal density of lived experience. Obviously we are dealing with a *hysterical commitment:* the old vow to collapse is present in the midst of these disorders as a teleological intention, but we have seen above what form intentions take in passive agents: they become *prophetic beliefs*. On the surface, Flaubert believes that *in this very crisis* he will go to the end, but *beneath* this belief there is the implicit knowledge of unsurpassable limits (it can neither produce death nor structure itself as insanity), so that his actual pithiatic belief, deep down, is that the symptoms will maintain themselves indefinitely, which is equivalent to the commitment to repeat them as often as he must. Thus we shall better understand Gustave's terrors and his feeling of sinking into the atrocious: what terrifies him is not really the conviction that *this time* he is going to sink to the bottom, it is his commitment-belief, in short, his conviction that the present disorders are equally more of the future, and that hc is in the process of living the totality of his future in anticipation. The fall *had* to bring Gustave to the point of no return, which is just what it did: not in that moment—when it was merely a metaphor—but in signifying to him by some ghastly flavor of lived experience that the point of no return resides in the repetitive structure of the suffered event. The immediate future (I am dying, I am sinking) becomes the symbol of the distant future, believed and dreamed in a terror itself imaginary. Gustave's whole life will be changed from day to day by the intermittent resurgence of disorders that are always similar and whose referential character is present even in the original attack, although veiled by the desperate and sadomasochistic haste to radicalize everything instantly. In this sense, of the two radicalizing metaphors it is death that will henceforth obsess him: it will appear to Flaubert on the level of metaphoric reflection, and in the light of the referential disorders, as the most appropriate symbol of his state. For after January '44 the young man can no longer doubt it: *he is not mad;* aside from brief attacks he has all his reason, and henceforth he will go around repeating that he has had a brush with madness but that, thank God, he was immunized. The one who is dead—Gustave returns a hundred times to this subject in the letters to Louise and in the first *Education*—is the young man who was still healthy but tormented by the paternal curse. The one who rises from the grave and allows himself to be defined by the repetition of the attacks is the young man with a *nervous* illness whose sensibility, as we shall see, has suffered a radical modification and who must forever renounce the "active and passionate life" of his youth. Thus the collapse—undeniable *from the point of view of others*—far from realizing itself in a lightning flash as radical irreversibility, will be lived and suffered on a daily basis. The attacks, the affective void they provoke, which is at the same time the very setting in which they can be engendered, the affliction as an objective definition of Gustave's state by the paterfamilias, the sequestration—everything comes from the secret and terrifying commitment to *maintain* this state through symptoms suffered in the measure of the most perspicacious witness, the man who slices through lies with a scalpel and makes them fall to pieces at his feet.

Here the objective of the passive enterprise is manifestly clear to us: what Flaubert could not achieve in 1841–42 because he had not decided to *believe in it,* he now believes, and as a result he achieves it in earnest: by accepting himself as the shame of the family, he manages to remain in it indefinitely, realizing at last the way of life to which he had been aspiring in vain for many years: semisequestration.

F. Neurosis as Regression

The moment Flaubert felt threatened, as we have seen, he hastily left Paris and took refuge at the Hôtel-Dieu. Not to avoid a disaster he believed inevitable, but so that his mother, his father, his brother, and his sister could be witnesses to it. This reaction shows an explicit and immediately recognizable intention. Many people tear themselves away from solitude and return to die in the midst of their family, if they can. It is not so much that they are seeking physical help, but they don't want "to croak like rats in a hole"; in short, they want to recuperate their death by socializing it as a communal adventure of the group from which they came and which will survive them. Death will no longer be the pure abolition of an existence: recaptured and, if possible, transmitted from generation to generation, it will become a dated event in the family history, a determination of communal life surpassed but preserved, *instituted* as an imperative of the sensibility and as a repetitive ceremonial. The dying person desires to live his death as a passage to eternity by discovering it in the eyes of those near to him as an archetypal event that will henceforth be maintained in the form of a celebrated eternal return. Flaubert feels the weight of a terrible threat, but he hesitates with regard to the nature of the peril; in any case, he rejoins his family. Since he has wanted the group to institute the catastrophe that will crush him, the immediate proximity of the family setting is a direct entreaty: the attack strikes him down *here and now*, in urgency, because soon *there will be no more time*, because he has only two or three days, and once he has passed this ultimate limit he will have to suffer the attack in solitude. In short, he abandons himself to it at Pont-l'Evêque so as not to be its victim in Paris.

Beneath this first intention—so common that it does not permit interpretation of his illness in its singularity—we shall easily discover another, which is more personal to him: he harbors the desire to plunge his family into remorse—they will be seized with horror if they see him struck down at their feet. But, in a way, this negative intention aims at something imaginary: Flaubert is inclined to give himself the (unreal) satisfaction of moving Achille-Cléophas to a repentance that, in any event, the father will not feel. This bitter and insubstantial pleasure can be lived only in the most atrocious solitude, at the price of a difficult *derealization*—at the edge of autism and madness. He will come to it, as I shall show in this chapter. But we know the ambivalence of his filial feelings. Nor should it surprise us first to encounter in him another, more positive intentional level. Indeed, if we reread the letter to Ernest, one sentence stands out dramatically: there is a kind of felicitous fatuity about it, out of place as it is in the sad enumeration of Gustave's ills: "I nearly popped off in the hands of my family." To communicate the simple news of his "congestion," three words would have sufficed: "I nearly croaked." But— whether or not he is explicitly conscious of it—this dry information could not satisfy Gustave, it would not take account of the concrete event in its synthetic unity, it would be an abstraction. The originality of the crisis is expressed in these strictly inseparable terms, which must be read as a single movement: "pop-off-in-the-hands-of-my-family." His false death is familial, it is a *restoration* of the Flaubert group through the sacrifice of the younger brother. Until then, this student, past his majority and enfranchised, by spending several days with his relations could be said to be living *with* them or even, strictly speaking, to be living off them. But he was about to leave, take his exams, enter a profession that would permit him to reproduce his life through his work. And now the catastrophe has put him back "in their hands." These words at first suggest the anxious solicitude of *all* the Flauberts, gathered at his bedside, clutching his body with their eight pairs of hands to wrench him away from death. From this point of view, the intention is clear: unloved children injure or burn themselves to reawaken love. So it is with Gustave; we know that he dreams of making his father weep; here is the chance to do it. When Maxime came to pay him a visit, Achille-Cléophas was still tormented, but the family no longer feared for the life of their younger son, nor even for his reason. It was Flaubert himself who informed his friend that the paterfamilias "was desperate." What gives Du Camp's narrative its strange flavor,—even if we take no account of this author's malicious intentions—is the juxtaposition of contradictory information obviously furnished by Gustave alone: "He saw no other remedy than bleeding to excess"—that is what satisfied the younger son's *resentment*. In the "father's despair" we have the fulfillment of his frustrated desire as loving vassal. The father weeps, and the patient, immobile and mute, thinks ecstatically: "So he did love me!" The letter to Ernest confirms this, the tone of certain passages does not deceive: "My father wants to keep me here for a long time and to treat me attentively, *although my morale is good.*"[20] You have read cor-

---

20. My italics.

rectly: Gustave, if it were up to him, would take several weeks of rest and gaily return to Paris. But it is the father who *wants* to keep him: a superfluous precaution, no doubt, but one that Gustave accepts as an act of love. The slyboots! Look how he has reversed the situation! Now it is his father who orders him to interrupt his studies, and it is Gustave who *agrees, out of obedience,* so as not to plunge the family into anguish, not to return to his beloved room in the rue de l'Est, to interrupt *sine die* his passionate reading of the Civil Code. And the strange thing is that it is true: by the sacrifice at Pont-l'Evêque, he has compelled the head of the family to withdraw him from the world and from active life. With what delight does he submit to the decision of his master!

But what makes his comfort complete is the promise that accompanies this decision: "My father wants . . . to treat me attentively." It is not simply a question of keeping him at home: Achille-Cléophas is constantly engaged in caring for him; here he is, that overworked physician who had eyes only for Big Brother Achille, finding the time to watch over his younger son attentively, to pay *attention* to him. Gustave's triumph—discreet but visible—enlightens us as to one of the chief meanings of his collapse: when he is struck down at his brother's feet, it is not only out of masochism. Death and madness, no doubt, transform him *into an object.* He is *pliable,* and if he "nearly popped off," it was in the hands of his rival, the detested usurper. But he makes himself an object in order to *become the object of care.* Since he does not go to the end of either death or insanity, the two doctors Flaubert must try to cure him. Certainly he is ashamed to entrust his destiny, his life, to his enemy brother, and his fall is a prostration. On the other hand, he compels Achille-Cléophas's representative to behave as his father would have done, to bend over his younger son, to fear the worst, to try everything to save him. In short, he restores to him his function of benevolent big brother. Adult, married, a father, waiting to inherit the responsibilities of the chief physician, Achille leads *his* life; always bound on the deepest level to Achille-Cléophas, he has taken his distance in relation to the other Flauberts. Gustave compels him, by means of the care required by his condition, to reenter the family circle, of which the younger brother has suddenly become the center through his unforeseen fall. The tormented face of the young Doctor Flaubert at this moment prefigures that of the paterfamilias, until now excessively severe, ironic, and often irritated; that of the mother, austere, a bit distracted, and too often glacial; that of the traitor Caroline, who forgets him for a Hamard—all those faces that in a few hours will be turned toward Gustave, anxious or imploring. An object, certainly, since mute, blind, paralyzed, he mimics the inertia of an object, but an object of love, *at last*, he awaits the gentle murmurings at his bedside, the respectful silences, the looks filled with tenderness. He goes still further, and if he abandons himself to false death it is not in order to "pop off" but to abdicate "in the hands" of his family. He feels a certain self-indulgence in writing: *"They will make me* take the sea air early this year, *they will subject me* to a good deal of exercise and especially to a good deal of calm." This reveals the underlying meaning of his passive option: naked, fragile, defenseless, his powerlessness as patient must restore to him the powerlessness of the nursing infant. Through death and madness, he aspires to *regress* to his protohistory. He prepares to receive the expected medical care *in the same way that he received the first maternal care.* These practices, conscientious, expert, and without warmth, have affected him, we know, with a constitutional passivity. But, precisely for that reason, he aspires to pure passivity. It is no accident that the crisis took the form of a *fall*, followed by paralysis: he has lost the use of all learned gestures, he can no longer speak, or walk, or even stand upright; Achille is bringing a newborn back to the Hôtel-Dieu. In that "fatal moment," is it out of antagonism to the paterfamilias (who condemned him to activity) that Gustave returns to his first infancy? Is it from his mother that he seeks to retrieve the firm authority that prevailed before the reign of the father by retracing the course of time back to this golden age? No, or rather not only: she had charge of him then, it's true; but now the father alone can give him the care Gustave demands, which is quite as intimate (he is "sodomized by the syringe"). Indeed, one intention of the fall—highly ambivalent, as we shall see, but we are examinining here only its positive aspect—is to compel that forgetful and unjust father, that terrible, virile Moses, to become *maternal*, to treat his son manually, as Madame Flaubert did, to *reconstitute the collapsed, decomposed body that she had constituted in 1821—in short, to leave his lordly, masculine authority at Gustave's door and to enter his room in skirts, to manipulate or sodomize him with a feminine gentleness.[21] To transform a progenitor into a progenitrix is no small matter: this, however, is what Gustave is set on doing from the moment of his crisis, and it must be acknowledged that the operation, promptly executed, will be crowned with success, at least until the end of the summer of '44. Above all, he at-

21. Which Madame Flaubert certainly had not had in 1821.

tempts to start his protohistory over again by improving it, and to create a tender, intersubjective setting around himself of which he will be the principal purpose and which will make *all decisions* for him, out of love.

Here he is undoubtedly pursuing two complementary ends: to make himself the beloved child he never was by sowing anxiety through a sudden regression; and to palm off onto the Flaubert community all the responsibilities that crush him—including the obligation to wash, shave, defecate, etc. This second objective is perhaps the more important, because it concerns Gustave's mode of *existence*, in other words, his ontological relations to temporalization and localization.

We would be wrong to believe that he aspires to the condition of object as a lesser evil, or only to elicit love. He also seeks it for itself. When in Paris, he suffered his own activity as an alien force that he did not recognize yet had to claim as his own. He made no decisions by himself yet had to internalize the decisions of others and assume them because others needed him to turn himself, in the heteronomy of his spontaneity, into the conscious means of their enterprises. Thus, subjective intimacy was his damnation, for it was reduced to the internalization of instructions, which immediately became his freely accepted responsibilities. It is easy to see how, leaning over the chasm at Pont-l'Evêque, he could be seized by the vertigo of irresponsibility. If he finally fell like a ninepin, it was also to free himself from subjective intimacy and thus from the prison of internalization. Let others decide in his place, as they have always done, but let them execute those decisions themselves. Gustave will remain external to himself, he will have no more self, he will make himself the provisional incarnation of being-in-exteriority; he will receive from the outside the motor impulses that will be prolonged in movement if nothing from the outside comes along to oppose them. But this motive power will no longer have an "inside" to take charge of these impulses. Let them do with him what they will, let them purge him, let them raise him up or lay him down, set him aside or carry him: Gustave will offer no resistance to them—except that of his weight; he has made himself unable to lend his assistance. What mortuary calm: he loses both the possibility of obeying and the dream of an impossible revolt; the ninepin declines all responsibility. For want of being a ninepin, the cadaverous state will serve his purpose better than insanity. Not only because it represents the return from the For-itself to the In-itself, but also because the theme of the becoming-thing of man has always haunted Gustave: Marguerite ends up on a dissection table, and an autopsy will be done on Charles Bovary. In between, what sullied, profaned deaths: the great man now a carcass manipulated by the gravediggers in front of a crowd; Djalioh is impaled; Mazza is naked, dead, violated by the obscene gaze of the commissioner, etc. This motif has a masochistic meaning that allows him to link the temptation of death to the desire to collapse. But it also contains a meaning from much earlier times, born in the days when Gustave and Caroline, by hoisting themselves up, could surprise Achille-Cléophas at his labors of dissection. The cadaver is an eminently *manipulable* thing; it is undressed, laid out on a table, its belly cut open; this primitive vision surely played its role in the crisis. The intention of death did not aspire so much to the abolition of consciousness as to a cadaveresque survival *in exteriority* during which Gustave, delivered up to his relations, would become the innocent object of all their enterprises. Starting here, the syncretism of the crisis appears clearly, for the madman, the cadaver, and the nursing infant represent in varying degrees a manipulable but *still human* irresponsibility. In death itself, the family tie—Gustave's *constitutive* relationship—is maintained: the body is, at the very least, determined as an object of ceremonies. Things will not go that far, of course; Gustave will survive, he will not fall back into childhood. The essential point is that he has had the radical intention of abdicating his humanity: nothing less was needed for him simply to be *ill* again, for his secondary attacks to be always suffered and never simulated. At the same time, the result he obtains—that incurable illness which defies Achille-Cléophas's diagnosis—while greatly inferior to what he expected, remains homogeneous with it: since the cadaver or the idiot represents *irresponsibility within the family*, his nervous affliction is a way of *living* this irresponsibility. Though not reaching back as far as his protohistory, as he would have liked, this regression is no less effective: it leads him back to his adolescence. This chronic patient is maintained by his illness in a state of extreme dependence; an accident has reduced him to the condition of the eternal minor, in other words, to the female condition.

In this sense, the attack at Pont-l'Evêque is the crucial episode in his battle against temporalization. For several years now we have seen him determined to destroy the future—*his future*—whether by tearing himself away from human duration, turning himself into a panoramic consciousness and establishing himself in the Eternal, or by plunging into the pure present through hedonism ("the future will be black, let us drink") or through stupor. In vain. Eternity is not accessible to him, and even in a drunken state his present is structured by his future condition, his life is implacably oriented; he can *forget* the Future but not suppress it, and when he forgets it for a moment, he merely lets himself be carried blindly toward the ignoble end that awaits him. Made and suffered, temporalization is the woof of lived experience, its law. A sole means remains to him, the one he chose at Pont-l'Evêque: to kill a boy with a future and, by the same stroke, give birth to a man without a future. The man contemplates the boy; indeed, he has no other purpose than contemplation: empty, without passion, without character, without interests, he is merely the beam of light that explores a memory. His own? No; he says expressly: that of another. Nothing will ever happen to him because he has been made in such a way that nothing—except death—can happen to him. In other words, it is a matter of constituting, by means of the attack, an entire life of passion, hopes, rage, and horror as a *before* so that the other, the survivor committed to contemplating it, may have no other temporal determination than that of being his *after*. And certainly Gustave is compensated for knowing that every moment lived in the present is dialectically constituted as a *before* to the same degree that it is lived as an *after*. But, as he will say later, arrogantly: "We are not made to live." Who is this "we"? And what does he mean by "live"? We shall soon see. Here we should merely note that an *after* without a *before* can be only an abstraction, that Gustave is convinced of this, but that by means of the catastrophe of Pont-l'Evêque he aspires to constitute an absolute *before* (his defunct youth, which will have no more *after* even as he annihilates himself by totalizing it) and, by the same token, a *pure after*, which, reduced to a pure remembering consciousness, can in no case be the *before* of anything of anyone.

This is the dichotomy of *Novembre*, realized by the false death of January '44. For the operation to succeed, he had to believe passionately in dying; and this same belief had to contain the intention to resuscitate the *other*, emptied of his richness and even of his personality, a pure transcendental ego, recording and unifying the debris of an experience totalized in a sudden lightning flash, then scattered by death. But let there be no mistake: it is not the dead young man that interests Gustave, it is the other, his archaeologist; he kills the first in order to save the second. This second, of course, can only be an old man. From the letter of January '44 on, the first in which he mentions his "congestion," the theme of old age, familiar to his adolescence, reappears in all its force: "I must be boring you stiff with the story of my pains. But what do you expect? If I already have the afflictions of old men, I shall surely be allowed to ramble on the way they do." This leitmotif has a multiplicity of functions and meanings in Flaubert. Here it recalls the "I would like to be already old" of *Mémoires d'un fou*, and its principal purpose is to burst the structures of temporalization: an old man is a man who turns toward his past and has no more future. Everything had been prepared; the day after the crisis that must strip him of his future, Gustave already knew the role he had to play to profit from it: he would live his affliction as a precocious senility. That would not be difficult for him; it is commonly said of people who have suffered or will still suffer a physical affliction that they are old before their time. And his other phantasms would accommodate themselves rather well to this new metaphor: an old man falls back into childhood; he is, like children, the irresponsible object of care and concern; everything is decided *for his own good* and without consulting him.

Here he is, then, immovable. In reality. So he has won against the world. We know that this theme is not new for him; he triumphantly takes it up again after the crisis and emphasizes it. "As for your servant, it is always the same story: neither better nor worse, neither worse nor better; as you know him, have known him, and will know him, always that same *kid*, rather boring where others are concerned, and even more so for himself, although he has had some good moments in society, in liberal society, especially, and is hardly prudish."[22] A little later, after losing his father and his sister, he was to repeat to Maxime: "It seems to me that I am in an unalterable state. It is an illusion, no doubt, but I have only that one illusion left, if it be such. When I think of everything that can unexpectedly occur, I do not see what could change me; I mean the basics, life, the ordinary sequence of days."[23] The superficial meaning of this second passage is clear enough: *after these two bereavements,* I have fallen into a lucid and permanent despair which can be neither increased nor diminished. And certainly this is what he wants to convey to Maxime; but we know very well that he truly mourned neither Achille-Cléophas nor Caroline. Besides, at the end of the same sentence he adds: "And then, I am beginning to take up a habit of working, for which I thank heaven." From the time of his adolescence he had desired immutability against his bourgeois destiny, and it was not the death of others that gave it to him but his own death in January '44. From that time on, he no longer changes, and the passing days are all the same:

22. To Ernest, 11 November '44, *Correspondance*, 1:157.
23. To Maxime, April '46, *Correspondance*, 1:204.

"Each day is like the other. There is not one that stands out in my memory," he writes to Alfred in September '45. He is not complaining, quite the contrary, since he adds: "Isn't that the right way to live?" The whole of the letter is moreover devoted to explaining the reasons for his serenity. Ten years later, returning from a journey to Trouville, he writes with pleasure: "Thus begins again another series of days like other days." And a little further on: "Nothing more effectively proves the *limited character* of our human life than *displacement*. The more our life is shaken, the hollower it sounds. Because we must rest after moving about, because our activity, however diversified it may seem, is merely a continual repetition, we are never more convinced of the narrowness of our soul than when our body sallies forth."[24] This remark takes on its full value when we realize that it was made *after* his journey to the Orient. It is striking that, returning in the middle of the night to Pont-l'Evêque ten years after the crisis, he said to himself: ten years ago, I was there. "And one is there, and one thinks the same things, and the interval between is forgotten. Then this interval seems to you like an immense precipice with nothingness whirling below. Something indefinite separates you from your own person."[25] Indefinite because empty: one same, solitary day, colorless, endlessly begun anew. What separates him from himself is pure time, stripped of all content. Neither his bereavements nor Alfred's betrayal nor the meeting with Louise nor his journey have filled *his* duration. Everything has slid by without altering that "limited character" he gave himself in January '44. He is referring explicitly to the night at Pont-l'Evêque, for that is where he gave himself immutability. Beginning in '44, he is conscious of it. To be convinced of it we have only to reread the end of *L'Education sentimentale*, which he started writing in July. Jules, of course, has had no crisis. However, without our knowing exactly the reason, a break has taken place in him: "The calm in which he wanted to live . . . distanced him . . . abruptly from his youth . . . His heart [was] almost petrified." Turning back to his past, to the life he led *before* the break, he is "frightened by the vividness of his memories, rendered more vivid still by the presence of those places where they had been facts and feelings; he wonders if all of them belong to the same man, if a single life could be sufficient for them." Then he was not the "skeleton" he has now become: at that time, he *was changing*." "He looked at himself with astonishment,

24. To Louise, 2 September '53, 9 o'clock, *Correspondance*, 1:331.
25. To Louise, 2 September '53.

thinking of all those different ideas that had come to him." But a little further on—several years have passed—speaking of the present life of his hero, Flaubert writes: "His life is obscure. On the surface, sadly for others and for himself, it runs on in the monotony of the same labors and the same contemplations, nothing recreates it or sustains it." [26]

Immutability—desired, proclaimed since adolescence, realized at Pont-l'Evêque—is, in a sense, the irruption of eternity in time, and as a result the bursting of temporalization. Gustave has chosen: to be *merely that*, but to be it *forever;* to define himself—in great part by negation—but to give himself through this minimum of distinctive traits a rough carapace, so crude that it resists everything. As we see it, Gustave's effort is to *change time*, at least insofar as it concerns him personally. If he is no longer anything but a mechanical system given once and for all, if he assumes the being-in-itself of things and of the past, then the irreversibility of temporalization made and suffered gives way to the homogeneous milieu of succession, that is, to the time of Newtonian mechanics. The time of history is abolished; the time of mathematics replaces it, a simple, indefinitely divisible recipient that possesses no efficacy in itself, that can exercise no action on its contents. From this perspective, the future, the present, the past are not differently structured "existential" elements: we already know that the future moment—considered in its temporal *form*—will be identical to the present moment and to moments gone by. Flaubert goes still further: immutable, he claims that, for him, the future content will be nothing but the present content itself. Death and inertia constitute the sole means of destroying the primacy of the future and of affirming the perfect homogeneity of the temporal "container." Gustave has understood that time was *himself;* it crumbles, congeals, and thus deinternalizes temporality. He dehumanizes it as well, since it is no more than a universal and totally inert setting. To choose the moment, that infinitesimal suspense when the before and the after neutralize each other, the temporal image of Eternity—this choice is to cling to the present, to affirm that beyond the lived moment there will be nothing other than the restitution of that same moment. It is to deny his life the atrocious yet human meaning that he gave it under the name of Destiny. Destiny is dead: that dreamed destiny of the Artist-Genius as well as that destiny, so dreaded, of the great man *manqué*, the notary in Yvetot. Flaubert's existence is no longer *vectoral,*

26. *On the surface;* deep down, there is a counterpart to which we shall return.

it has irreversibly lost its irreversibility. Better, it is a succession of empty presents, for the surviving old man can only be defined in himself as an inert lacuna. What characterizes him is the contemplation of the dead young man that *he is not*. Thus, since he is *nothing*, nothing can reach him; and as for the deceased, despite all his richness, time is without power over him since indeed he no longer is, or, which amounts to the same thing, since he *is-in-himself*. This choice of the moment could only be realized as the choice of *a* moment: a *fatal moment* had to manifest the madness of all human activities, destroying by its instantaneous lightning flash all the Flaubert son's projects; Eternity, by its sudden irruption, had to cause an instantaneous disconnection from our wretched duration. Indeed, if temporalization is the very woof of praxis, instantaneous options are by definition destructive. Thus Gustave, at Pont-l'Evêque, chose to privilege a moment, the intratemporal negation of temporality: *something happens to him* (the moment is also the suffered time of the event) *so that nothing more will ever happen to him*. The crisis is born during that night, at that hour, out of Gustave's pithiatic fascination with the moment: he has stretched autosuggestion to the point of detemporalizing himself, that is, to the point of no longer even comprehending the reasons for that perpetual *postponement* which belongs to human reality, and to the point of finding the absolute in the demands of the immediate.

This passive option does not aspire so much to death as to death's view of life. Be that as it may, to achieve his purpose, Flaubert would really have had to die. He accommodates himself to survival because, behind that radical goal of the impossible, there is another one, more modest but realizable: to substitute for the vectoral time of history the rural and domestic time of circularity. Indeed, repetition too is a fine image of eternity—as the myth of eternal return demonstrates well enough; that which returns indefinitely at a fixed date is a temporal equivalent of immutability. And by mutilating himself in order to become petrified in the family setting, Flaubert was plunging into the universe of repetition (meals taken in common at set hours, ritual pleasantries, collective customs, holidays, birthdays, etc.). And this repetition—with the ambivalence we have underscored—was the deepest object of his desire, as it represented his return to childhood. For this reason, as we have seen, the first attack bore in it, as an essential structure of its *meaning*, the intimate, *organic* commitment to repeat itself. Indeed, the subsequent attacks are exact replicas of it. Each is a reproduction of eternity or, if you will, of the fragmentation of practical time lived as instantaneous. Their unpredictable but frequent returns[27] somehow maintain the predominance of cyclical time, of reversibility, and of permanence over the oriented time of the Act. The subsequent attacks, recur, always similar, like calendrical holidays, and finally they *are* holidays. Dreadful holidays, certainly—although less and less terrifying—but celebrating them has the purpose of maintaining Flaubert in the setting of repetition and *symbolizing* familial repetition. Indeed, since he suffers family practices in dependence and inactivity, the intermittent reappearance of a collective practice *affects* him—whether he takes pleasure in it or not—as would an attack. Conversely, these referential attacks, "under the aspect of memory," have meaning for him only if they take place in a cyclical setting. When Achille-Cléophas is somewhat reassured, when they know—or believe they know—what must be done to remedy them, the attacks themselves become collective habits mobilizing the entire family, they punctuate Flaubert's slow vegetative life and that of his parents, as do birthdays and public holidays. Gustave understands very well that cyclical time is the degraded image of eternity, for he writes to Louise, in a letter I have already cited, that "our activity is merely a continual repetition, however diversified it may seem," which amounts, this time, to laying the blame directly on acts, denouncing them as illusions and showing beneath their claim to *invent* solutions to new problems the old circularity of routines and habits.

It is true, he will never change again. This choice of the immutable, in January '44, was not dreamed: it produced a real metamorphosis, a definitive blockage in Gustave of all living forces. Maxime, in his *Souvenirs littéraires*, writes: "As I found him in February '43 [*sic*] at the Hôtel-Dieu in Rouen, so he was to be all his life. Ten, twenty years later, he admired the same verse, sought the same comic effects, admired the same things, and, despite the true chastity of his life, en-

---

27. It is unlikely that the referential attacks arise spontaneously, without external provocation, like certain organic disorders that periodically reproduce themselves. It must be supposed, on the contrary, that Gustave, while maintaining his hysterical disposition to repeat the attack at Pont-l'Evêque, does not become convulsive unless family events more or less faithfully reconstitute the situation of January '44—or at the very least dispose him to relive it. One surmises that such occasions are not lacking: the activism of the paterfamilias is perpetual provocation, as are, to a lesser degree, the presence or the words of the two "Achilles" when they come to the Hôtel-Dieu, the projects they are involved in, the future they imagine. We must take into account as well "Caroline's betrayal" and her engagement, the visits of Hamard, the friendship Flaubert is compelled to show him. When all these givens, in one way or another, converge, when his present state is *put in question*, when he feels observed, spied upon, when allusions to his comrades, to his future life reawaken dormant frustrations, in short, when the pond is disturbed and the slime rises to the surface, he reacts by becoming convulsive.

joyed readings of obscene stupidity which never managed to disgust him . . . He seems to have had all his conceptions around twenty years of age and to have spent his whole life fleshing them out." The author's purpose is clear: he appears to pity Gustave, and all he does is disparage him, concluding: "My conviction is unshakable: Gustave Flaubert was a writer of rare talent; without the nervous illness that had him in its grip, he would have been a man of genius." Or, as he says elsewhere: his friend's "creative faculties" were "knotted up." On the other hand, he sees Gustave's immobilism as the rigorous and nonsignifying effect of an affliction suffered totally by the nervous system—hence external to Flaubert's *person*. On these two points he is mistaken. If Gustave has congealed, it was intentionally, as we have just seen; and his refusal to change exists only on the level of daily life: the same readings, the same jokes, etc. From her early childhood, his niece felt the life of Croisset to be a return governed by the same daily rituals. But it should not be concluded that Gustave's creative faculties suffered from this; we shall see in the next chapter that it was quite the contrary. It is true that he showed evidence of a rare precociousness; yet he did not possess "all his conceptions" at the age of twenty but, rather, at fifteen. And the illness did not in the least *arrest* him, since its purpose was not to discover other conceptions but to utilize those he already had to produce *beautiful* works; if one could say of Hugo that he was a form in search of content, Gustave, from '41 on, might be called content in search of a form. Moreover, Du Camp's testimony, biased as it is, confirms the evidence Flaubert has given us in his correspondence. For many years he rejected maturity and its obligations, desiring a prolonged childhood or sudden senility: time was running on, however, carrying him toward the adult he did not want to be. In '44, he works things so that he can remain eternally what he is, and his false death symbolizes and realizes, at one and the same time, his passive choice of *living minimally* in order to change as little as possible.

This denial of temporality must be lived simultaneously as the choice of a new localization or as the restoration of a former *situs:* in effect, inertia is a spatio-temporal determination. The choice of *being-in-itself* is a passive refusal to realize life as an adventure, lest it become a destiny; so it must manifest itself as a pithiatic attempt to substitute for "being-in-the-world," which defines transcendence, being-in-the-midst-of-the-world, which is the characteristic of things. Facticity—anchorage—a contingency perpetually surpassed and preserved by the project, must, if the project tends to negate itself, become degraded as a material *being-situated*. To tell the truth, the object is never situated by itself: *it is the project* that a situation confers on it in our practical field.[28] But when transcendence is inverted and seeks to make facticity into inertia,[29] it must define it by an unlimited *situs*. The result is double confusion: interiority will be lived as exteriority, and vice versa.

This is precisely the *spatial* meaning of the passive choice we are examining. The collapse and the illness are aimed at integrating Gustave into the family setting. On one level, his motivations are to be sought in his relations to his father and to his older brother: Achille, the preferred son, is no longer *in* the family; he has started a family of his own and is earning his living. Gustave takes his revenge against the usurper by choosing for his *situs* the secret center of the temple; through his weakness, his fragility, his dependence, he claims a prominent place *inside* the group and thus avenges himself on the future heir, who, through his intelligence, his strength of character, etc., is outside it. On another level, however, the process of integration takes on a more profound and radical meaning: it can be lived to the end only in the form of *sequestration*. Not only because Gustave, upon re-entering the bosom of the family by means of the spectacular crisis of '44, is tacitly committed to *never leaving it again,* but also because the collapse, once accepted, exacerbates his misanthropy and makes any dealings with others, with the exception of the family, intolerable to him. In this sense, not only does he seek refuge at the Hôtel-Dieu in

28. Obviously, to *situate* things is not the equivalent of an idealist designation: one discovers them as they are and in their real relations, but insofar as this set of relations is grasped as a practical environment by the agent. The discovery of an oil deposit immediately *situates* this stratum in relation to other strata (possessed by others), to means of transport, to drilling instruments, to the costs of exploitation (which result in great part from the above-mentioned determinations), to available capital, to economic conditions, etc. Be that as it may, the stratum has not awaited this discovery for its *being-there*.

29. None of this can be understood if we forget that praxis necessarily comprises a moment in which man (and beast) is turned back toward his own inertia (for the living being is inertia surpassed but preserved) in order to make it the unique means of working the inert (I have described that moment of praxis in the *Critique of Dialectical Reason*). Inertia is a certain structure of the living and consequently of action. Thus the inversion of transcendence—a typical but deviant moment of the pithiatic option in Flaubert—does not have to *invent* the inert. It restricts itself to making it an end when it was merely a means. We shall see further on, once again, how Flaubert *utilizes* this inertia. Not to gain leverage or to shoulder a weight, but—this is the positive aspect of the option—to free the imaginary from its practical matrix and to construct the unreal adventure of the artist. What I want to emphasize here is that, while the crisis of '44 is in itself derealization, its real elements are given in the very structure of praxis. Gustave, being a passive agent, exploits his inertia to other ends, that's all.

order to ask his family to care for him and to protect him against new attacks, but he *hides there*. Thenceforth, *place* takes on a crucial importance: walls must be built against men; certainly, it is primarily the family that *acts as his ramparts;* but walls, authentic and inert ramparts, become the objectivization of the family and, above all the objectivization of Gustave—his shell. Later, he will often lay emphasis on what a bourgeois tradition calls the "impenetrability of others," which he compares—as many others have done before or will do later—to the insularity of a group of archipelagoes. But an island can even more effectively symbolize the *domain* and the high walls that encircle it. Neither man nor things are impenetrable, but the impenetrability comes through things to man when he uses their exteriority to create for himself an interiority from which he excludes other men. By the act of appropriation of a house and a piece of land, the property owner unites, in a magical relationship of belonging, a set of material elements whose actual relationship is one of reciprocal exteriority; by an equivalent act, he presses these particles together, pushes other men out, and encloses himself in his thus delimited bit of space. In this way, man particularizes the thing possessed; but conversely, the singularity reverts from the thing to the man. By realizing *through gestures* the synthetic unification of the room and the house as the unity of his property, Gustave transforms himself into the *proprietor of that thing;* which means that his essence is outside him, in the possessed object. By conferring interiority on matter (each part of the house, insofar as the act of appropriation transforms it into a human whole, is *interior* to everything), he confers exteriority on himself; and that house becomes his exterior, through it he gives himself interiority as internalization of that exteriority. He has an "interior" which is simply the interior face of the exterior; he has an "interior life" which does not take place inside his head but in his interior, by synthetic connection with objects possessed. Flaubert's life of the interior will become the basis and the reality of his inner life. It will be defined by its singularity, that is, by the singularity of the "interior" in which it takes place; walls will shield it from sight; light will come in through apertures opened by design; the present, as for Bergson, will be merely the extreme point of an upended cone that is totally occupied by memories because the object possessed emerges from the familial and historic past in order to be seen at the level of the present.

This interior life will have its "depth," its "mystery," which represent purely and simply the opacity of its "contents" (namely, rooms and furnishings). Alienated from his room, Flaubert chooses to *be* rather than to *exist*, and to *have* rather than to *do*. At the same time he demands that a familial pact and a social contract acknowledge that in his room he is "at home," that others take responsibility for the impenetrability of the walls—the symbol of his own impenetrability, and, reciprocally, his desire for eternity. His passive choice of inertia, his choice of *being*, manifests itself not only by the decomposition of time into identical molecules, it is *materialized* by the lived assimilation of his existence with the *inert-being* of the thing. So the extreme solitude of the failed man, realized through illness, is merely the realization pushed to the extreme of *appropriation*, grasped as the movement of isolation that engenders solipsism, its most radical ideological manifestation. The false death at Pont-l'Evêque is Flaubert's transformation into *domus* (at once into grave and into domain); it is the proprioceptive act (or rather its imitation) insofar as it realizes property as an enchanted thing becoming the objectivization of a man. The appropriation of the domain is what constitutes the infrastructure of the dream in *Novembre:* when Gustave envies the reclining mortuary figures, and when he wishes to be nothing but matter while remaining conscious of no longer being, he defines the condition of the property owner whose life, reproduced by the work of others and punctuated by the eternal return of income from properties, falls outside of praxis and makes clear what it has become through the real property that it unifies synthetically. In other words, the desire of the proprietor is ultimately to become the pure synthetic consciousness of his properties (of their internal-external *limits*, the inorganic inertia of the terrain, the vegetative life of the grain, the cyclical temporality of seasons and labors). We have recognized Gustave's old desire: he withdraws from the world of activity and of production in order to reconnect with the feudal form of society, where the emphasis is put on consumption and where work is disqualified or passed over in silence. He agrees to become a great man *manqué* and, worse, a *failed bourgeois* so that he may be transformed into a member of the landed gentry. His affliction will become identified, over time, with the house at Croisset; when it erupts, it is the conversion of a bourgeois to feudal parasitism within the framework of bourgeois property. Indeed, Achille-Cléophas does *not* live off the income from his properties—although it is rather considerable; he lives primarily by his work. When he buys lands or decides to build houses, he is merely following the general current of investments. If he "rounds out" his domain, it is neither through inheritance nor through marriage nor through seigneurial gift: he buys land with money that he earns by practicing his profession. As soon as it is spent, the money effaces even the memory of the former owners, and nothing remains of the complex relations of family or vassalage which from a certain point of view "humanized" feudal appropriation. This shrewd man is making investments, that's all. His fixed goods are his *real* property: the bond that unites him with the thing possessed—*jus utendi et abutendi*—is immediate and absolute.

For Gustave, everything is different: as a sick man he lives not off his own properties but off those of another; his attack forces his lord and father to support him indefinitely; he has the joy—at Achille's expense—of inheriting by anticipation; by supporting him, his father gives him an advance on the inheritance. The young man is a property owner by procurance, by *gift*, which restores the human relation of vassalage between him and the goods he uses. Moreover, he knows he will not keep that room in the Hôtel-Dieu where he wants to sequester himself. One day, on his father's death, Achille Flaubert's household will come and settle there. Thus the movement of appropriation is an effort of petrification that knows its own futility. Certainly, as early as June '44 the chief surgeon acquired Croisset—where the family was definitively to settle only a year later. But when Gustave moves in, he must already know he will not inherit it: it will be his sister Caroline's portion and after her death will revert to her daughter. Thus, from one end of his life to the other, he will have never been *at home*. This does not mean he did not appropriate *his* room at the Hôtel-Dieu, or, even more important, the one at Croisset. What it does mean is that his possessing goods owned by others, goods whose use is conceded to him—provisionally or until the end of his life—will facilitate through its ambiguity the wide oscillation that makes this bourgeois now an aristocrat, now a saint. We shall have occasion to return to this point. For the moment, it is sufficient to observe that when Flaubert feels himself kept between the four walls of his voluntary prison by the express intentions of other members of his family ("my father *wants* to keep me near him"—later his mother's last wishes will be that they allow Gustave the use of Croisset until his death), he lives this actual nonproperty as a feudal proprietor and identifies with the *thing* insofar as it is already humanized and familial. In this way he can feel he is a lord in the essentially bourgeois moment of his reification. The room is *his* room insofar as it proclaims the seigneurial will of his father and the depths of a collective past.

He sequesters himself in it, but all *his* world is already contained in it. By contrast, when he does emphasize the fact that he does not really possess his *situs*—and this happens frequently—he experiences the bitter pleasure of poverty.[30] Its walls and furnishings refer him to his image; long years have structured the hodological space of his study and of the house in such a way that his gestures and thoughts are stirred up in an order defined by the innumerable bonds he has forged between his armchair, his work table, his divan, etc. At Croisset, the room he has chosen on the first floor materializes the impulse of "rebound," the vertical ascent that must perch him above the world. And the "point of view of the absolute"—which will be *style*—has as its infrastructure the plunging perspective he has to take, from above, onto the garden, the Seine, and the opposite bank. But this objectivization of his person, even while imposing itself as his inert or repetitive being-in-itself and directing his very dreams, preserves some kind of slippery inconsistency, does not adhere entirely to the rooms, to the objects that surround him, simply because nothing belongs to him completely, and because the *situs* that characterizes him so deeply in his very interiority is at the same time outside him, in the hands of others, and on loan to him out of tolerance. Hence Gustave, carried away, can persuade himself that he has definitively broken with the bourgeoisie—defined in his eyes by real property—because he lives in a cell, conceded to him by the good will of a community, which could at any moment be taken from him; in short, that he is a monk, a saint, and has cut the last bonds that held him to our world.

Thus the attack at Pont-l'Evêque has all the characteristics of a conversion: instantaneous, shocking, and long in the making, it renders Flaubert an heir, a vassal, a monk, even as it ties him to his room and leads him to objectify himself—a cadaver under a spell—in a real property, scarcely disguised, which will become the inert infrastructure of his immutability. *To be,* for him, means announcing what he is through his permanent possessions and hiding from himself the bourgeois character of this appropriation while compelling himself, at the cost of the worst collapse, to *receive as a gift* what he was being required to earn by work. And, of course, Gustave is also tempted metaphysically, for reasons we are familiar with, to abandon the dimension of the For-itself and to sink into the unlimited In-itself. In

30. Obviously this is untrue: the inheritance will be divided into three equivalent portions. It is true that Gustave does not own Croisset, but he has other properties from which—until Commanville's ruin—he draws a comfortable income.

this pantheistic form the boundaries of property are suppressed. But this aspiration can be realized, according to his belief, only as a surpassing of appropriation. Appropriation must turn Flaubert into *this* matter so that he may accede thence to the material condition, hoping to surpass it subsequently toward infinite materiality, not by a real act but by a *mental disposition*—that is, ideally. Indeed, the nonreal, nonpractical character of the appropriation—since what is involved at the Hôtel-Dieu, as at Croisset, is the property of others—will permit the proprioceptive act to slide toward pantheistic ecstasy. Work is objectivization; joy is internalization. The moment when Flaubert in order to interrupt an odious labor, falls head first and hits the floor, he abandons himself to passivity, and that passivity is given him as the sign of his deepest being, of his constitutional inertia. But this negation of activity, despite itself, involves a *surpassing:* it is proposed as a capturing and internalization of the inorganic—in other words, as possession or, better, as the reciprocity of possession (property possesses its owner at least as much as he possesses it; the only difference is that the possession of man by thing is demonic, something we have elsewhere called *an inverse possession*). The choice of being nothing more than a house in the midst of a domain bounded by walls could not even be conceived if this inert whole did not already present a multiplicity of human meanings: work—crystallized in its products—and especially *patria potestas*, the authority and glory of the progenitor. But these meanings, which assert themselves and demand to be internalized, are themselves fixed: inert demands, they put their stamp on material inertia; Gustave is penetrated by them insofar as they are the inhuman reverse of human significations. In January '44, when Gustave abandons himself to his constitutional passivity, he falls headlong into property.

I may be accused of going too far, of giving the crisis at Pont-l'Evêque economic motivations which—in whatever form—did not exist for Flaubert at the time. To which I respond simply: in the course of this book, haven't we seen Gustave dream a hundred times of *inherited* wealth? From '39 on, wasn't he calculating the income from properties his father would leave him, and didn't he see himself living off them in Naples, where life is less expensive than in Paris, *without doing anything?* If the situation of the Flaubert family had been different, if the paterfamilias, while disinheriting his younger son *morally* to the advantage of the older son, had not had the means to support him even after his own death, can we believe that the cursed child would have become a one-hundred-percent permanent invalid? The frustrations would have remained, and the despair and the constitutional passivity, but the neurosis would have taken another course. We shall understand nothing of the illness that struck the young student failing his exams unless we interpret it primarily as the "stress" of a *son of good family* for whom money *earned* is necessarily vulgar and who can accept only *bequeathed* wealth. It is not so surprising, then, if by means of a collapse that bears in itself a commitment to sequestration he resolves to live his condition of legatee in advance.

Through the atomization of time and the identification of his person with the *situs* that conditions it, has he really escaped temporalization? No, for what is involved is an existential structure. He will live it beneath a mask, however, as an *exterior* determination of his life which he must suffer and is powerless to influence. In other words, oriented time has not disappeared, and the cyclical time of repetition is merely its superficial representation. This underlying duration is now defined as the time of degradation and involution. In a sense, none of this is very new: Gustave, turning toward the lost paradise of childish loves, has never seen in temporality anything but its negative power: it distances, separates, exploits. And his passivity forbids him, of course, to instrumentalize it. But until the crisis, vectoral duration was *in him* like an enemy force, it was confused with the authority of the symbolic father, and even while reducing him through fatigue to a precocious senility, it carried him swiftly toward that other-being that was awaiting him and that he dreaded: his Destiny as bourgeois, as mediocrity. In '44 it becomes a slow stream that bears him *toward ruin*. The immutable, by dint of being tossed about by the currents, suffers passively the slow deformations that are imposed on it from the outside: inert, external forces destroy it without its having any power to resist them. Or, if you will, he foresees that by their very return, the repetitions of cyclical time are going to harden, to ossify. Ruin is the thing that haunts the landowner: having made the exterior his interiority, he finds himself threatened by universal exteriority, even in his interior life. It is also the thing that haunts Gustave: his letters bear witness to it—as do his novels, whose heroes die ruined. Later, we shall demonstrate more effectively the meaning of this long sliding of things and beings toward decadence, and the course that the author will take in *Madame Bovary*. Here we need only show that he tries, beginning in '44, to duplicate temporalization and to replace Destiny (concurrence with his being) with Ruin (progressive deterioration of an inert motor by friction and deceleration).

110

G. Flaubert's Illness as "Murder of the Father"

If we wish to restore the fundamental unity of these multiple intentions and see all the attacks in their true light, we must understand that they represent above all a crucial moment in Gustave's relations with the paterfamilias. All the rest—whether the masochistic impulse that throws Gustave at the feet of his triumphant brother or the underlying connection between sequestration and income property—necessarily refers to the "object relation" that both binds Gustave to the chief surgeon and sets him against him. Indeed, until '44, in the very measure that Gustave has been constituted a relative-being, that constitutive relationship is established in relation to a double personage who is—simultaneously or by turns—the symbolic Father (at first positive, then negative) and the empirical father, a little too nervous, choleric, sometimes whining, often "lead-assed." In this relationship, Moses is the independent variable, the absolute being; dependence and relativity are on Gustave's side. Hence, the essence of lived experience for the child, then for the young man, must be envisaged as a discourse with the Father that can never take place.[31] A negative but unreal discourse, since the locutor has no affirmative power at his disposal and consequently no power of negation. A dialogue of the deaf that has been going on for twenty years; even through Alfred, Gustave is still addressing himself to the father. In vain; the definitive heart-to-heart talk will never take place, the fault lying as much with Gustave, a mute who wants to speak, as with Achille-Cléophas, who understands nothing about his son and does not care to understand him. In other words, Gustave's neurosis is the Father himself, that absolute Other, that Superego inside him who has constituted him as impotent negativity (this negativity cannot be changed into negation and is inclined only to *positive* behavior—obedience, respect, haste—to achieve its ends, that is, to *deny* imposed Destiny). It is easy to conclude that Gustave's body takes charge, in its fashion, in the form of suffered disorders, words that cannot be pronounced: the fall at Pont-l'Evêque *says something* to the Progenitor. By mutely denouncing the vanity of activism, it symbolically condemns the activist in charge, first of all by forcing him to assume the consequences of a voluntarist education—this is what you've made me—and then, more profoundly, by challenging the virtues of any activity. What the agent takes to be acts is merely superficial fidgeting; one makes a fool of

---

31. In contrast to Kafka's *Letter to Father*, which was never received by its addressee.

oneself believing that one is autonomous, hard reality takes on the job of disabusing us: we are matter, therefore incapable of spontaneity, and the impulses that animate us come from the outside and disappear while being communicated from the outside to other bodies. In short, there are two levels of meanings. One is restricted: I *am* passivity, I cannot act. The other generalized: and as for you, you are merely an inert mass, buffeted by external impulses. Without being opposed, the two meanings, if expressed simultaneously through discourse, would merely serve to undermine each other. For the first meaning aspires to specify Gustave's singularity, as it was fashioned; it does not put the sources of activity in others in question and simply shows that Gustave—is it an anomaly?—is not made to act, that he has tried loyally, as a conscious subject, and that his "nature" has reduced his efforts to nothingness. By contrast, the second meaning, aimed directly against the father and rejecting the very idea that a man can be an agent, risks conceding the argument to Achille-Cléophas by affirming that under any circumstances one is *acted upon:* if we are all equal, you are not anomalous, and despite our universal passivity you can, like me, win over the animating cosmic forces. But Gustave, who in his writings is not embarrassed to expound two ideas simultaneously,[32] is careful not to express them together here. He uses all the means at his disposal against the progenitor: he tells him simultaneously, you are torturing me, I am not made for the destiny you impose on me—and, like me, you are merely a puppet; with action denied to man, activism is a ridiculous frenzy. Thus the fall as the offensive return of passivity aims at nothing less than destroying the very authority of the father; we shall understand this better by examining these two "languages" one by one.

We shall pass over the former quickly: his "death" at Pont-l'Evêque proves that he was not made for the future that had been imposed on him. Error or cruelty, the paterfamilias bears full responsibility for it; in a word, this is the discourse of resentment. The point here is to plunge Moses into remorse, and so Gustave must survive to enjoy his pain.

The second intention is more complex. We have seen Gustave set against the empirical father who destines him to that minor hell, mediocrity, the ferocious Progenitor who has sworn him to abjection, death. The crisis called him from the former to the latter. But at the same time, it has another objective: to kill Moses after using him, and

32. Jules is not made for action. But Henry, who seduces a woman, carries her off, and leaves for the Americas with her, is in fact led by chance every bit as much as his friend. Cf. above.

to allow a pathetic, highly excessive, and rather grotesque fellow to survive. As we have seen, the *maternalization* of Achille-Cléophas already betrays the ambivalence of Gustave's feelings: it signals the unloved young man's deep need for tenderness, but there is obviously a malicious intention as well, to ridicule his Lord by feminizing him. He goes much further, though, and gives himself the bitter and triumphant pleasure of being *badly treated:* "[I am doing] very badly, [I am] following a stupid regimen; as for the illness itself, [I] don't give a damn."[33] I have observed above that Gustave was contesting not so much the regimen as the diagnosis. Certainly he complains of being uselessly tortured, deprived of wine and tobacco, immobilized by a seton. But this is not the essential thing: he is being treated for a miniapoplexy—by multiple bleedings, which weaken him—when he is suffering from nerves. To tell the truth, Achille-Cléophas's mistake is imposed on him by the illness itself, which at the time can only elicit a false diagnosis since the nature of hysterical diseases is to look like what they are not. Gustave rejoices in being more in the know about what is happening to him than the illustrious surgeon of Rouen. Not that he is amusing himself by tricking his father—we know he is not simulating illness. But his affliction implies a certain understanding of itself, whose consequence is to demonstrate the incompetence of medicine—something beyond Flaubert's wildest hopes, which will be manifest *in action* through his daily martyrdom: in short, it is *as if* the patient were fooling his doctor.

Maxime reports—he takes it from Gustave himself—that Father Flaubert, in the course of one of the referential attacks, was so distracted that he spilled boiling water on his son's hand. Gustave complains of it in his letters: it hurt terribly. He never denounces the clumsiness of the philosophical practitioner. Yet after the father's death he speaks to Louise about his scar in these curious terms: "You do not ask what I went through to arrive where I am. You will never know it, nor will the others, because it is unspeakable. The hand I burned, where the skin is withered like a mummy's, is less sensitive than the other to cold and heat. My soul is the same; it passed through fire—is it so surprising that the sun doesn't warm it? Consider this a kind of infirmity in me."[34] The third sentence is incorrect:[35] he should have said "the hand my father burned" or, if he had

33. To Ernest, 9 February 1844.
34. To Louise, 20 March 1847, *Correspondance*, 2:12.
35. Even though the use of the verb "to have"—instead of the verb "to be"—seems in certain cases governed by a local particularism, Alfred writes: "*Je m'ai promené*" in-

113

to lie, "the hand I burned myself." But as usual he intends neither to betray the truth nor to reveal it. For Louise, Doctor Flaubert must remain one of the glories of medicine, and in several other letters to her he vaunts Achille-Cléophas's competence. Therefore, his burn comes to him neither through his own fault nor through that of others: he *has* it, he bears it and *suffers* it without protest, as he has suffered everything. But this itself is suspect: after all, his father is guilty only of clumsiness; he might have mentioned the source of the burn without damaging his father's memory; he does not mention it precisely because the scar means much more to him than a mistake committed out of "distraction." Distraction is a good enough explanation to give Maxime: it implies the power of the emotions that Gustave's state provoked in his father—he confides in Maxime in the early months of '44. With Louise, he makes no such suggestion; an intentional ambiguity is manifest through an incorrect statement. Yet they have known each other since the summer of '46; they are lovers; she has surely asked him about the scar. What did he answer? He most likely said it was some accident during the treatment of his nervous illness. Even if he was telling the truth in those early months of intimacy, he has no intention of returning to it; this transparent mystification suffices to show the importance he attaches to his "infirmity": it symbolizes his father's medical incompetence, and, at a deeper level, it is the indelible mark of the paternal curse. After all, it appears here as the first term of a comparison which involves his entire life: the hand I burned is half-numbed; my soul, which has passed through fire, is even more so. Another image, borrowed from a previous letter, gains its full force in the light of this one: "The Numidians, says Herodotus, have a strange custom. One burns their scalps with coals in infancy to make them less sensitive to the action of the sun, which is scorching in their country. And of all people on earth . . . they are the healthiest."[36] The tone is different: the comparison here functions specifically to highlight a certain *positive* aspect of his youth: Gustave was not born insensitive; he has been desensitized. Louise has just given herself to him, he left her less than a week ago; she is already complaining a little, but he is not yet fending her off. Far from being backed into a corner, forced to find an excuse for his coldness in the negative side of his mental constitution, he struts before his mistress,

---

stead of "*Je me suis promené.*" But even taking this into account, the indeterminacy remains.

36. To Louise, 8 August 1846, *Correspondance*, 1:227.

"poses" a little, as she will tell him later, and, although recourse to the Numidians is motivated at bottom by a defensive prudence, he tries to make her believe that he has hardened so as more surely to convince himself. Be that as it may, whether insensitivity is an advantage, as in this first letter, or an infirmity, as in March '47, the meaning of the comparison is the same in both passages. Boiling water and burning coals, it's all the same: one becomes indifferent only after suffering the most atrocious torments. Both images are structured according to a unique experience (the burned hand) and the meaning Gustave attributes to it: in the first text we encounter a mistake in thought which corresponds exactly to the grammatical mistake found in the second. The Numidians, he says, have a strange custom: we expect him to say, "They burn their childrens' scalps," for it is *they* who "have" this custom and who observe it. Instead, we have "One burns them," which severs the burners from the community of the burned. Rather as if one were saying: the explorers have a strange custom: when they go among the cannibals, one cuts them into pieces, cooks and eats them. Looked at more closely, however, the apparent absence of sequence in his ideas manifests the ferocity of Flaubert's rancor. The custom reported by Herodotus is characterized by commutability (what the fathers do to their sons, their fathers formerly did to them, and the sons will do to their children), a kind of diachronic reflection of reciprocity. But Gustave cannot accept this commutability: the father-burner is not a former burned child, nor is the burned son a future burner. As often happens to him, he breaks the metaphor by abruptly introducing the compared into the comparison: *one* burned me, he says. And this anonymous subject is none other than Achille-Cléophas, who slipped incognito into the sentence in the same way he later slips into that strange, passive "the hand I burned." *One:* not a Numidian, even if he were the tribal chieftain or king; but someone from elsewhere, the grand torturer of the Numidians, whose only custom is to suffer torture passively, unable to revolt against their executioner. My father, that stranger who burned my hand . . .

Of course, he adds: "Imagine that I was raised in the Numidian fashion." But this sentence—in which, moreover, the Progenitor appears no more directly than in the other two—is merely a variation on a proverbial locution, "I was raised in the Spartan fashion," whose pattern alone is preserved. As a result, we are put on our guard: if this is what he *means,* why doesn't he say it? Why does he have to go looking in Herodotus? To disguise a commonplace? There is something in

115

this: Gustave is an old offender, and we know why. However, the real reason is that Lacaedemon [ancient Sparta] educated its children harshly but did not torture them. Gustave, toadyish and hypocritical, wants to make us believe the moon is made of green cheese, and that the Numidians' forms of torture are equivalent to the rough training of the little Spartans. He pretends to vaunt his father and the education he received; he vaunts them, indeed, but what he intends to communicate secretly to Louise is a physical and intolerable horror of those burning embers that inflict their sting on the innocent scalps of the newborn. In any event, we know now that his burned hand symbolizes the paternal curse. That allusive, hypocritical little sentence refers us on the one hand to the distant time when Gustave, distraught with shame and frustrated love, learned to read under the rod of the paterfamilias and felt accumulating in him the rancor he later expressed in *Un parfum à sentir* by embodying himself in a young inept acrobat who bleeds under the paternal whip. On the other hand, the sentence—but only for the writer—refers to the ultimate mistake of a barbarous father doubled by an inept physician, to that scar which seems to him the symbol and conclusion of his dead youth, or rather that youth itself transformed into dead skin and sealed onto his hand. In this light, the second text delivers up its secrets: it is not by accident that Gustave compares his soul, which "has passed through fire," to the "mummy" that hangs at the end of his arm: that soul too has been *mummified* by the clumsiness or ill will of the Educator. Gustave still boasts a bit: he keeps the arrogance of the black stoicism he invented and refined for himself alone. Never mind that an Attila ravaged his heart. He doesn't even need to say it to himself: it is enough to contemplate his hand. What masochistic revenge! And what joy if Achille-Cléophas shuns it or looks at it contritely! *That* was the purpose of the crisis: the intention to die is joined to that of survival in order to see the look on his murderer's face.

Undoubtedly the second-degree burn was entirely fortuitous. The chief surgeon would have acquired his reputation or would quickly have lost it if he had gone around scalding his patients. But by an incredible stroke of luck, he reserves this favored treatment for his son alone, for his cursed son. At Pont-l'Evêque, Gustave did not throw himself at his brother's feet *in order* to obtain this supplementary proof of paternal barbarism; but by means of the commitment we have described he became *a patient to be treated* and thereby constituted the framework and the setting in which *any error* by Achille-Cléophas would expose itself as a crime; and if, as is the case, it were to be revealed as irreparable,[37] that error would become the very symbol of the irreversibility, the misdeeds, of a bourgeois education and their result. It would also be proof of what the patient always suspected: for want of having studied the strange correspondences between body and soul, for want of conceiving that which would later be called the psychosomatic, and which Gustave knew and understood from *experience*, medicine is powerless to cure him. This is what he sought at Pont-l'Evêque: to obtain from one of medicine's darlings a certification of his incapacity to live. He has fallen, blocked in advance from any cure, and has turned himself into a living cadaver in order to denounce through the inefficacy of the treatments lavished upon him the absurdity of analytic rationalism, of mechanism and of positivism, the unhealthiness of the utilitarian ethic; and in order to reveal that Achille-Cléophas's activism—and consequently any human activity—is nothing but pointless agitation with unpredictable consequences. In short, the crisis of Pont-l'Evêque is at bottom *also* the collapse of the symbolic father. But Gustave, the passive agent, could realize it only by making himself a martyr, by killing himself first.

He had little trouble doing so: from his adolescence on, everything had been set in place. And the theme of vengeful self-punishment, which first appeared in *Matéo Falcone*, and which Gustave subsequently evoked a thousand times in his reveries, quite naturally became in January '44 one of the guiding themes of his neurotic behavior.

Achille-Cléophas, one suspects, would never know that he was forever discredited, or that his son had risked everything to free himself from paternal authority. He felt no remorse and acknowledged no incompetence on his part: he was too conscious of the limits of medical science, had too much confidence in the future of medicine, not to regard his gaps in knowledge as the historical expression of a transitory moment in the development of scientific disciplines. After all, this overworked practitioner, despite his students, his patients, his clients from the upper reaches of the Rouen bourgeoisie, still found time nearly every day for research. Like most of his colleagues, he had to believe in progress and—beyond the immense Flaubert

---

37. Gustave permanently lost partial use of his hand: he could no longer clench his fist. As a writer, this slight impairment did not disturb him. As a practitioner, he might have had to give up his profession. We can well imagine that the young man, with his share of bad faith, told himself that his father's clumsiness definitively proscribed for him the career of surgeon.

pride—took humble pride in contributing to it. Still, resentment is passive and charges the external world with assuaging it. Gustave cares little for his father's real feelings; it is enough for him that, through his own sacrifice, he has put him in a situation which he judges to be objectively untenable: guilt and discredit come to *Achille-Cléophas* from the outside, they constitute him in his being, even if no one perceives it. This father is cruel and incapable *in the absolute*, that is, in himself. It would, of course, be desirable for him to internalize these new qualifications and live them in shame. But not only does he fail to do that, he does even worse: his patient's permanent nervousness, the potions, the bleedings, the burned hand, the seton, everything condemns his derisory agitations and *he does not know it*. Alone, his younger son, docile clay between his hands, an eagle perched on a summit, casts a surgical look upon him that pierces him to the bone. For the younger son, Achille-Cléophas is a poor man dominated by a situation that bewilders him. And the conviction of having discovered the true face of Achille-Cléophas delights Gustave all the more in that his discovery is uncommunicable. He will be its guardian, he will share it only with God, if God exists. Later he will recall these bitter joys when he shows us *la* Bovary, as Charles furiously works away at the clubfoot, mute, seemingly helpful, and savoring the pleasures of contempt.

Let us acknowledge, however, that these satisfactions can be experienced only in the imaginary. First of all, he must unrealize his perception according to certain rules: in order to "maternalize" the father, Gustave must make a certain use of his passivity (he is in his bed, weakened, immobilized by his seton and his bandages) and must block his perception, remove its "seriousness." That is not too difficult for this absolute quietist; perception is a moment of praxis and delivers its stubborn reality to the enterprise; disinterest can allow it to be treated as a dramatic scene and to place its reality between parentheses. One can thereby charge the actors or the objects with more or fewer gratuitous significations. Similarly, when the doctor examines him, his medical behaviors, precise and skillful, surely have nothing grotesque about them. But it is sufficient to see things as theater, to derealize this surgeon, to recall with bitter delights the hand "he burned," to *represent* him as a bewildered practitioner deceived, despite all his precision, the sureness of his diagnoses, the promptness of his therapeutic decisions, by an illness that goes beyond him and is not within his competence—resentment is satisfied. Yet, just as his *vision*, at first perceptive, must be unrealized, so the father

Flaubert, if he must play the role of Diafoirus, must be stripped of his terrifying, singular reality, which has the same opacity as his son's "dreadful depths"; Gustave is constrained, at the cost of a tension that he will not be able to bear for long, to maintain him in the status of mere appearance, as a flat character. For this reason, the pleasures he experiences are neither true nor false: lived but unreal. Irritating.

What is indeed real, by contrast, and continually destroys the patient's phantasms, is Achille-Cléophas's inquisitorial gaze. Inquisition or solicitude? Both, since his very anxiety discloses a permanent demand: the troubles must recur or Gustave must take the road to Paris. The paterfamilias is obstinate: he has already lost too many children to consent to the mental infirmity of his younger son. He will cure him so that he can take up his manly vocation, as all the Flaubert males have done. The practitioner scrutinizes him for signs of improvement. From morning to night, entering at whim, he stares at his son, takes his pulse, casts that "surgical gaze" upon him that detects all lies. Not, of course, that he suspects him of faking; he wants to understand the evolution of the illness. Be that as it may, his conduct suffices for the situation to reverse itself and for the mute addresser to feel himself questioned by the supercilious addressee. Gustave is *under observation,* he lives under surveillance. On the surface he is meekly in agreement with Achille-Cléophas: he must certainly be cured. But the practitioner's scrutinizing gaze shakes him to the core. Gustave believes he is suspected and hence "receives" the intuition of his deep commitment, the vow he has made to remain forever afflicted. The referential attack—not on the spot, of course—stems largely from this; it is a protest against the suspicions he attributes to his father, against those he harbors himself: but you can see, you can see that I am very sick, *I'm still just as sick.* He defends himself against guilt—too often tied to the father's gaze—by reaffirming his illness. Or, rather, to defend himself, he abandons his superficial will to be cured, he makes himself vulnerable to his discomforts, he delivers himself to his body: nothing easier for this pithiatic type, insofar as it is merely a matter of falling, of imitating the crude yet precise archetype of Pont-l'Evêque.

But let us not thereby conclude that the referential attacks are simulated. It may be, as I have said, that Gustave reproduced them a few times out of curiosity, in his room, with all the doors closed, or, at the very most, in front of Maxime, to fool him. In the great majority of cases, they take him by surprise. In fact, they precisely express Gustave's fidelity to his enterprise, his continuing faith in the irreversibility of the drama of Pont-l'Evêque. This organic belief masks for him his passive option: insofar as he believed, in the carriage, that this event was going to change his life—insofar as he rediscovered, by turning inward to understand it, the fatality he had put into the event, he can only reproduce it. For he has not left it behind, he has remained overwhelmed by that nocturnal audacity and by his obscure vow. At Pont-l'Evêque he fell *once and for all;* his fall is eternal, and from this point of view no cure is possible before the affliction has caused irreparable damage. Thus, it is his archetypal attack that produces the referential attacks or, rather, reproduces itself in them. They are not the consequences of the first but its renewal, not the symptoms of a hidden illness but the illness itself reaffirming its integrity and hence committing itself to its reaffirmation. He takes the trouble to add a few novelties, the convulsions, for example, which compensate by their pathetic violence for what the fall itself offers, in the long run, as stereotype.

We might say, then, that in the silent dialogue that sets them against each other, the basic intention of the referential attack is not to trick the father by exaggerating the importance of Gustave's nervous disorders but, quite the contrary, to reassure Gustave—troubled by Achille-Cléophas's gaze and always ready, out of habit, to accuse himself of insincerity—of the depth and truth of the primal attack by reproducing it unexpectedly and without the least conscious compliance on his part. And, of course, to the very extent that these attacks solicited by the chief physician and elicited by Gustave's inner discomfort, convince him of his sincerity, they even more effectively fool the paterfamilias, who is seeking organic causes for what is clearly neurotic behavior. So by a new turn, the son, assured of the permanence of his commitment, is delighted to humiliate Moses by obliging him to advance a new diagnosis—epilepsy—which he intuits is as false as the previous one. In short, the father is pathogenic: his mute and permanent interrogation directly induces the disorders. These exhaust and weaken Gustave by their repetition, and although he is their secret author, he ends up afraid of them. Don't they threaten to compromise the integrity of his mental faculties in the long run? What if he were to lose his reason as a result?

These fears are not unfounded. If the chief physician had died before '44, his son's neurosis would hardly have remained latent: he would simply have sequestered himself while being economical with the attacks. But between '44 and '46 there is no indication that Achille-Cléophas does not have twenty years of life before him: What will happen to him? Doesn't Gustave's illness, so long sustained, risk extending to all sectors of lived experience? Won't the young man be required to give proofs a hundred times over, all the more violent, perhaps, in that their meaningful content cannot avoid being impoverished? No doubt he will be cured while Achille-Cléophas is alive, but as late as possible, not before gaining—at the age of thirty or forty—the certainty that he will enjoy his income and be allowed to entrench himself in his family: he will work like mad against himself until he becomes a useless piece of debris. Is that what he desires? So it seems, when he abandons himself to the masochism of resentment. But strategically—as we shall see in the next chapter—he has chosen the neurotic response so that one of his works may succeed. And the tactic of renewed attacks, by leading—he thinks—toward senility, can only harm the neurosis strategy. Certainly he has the leisure to complete the first *Education*. But for the whole of 1845 he does nothing. This idleness is prolonged beyond the decease of the Great Witness, and we shall see why. In the meantime, while Achille-Cléophas is alive it is established and consolidated. As if to imply that his leisure has a primarily negative and tactical meaning, as if Gustave had feared that the abundance of his literary works would suggest he was cured.

For despite the efforts of resentment, which is determined to humiliate him in the imaginary, the philosophical practitioner remains a powerful and dreaded personality. He is no longer Moses, of course; Moses was nothing but a primitive category expressing the complex structures of family life as they are lived in the impotence of early childhood. But to create this imaginary Lord, Achille-Cléophas furnished all the materials—power, glory, authority, universal knowledge, capricious omnipotence, unjust justice; all Gustave had to do was carry them to the absolute. In this sense, the empirical father was never closer to the symbolic father and never contributed so strongly to personalize him. Now that a radical but passive option has in principle separated them, the real father, even reduced to himself, preserves his intolerable virtues, each experienced by his younger son as a permanent aggression. But these virtues no longer contain the infinite within them, they no longer have the power of representing, by turns, radical Evil and the plenitude of Good. Limited, evaluated, reduced to their empirical manifestations, as distant from the paradigmatic qualities of Moses as palpable objects are from their Ideas in the thought of Plato, they nonetheless remain Gustave's radical challenge. A bond is severed; but this subjective liberation does not, for all that, settle the judicial problem of *patria potestas*. As a father, Achille-Cléophas is endowed with a certain number of rights, of which he means to make full use. Thus, in order to play himself now, the drama remains basically unchanged: if he is cured, the younger Flaubert son will embrace a career. For the young man—who has paid a heavy price for the right to be lucid—these whims no longer contain anything satanic or absolute: this blind bourgeois father wants bourgeois sons who work and live in a bourgeois fashion; he is mistaken, it's quite plain, he is not Satan, he is a strong man blinded by the prejudices of his time and his adopted class—Gustave is fully conscious of this. But even if he were to repeat it over and over to himself, that knowledge would have no bearing: he would have to convince his father—and the two men do not speak the same language—or resist him—and this is what he has never been able to do. For Flaubert to escape the career of attorney, there is only one solution: either father or son, one of the two, must die. The son regards himself as already dead: he merely has to prolong his death until that of the Other. From this point of view, the affliction of '44–'46 can be considered a "long patience," an *expectation*. An expectation lived, assuredly. Can we say that it is fully conscious of itself? Often: he expresses himself through monologue, with ruminations on the future death of the head of the family—those ruminations Flaubert mentions a little later.[38] This was surely not the first time Gustave dreamed of this liberating death: as we have seen, between '40 and '42 he was thinking of settling in Naples with several thousand pounds' income, which obviously he could only inherit from his father. But at this period, I imagine, his desires were more masked;[39] they had to present themselves, in the course of morose musings, as bouts of anguish rather than as wishes. From '42 to '44, in Paris, anger was able to reveal their

38. When he says he had often thought (in anguish, to be sure) of Achille-Cléophas's death and was not greatly surprised when it occurred prematurely and unexpectedly.

39. Yet much earlier, in *Agonies*, he had articulated a highly ambiguous fantasy. Who was this great man, now a mere skeleton, whose disinterment the crowd is enjoying? Of course, the story is primarily an apologue meant to show the vanity of fame and hence the absurdity of our ambitions. Gustave rebukes himself harshly: you want fame, idiot? Will that prevent you from rotting in a coffin? But it must be observed that the only celebrity he knew then was his own father. The adolescent only longs for fame: the great man necessary to the apologue must possess it *in fact*. Can we not express the morality of the fable as follows: "You want fame, idiot? Look at your father: he has it, that won't stop him from dying like a dog!" In this case, Flaubert might feel some complacency imagining the famous philosophic practitioner in the form of the "unnameable thing" he describes in *Agonies*. And let us not forget that, despite the metamorphosis that changes him into his own son during his last hours, it is Achille-Cléophas who dies under the name of Mathurin.

real meaning, at least at moments: Of whom, of what "ferocious dramas," was he dreaming at the morgue in his moments of "unhealthy" meditation? From '44 on—as I shall soon demonstrate—they present themselves openly. For by the end of '43 Gustave has begun to conceive his life as a fight to the death against his father. His father, of course, suspects nothing: he judges himself neither obstinate nor severe, and perhaps after all only a categorical refusal would make him change his resolve. But Gustave is heading for the worst *for want* of the power to summon this refusal. The most convinced parricides—in dream—are those passive agents who desire the annihilation of the obstacle because they are incapable of either getting round it or displacing it. Is Gustave a parricide, then? Yes, a passive one. If he were to die thinks the young man, that would be the only way out. Maybe he sometimes cries out: Croak! Go ahead, croak! But without raising a finger, he trusts in the order of the world, the grains of sand that enter urethras, black Providence and—who knows—perhaps his star,[40] to fulfill his desire.

On 15 January 1846, Gustave has the chance of a lifetime: he becomes fatherless. The dialogue will have no end. But it will: by dying, Achille-Cléopas leaves his son the last word. That Flaubert had experienced this death *quite consciously* as a deliverance is clearly shown by three changes produced in him in the six months following. First—Gustave says so himself—the day after the burial he declares himself cured: "Perhaps it affected me the way cauterization removes a wart." The death of his sister follows close behind. Then he cries in triumph: "At last! At last! I am going to work!" Alone now between Achille and his mother, he will not need to make himself sick in order to impose his decisions: the former is merely a usurper, and Gustave will find in his rancor and contempt the strength never to obey him; the other was but the father's mouthpiece: since death has closed her husband's mouth, she has no more orders to transmit. On this point, however, Gustave is not so reassured: she intimidates him, and he blushes when she speaks to him. While he is staying with her shortly after Caroline's death, he goes so far as to wish that Madame Flaubert will succumb to her grief. He will write to Maxime, somewhat disappointed: "My mother is doing better than she might. She is busy with her daughter's child . . . ; she is trying to be a mother again. Will she succeed? The reaction has not yet come, and I fear it greatly."[41] Then,

40. Has he a star, then, this cursed young man? Yes: *now* he has one. We shall establish this in the following chapter.
41. To Maxime, 23 or 24 March 1846, *Correspondance*, 1:197–98.

as always with him, the wish becomes a prophecy: "There is neither word nor description that can give you an idea of my mother . . . ; I have a sad presentiment on her account, and unfortunately I have every reason to believe in my presentiments."[42] He cheerfully organizes himself in view of this sad prospect: "If my mother dies, my plan is made: I sell everything and go and live in Rome, Syracuse, Naples. Will you follow me?"[43] That is called making a clean sweep.

The third change is no less significant: *at least* since January '44, Flaubert has had no sexual relations. Indeed, we may well ask whether we should not date his hysterical castration from the autumn of '43. In the spring of '45, Alfred passes on to him Pradier's advice "to get back into normal life," that is, to take a mistress. In June–July '45, Gustave declines the sculptor's proposition—for it is a proposition: Pradier's atelier is a pond full of pretty trout, they would save one for him; young, strong, handsome, romantic, she would not be cruel to him. Certainly, he still feels desires, stirrings (or are they merely memories?), but he is not made for pleasure, a woman would upset his life. In January '46, the father disencumbers the Hôtel-Dieu, and within six months the young man takes the path to the atelier, conscious of what awaits him and entirely disposed to let himself be seduced: Louise will make but one mouthful of him. It is just as if Achille-Cléophas had been the actual castrator.

Of these three characteristic changes—declaring himself cured, wanting to work, making love—we shall concern ourselves here only with the first, which was crucial with regard to the evolution of the neurosis.[44] In fact, as was said above, scarcely has the chief physician been put in his coffin than Gustave deliberately takes the road to recovery, which presupposes a complete reversal of his intentions. Certainly in psychic as well as social behavior, what is constitutional contains a certain inertia, and real deliverance can follow at quite a distance from the actual liberating event. Still, Flaubert's state is markedly improved. In the letter where he makes this very lucid admis-

42. To Ernest, 5 April 1846, *Correspondance*, 1:199.
43. To Maxime, 7 April 1846, *Correspondance*, 1:203. He also says: My mother is so unhappy, and I love her so much, that if she wanted to throw herself out the window, I would not stop her from doing it. In a sense, he is not wrong, and the life of the "poor old thing," after two bereavements, seems to have become nothing but prolonged suffering to be purged (even though she had transferred to little Caroline some of the feelings she had for her daughter). But it is preferable, no doubt, to inspire feelings that are less constrained, blinder, and to a certain degree more egotistical. To be loved for oneself feels very good. On the condition that the other also loves you *for himself*.
44. The second characteristic will be the subject of the next chapter.

sion, he explains his recovery in part by the whirlwind of activities into which his bereavement has thrust him. Everything has had to be put in order; Caroline, who was ill, had to be cared for; and *above all* the transmission of Achille-Cléophas's powers to Achille had to be assured: the older son's qualifications were being challenged, a colleague was conspiring against him, in short, his nomination to the post his father had reserved for him was not assured, despite the chief surgeon's last wishes. Happily, Gustave is there. He looks after everything, makes visits and overtures: thanks to him, Achille sees his father's responsibilities conferred on himself—in a slightly diminished form, which is the normal consequence of his youth. You have read correctly: Gustave *has thrown himself into action;* this invalid, this hermit, this quietist has gone on his own initiative to see highly placed adminstrators and distinguished doctors, has known how to speak to them—using that practical language which ordinarily plunges him into a stupor or seems foreign to him—in short, Machiavellian and courteous, he has them eating out of his hand. All that to assure the hated Usurper the usurped patrimony. What are we to make of it?

First of all, that the facts are probably correct. Gustave did make visits. That goes without saying—who else could make them? Not Achille—that would have been blatant. Nor Madame Flaubert, lost in her grief. Nor Hamard—who was not sufficiently informed about the intrigues. The younger son was left. This enterprise filled him with pride. He refers to it later, in his letters to Louise: it was to him, Gustave, that Achille owed his post. And this episode—almost unique in his life until the time when he would take it upon himself to have the plays of his deceased friend Bouilhet performed—allows him to present his passivity in the most flattering light at times: what he feels deeply and willingly admits is that he is not made to act. He repeats from time to time, when he recalls his role in the "Flaubert succession," that he is *above* human agitations: a quietist by excess, not by default. But—a Flaubert adage—he who can do the most can do the least: if the circumstances demand it, he rolls up his sleeves, puts "men of action" to shame, reaches his goal in "record time," and reenters his hermitage with the honors of war. On condition, he implies, that the enterprise is *gratuitous* and that he puts himself, through generosity, at the service of interests that remain alien to him. Therefore he is convinced that he has put his brother in the saddle. What is the truth? He made visits, but did he really strike home? Was he really the one who clinched the deal? Was there actual resistance? Did he confront it and vanquish it? We cannot be sure, but if we take into consideration Achille-Cléophas's enormous prestige, the favor Achille enjoyed, and, conversely, if we recall the clumsiness of the solitary younger son, made for shouting with his comrades rather than for manipulating aging administrators, it will seem to us more likely that the game was won in advance. No doubt there were cabals. But they *had* to fail; at most they worried the Flauberts for a few days. In all likelihood, Gustave played the busybody. Not entirely, however: etiquette demanded that he made certain contacts; he did make them. He managed to acquit himself reasonably well because the action was merely a courtesy—just a role.

Still, he *believes he is acting,* serving the aims of the detested usurper to his own detriment. We shouldn't find this surprising. If he were passively witnessing the transmission of powers, he would feel despoiled. But if he is the one who disdainfully leaves his monastic retreat in order to give his brother a secular power which might be coming to him but which today he scorns, the frustration disappears—and Achille's merit and rights disappear likewise. Two factors are at issue, and only two: the glory of the dead father and the maneuvering ability of a younger son who remains submissive to him out of free obedience. Nothing more was needed to clinch the deal and change Achille—in Gustave's eyes—into an inert beneficiary. A few whispered conversations and the water is changed to wine, and vice versa: the active passivity and activism of Achille—aping the paternal praxis—reveals its true nature, the passive expectation of an undeserved gift. In any case, doesn't the younger son suffer by ratifying the father's unjust preference? This question leads us to the essential fact: no, Gustave does not suffer by it, for in this circumstance he is playing the role of head of the family and, as a result, substituting himself for a father absent by death; he *is the paterfamilias* in flesh and blood. In his own eyes, of course, and no one perceives it: Achille does not seem to have felt any gratitude for his interventions; he still thinks of him as a *minus habens* whom one does not invite to formal dinners; and Madame Flaubert has perceived nothing. Be that as it may, Gustave is delivered from the father only after having taken his place for several days. Is this parricide? Yes. Precisely. For the old warrior has bitten the dust; like his younger son in January '44, he is nothing but a reclining mortuary figure. His grim, sadistic wishes have no more importance than the whims of an infant in the cradle: Gustave must *decide* to take responsibility for them and thereby make himself father to his father. It depends on Gustave whether these wishes of the dead, the "*last*" wishes, are or are not flouted. By substituting his own wishes, alive and effective, the young man executes them but degrades them, for his obedience to the dead, far from being submission, is explained by an undeserved love that strongly resembles pity. And when he returns to his monastic life, the paterfamilias, sidetracked, surpassed, will have no other life on earth than that of Achille, his pitiful incarnation, a striking and lasting punishment for his ill will, just as the second Napoleon, according to Victor Hugo, was the the great Napoleon's punishment. Gustave, after his generous revenge, will turn his back forever on father and older brother.

Here he is, delivered. If the objective reason for this deliverance resides in the abolition of a dreadful, perspicacious and all-powerful Lord, he must also *live* it, that is, internalize it through subjective structures which, as such, comprise liberating elements. Gustave could tear himself away from Achille-Cléophas's grasp, even in death, only by playing at dethroning and replacing him. In other words, this primary and long-awaited event had to be lived by him as the ritual murder of the father. Like all the children of man, he has had to kill his progenitor and take his place for a moment in order to be rid of him. But because the acts he believed he was engaged in were in fact mere gestures, the sacred crime is reduced to a criminal imagining.[45]

This may be the reason that the parricidal intention, from '45 on, is so conscious of itself in Flaubert. Maxime, in *Souvenirs littéraires*, tells how he often kept his sick friend company during this period. One day the two young men went as far as Caudebec and entered the church; Flaubert, having noticed a stained glass window that retraced the life of Saint Julien, "conceived the idea for his story."[46] After which there is absolute silence until '56, not a single reference to Julien in Flaubert's correspondence. Not even to Maxime, who was privy to his project. This is surely intriguing, inasmuch as he does

45. I do not mean that for others the murder of the father can be *really* accomplished with a revolver or a knife. For practical agents, what is *real* is the sequence of acts by which they dethrone their Moses and substitute themselves in his place by founding a family in their turn or by replacing him as head of the business, or by rising higher than he in the social hierarchy, etc. Thus the homicidal intention is sustained by a symbolic but real praxis, which gives it substance.

46. Maxime, as usual, mixes everything up. The stained glass window was in Rouen, in the cathedral. At Caudebec there was only a statuette of Saint Julien. We can therefore venture a hypothesis that Gustave did not "conceive" his narrative that day—the statuette could hardly have inspired him—but that at Caudebec he *told* the life of the saint as it was seen in the stained glass window at Rouen, and confided to Maxime that he hoped to make a story of it. Maxime, typically, has dramatized the episode.

not refrain from talking to his friends at this time about what he plans to write. Yet the project is not abandoned: he has spoken of it to Bouilhet, for *ten years afterward*, on 1 June '56, he writes to him, without saying anything more specific: "I am preparing my legend, and I am correcting *Saint Antoine*." He was thinking at the time "of returning to Paris in the month of October with *Saint Antoine* finished and *Saint Julien l'Hospitalier* written." For what reason did he decide to take up this tale? To "provide, in 1857, something modern, something of the middle ages and of antiquity." This motivation is not superficial: he always dreamed of showing all three strings of his bow together, and for this reason he would write the three tales between '75 and '77, of which the first to be finished was *Saint Julien*. In '56, however, he does not seem to be taking his "legend" seriously; he is using it largely as a pretext to read works on hunting and to revel in archaic words. For he leaves everything in outline and does not speak of *Saint Julien* again until '75. He must have been lacking some emotional reason for undertaking his narrative. When he sets himself to it in earnest nearly twenty years later, the situation has changed: he is at Concarneau, alone with Pouchet; ruined, hagard, miserable, "devoured by the past," he stops thinking of "those cursed business matters" only to "mull over his memories." When he conceived *Saint Julien* and, much later, executed it, he seems to have been prey to unhappiness, to anguish, and—we shall return to his inclinations of '75—to his family. His "legend" is nourished by storms; it is very close to his heart since it appears when this heart, a calm pond, is stirred by the wind and the "slime" rises; the rest of the time, it is not even mentioned.

In any event, between '44 and '47 the subjects that attract him are lyric: he wants to totalize himself, gather his life into one work, which is what he has done in the last pages of *Saint Julien L'Hospitalier*. What fascinates him in the story of Julien is not merely its picturesque medieval character. It has to have some *meaning* for him. And what is this story about? About a saint whose hard daily penance makes him the equal of Saint Antoine, and who is determined to expiate the most unpardonable crime: in his youth, he *killed his parents*. We are not altogether certain how Gustave might have presented the thing had he written it in '45: surely the tale would have been profoundly different from his 1875 version.[47] What is certain is that the parricide-sainthood connection (long patience, terrors, genius) came to him on the spot in

47. I shall return to this subject in the following chapter.

all its complexity. And what is equally striking in the definitive text is that the murder of the mother—although Flaubert had often wished for his mother's death—seems of secondary importance: she will die like the progenitor, clearly so that a second murder should mask the ritual importance of the first.

Let us observe, first of all, the misunderstanding that explains the parricide. In Julien's absence, his parents, whom he has fled for so long, come into his castle, make themselves known to his wife, who, to honor them, gives them the marriage bed. They go to sleep in it; Julien, returning late, half mad from an infernal hunt, leans over them in the dark and, thinking he is meeting his wife's lips, "has the impression of a beard." Mad with rage, he seizes his dagger and repeatedly stabs the two bodies. Thus the cause of the double killing is *adultery*. "A man in bed with his wife!" This adult cry of fury echoes a distant fury whose traces we have found in many of his early works, "a man lay in my mother's bed"—the classical Oedipal situation. In this case it is the man who is the criminal, it is the man who has sullied the relations between Julien and his wife. It is he who must be slain; the mother has her turn too, but as part of the bargain. Or, rather, she is expiating a real sin but one with which the man first tainted her. And when Julien, fleeing the stag's curse ("One day you will kill your father and your mother"), waged war across the world—half knight-errant, half adventurer—it was *his father* he feared to murder: "He protected people of the church, orphans, widows, and, most important, old men. When he saw one of them waking in front of him, he cried out to him so that he might know his face, as if he were afraid of killing him by mistake." And when he has accomplished his heinous crime and remorse pushes him to suicide, it is the sudden apparition of his father's face that deters him: "As he was leaning [over the fountain] . . . he saw an old man appear in front of him, utterly emaciated, with a white beard and such a pitiable look that it was impossible for him to hold back his tears. The other was weeping too. Without recognizing his image, Julien confusedly recalled a face resembling this one. He uttered a cry: it was his father; and he never again thought of killing himself."

In other words, Julien, aged by suffering and by the hard life he leads, leans over the water, sees his own image, and takes it for that of his father. The progenitor is killed, and now the son resembles him: Gustave has transformed himself into Achille-Cléophas by the very fact of having slain him; and on his own cheeks he finally manages to shed the tears he would like to have wrung from the medical director.

Perhaps at least once, during the terrible months of '44, feigning sleep and watching through his eyelashes as Doctor Flaubert observed him, Gustave saw those tears burst from the terrible "surgical" eyes. We shall note that these feelings of remorse in '75 are linked to the resurrection of childhood. At the time when Gustave, at Concarneau, is writing to all his correspondents that memories are suffocating him, that he is being "devoured by the past," he writes in his legend:

> Months went by without Julien's seeing anyone. He often closed his eyes, trying through memory to reenter his youth—and the courtyard of a castle would appear . . . with . . . a white-haired adolescent between an old man covered with furs and a lady with a fifteenth-century headdress. Suddenly, both bodies were lying there. He would throw himself face-down on his bed and repeat, weeping: "Ah, poor father! poor mother! poor mother!" And he would fall into a somnolent state in which the visions continued.[48]

It should be noted that the parricide is at once a crime and a punishment. If Julien's destiny is to kill his father and expiate the crime—just like that of Oedipus—it is not gratuitously, as in the Greek legend, but in order to punish his pathological desire to kill animals. If we recall the numerous passages from his early works in which Gustave speaks to us of his *meanness*, and if we remember the fascination animals hold for him, the respect Gustave has for "animality"—in himself as in the beasts called "wild," indeed the love he feels for dogs, we can understand that this bloodthirsty taste for the hunt represents his arrogant and mean-spirited hatred of men, announced in his twenties, and the violent, murderous impulses to which he testifies even in *Novembre*. Yes, a hundred times, a thousand times, Gustave, beside himself with wretchedness and fury, wanted to kill. And it is this same criminal impulse that made him desire the death of Achille-Cléophas. There is a revealing passage in *Saint Julien*. A dying stag has prophesied in a human voice: "You will kill your father and your mother." Julien has come home. The following night he is haunted by this prediction. "Beneath the swaying of the hanging lamp, he kept seeing the huge black stag. Its prediction obsessed him; he struggled

---

48. Flaubert, *Oeuvres* (Pléiade ed.), 2:646. Madame Flaubert had died shortly before. Cf. the letters from Concarneau, *passim:* "I have much trouble writing, physically, and I am chocked with sobs . . . My nervous debility surprises even me and humiliates me . . . Many things that I see here reawaken memories of my travels in Brittany and give me no joy. I think only of the years gone by and of people who cannot return. I daydream, I ponder my memories and my sorrows, and the day goes by . . . Can you believe that I dream of Croisset or of some of my dead friends every night? Last night it was Feydeau," etc., etc.

against it. 'No! No! No! I cannot kill them!' and then he thought: 'But what if I wanted to?' And he was afraid that the Devil would inspire him with the desire to do it."[49] These lines illuminate the entire tale. We might be surprised that Julien, after the catastrophe, is determined to expiate a crime he has not even committed; in fact, it was merely a grievous misunderstanding. His remorse will doubtless be explained by the objective enormity of the event. A son has killed his father: this is utterly unacceptable, whatever the murderer's intentions. Flaubert would have wished to underscore the preeminence of things done in such primitive and absolute souls: the examination of conscience will come later. Oedipus did not *want* to kill his father or to fornicate with his mother. Should that prevent him from gouging out his eyes to expiate the crime? It would have been to show the monumentality of the antique and medieval world, entirely in exteriority.

Is this certain? First of all, Gustave distinguishes perfectly between the Rome of the Caesars and the Middle Ages: "Christianity came this way"; that is, for him, the way of conscience, interiority, self-reflection. Indeed, the modern Oedipus is not he who becomes a parricide without knowing it but he who dreams of killing without going so far as to commit the crime. In short, it is as if Gustave, Freudian in advance, grasped the true meaning of his hero's remorse: if it is perfectly intolerable to him to have killed his father by accident, it is because he knows in his heart that he is not innocent; the crime has all the *appearances* of an accident, a matter of mistaken identity. But wasn't he afraid all his life of *wanting* to commit it? Did he not flee the paternal residence because he was not sufficiently certain of vanquishing his bad thoughts? He chose to make it physically impossible to realize the stag's prophecy himself because he hadn't the necessary love and virtue to create in himself the *moral impossibility* of accomplishing it. Of course, there are accidents, made more frequent by family life; there is the sword he takes down, which gets out of control and nearly cuts off the father's head; there is the arrow he shoots at a bird but that pierces the maternal bonnet. Yet who can say that these accidents do not simply conceal ill will? The second incident is especially suspect. The prophecy coming from a dying and enraged stag, Julien "is determined to do no more hunting"; nothing could be better, it's a bargain: I'll never hurt animals again, and my parents' lives are saved. But how shall we interpret the sudden resurrection of his murderous impulses: "One summer evening . . . he saw two

49. Flaubert, *Oeuvres* (Pléiade ed.), 2:632.

white wings. He had no doubt it was a swan; and he threw his jave-
lin. A rending cry was heard. It was his mother, her long-feathered
bonnet nailed to the wall."[50] He had not doubted that this was a bird:
we take him at his word. But since he now knows that parricide is
indissolubly linked to his cursed hunter's instincts, isn't killing a beast
even once an assent to killing his parents? In short, when he abandons the castle forever, it is himself he is fleeing as much as his family.
Without leaving himself, however. Son-in-law of the emperor, he falls
into melancholy: he refuses to hunt, "for it seemed to him that on the
fate of the animals depended the fate of his parents. [One day], he
confessed this dreadful thought [to his wife]." Things have come to
such a pass that "his other desire" (to make animals die) becomes unbearable without diminishing his fear of parricide. And one night,
yielding once more to the desire to kill, he departs, his heart quite
black, already feeling criminal and yet incapable of resisting: it is on
his return from this hunt that his parents will be stabbed.

But Gustave goes further still, for he traces the origin of the crisis of
'44 to his sudden terrified certainty that he will murder Achille-
Cléophas. In telling us the effects of the stag's prophecy, he has
shown us Julien "struggling against it." It is night: "'But what if I
wanted to? . . .' And he was afraid that the Devil would inspire him
with the desire to do it." At which point he passes to the next line and
continues without any transition:

> For three months his mother, in anguish, prayed at his bedside,
> and his father, groaning, continually paced up and down the cor-
> ridors. He summoned the most esteemed masters, who ordered
> quantities of drugs. Julien's illness, they said, was caused by a
> deadly wind, or a desire for love. But to all questions the young
> man shook his head. His strength returned; and they walked him
> in the courtyard, the old monk and the good lord each holding
> him by the arm.

This misunderstood nervous illness is familiar to us: it devoured
Flaubert after a night of horror; it was attributed to a bad wind, to a
stroke, and the good Phidias in his atelier said it's because he needs to
make love. But Gustave knew and kept to himself the causes of his
apathy; he knew—at the moment when the entire household assembled at his bedside, and when his good Lord was solicitous
enough to support him with all his strength, as though Gustave were
a child taking his first steps—the deep and unbearable grievances

50. Ibid., p. 633.

that would make him the principal agent of the "fall of the House of Flaubert."

Of course these pages were written more than thirty years after the crisis: the man changed, and his memories did as well. Tortured by the present, incapable—as he repeated endlessly to his niece—of "beginning his life anew" and of facing the future, he took refuge in the past and delighted in embellishing it. We shall find in the legend neither Doctor Flaubert's satanism nor his wife's distant coldness; their son turned them into sweet old people, tenderhearted, naive, and mildly absurd. How they loved him![51] Julien, in flight, bewildered, wandered through a thousand places; and those good parents, aged and weary, wandered through them in his wake. They are *seeking him.* What wouldn't he have done, our Gustave, for Achille-Cléophas to go off in search of him, if only for one day. In short, he gives Julien's parents all the "feudal" virtues he would have liked to find in his own parents. This was the time when he began to weep over himself in his room at Concarneau: evidently he was unable to complete this falsely naive portrait of loving parents, who—by a just reversal—are turning into the relative-beings of their child, without bursting into tears. In consequence of this permanent compassion, the story is once again incomplete: hidden from us are the "dreadful and disturbing" reasons for the murderous appetite so suddenly revealed in Julien. The work does not suffer from it: it suits its naïveté to give us the facts without much in the way of commentary. One day the child killed a mouse; he enjoyed doing it, he went on doing it, that's all. He was made that way, perhaps, or else it will turn out to be the Devil that made him do it. Whatever the case, when we find Julien again, as an adult, a great captain, son-in-law of the emperor and possibly his future successor, and we see him sad and solitary, "resting on his elbows at an open window, remembering his former hunting trips" or dreaming that he is "like our father Adam in . . . paradise among all the beasts," that he has made them "die by stretching his arm," our modern reader's sensibility is troubled by these obsessive and monstrous nightmares. This poor Julien—we agree to be ignorant of the origin of his troubles, but we cannot doubt that he is powerfully affected. It is quite simply that the author, by falsifying his childhood, consciously deprives us of the key to the mystery. Julien was so afraid of being a parricide because he believed he had good reasons for kill-

51. It is to be observed, however, that his father does not understand him and wants to make a warrior of him (the man of action par excellence), whereas his mother, more perceptive, would like him to be a saint (an artist).

ing his father, some of which arose in his earliest years. At fifteen, Julien is Garcia in his blackness, but with no allusion to his brother François.

How would Gustave have shown us the parents of the cursed hunter if he had written the legend in his mid-forties, when he mentioned it to Maxime? Wouldn't the "good Lord" have furtively resembled Cosme de Medicis or Doctor Mathurin? This remains uncertain: Gustave, as we know, is adept at creating confusion. Besides, when he fell to daydreaming before the stained glass window of the cathedral, it was himself he was seeking and not Achille-Cléophas. Sainthood attracted him: sainthood conceived not as an inborn elevation of the soul but as a formidable victory over corruption. What he liked about this story was that radical, original Evil is conceived in it as a condition of the Good. Mean-spirited and bloodthirsty, then ascetic and turning his rage against himself, Julien is never *good;* he has nothing of that virtue, which seemed insipid to Flaubert. He saves lives, empires, renders service to men, but does so in expiation, not out of love. In the next chapter we shall examine what salvation means in his case. For this is the other intent of the legend and—as we shall see— of the crisis: to show how Gustave can be saved. For the moment, it is certain that Julien, Flaubert's new symbol, creates his salvation not in spite of his parricide but directly *because of it* and because of the cleansing effects it has on his impassioned soul.

Indeed, Gustave, facing the stained glass window in 1845, could not imagine salvation without thinking at the same time of Achille-Cléophas: the philosopher-physician had so spitefully fashioned him that the angry young man could tear himself away from the paternal curse only by a symbolic murder. The life of Julien served him beautifully: there was a misunderstanding, an accident, the stabbings were aimed at the wrong target—and, indeed, by collapsing at Pont-l'Evêque, Flaubert did not for one moment want to make the edifice of paternal dictates crumble by means of simulated attacks. Yet Julien in horror, and Gustave in shriveled pride, recognize their guilt: before the crime there were dreams, abominable temptations, projects which, though embraced and then rejected, became stratified in their "dreadful depths" and which, unrecognizable, almost inert, must have reawakened at the most fundamental levels of motivation. Innocent and responsible: this is how Gustave, taking a nosedive toward the floor of the carriage, intended to define himself. And the fall itself in '44 had to have the insignificance of an accident and the multiple meanings of a passive action. This action, in any case, is *turned against his father:* it defines him as a demonic father in his own eyes by seeming to be the result of his curse; by the same token, it obliges him to go back on his pitiless dictates and even to denounce them, with remorse, as mistakes; finally, it takes away his role as symbolic father and forces him to give maternal care to his victim: and even in these new functions it makes him ridiculous since "drugs," his specialty, are ineffective, and he makes an incorrect diagnosis. All this is confusedly implied in Gustave's intention, but nothing must be *done:* everthing, from the fall to the silent contempt, is imposed; and when the father becomes ridiculous, Gustave's luxurious disappointment is *suffered.* This is why the parricide must be at once an unforeseeable accident and an action manifesting itself solely through the halo of meanings that surrounds the opaque body of the event.

Before the fall there were two beings in one: the symbolic father and the empirical father coincided. This was Achille-Cléophas, that tall, thin, bearded man with his goatskin cloak, who had cursed Gustave before his conception and who charged himself, from day to day, with administering the curse. Of course, this did not entirely apply: the father had moments of tenderness; everyday relations were established between Gustave and Achille-Cléophas, which consisted of "serious" discussions and ritual pleasantries. But this good fellowship—highly intermittent—did not suffice to distinguish the man of flesh, with whom Gustave dined daily, from the *persona* who had once cursed him. Moses was the *Truth* of this man; the symbolic father was never there, but he seemed still more dreadful in his absences: he was the obscure carver of cadavers, the scientist who cured the living thanks to a fearsome knowledge acquired each day in his commerce with the dead, the dreaded professor who stole his students' souls and dispatched each year, into every region of the country, twenty robots who aped their master; he was the philosopher who said that everything is matter and matter is nothingness. This personage was *everywhere* but in his Rouen apartment. Beginning in 1841, the two inhabitants of the chief surgeon became distinct from each other without either posing clearly as himself. As we have seen, the bourgeois ambitions of Achille-Cléophas—who wanted an attorney son—although still more distressing to Gustave, did not coincide with the diabolic intentions of the paterfamilias, who required his younger son's supreme collapse followed by an even more dishonorable death. In 1840–41, Gustave, the imaginary invalid, was fooling

135

the good doctor, who transmitted his errors to Moses, more distant at the time, and shared them with him. In January '44, Gustave was reduced to setting them against each other: by his degrading fall into a mad death, into a mortal madness, he appealed to Moses and charged himself with executing the original curse in order to escape the stubborn notions of the empirical father. Now the hand had been played and won, the curtain drawn. But by the same stroke, the black Lord disappeared: all that's left is a poor man overtaken by events, who *means well*. But he is not the man Gustave blames; it is the Other. And every time he believes he can verify the collapse of the symbolic Father, at that moment Moses disappears: he escapes ridicule by his very nature, he is the Law. Gustave does not choose between the two fathers, during this period; his confidences to Maxime, his letters to Ernest, are aimed at the empirical father. Later, however, his letters to Louise (the burned hand, the Numideans, etc.) will indicate that even after his death the black Lord is not yet relegated to the storeroom. Finally, on 15 January 1846, they both die. In consequence, Gustave's old, prelogical depths revive in order to make him assume entire responsibility for a death he had summoned with all his wishes. By his crisis of '44, he wanted, he thinks, to bring about the collapse of the diabolical Lord, to compel him to relinquish his monstrous powers. But what does it mean for his ruling Lord to abdicate? To accept the tonsure and the monastery? To croak, rather. And he does croak, in effect: first of all, he withdraws, leaving Achille-Cléophas to stew in his own juice. And then, finally, by the suppression of the empirical father, he cuts the last ties that bound him to the earth, thus persuading Gustave that the suicide mimed in January '44 is, like many real suicides, a murder in disguise.

Is this to say that Moses, once dead, ceases to be? On the contrary: like his son's passional life, he suffers an ontological transmutation. That is clear, for he is indissolubly linked to that life and haunts the memory of the impassive survivor in the same way as the life itself does, as the original, fundamental factor of all remembered episodes. Thus the deceased Gustave junior and his father, victims of a double murder,[52] accede together, inseparably, to the supreme dignity of Being-in-Itself. The father will always be the *Other* in that young, vanished heart. But an impotent other—although possessing the opaque density of past-being. Restrained, mute, incapable of acting on the

52. The father has killed the son whose death kills the father: there we have one of the meanings Gustave gives to his fall. Conversely, the death of the son, a little too much sought after, allows in his own eyes the project of killing his murderer.

eternal present, which contemplates him, Moses is no more than a genie in a bottle. His son's youth, which he has systematically destroyed, encloses him and totalizes him by totalizing itself. Caught in his own trap, the Demon will fall victim in his turn to the incisive gaze that he has been directing onto his prey and that now nails him, like the abstract survivor of a shipwreck, to every past event, full, empty, present, distant, surpassed, endlessly remembered in his absence, like a butterfly on a cork. To the extent that the "creative" imagination draws its schemes from memory, the old unrecognizable Lord will be in all his son's future books; and by that I mean not only that he will be exploited as a *character* (Doctor Larivière, etc.) but that he will represent for each of the heroes the curse of Adam, destiny, the implacable and flaccid time of the collapse, analysis, making their emotions look absurd, the abundant prophecies by which things announce the worst. But to the degree that each individual obscurely, negatively, surpasses him in silence—if only through pain—he is vanquished each time in his very victory. Thus, henceforth every work of Gustave's—among other functions—has the task of renewing in the imaginary the original crisis, namely the passion of the son and the murder of the father.

So he is a parricide. Yet despite his obscure allusions in the letters to Louise, and his discourses on the *real* efficacy of the imaginary, he has no remorse. On the contrary, he is rather fond of this murder by magic spell: it makes him still more gloomy, more cursed; it gives body to his role as fatal man, hiding in the depths of his heart unspeakable wounds and unknown crimes. At this time, his father's death has not yet appeased his resentment. But his *real* thought— perfectly right as it is—does not have these magical resonances. In a nutshell, it amounts to this: one of the two of us was superfluous; if I am a man today, it is because I have bought my freedom with his life. This is why Gustave is attached to the legend of Julien, who only accedes to sainthood *because* he has stabbed his progenitor; it is that doubtful error which arouses his self-hatred and pushes him to extreme destitution; likewise, Gustave will receive genius only with the premature death of Achille-Cléophas. Much later, when fame has come, the black Lord of the Flaubert younger son becomes the "good Lord" of that only son, Julien. Gustave's rancors are appeased; the ruin of the Commanvilles compels him to take refuge in his childhood: he wishes, now, that it had been good. In Achille-Cléophas he sees no more than the man who knew how to take his leave in time.

Have we exhausted the significations of the crisis in this initial examination? And should we attempt to see it as mere negation, to describe it as a simple tactical defense whose principal objective was to rid Gustave of the obligations of his class, that is, the dictates of a bourgeois father, by revealing a radicalized passivity through a fall that would cast him below the condition of man? On the level at which we have elected to study it thus far, it is clear enough that the "attack" at Pont-l'Evêque is *first of all pure negation* of this kind, and that it was certainly lived as such. Flaubert himself sometimes appears to see in his attack of '44 and the life he made for himself as a result—sequestration, accepted deprivations, etc.—as merely a tactical and purely negative means, even in relation to art. For example, in 1875, at the very time he was writing *Saint Julien,* he seems in his letters to ascribe a merely practical and rather egocentric meaning to his "monastic" life. We know that he reacts to the ruin of the Commanvilles—which touches him materially and threatens him in all he holds most dear, namely Croisset, which belongs to his niece and which she can sell—with tears, extraordinary nervousness, a kind of prostration which in his eyes signifies nothing less than the beginning of senility. His niece tries to combat this extravagant despair—from which he is literally going to die after precocious aging—by making some rather comic appeals to him for stoicism. She merely succeeds in irritating him. He is especially annoyed when she enjoins him to "toughen up," or when she suggests that he should begin his life anew or to "begin a new life." She does have a point, however: Hasn't he claimed all his life that one accedes to Art only by detaching oneself from the goods of this world? Didn't he pose as a stoic? He answers her with passion; he's through with stoicism—that was fine before, during his youth and his maturity: "My sensibility is overexcited, my nerves and brain are infirm, very infirm, I feel it . . . You should know that old veins of granite sometimes become beds of clay . . . But you are young, you have strength, you cannot understand me." In another letter, he vehemently protests: they *have no right* to demand an attitude of resignation on his part.

> I have spent my life depriving my heart of the most legitimate nourishment. I have led a hardworking and austere existence. Well, I've had enough! I feel at the end of my tether, the tears welling up suffocate me, and I open the floodgates. And then the idea of no longer having a roof over my head, a home, is intolerable to me. I now look at Croisset with the eye of a mother who looks at her consumptive child and says: How much longer will he

go on? And I cannot accustom myself to the hypothesis of a definitive separation.

With such concerns, work is impossible for him: long before departing for Concarneau, he abandons *Bouvard et Pécuchet* and "dissolves in dreadful inactivity." He recognizes, however, that the financial disaster does not put him entirely in the gutter, but it immediately prompts him to affirm that his "broken heart" condemns him to sterility. "My existence has been overturned, I shall always have something to live on, but in different conditions. As far as literature is concerned, I am incapable of any work." When he allows himself to hope, what does he require in order to return to his writing desk? That after the liquidation he should still have ten thousand pounds in income, as well as Croisset. At Concarneau he declares that if he had to live there, six thousand would suffice, strictly speaking. But right away he falls back into his black thoughts. Exactly what is he complaining about? He tells a few close friends. To Madame Brianne, for example, on 18 July 1875: "I have sacrificed everything in my life for the freedom of my intelligence! And it has been taken from me *by this reversal of fortune.*[53] It is this above all that makes me despair." Sacrificed everything? Yes, *except* Croisset. He says in the same letter: "If Deauville remains to me . . . and we keep Croisset, existence will still be possible. If not, it won't." Deauville and Croisset assure him the "peace of mind" that makes inspiration *possible* for him: as long as he is afraid of losing his income and his roof, he will feel "empty." "I ought to feel enthusiasm for an idea, for a subject, for a book. But Faith is no longer there." The idea takes shape beneath his pen: "I had sacrificed everything since my youth for my peace of mind. It is destroyed forever . . . and I believe that never again will I be capable of writing two consecutive lines." This curious sentence is aimed at the whole of Flaubert's life from the time of the crisis, and consequently at the crisis itself, which, with its subsequent attacks, is presented as a sacrifice: in January '45 Gustave deprived himself of "legitimate nourishment for the heart" by proclaiming himself incapable of action, a subman, and by acknowledging that he was "not made for pleasure." No more desires; hence *calm.* But on condition that his objective being be preserved, that is, Croisset and some income. The contradiction will be noted: if he has sacrificed *everything* to his soul's tranquillity, nothing and no one can take that tranquillity from him. It should

53. My italics.

therefore remain to him even if he becomes a hobo and sleeps under bridges. But that's not so at all: the search for destitution can be conducted only on the basis of bourgeois property. He takes up the theme again in a letter to Madame Brianne of 2 October '75. This time his thought seems complete:

> I am a "man of decadent times," neither Christian nor Stoic, and certainly not made for the struggles of existence. I had arranged my life so as to have peace of mind, sacrificing everything to that end, repressing my senses and silencing my heart. I recognize now that I was mistaken: the most sensible precautions have served no purpose and I find myself ruined, crushed, numbed . . . *To create art*, one needs *to be unconcerned with material things*,[54] an attitude that I shall henceforth lack! My brain is overburdened with base preoccupations. I feel defeated! Indeed, your friend is a man who is finished.

This time, everything is said. To create art—thus to soar above life—two things are required: the systematic practice of anorexia (chastity, temperance, denial of ambition and of human passions) *and* unconcern with material things that comes only with a private income. The candidate is required to renounce *desires;* in exchange he has the right to demand the automatic satisfaction of his *needs.* To George Sand on 10 May 1875, to Georges Charpentier at the beginning of August of the same year, he says the same thing in the same terms. "To write good things, one needs a certain alacrity! What can be done to recover it?" "To write well, one needs a certain alacrity, which I am lacking. When shall I again take possession of my poor aching head?" Alacrity: the word is carefully chosen, and its reappearance three months later proves the importance Flaubert attached to it. Alacrity is the positive aspect of ataraxia, the reflexive feeling of the readiness of the emancipated soul, the calm contentment of seeing it wholly gathered together, strengthened by spiritual exercises, and the resulting generous desire to employ it to suprahuman ends. In sum, this is the alacricy of the athlete at rest who neither drinks nor smokes nor makes love and takes pleasure in his strength; it is the full and conscious possession of what he calls, in another letter, the freedom of his intelligence. In '75, with the resurrection of the Future—which he thought had been killed in January '44—worry makes an abrupt entry into his life, cheerful tranquillity vanishes as soon as he must "think of tomorrow."

54. My italics.

Is it certain that Gustave in 1875 understands what happened in 1844? When he writes to his niece or to George Sand, disheartened and angry, he focuses on the ataraxia that he is about to lose, which, despite several allusions to his work as a writer, consequently seems to him the supreme good. He is the unyielding bourgeois, the plundered landowner. He returns to this continually: at his age, a man cannot remake himself, he has habits he cannot give up without dying. I am an old man, he says; I am not going to change. And this time it is true. Moreover, in this spring of '75, his crazy project *Bouvard et Pécuchet* fatigues and bewilders him; he is losing his way in it and thinks of abandoning it. In short, for a moment Art ceases to be his major concern: what he regrets is his *life*, his poor solitary, regulated life with its comfort and the eternal return of celebrations and seasons. He is "emptied," and he undertakes *Saint Julien* at Concarneau, he says, "only to occupy myself with something, to see if I can still turn a phrase, which I doubt." [55] We may suppose that, under these conditions, Gustave is escaping from himself and no longer understands his principal option. He is rarely truthful when speaking directly about himself. Yet, is he not otherwise sincere and profound in *Saint Julien*, which was begun without much enthusiasm and yet gradually captivates him? Doesn't it furnish a difficult and complex but direct link between meanness, crime, self-hatred, and the hopeless desire to kill himself in order to make expiation and sainthood— Art found at last? In these few pages all the components of the primal fall are set in place. Reading them correctly, we understand that in '44, when Gustave fell in the night, he sacrificed himself at once *against the Father and against the younger son*, the odious "great man *manqué*." How could it be otherwise? To take his whining at face value would be to forget that, in his youth, passive resistance to the bourgeois destiny arranged for him was always coupled with the ardent and vain hope of being reborn a genius. As we have observed, his hatred of the bar was all the more intense in that his literary hopes were more bitterly disappointed. In January '44, what makes his return to Rouen, then to Paris, *impossible* is his certainty of being merely a failed bourgeois. His fall at Pont-l'Evêque, therefore, is at once *against* Destiny and *for* Art. Doesn't this humiliating sacrifice, far from merely providing him with the leisure to write, aim directly at defeating bad luck with a holocaust in order to give him access to the

55. To Madame Roger des Genettes, Concarneau, 30 October 1875, *Correspondance*, 7:267. He has other motives, as we shall see. He minimizes his enterprise.

glorious host of artists? We have just indicated that his neurosis at a certain level was organized as a passive expectation of the death of the father. Might it not also be an *expectation of the masterpiece to come?* Even so, we must be clear: the first expectation, purely negative, appeared to be an internal effort to come closest to pure passivity, to become that pure block of granitelike eternity over which time will flow without leaving any trace. But there are active expectations; the expectation of the Idea is not only the trust placed in the void, it seeks to be a trap by the very fact that it expects; in other words, it constitutes itself as an oriented opening. Is the neurosis of pithiatic expectation, which is structured in '44 in relation to art, a simple negative instrumentalization of passivity, or must we see it as an internal, prospective relationship to the future masterpiece?

Let us come back to that curious tranquillity of soul which Flaubert begins to exhibit at the end of January. We have just shown that he somehow divined "just how far he would go in excess." A calm of that kind is proper to hysterical afflictions, when the body takes charge of anxiety. Be that as it may, *before* the crisis he was anguished because the collapse, a dizzying and terrible outcome, became more menacing each day and because he denied the intolerable humiliation with all his strength. Now it is done, Flaubert is *objectively diminished*—he should cry out in rage. All the more so because he can no longer even take refuge in a dream of glory: for the first six months they will refuse him the right even to take up his pen. Does he even know whether he will one day find the strength to write again? *Why is he not humiliated* if he has lost everything, even that?

May we not contend, then, that Art is directly at stake? And what if the meaning of the crisis were not only to procure for Flaubert, through sequestration, the leisure and isolation he judges necessary to do a book but also to make him *internally capable* of doing it? What if the other objective—the principal one, perhaps—of the "particular system made for a special case" were to surpass the inhibitions and inadequacies of the "great man *manqué*" and to transform him into an *artist?* The conception of *Smarh* was not separable from the transformation of Gustave's mental attitude toward the world and himself. Conversely, might not the change of attitude provoked by the collapse and false death be preparation for an aesthetic ascesis? Flaubert's position is complex: his allergy to the Code has no meaning by itself; in order to understand it, we must link it directly to the literary impotence from which he believes he suffers. An uncontested genius—who is therefore certain of escaping the bourgeois condition—

he would pass his exams effortlessly, as he did in the autumn of '42 after finishing *Novembre*. Isn't the collapse, which thrusts him into subhumanity, meant to help him realize in himself the super-humanity of the artist? The essential thing, in this case, is to be non-human—whether beneath or above humanity is unimportant and may even amount to the same thing. He must make himself incapable of sharing the aims of the species: with this, Art begins. Or idiocy. At Pont-l'Evêque, Flaubert no doubt made an audacious wager: with the possibility that the fall could bring him genius or insanity, he fell, betting on genius. If we accept this working hypothesis, we understand that the humiliation must have grazed him without crushing him: first, because he would not have experienced his crisis as the simple realization of his collapse but as a condition necessary for his internal progress; and then, even more important, because the renunciation of human ends, provided it is wholehearted and sincere, involves ipso facto the disappearance of shame.

Gustave always contested human aims. Yet he adhered to them, more or less. Served by an excessively docile body, he denied needs, but sooner or later and for good reason they returned at top speed. He scorned ambition, but the Flaubert family had infected him with its formidable arrivism. He detested his studies without remaining indifferent to success, even admitting in his *Souvenirs* that he sometimes yearned "to shine in the salons." The primary result of his neurosis is to burn all his bridges. In September '45—twenty months after the first attack—he writes to Alfred:

> There is now such a gap between me and the rest of the world that I am sometimes surprised to hear the simplest and most natural things said. The most banal witticism sometimes holds me spellbound. There are gestures, vocal sounds, that I cannot get over, and trifles that make me dizzy. Have you sometimes listened attentively to people who were speaking a foreign language you did not understand? I am like that. By dint of wanting to understand everything, everything makes me dream. But maybe this wonderment is not so stupid after all.[56]

This text makes explicit the reasons for his estrangement: Flaubert wants to understand the interests and passions of men, but he cannot without participating in them. And here he has withdrawn himself from the species: a "gap" separates him from it; comprehension turns into confused contemplation. It's all there: actions, their motivations,

---

56. To Alfred, September '45, *Correspondance*, 1:191.

their objectives; he can reconstitute the linkages, but the entire process remains opaque to him because he has not put himself *inside*. This was underscored by a much earlier text, which translates Flaubert's impressions during the first six months of his neurosis. In chapter 26 of *L'Education sentimentale*, Jules observes:

> Anyone engaged in action does not see it as a whole, the player who is in it does not feel the poetry of the game, nor the debauchee the grandeur of the debauch, etc. If every passion, every dominant idea of life, is a circle that we follow around to see its circumference and extent, we must not stay closed inside it but must put ourselves outside it.

There seems to be a contradiction between the text of *L'Education* and that of the 1845 letter to Alfred, for in the earlier one the "gap" leads to a panoramic comprehension, global and totalizing—the entire circularity of our behavior is seen—and in the more recent text it leads to estrangement. But this is because, from January '44 on, Gustave keeps vacillating between optimism and pessimism. Beginning at this time we find letters in which Art is presented as an absolute point of view on the world, alternating with others in which it is reduced to the least boring occupation of a bourgeois who lives in the country. We shall return to this. The positive view wins out, however; even in the letter to Alfred, Flaubert refuses to assimilate his daze to stupidity. His incomprehension is a superior comprehension, which comprises, beyond the clear vision of human actions, the stupefied consciousness of their vanity.

To tell the truth, there is nothing new here—at least in appearance—and we have once more caught him contemplating the actions of the species with the same stupefaction. It is the "rebound" of pride and the use of the negative infinite: "Climb a tower . . ." In fact, what is involved is a new utilization of what we have called panoramic consciousness: it is himself, first of all, whom he claims to leap beyond, as these two texts from the first *Education* indicate, one of which—possibly written the very moment he returned to his manuscript—shows the *means,* and the other the result:

> [Jules] seemed to take pleasure in debasing himself and dragging himself in the mud, as if he had wanted to take revenge against his own person; nevertheless, his was preoccupied only with himself . . . analyzed himself down to the last fiber, looked at himself under a microscope or contemplated himself as a whole. It was as

if his pride had placed him above himself and he was viewing himself with pity.

Here we find once again the theme of *Novembre*—"I am too small for myself"—replayed in exasperation. But we see the ascesis as well: dragging himself through the mud, *taking revenge on himself*. And this is what follows: "The calm in which Jules had wanted to live, through egotism and the arid heights on which he had placed himself in a spasm of pride, had distanced him *so abruptly*[57] from his youth and had required of him a will so harsh and so sustained . . . that his heart was almost turned to stone." Two words are striking: *so abruptly*. Since the ascesis is the object of a *sustained* will, one would expect the change to be progressive. But the emphasized brutality of the metamorphosis leaves us no choice: it is an allusive reference to the crisis—which Flaubert never mentions directly in this novel. In this case, the will would come *afterward* to finish the job. This interpretation is confirmed by a letter from 1846 cited above: "I was not like that formerly. This change came about naturally. My will counted for something in it as well. It will lead me further, I hope." In short, he has avenged his mediocrity by inflicting ghastly tortures on himself which result in the memorable plunge of 1844. It hardly matters whether he was then perched above himself or had fallen beneath his pitiable particularity: the plunge was meant to free his arid and arrogant pride from his singular person. When he takes the leap, he does not, of course, succeed in stifling his anomaly, but his heart is turned to stone: in other words, the origin, the result, and the aim of the original attack is nonadherence to the self, a certain distancing which releases Gustave from his *reality*.

The first attack did not occur before the development in Gustave of a passive consent to the worst: it is not enough to tear apart his own heart; he will take vengence to the point of condemning himself to abjection. But by the acceptance of the worst, lived as belief, he has already in part broken solidarity with the corpse or the madman he has condemned himself to become, as if the disproportion between the aspirations of his pride and his capabilities were already so accentuated that it mattered little to him whether it was exaggerated still more. But since it is pride that does the sentencing, it is pride that will be witness to his execution: something sinks to Achille's feet, something *must* soar above the disaster and observe it with indifference.

57. My italics.

This is why he never loses consciousness: fainting, pure and simple, would symbolize total abolition. Gustave intends some vigilance to remain: "I clung to my reason, it conquered all, however besieged and battered." Not that this Reason seeks to combat madness hand to hand: it remains above the fray, a futile, stupid affirmation of the universal, of the stoical "I think." Pride was, willy-nilly, in solidarity with the anomaly, a contingent and finite determination but an ordered totality; it can no longer be in solidarity with the disorder of images into which the anomaly seems to have dissolved. Distancing, a self-denial long contemplated during the autumn of '43, has favored the crisis that has cut this captive balloon loose from the concrete Ego, which is atomized.

Flaubert had a long struggle with his double: Almaroës, cold analytic reason, scuffled with Satan the whimperer, tortured memory. The fall separates them: present reality is swallowed up; Satan, deprived of this support, is converted into pure memory. Almaroës, losing his body, is no longer anything or anyone and can feel nothing except in the imaginary. Lived experience congeals, closes over his sufferings: it belongs to a young dead man. What remains is an imagination fixed on a memory and a pride that is mad but disembodied, derealized.

As the origin and result of the crisis, isn't such distancing, at bottom, its positive aim? In this case it would be identified with the crisis itself, as its teleological intention, its orientation, and its meaning. Indeed, Gustave, despite a few relapses, is soon to break with the impassioned eloquence of his first works: Art, beginning with the last chapters of *L'Education*, will be affirmed as the supreme distancing. Isn't it *to be reborn as an artist* that Gustave has severed his bonds to immediate life?

One cannot answer these questions if one continues to limit oneself, as I have just done, to examining the initial crisis and describing the referential attacks. If the tactical intentions, whose objective is short-term, can yield immediately to existential analysis, the strategic intentions can be grasped only in their temporal development. Not only is their objective distant, but they are by themselves neither repetitive nor instantly summerizable, no matter how privileged; they must be considered temporal unities whose meaning is in the process of *becoming* to the extent that they are temporalized. In order to describe the strategic orientation of this neurosis—if it has one at all—the patient will have to be observed during the three months that follow the first "attack," that is until his decision to write the first *Saint Antoine*. We must not limit our study to the referential attacks— which seem to have become stereotyped rather quickly and which unfortunately we know hardly anything about, other than what Maxime says—but, quite to the contrary, we shall try to comprehend and to fix in words the way that Flaubert lived these years, what he did, what was done, what he did about it, what was felt, what was written, what he wrote *about it*. Indeed, during this entire period, his illness, although diminishing, never leaves him; it remains as exis, at once lived and patiently deciphered, even in the interval that separates the two referential attacks. In this sense, it is *his life:* he *lives* the hysterical neglect of living.

But isn't it true that his relations with Art and culture, as these are manifest through feelings, thoughts, behavior, and roles, also represent the essential part of his existence? And are they separable from his neurosis? The neurosis, despite its apparently crude and rudimentary character, cannot be regarded otherwise than as the "illness of a writer" or the neurosis of a man of culture; the cultural world, and especially literature, furnish and maintain the meaningful setting in which Gustave must live his illness. Conversely, these manifestations of the *objective mind* are determined in Gustave in relation to his disorders. We shall therefore have to examine the dialectical movement by which the artistic project and the neurotic project mutually condition each other to the extent that writing becomes neurosis and neurosis literature.

This examination alone will be able to answer our question of principle. It is what will allow us to decide which of two possible responses comes closer to the truth. A choice must be made. *Either* the fall is none other than a moment of dialogue with the father—one in which unspeakable discourse is replaced by a somatization—in which case the neurosis-writing unity will not be significant. Certainly the relations between the one and the other will not be those of *exteriority*, but their single foundation will be the totalizing unity of lived experience in which even external relations are constituted as internal bonds of the parts with each other throughout the whole. In other words, the literary project and the neurotic project, far from being limited to coexistence, will condition each other. But it will nonetheless be the case that each is born outside the other; an exhaustive expression of the neurosis will not be found in the writing, nor will the fundamental intention to write be found in the origin of the neurosis.

Or the two intentions will reveal their original unity. The neurosis will appear, then, *on a certain level* as a tactical and negative answer to the father, provoked by an urgency nonetheless long in the making, and *on the deepest level* as a strategic and positive answer to the question posed by the necessity and impossibility, for Gustave, of being the Artist. In such a case, the neurotic project would aim at a radical metamorphosis of the person, accompanied by a new vision of the essence of the Beautiful. Strategically, the fall would then seem to be a conversion, in which Gustave need do no more than develop the consequences. This transformation, at once fully lived in a lightning flash and temporalized in the following years, would be the conversion to optimism. But an optimism according to Saint Flaubert; in other words, more than ever would the worst be certain, but the radicalization of the defeat would be nothing less than a victory. Is this the original exteriority of two projects subsequently unified by their contingent belonging to the same whole? Or a fundamental conversion and *one* in which the tactical and the strategic levels would be in a relation of reciprocal symbolization? That is what we must determine by following Flaubert step by step through his years of somnolence.

Elbehnon, or the Last Spiral

BOOK TWO

*The Crisis Seen as a Positive Strategy
in the Light of Subsequent Facts*

or

"Loser Wins" as a Conversion to Optimism

EIGHTEEN

"Loser Wins" Rationalized

At the first remission in June, 1845, Gustave takes up *L'Education sentimentale* and completes it. In the last chapters of this work, originally written in January '45, the influence of the illness is undeniable: the role of Jules is suddenly amplified and he becomes the book's main character. We should read these pages with care: they constitute the author's first account of his illness. In the six months during which he did no writing, he had time to meditate on what was happening to him; he questioned himself continually, he read works of mental pathology; above all, he familiarized himself with his attacks and acquired an ever deeper understanding of them. Primarily, however, he writes in order to recuperate his neurosis. Certainly he never speaks of it directly, but he discovers in Jules's life a sort of providential intention that governs it and primes him, from one disappointment to another, for his "extremely abrupt" conversion and, beyond that, his victory. Jules's adventure, in effect, is achieving genius through absolute failure. Not by accident but *intentionally*. In other words, Gustave's illness has a meaning. But if he senses that there is a subjective finality in his previous misfortunes, he is neither eager nor able to know it; he prefers that the solicitude gently and implacably guiding him toward future masterpieces should act on him from the outside. Before '44, he had transformed his father's mechanistic determinism into a prophetic fatalism that better corresponded to his pessimism: facts were linked together from the outside according to strict laws, *but* the whole process was oriented by an *other* will toward an objective that was nothing less than the worst. After '44, fatality is turned into providence: the confusion remains between the external rigor of causal sequences and the teleological necessity which, in a calculated enterprise, links the means to the end. That necessity has merely changed signs—it has become positive. In this way Gustave, without too much bad faith, can call himself both the innocent victim and the chosen bearer of an illness that devours him and that he himself has secretly fashioned: obviously this projection of his neurotic intentions into the objective ream is required by the neurosis itself, which could not survive any discovery of its strategic intentions. The profound understanding exists, but he is forbidden to make that knowledge explicit.

As it is, this text—all the more important as it was, so to speak, written "in a white heat"—has something singular about it, for it was the only song of triumph Flaubert could permit himself in his entire life's work—including his correspondence. That is quite striking if one considers the circumstances that accompanied and frequently interrupted his work: when he resumed work on *L'Education,* he had already got quite far with it; six months to complete it—if we recall the author's fecundity—is considerable. So the referential attacks must still have been quite numerous, and each of them must have compelled him to take several days of bed rest—as Maxime's testimony confirms. In this miserable state, in utter insecurity, not knowing even as he writes whether an abrupt return of the "epilepsy" will at any moment crush his pen onto the page and hurl him to the ground, Gustave dares to make Jules equal to the greatest writers, perhaps even to Shakespeare. He abandons himself to convulsions, falls into a deep sleep, keeps to his bed, and when he gets up again, he returns to his writing table exhausted, and cries in jubilation: at last! at last! I am an Artist. It goes further still, for these final pages contain, although he denies it, a poetic Art that would serve as manifesto to the post-Romantic writers, and that brilliantly defines Flaubert's future work. It may be said that we still have not established whether he discovered a positive strategy in his neurosis or whether he simply *attributed* one to it in a rebound of pride. To that I answer that we shall not be able to settle the question without rereading the end of his novel and without comparing it to the letters he writes at the same period. If it can be shown that his conception of Art, without being neurotic, necessarily implies his neurosis and would be incomprehensible if it were not its result and did not reflect it even while transcending it, we shall see clearly: Gustave will be shown to have plunged into abjection at Pont-l'Evêque in order to be transformed into an Artist—in other words, to have utilized his pithiatic constitution to reinvent the art of writing.

Who is Jules? A young provincial, the "foil" to Henry. In the first part—more precisely, in two-thirds of the novel—he appears as a mediocre fellow and cuts a pale figure next to his brilliant comrade. Gustave has not favored him; even his sorrows are ordinary: an unhappy love, some literary disappointments, the author also mentions betrayed friendships. He burdens him with an adversity from which he has just escaped but which is so common it is scarcely distressing: Jules *works*, imagine that! He has taken a job to *earn his living*. After all, he is a dreamer, a poet without great talent. He does not lack for pride, however: he is another one who is too small for himself. All this is indicated to us casually: the character has only a relative being, there is no point in taking the trouble to give him depth, he is a pale remake of the hero of *Novembre*. And then, all at once—Henry is long since in America, Madame Renaud is beginning to bore him—the poor boy's vexations are immeasurably inflated without our being able to know whether he has suffered other disappointments or whether they are the same ones that Flaubert has suddenly charged with representing the hell of suffering in noble souls. In any case, far from attributing these misfortunes to chance, the author takes such care in revealing their meaning to us that he refers to them several times: "He was slighted, derided, hissed, abandoned by his friends, outraged by himself. His zeal was attributed to his egotism and his sacrifices to his cruelty; he failed in all his projects, he was repelled in all his impulses, he witnessed the agony of all his emotions." The subsequent paragraph, which Gustave devotes to Henry, suffices to show that this collection of calamities, far from defining the human condition in its generality, serves an elective purpose. Jules could not endure such reversals without being made the object of a particular designation, since his friend Henry, "supple and strong, hardy and clever, is . . . the Frenchman in all his grace . . . Women love him because he flatters them; men are devoted to him because he serves them; he is feared because he takes revenge; he is deferred to because he bullies; people are drawn to him because he attracts." We are bound to conclude that what designates Jules as the martyr is his being itself: he is made in such a way that he fails at everything and displeases everyone, beginning with himself. Indeed, while writing to Henry he revels in self-abasement as though to get even with himself.[1] As a result, he is more interesting, and rather surprising as well:

---

1. Curiously, he also drags through the mud the great love of his youth, not in the letter to Henry but much later, when he has detached himself from the world and has produced his masterpiece: "Jules loved to chat about her, to hear fom Bernardi's own mouth a thousand intimate details that degraded her, a thousand facts that violated the memory he had kept of her . . . By dint of satisfying this singular need, he finally no

we would not have expected it of this gentle daydreamer. Is it because the author jumped into his character (just *before* the crisis? Six months afterward? Nothing can be known for certain). This mediocre fellow is transformed into a wildman, he tears at his chest with his nails, he ravages himself: promoted to the dignity of "great man *manqué*," he has a mandate to experience the raging self-hatred harbored by Gustave himself. This is what has transformed him. Previously, he took some satisfaction in suffering, as his creator once did: "Formerly, he fled [in his sufferings] from pleasure with the desperate obstinacy that is the essence of Christian and Romantic anguish." That's all finished: in January '44 at Pont-l'Evêque, Romanticism is dead, the post-Romantic generation has come of age. Suddenly Jules's misfortunes are different in kind: they are the atrocious wounds of pride provoked by repeated failures. Skewered on the vertical negative that structures Gustave's space, Jules falls, rebounds, falls again, enraged by the "humiliation of these falls, deeper each time."[2]

---

longer felt it; when he had properly dragged through the mud, turned around, and broken in all its articulations the tender and painful love of his youth, and when the ferocity of his mind had been sated by this spectacle, he found less charm in Bernardi's company." This episode throws a singular light on the pleasure Gustave took in Schlésinger's visits: Bernardi is the lover of the actress Jules loved; he is a comic and vile actor, like Schlésinger (according to Gustave), like Arnoux. If we recall that the young Flaubert, even at Trouville, likes to place his dear "phantom" in obscene and grotesque postures, to sully her in imagination by delivering her up to Schlésinger, our reservations concerning the nature of his "great love" will be understandable, as will the fact that we saw it, *at least in part,* as a myth, if not a mystification (concocted by Gustave himself to pique the jealousy of the Muse).

2. In this passage, Flaubert speaks in full of the *"humiliation"* that his *falls* provoked in him. The sentence would seem obscure (why are these falls each time more extensive? How is it that after each of them he finds himself higher than before?) if we were not already familiar with the self-defensive mechanism of the *rebound.* In any case, Jules speaks of it *in the past:* the last and most extensive fall obviously corresponds the crisis of January '44. It managed to kill his heart or, as he says, to "armour it in the sensitive places." From one disapointment to the next, the amplitude of the downfall increases; the intensity of the humiliation decreases and ends around zero. The author takes up his idea a bit further on, but this time the Romantic finery masks or distracts his thought: "Do you know what makes the flesh of those Strasbourg truffle patés you are gorging yourself on at lunch so delicate to the palate? The animal destined for your table was made to jump up on the bloodied marble slabs and was killed only after its liver was sufficiently inflated and swollen to make good eating. Never mind its sufferings, provided it abets our pleasures! It is in slow suffering that genius is cultivated; those heartfelt cries you admire, those lofty thoughts that make you leap have had their source in tears you have not seen, in anguish you do not know." On a quick reading, one might think he shares Alfred de Musset's opinion: "The most despairing songs are the most beautiful." Yet he means just the opposite: let us not forget that sufferings have killed the animal with the hypertrophied liver, and that we do not taste its flavor until it is dead: the genius is a dead child who has suffered from an enlarged heart but

Yet he suddenly finds himself on the other side of an abyss. What has happened? We shall not know directly: in *L'Education* there is no *realistic* equivalent to the accident at Pont-l'Evêque. On closer examination, however, there is a whole chapter which *symbolically* describes Jules's break with the past, the moment when the convert, in fear and trembling, sees his life totalized in all its ugliness, is tempted to cling to it again, then flees it by sequestration. This is the dog episode. Flaubert wanted it to be "fantastic" precisely in the way he will define several pages further on: "Understood as a development of the inner essence of our soul, as a superabundance of the moral element, the fantastic has its place in art." And, of course, Faust's spaniel is of some influence.[3] One evening, Jules, already quite far along the road to conversion, meets "a skinny beast, lean as a wolf; it had a wild and miserable look, dirtied by the mud, its skin, mangy in certain places, was scarcely covered with a sparse, long coat of fur . . . It was lame in a hind paw." This wretched animal "rushed upon him, yapping and licking his hands; its eyes fixed on Jules with alarming curiosity." Jules "at first feels horror, then pity." He sees the animal "merely as one of those dogs that have lost their master, that are chased off and roam in the country, and are found dead at the roadside." We recognize the scheme: previously it was Marguerite whom the crowd hooted down and who, abandoned, slipped into the river. Now it is a dog. But this dog, in every respect so repulsive, so ill-favored, represents Flaubert's own life neither more nor less than the poor drowned acrobat. Indeed, Jules tries in vain to chase it off, he ends by throwing stones at it; but the beast comes back to him so "stubbornly" that the young man is intrigued: has it seen him before? can it be Fox, the spaniel he had earlier given to Lucinde, the woman he loved, who slept with a clown and went away as she had come, without granting him anything—in short, a malicious caricature of Madame Schlésinger? He feels "an infinite compassion for this inferior being that looked at him with so much love,"[4] but this inexplicable love scares him. Repulsed by the ugliness of the "horrible beast,"[5] he

---

suffers from it no longer. Later, when he writes to Louise, Gustave shows the negative aspect of his malady: if I had had a stronger mind, my pain would have remained in my head instead of slipping into my limbs. But in '44, pretending to speak only of his character, he reveals its other side.

3. And doubtless also the memory of some encounter with a lost dog. He often mentions the fact—to Louise—that children, idiots, and animals attach themselves to him, and recalls "curious" episodes which he unfortunately told her only in person.

4. Everything is there, even the bond of vassalage.

5. This disgust with ugliness is entirely Flaubertian.

forces himself not to see it, but an "insurmountable attraction draws his eyes to it." The dog "seems to beg him to follow it." "It runs back and forth, approaches Jules, draws him after it" and finally leads him onto a bridge. Surprised, the young man "recalls that one day—oh, it was long ago—he had come onto this bridge and had wanted to die. Was that what the dismal beast circling around him is trying to say?" Or is it trying to convey that Lucinde is dead? The cursed dog and the man "frighten each other; the man trembles at the gaze of the beast, in which he believes he sees a soul, and the beast trembles at the gaze of the man in whom it believes it sees a God." Jules starts to beat the dog, it draws back, he runs away. Returning home, he "reflected on what had just happened to him."

> In all that had passed between him and the monster, in everything that was connected with this adventure, there was something so intimate, so profound, so clear that at the same time it was necessary to recognize a reality of another kind, one as real as everyday reality though seemingly inconsistent with it. Now *all that was tangible and perceptible in existence disappeared in his thought as secondary and useless, as an illusion that was merely superficial.*[6]

He has a hunch and a curious desire to take another look at the dog that has pursued him; he goes downstairs and opens the door: "The dog was lying on the threshold." These are the last words of chapter 26. The next chapter begins with the sentence: "That was his last day of pathos; henceforth he was cured of his superstitious fears . . ."

The dog is the temptation of the pathetic; at the same time, it is his past life, his loves, his vexations, Lucinde, the desperate hours when he dreamed of suicide, a few moments of an illusory happiness. It clings to him, this life, as if to tell him: *I am yours*, claim me, I will die if you abandon me and I will live if you continue to live *me*. Jules is fascinated, but at the same time he sees it implacably as it was—symbolized very effectively by this frightful, abject creature. In truth, he is never *tempted*; this sudden encounter with his life corresponds to the crisis (it is his *last* day of pathos): he discovers it as an alien life and it hypnotizes him; the bond is not severed because there is "something so intimate, so clear and profound," between him and the monster. But it is during this very night that the bond is broken. Curiously, we are not witness to the definitive rupture: Jules goes downstairs again, opens the door, the dog is there; what happens? It is highly significant that Flaubert doesn't breathe a word about it, and that he de-

6. My italics.

clares in the following chapter: "That was his last day of pathos." As if the *real* crisis took place between the last lines of chapter 26 and the first of chapter 27; indeed, given the state of his nerves, when Jules found the dog in front of his door—as he feared, as he hoped—he could have fainted or fallen in a "flood of fire" and believed he was dead. Neighbors came, perhaps. They bled him. He opened his eyes. We can imagine anything except that, seeing the creature, he calmly shut the door and went back upstairs to bed. For he was *still* "pathetic" at that moment. What happened, that the next day he should forever have ceased to be so? The encounter with the dog is the *screen event* that both reveals and masks the true event at Pont-l'Evêque. What is striking is that Flaubert, in passing over the actual event in silence, has managed to give it a supernatural dimension. The perceptible, the tangible, "disappeared in his thought as secondary and useless, as an illusion." He recognizes existence as a "reality of another kind, one as real as everyday reality though seemingly inconsistent with it." This surreality is not quite the same as the sacred but closely resembles it. And this way of reporting his experience to us is quite similar to what a convert might adopt: the real—assimilated to quotidian banality—falls away; the surreal appears, radically contradicting it. We can therefore confidently assert that Flaubert—*at least* during the summer and autumn following his attack—considered it an authentic *conversion* in the metaphysical, if not the religious, sense of the term.

Reassured, drained by his surreal experience, Jules dares to look backward, and consequently his thought goes further than his author's had gone until then. Rather, it is the author, reassured by "recourse to the third person" and taking up once more the method of his adolescence, who projects himself into the milieu of alterity so as to follow his ideas to the end while pretending to discover them in his character. In Jules, therefore, the *positive* aspect of the "attack" is revealed:

> From all that, however, his present state resulted, which was the sum of all these antecedents and allowed him to review them; every event had produced a second one, every sentiment had been based on an idea . . . Moreover, he told himself in order to justify himself, wasn't denying a period of his existence a demonstration that he was as narrow and as foolish as the historian who would deny one of the periods of history, approving of this part, disapproving of that . . ., putting himself in the place of Providence and aspiring to reconstruct its work? Therefore, everything

he had felt, experienced, suffered had perhaps come about for unknown ends, with a set and constant purpose, unperceived but real.

Nothing could be clearer. Rereading this passage, I cannot help recalling the Kierkegaardian concept of "repetition." At the moment of conversion, Flaubert consents to lose everything, and precisely for that reason all is abundantly returned to him. He hated his life—at least certain aspects of it, certain periods—as long as he still clung to it; he relaxed his grip, collapsed, and—divine surprise—*from the other side of the false death* he can love it wholly, as past, since it was destined to lead him, "by everything he felt, experienced, suffered," to the sublime purpose that Providence had assigned him.

First degree of ascesis: Jules-Flaubert no longer suffers: "He was hardened against tenderness and his heart was almost turned to stone . . . In this nearly superhuman stoicism, he had come to forget his own passions." These lines contain precious information on Gustave's state during 1844–'45. He does not tell us that he is *delivered* from his passions, that he has strangled them, and that his calm is born of the real emptiness of his soul. He insists, to the contrary, that they still exist but that he forgets them. This means, to be exact, that he lives in relation to them in a state of *hysterical distraction*. Indeed, how can it be allowed that from one day to the next one can stifle such harsh and violent impulses (resentment, self-hatred, shame, rage, the frenzied desire to kill or to kill oneself, mad ambitions) without being affected by a pathological mentality? I said earlier that his tranquillity came mainly from his Pyrrhic victory, which allowed him to escape from his bourgeois being, from his destiny, from time, and, moreover, that by renouncing human ends he had freed himself from shame. So be it. Yet one must *be able* to live this abdication. Breaking with a friend, with a beloved mistress, is possible under certain conditions; but it is not possible to avoid the sorrowful regrets, jealousies, temptations to begin again, etc., which ordinarily follow such decisions. *Sticking to it*—everyone knows what that costs; the work of rupture is often as long, as exhausting, as that of mourning. Now, in the grip of passion, Gustave and Jules claim to have broken a liaison of ten years and not to have suffered from it. Yet it is clear that Flaubert's fundamental impulses have survived his attacks: pride is intact—as we shall see when Maxime and Louis pass judgment on the first *Saint Antoine.* Long afterward, Bouilhet spoke to the Goncourts almost with terror of his friend's unbelievable susceptibility; resentment, sadism, masochism, envy, as many an episode testifies, never disappeared. As for literary ambition and the despair it so often provokes in Gustave, we shall take these up again a leisure. The truth is that he *believes* he is delivered. Not that this belief isn't secretly given the lie by the understanding of his illness; indeed, the image of the clear pond—its slime rising to dull the surface when the wind stirs it—corresponds perfectly to the previously cited text: the pool has *forgotten* its slime, as Jules has forgotten his passions. How are we to understand this? First of all, the "distraction" will be preserved only by means of inifinite precautions. It is the system designed for one man. Then, if he is again tempted to yield to envy, to hatred, the body intervenes, takes all the problems in hand, and somatizes them as convulsions. The conclusion is self-evident: Gustave was already more than half imaginary: after the crisis he becomes entirely so, to the extent that pithiatic belief produces in him a lived but unreal ataraxia. Or, conversely, to the extent that he escapes *pathos* only by unrealizing himself. Everyone has experienced the ability to suspend a torment provisionally (but not its cause) by *thinking of something else*. This turn of mind will be pathological only if it is sustained. For Gustave to persist in forgetting the passions, he must be forcibly motivated by *something else*, which continually makes itself the subject of thought. What? We shall attempt to find out. Let us observe at the outset, however, in order to clarify our research, that when a real man becomes entirely devoured by the imaginary, yet doesn't lose his reality, what he calls his mind tends to coincide with his imagination. As a result, the sole object with which he can have an exchange is the real world insofar as this allows itself to be derealized. Gustave writes to Louise that he pities those who are incapable of maintaining themselves each day, all day, in what he calls the "aesthetic attitude." He doesn't elaborate, but his letters of 1844–46 and *L'Education* help us understand that he is referring to a pithiatic absenteeism which allows him simultaneously to unrealize himself in order to derealize the world, and to derealize the world in order to unrealize himself. In short, *being must be imagined*. We shall look more closely at what this means.

Let us return to Jules. Flaubert does not conceal the fact that Jules *intentionally* maintains his interior emptiness, and several of his procedures are enumerated for us:

> When something had entered into him, he hunted it down pitilessly, like an inhospitable master who wants his palace to be empty in order to walk there more at his ease, and all fled beneath the flagellation of his irony, a terrible irony that began with him-

self and was all the more violent and cutting to others . . . Unjust
to his past, hard on himself, in his superhuman stoicism he had
come to forget his own passions and no longer to understand very
well those he had had . . . There were still moments when he was
tempted to live and to act, but irony was so quick to place itself
beneath the action that he could not complete it . . . He descended
so quickly into everything that he saw the nothingness in it at first
glance . . . Abandoned, sterile even on its first levels, deprived
of cool shades and murmuring springs, Jules's existence is as calm
as the desert.[7]

In short, he is *nothing*, feels *nothing*, wants *nothing*. This "distraction," considered in itself, remains on the level of a negative tactic.
Jules has killed his heart, we are told, because he could no longer bear
to suffer. But this position is soon surpassed: desensitization is presented as an indispensable moment in the conversion to Art. "Would
he have had this idea of Art, of pure Art, without the preparatory anguish he had suffered and if he had still been enmeshed in the bonds
of the finite?" To be someone is to be the slave of one's determination—as Gustave has long been saying. To be no one is to choose absolute indeterminacy, which presents itself *primarily* as an analogue
of the negative infinite; we shall come back to this. But above all it is to
disentangle the relation of the microcosm to the macrocosm from the
raging will-to-live which denatures and obscures it. Gustave shows us
Jules at a later moment of his development, "striving to make the seriousness of sensation vanish as rapidly as the sensation itself." *Seriousness:* what a happy discovery! Yes, sensation is *serious* when the
spirit of seriousness possesses it, when it testifies to the crushing reality of the world and the dangers that threaten us, when it appears in
our enterprises like an alarm bell indicating the adversity coefficient
of things, or like a forest fire at the edge of a narrow corridor of possibles. It is serious when it invades and dominates, when it feeds on
all our interests, when it reflects to us our desires and fears, in a
word, when it shows us our anchorage, when it reveals to us the external world as the basis of our inner reality. Serious for all those who
share human ends, it loses its practical depth for whoever is constituted in such a way that he no longer shares them. And a perception,

7. One is converted to what one *is* by privileging and radicalizing some essential tendency which, however, before the metamorphosis, held in check by other impulses,
could not achieve its full development. Let us recall that Flaubert, beginning in 1839,
depicts himself as a quietist discouraged in advance by his ironic skepticism from all
the enterprises into which he dreamed of launching himself. The attitude is now generalized, lived as permanent: disinterest becomes an exis.

when it is deprived of that dizzying gravity and no longer reflects either our life or our death or our needs or the community of men, is nothing but *representation*. One thinks here of a philosopher unknown in France in Flaubert's time and whose work Flaubert did not read before 1874,[8] Schopenhauer. For him, the *reality* of the world comes from the will to power. It is the violent *conatus*, diversified into millions of consciousnesses, that gives our environment its weight of menace, of desirability, of instrumentality, in short its being. For him who succeeds in suspending for a moment this headlong impulse, the universe is nothing but a collection of representations whose unity lends itself to disinterested—that is, aesthetic—contemplation in the form of the *Idea*. From this point of view, Gustave's crisis appears as a gigantic effort to combat the will to power in himself—in other words, Flaubert ambition and pride—by setting against it a decline from which he will not recover. He frees himself of desires by ridding himself definitively of the means to satisfy them, so as to have no more than a "glancing acquaintance" not only with men but with the things of this world. But his intention is not to transform the real into a collection of "representations" that would reveal their true structures to passive contemplation: he aspires to recondense the disorder of the world and to constitute the cosmos as pure appearance by the very order and formal unity he will give it. From this point of view, he has not changed since *Smarh:* the Beautiful derealizes to the extent that it informs. In 1839, however, the derealization had to be effected on the level of the work through the labor the artist performs on language. In '44, his literary failures have convinced him that a work of art—which preserves its function—*will not be* if its future author, on the level of lived experience, does not first grasp his experience as an unreal synthesis, a symbolic integration of the diverse. In short, in order to make the macrocosm his phantasm, the young man has made the passive choice of falling headlong into the imaginary and being swallowed up in it.

Certainly he has long been accustomed to fleeing the inconveniences of the real "on the wings of imagination." We have seen him take revenge on his family, on his comrades, and on his teachers by dreaming that he was Nero or Tamberlaine; or he would transport himself to the Orient, to India, to get away from the room or the study hall in which he was confined. In *Novembre* he informed us of his

8. Not a single allusion in the correspondence before this date. He mentions it in '74 only to say that he writes badly and thinks the wrong way. He surely did not see then how he could take advantage of it to buttress his theories on Art.

techniques. This fantasizing—as much as his pithiatism and his desire to be an actor (which are one and the same)—led us to see him as a child who is more than half imaginary. The difference between the young hunter of images who was writing *La Peste à Florence* and the "Old Man" who survives the crisis at Pont-l'Evêque is this: Gustave shifted from one to the other when he believed he could attribute his literary failures to the fact that his images themselves were too "serious," an affective charge that reduced them to bringing an illusory satisfaction of his desires, and consequently prevented them from being posited in their aesthetic truth. If he saw himself in Nero it was *to assuage* a tenacious and very real resentment, a constitutive trait of his own singular person; if, with the wave of a wand, he turned himself into an Indian rajah, it was *to satisfy* his violent desire to escape from the bourgeoisie and to enjoy the omnipotence that wealth confers. François de Médicis disemboweled by a dagger; Djalioh a murderer, struck down and stuffed; Mazza poisoning her family—all the morbid tales he invented for himself at the morgue, contemplating the cadavers—those humiliated images abdicating their radiant purity, their magnificent inutility, to serve the morose ruminations of a child of man, of a being of flesh who—despite his anomaly—was still affected by the concerns of the species. In other words, he rebukes himself for having used his imagination to masturbatory ends and hence for having deterred its creative functions. In *L'Education* he writes: "The poet, even as he is poet, must be man, that is, resume humanity in his heart and be himself some part of it." It is on the level of poetic research and innate knowledge of the human heart that image has its role. But the "ordinary run" of humanity has no right to make use of it for its all too human ends: as we have seen in *Smarh*, Gustave forced himself to view that "run," as he has all others, from the the perspective of the infinite; in short, he sought to free himself from it by a flight of pride, to diminish it beneath his eagle's eye. A futile effort: this divorce was *playacted* if not purely verbal. And until '44, the run of humanity kept its singular passions, its traits, its interests, its history. If Gustave has so long remained a "great man *manqué*," too small for himself, he thinks he now understands that this was a result not of his mediocrity but quite simply of his determination. It would have been the same if he had been determined differently: the Artist, creator of the universal, is nipped in the bud by the particularity of his conditionings. The January crisis is a radical effort to liquidate that determination definitively: let that half-portion fall at Achille's feet, let it croak from despair and humiliation—good riddance! As a consequence, there can be a feast of images, jumping like fleas, gratuitous at last, although the "rational-being"—humanity resumed—endures and dominates. This was the beast that embodied living and used the imaginary in order to perpetuate its life. Nothing lives anymore: the old passions are swallowed up; the imagination, swept clean, is surrendered to its free inhuman play of finality without end.

Gustave could not have sustained this *disinterest* for long if it had not been endured as a dream: it is the luck of hysterical "constitutions" to be so subject to autosuggestion as to *suffer* their own options. Not only does the *soma* react to excessively lively aggressions from the exterior with convulsions that save the young man's tranquillity, but it maintains a kind of somnolence in him, a torpor propitious to the aesthetic attitude. On this point we have Maxime's testimony, all the more significant for its silliness and malice. In *Souvenirs littéraires* we read:

> Increasingly he restricted his field of action and concentrated on the reverie of the moment; he sometimes went for months at a time without opening a newspaper, withdrawing his interest from the outside world and unable to tolerate anyone speaking of anything that did not directly interest him. The notions of real life escaped him, and he seemed to float in a permanent dream, which he could shake off only with great effort.

It should be noted that Maxime attributes his friend's behavior to epilepsy, which was then thought to be a lesion—fortuitous or constitutional, in any case organic—involving the cerebellum or the cerebrum. He was therefore struck by the extent to which it was involuntary: if it hadn't been for his illness, Maxime writes with a straight face, Gustave might have been a genius. The Flaubert younger son was preparing to become Shakespeare when an accident, bearing down on him, condemned him to repetition and plunged him into an oneirism "which he could shake off only with great effort." At the time, it all seemed—to outsiders and to Gustave himself (leaving aside some indefinable malicious and tacit vigilance)—as though his fall at Pont-l'Evêque had largely compromised his adaptation to the real. Indeed, his passive option implies that it is no longer merely a dream; it aims to rid him of the notion of true and false, already highly compromised, the sense of the real and the unreal. But we should not conclude, as Du Camp tends to do, that Flaubert resembles the hero of *La Spirale*, "capable of escaping

willfully from real life and peopling his fantasy with gilded and pleasant images,"[9] and finding perfect happiness in the asylum, in sequestration. The difference between Gustave and this happy painter
is that the painter turns away from the world and solicits his fantasy
to produce fine comic operas to *divert* himself; Gustave, on the other
hand, similarly changed into a dream, aspires merely to the rigorous
transmutation of the real into the precise unreality that corresponds
to it. In short, this dreamer is *lying in wait:* he is the mediator between
the world and the nonbeing of fantasmagoria; he is a "dual nature"
since he is alive: he has needs, specific surroundings, relations with
everyone, but this life has meaning only through nonlife, it reproduces and perpetuates itself only in order to evaporate in the rigorous dream that is nourished by it: "It folds itself around the idea
like a garment around the body it covers." For the real, *such as it is,*
must be devoured by images. The period of floods of flames, of fireworks, is past. By the very impulse of the illness, the imagination,
while preserving its gratuitousness, becomes a rigorous technique.
Jules, assessing the use of the fantastic in literature, contrasts his former mad inventions with the systematic exercises he is presently engaged in. The passage is worth citing in its entirety because it depicts
Gustave *before* and *after* January '44:

> Do we not experience at certain moments in the life of humanity
> and of the individual inexplicable transports that are translated
> into strange forms? . . . Our nature embarrasses us, we stifle it,
> we want to leave it behind . . . ; we rush at will into the unbridled,
> the monstrous . . . Calm once more, man no longer understands
> himself, his own mind frightened and appalled by his dreams, he
> wonders why he has created djinns and vampires, where he would
> want to go on the backs of griffons, in what fever of the flesh he
> put wings on the phallus, and in what hour of anguish he dreamed
> of hell. Understood as the development of the inner essence of
> our soul, as a superfluity of the moral element, the fantastic has
> its place in art . . . As for that which is engendered by the bias of
> the artist's fantasy through the impossibility of expressing his idea
> in a real, human form . . . , it denotes . . . the poverty of imagina-
> tion to a greater extent than is usually thought; the imagination, in
> effect, does not see chimeras, it has its positive aspect, as you
> have yours, it torments itself and turns away in order to give birth
> to this side of itself, and is happy only after giving it a real palp-
> able, durable, ponderable, indestructible existence.

9. Dumesnil, *Gustave Flaubert,* p. 481.

We have understood what Flaubert means by the *positive* aspect of the imaginary. Chimeras are pure nonbeing; they derealize nothing since they correspond to no living creature. "Positive" derealization derives its consistency from the being it annihilates: it is horses and men that must be ensnared by the unreal, not centaurs; women and fish, not sirens. Jules has forgotten his passions: "If he had not felt forced, as an artist, to study them and to seek them out in others, then to reproduce them in their most complete and remarkable form and to admire them beneath the plasticity of style, I believe he might almost have scorned them." They must, however, be understood. How does he set about it? It is very simple: "All the while irritating his sensibility by his imagination, he strove to make his mind annul its effects and to make the seriousness of sensation vanish as rapidly as the sensation itself." At first sight, these words remind us of what Husserl means by the "vision of essences" and the role that image is made to play as the support of eidetic intuition. But for that philosopher, concerned with pure knowledge, the imagination is put in the service of evidence. For Gustave, something quite different is at issue: in order to understand in others the passions he no longer feels, he must affect himself with them in the imaginary. This presupposes a double movement, first affirmative, then negative. If he wants to render concupiscence, he will evoke erotic scenes designed to provoke emotional disturbance. But instead of letting it develop sufficiently to provoke *serious* desire in him, which he would have to satisfy by masturbation, he stops in midstream; that is, he detaches himself from it through pride, refusing to let himself, the poet, coincide with that excessively emotional portion of humanity. As a result, what he feels is entirely imaginary. Here as elsewhere, I presume his body helps him: exhausted by convulsions and overwrought nerves, long affected by hysterical castration, if he reacts to erotic titillations it is at most by shuddering.

Does he at least manage to determine essences? Jules sometimes claims to do so: "Power has tastes unknown to the powerful, wine a taste unperceived by those who drink it, woman a sensuality unperceived by those who use her, love a lyricism foreign to those who are filled by it." These affirmations, so simple in appearance, become suspect when one examines them more closely. But they do have the advantage of highlighting the two great Flaubertian factors of derealization: frustration and memory.

In principle, therefore, everything is clear: an emperor is kept in ignorance of the real essence of his power precisely because he is absorbed in enjoying absolute power. Gustave, on the other hand, having dreamed of them for many years, has grasped "unknown tastes" because he discovered them on the basis of *privation*. The imagination of the frustrated man endlessly turns upon itself; impotent, in order to take pleasure, to assuage his desire deceitfully, he reviews all the possible uses a king can make of his authority; always harassed by his inextinguishable passion, he nourishes himself with history, gathers ancedotes on Nero's sensual pleasures, and takes sadism and pleasure further still, to the point where he finds himself alone and well above the dozen Caesars who were never so distant from him in invention and who never knew that pleasure beyond pleasure and that being beyond being, that shrill, tense aspect of the impossible. Gustave defines his method rather well when he writes, a little later, to Alfred:

> You are stifling? Be patient, O lion of the desert . . . Let the muse go and don't bother yourself with man, and you will feel each day your intelligence growing in a way that will astonish you. The only way not to be unhappy is to enclose yourself in Art and never mind all the rest; pride replaces everything when it rests on an ample foundation . . . Don't you think there are many things I lack, that I would have been as magnanimous as the rich, quite as tender as those in love, just as sensual as the orgiasts? Yet I regret neither riches nor love nor the flesh, and people are surprised to see me being so sensible.[10]

This passage is clear in its apparent contradictions: Gustave *lacks* fortune, love, and the joys of the flesh, yet he does not *regret* them. Meaning regret as a feeling *lived*—in sadness, in tears, perhaps, or, who knows, in fits of rage. Gustave the artist wants none of all that: the commotion would distract him from his task. Quite the contrary, *lack* seems to him necessary as an *ontological quality* not so much felt as structuring his relations to the world; or, more precisely, that ontological quality is constitutive of Art only if it is given to intuition as the limit between truly but *weakly* felt regret and vast *imaginary* regret. The role played by regret is to emphasize the *privative* aspect of the relation of the microcosm to the macrocosm. If one does not lack carnal pleasure, how is one to speak of it? And if deprivation drives one mad, one will say no more about it. Acted out against a background of malaise, on the other hand, it simultaneously throws into relief the artist's constitutional nonbeing as person and the nonbeing of the im-

10. To Alfred, Milan, 13 May '45, *Correspondance*, 1:171–72.

ages that replace the heights of pleasure. "I would have been as magnanimous as the rich." So much the better if he has no riches! His
magnanimity will therefore encounter no real limit. The rich man,
thinks Gustave, is enclosed in his wealth, which, great as it may be,
remains his negative determination, for the finitude of his goods constitutes his own finitude: he will take "magnanimity" just that far, no
further, or he will be ruined. Gustave can exceed any limit since he
hasn't a penny, provided he has neutralized Desire and preserves
only its ontological structure, by which we understand the transcendent relation to the macrocosm. Then, he thinks, he will reveal the
meaning of inherited money, which is to be dissipated by extravagant
spending. This is what he later writes to Louise: I dream of being rich
enough to give everyone the superfluous. Or, which amounts to the
same thing: in an Indian palace, in the midst of precious gems, I
would have no more hunger, thirst, or fatigue.

Has he really determined by these intellectual games the *essence* of
wealth? And is the sensual pleasure unknown to the rich man but
constitutive of proprioception the feeling of being freed from the necessary by the possession (or distribution) of the superfluous? It is hard
to believe. On the other hand, we see clearly that this conception is
born of an old dream particular to Flaubert: his relations with Alfred,
the man of luxury, have revealed to him that he is an average man, a
product of the middle classes; fortune, if it were to come to him in the
form of an inheritance, would pull him out of the round of means and
make him an end, or the essential means to the supreme end. In a
general sense, what are we to understand by "unknown tastes"?
Clearly, the objective reality of an emperor or a landowner escapes
him most of the time, and one need not be an emperor or a rich man
to know it. But when Flaubert speaks of the "taste" of their power or
their money, he has in mind their *subjective* reality: he puts himself in
their place in order to decide what they *must* feel. There are a thousand ways for *potestas* or wealth to *exist*, but in order to choose between them one must be already *in the situation of* the rich or the
powerful: it is from concrete experience, from conditionings some of
which go back to early childhood, that the great men of this world will
internalize their objective reality. A novelist, if he has frequented
them, can to some extent imagine what they feel, their "known
tastes"; in this case, as a realist he puts his imagination in the service
of practical knowledge.[11] If he aspires to discover "unknown tastes,"

11. Zola, in *L'Argent* or in *Son Excellence Eugène Rougon*.

that is, those they never felt, he will not express the subjective essence of the rich man but, rather, that of the poor man, of one who can *imagine himself* to be a millionaire because he has no experience of the historical conditionings that correspond to that situation. This means putting oneself as one is, *instantaneously*—without alteration, with the past of a poor man and a poor man's current desires—into the skin of a rich man without a past and not bound to his wealth, a rich man who has no money. By these observations I do not mean to devalorize Flaubert's "experiments"; it is merely a question of specifying their extent: and it is perfectly clear that these dreams of penury do not aspire to reconstitute essences but to invent them. Gustave is well aware—since that is his intention—of trying to derealize emperors, along with lovers or drinkers, since he seeks to constitute on the basis of real givens (power, money, wine, love) not men as they are, or even as they ought to be, but as they are not and never could be.

For drinkers, however, the business is complicated: Gustave has drunk wine, and although his regimen is still supervised, he knows he will drink it again. Be that as it may: "Jules lives in sobriety and chastity, dreaming of love, of sensual and orgiastic pleasures." Flaubert's other auxiliary is his memory—that is, the life of the dead child he carries in him after '44. Let us recall how he began truly to love Madame Schlésinger the second year, after being assured that she would not come to Trouville. What a depth of charm he found in the nonbeing of this phantom! It is the same thing which, ill and frustrated, he discovers in the sauternes he cannot drink. Here Gustave appears as the first of that long line that will end with Proust with his pure memory—which, when solicited at random and without practical intention, renders our remembrances as we never lived them, as irreducible essences, singular and *eidetic* in their idiosyncrasy. In 1844, Flaubert opted for the past against the future; he would remain until the end of his life turned toward that childhood and adolescence which, admittedly, he hardly loves, and we shall see him write to Louise, 4 March 1852: "I have just been rereading several children's books for my novel. When I looked at certain engravings, I rediscovered terrors I had had as a child, and I would like something to distract me . . . My travels, my childhood memories, all color each other, link themselves together and marvelously blaze up, dancing and rising in a spiral." What separates him from Proust is that Proust insists on the *reality* of pure memory (even if this type of reality is entirely different from daily reality), whereas Gustave though endlessly plunged into his memories, insists in addition on their imaginary aspect. Indeed, a reminiscence, on its dark side, refers to the event we have really lived. On its illuminated side it presents itself as an image that points to, rather than restores, a vanished past; an image whose existence we sustain with a certain tension; an image that in many ways escapes us, dissolves into the haze, and, in others, seems a logical reconstruction of something known. Only in the best of cases does an irreducible, but in itself indefinable, kernel still preserve the opacity of lived experience. For the rest, its structure is that of the image: an intention points, by way of analogue, to an absent or vanished object as it was given to our senses. Gustave profits from the ambiguity of the memory in order to raise it to a white heat by unrealizing it. The sauterne is better and richer when it is no longer drunk precisely because, in Gustave's eyes, memory is a particular sector of the imaginary; it too is *privation*. Far from restoring the sensation as a plenitude, it evokes it allusively, as a nonbeing that can be used at will[12] and mingled with fictional images precisely because it has no more reality than they do. In '44, Flaubert, unlike Proust, did not choose to revive his memory but to live it as a waking dream and to use it to nourish that other dream, the directed dream that he was to conduct from minute to minute until his death, feeding it with his daily life. I have shown above that Flaubert, at the time of *Novembre, dreams* of doubling himself: an old man will be the keeper of a dead young man; and we have seen that he *effects* this doubling at Pont-l'Evêque. We are now prepared to distinguish the dream of '42 and its actualization in '44. Though expressed by the same symbol, however, the two doublings have different meanings. In the first, the old man is the pure witness to a dead life, he wants to restore it in its truth; in the second, he vampirizes the young victim and feeds on blood not yet congealed by death. In other words, the memory of the deceased, treated according to certain methods, provides raw material to the imagination of the survivor; it is that memory which allows him, escaping from his abstract condition of "I think," to fill himself with concrete and imaginary riches. In 1842 the child was sinking, the old man was born: ceasing to suffer, he changes his life into memory in order to make it the reservoir of imagination. Such is Jules's choice: the condition necessary to becoming an artist is to dream his memory and to imagine his perception.

12. Recall that in the *Mémoires d'un fou*, Gustave experienced the pleasure of a demiurge in resurrecting his memories, in playing with them.

To imagine perception: open your eyes and ears, hold out your hand to touch, and the moment things surround you so closely that they seem to penetrate you, swallow them up alive into your dream, intact and derealized. This is undoubtedly the most delicate operation—impossible for most people. But Gustave has the good fortune to "float in a dream": for him, objects have lost their seriousness. They are pure presences, still glittering and fascinating but no longer moving—for he has forgotten his passions and the goals of the species—and he often no longer understands them. Imaginary, he need merely organize them as a function of the dream he pursues; they become imaginary themselves. The aesthetic attitude consists in great part of *imagining being,* of treating it in such a way that it is transformed in appearance: beneath the mental disarray Maxime observed in Gustave, a passive but intense activity is concealed. We shall penetrate further into both Flaubert's neurosis and his poetic Art if we dwell a little on the procedures he uses to effect this permanent transmutation.

Jules provides the norm and not the recipe. When he exposes the motivations of a justified recourse to the fantastic, he writes something that applies, in fact, to Gustave's general attitude: "One needs all that is not, all that has become useless: at times it is through love of life, to maximize it in the present, to eternalize it beyond itself." But Flaubert is more explicit in his correspondence. In a letter to Alfred of 2 April 1845, he writes:

> I have been to the Champs-Elysées. There I saw those two women again,[13] with whom I used to spend whole afternoons. The invalid was still half reclining in an armchair. She received me with the same smile and the same voice. The furnishings were ever the same, and the carpet was no more worn. By an exquisite affinity, by one of those harmonious accords, the perception of which belongs only to the artist, a street organ began to play under those windows as before, while I was reading to them from *Hernani* and *René.*[14]

The perception of the Artist is, as we see, synthetic: he is pleased to constitute this new moment of his experience as the simple cyclical return of Eternity. The situation lends itself: he has affection for Gertrude and Henriette, but it is a tranquil tenderness, he is not in

13. Henriette and Gertrude Collier.
14. *Correspondance,* 1:161.

turmoil at finding them again. The two young ladies, on the other hand, have hardly changed: he can only congratulate himself, for they are both more or less smitten with him, and he knows it. So far, we have not left the domain of the real. But suddenly the street organ begins to play: *as before.* This chance occurrence prompts him to gather things and people into a singular and fantastic totality whose secret purpose is to satisfy his desire for eternity. In point of fact, nothing has "returned," nothing at all: if the two women, in the service of cyclical time, seem to him *the same,* he has become *other,* profoundly so. And to make this lived whole an analogue of the eternal return, he must neglect the particular melody that comes in through the windows and must hang onto the abstract fact that *a* street organ has begun to play. But in this very moment he feels himself to be an artist because he has taken advantage of a singular fact in order to establish between all the elements of lived experience an "exquisite affinity" which he knows very well does not exist, and which he loves *precisely* because of that, because it structures reality as pure imaginary, or, if you will, because—without anything of the lived experience vanishing—it makes him *imagine what he perceives.* This is the meaning of that line from *L'Education sentimentale:* "Inaccessible equally to the man of science, who stops at the observation of facts, and to the rhetorician, who dreams only of embellishing them, there was for [Jules] a feeling in things themselves." He puts this feeling into things by living the real as a spectacle that he creates for himself.

A few weeks later, the correspondence offers us an example of a desire, which, first experienced in reality, is then transformed in imagination and serves simultaneously to reveal the imaginary character of the real. During the journey of '45, Gustave is often irritated and bored, tormented by vague sexual desires: "At Arles, I saw some exquisite girls, and on Sunday I went to mass to examine them more at leisure." But a few days later, at Genoa, desire has lost the "seriousness of sensation" and becomes an instrument of aesthetic unification; it no longer presents itself as covetousness but as a role to play. He has just evoked Don Juan, a "large symbol," and he goes on:

> Apropos of Don Juan, it is here one must come to dream about him; one loves to imagine him as one strolls in these Italian churches, in the darkness of the marble, in the rose-colored light that filters through the red curtains, looking at the brown necks of the kneeling women; for headdresses they all have great white veils and long earrings of gold or silver. It must be sweet to love there, in the evenings, hidden behind the confessionals, at the hour when

they light the lamps. But all this is not for us; we are made for speaking, feeling, and not for possessing.[15]

Between his desires and his calm, reflexive consciousness, a "symbolic" character has slipped, lending him his eyes; through this fictive gaze he discovers—as soon as he renounces *possession*—the hidden eroticism of an Italian church, a singular and meaningful totality that one can *speak of*, no doubt, but not conceptualize. The unrealization of sexual desire is by itself a refusal to live, but at the same time it reproduces that desire by giving it a symbolic meaning as a synthetic and derealizing scheme of reality.

This illuminates the line he writes to Maxime shortly after Caroline's death: "My last misfortunes have saddened me but have not surprised me. Without taking anything away from sensation, I have analyzed them as an artist." [16] And in the same letter he gives an excellent example of some techniques he uses to derealize an *event:*

Yesterday my niece was baptized. The child, the witnesses, I myself, even the priest, who had just dined and was red-faced, none of us understood what we were doing. In contemplating all those symbols that were meaningless to us, I felt as though I were witnessing some ceremony of a distant religion exhumed from the dust. It was so simple and so familiar, and yet I could not get over my astonishment. The priest hurriedly muttered Latin that he did not understand; the rest of us were not listening; the child held her bare little head under the water they spilled on it; the taper burned and the beadle answered, Amen! More intelligent, certainly, were the stones, which once had understood the whole business and had perhaps retained something of that understanding.[17]

Here Gustave is acting the artist. At the source of his attitude there are, of course, simple and real motivations. For him, religious practice is playing the fool, and the ceremonies of Catholicism are as much mummeries as the antics of fetishism. So there is nothing to prevent one from regarding the former as if they were repetitions of the latter, or, as a shortcut, from identifying each with each. But at the same moment, as we have seen, he knows that "the religious instinct" tends of itself to become particularized: thus, stupid as they seem, ceremonies

---

15. *Correspondance,* 1:169–70.

16. To Maxime, 7 April '46, *Correspondance,* 1:201. He takes nothing away from sensation, except that he derealizes it. Which means that those dead things have not taken him from his dream: his misfortunes have not aroused emotions in him but emotional abstractions.

17. To Maxime, 7 April '46, *Correspondance,* 1:202–203.

are inseparable from it—they incarnate it. One must therefore both mock them and be able to grasp in them "man's aspiration to the absolute." On the plane of the sacred, as on that of the grotesque, the basic equivalence of all these "mummeries" is encountered once again: the relic is as ridiculous as the amulet, but, conversely, religion is wholly incarnate in the cult rendered to the fetish—and equally in the cult rendered to the metacarpus of a saint. It is the ministers of the cult that Guastave despises. In his works, all of them, from the priests he sketches in *Agonies* to the Abbé Bournisien, have a fundamental relation to food, which is what makes his testimony suspect here: the priest has just eaten, why not? It is the afternoon. Is Gustave fasting? One may wonder whether the priest really was "red-faced," or whether Flaubert saw him this way because by definition he had to be so.[18] In any event, we have not yet left the terrain of real motives. As we see, they still exist, but in extenuated form: they serve here as guiding schemes.

This is how it works. In a first totalization, Flaubert derealizes the officiant, the baptized child, and the public. "No one understands what he is doing." From now on, he distorts facts: he embraces under the same rubric various ignorances, or rather he aligns them all on little Caroline's—radical—ignorance. For it is not true that the Flauberts don't know what they are doing: whether they are thesists (as Madame Achille may be), agnostics (as Gustave claims to be), or atheists (as Madame Flaubert surely has been since her husband's death), they are obeying a strictly social and utilitarian imperative: the greater part of the Rouen bourgeoisie is Catholic and would be shocked if Caroline were not baptized; doors would be closed to the family, Achille would lose clients. As for the priest, is he really unconscious? Is it true that he does not understand the Latin he mutters? Yet he studied it at the seminary. Certainly the priesthood is also a bureaucracy: baptisms and marriages are daily duties that must be swiftly expedited; but we are unaware of just how deeply the priest appreciates the *act* of baptism, the religious meaning he gives it— Gustave alone determines it, out of anticlericalism as well as a taste for artistic totalization. This very taste compels him to blend himself, a "portion of humanity," with the audience—unjustly. For if there is anyone who *is not unaware* of the meaning of the ceremony it is Gustave; we have just seen that he considers it to be the ridiculous

18. Or if the color of his face—actually ruddy—had no other cause but postprandial warmth.

incarnation, stereotyped by centuries of repetition, of our pure, and vague sense of the religious. Reading the text more closely, we see that he deliberately confuses ignorance and indifference: Gustave knows the Latin but does not listen; "these symbols" are quite familiar to him, he simply declares them "meaningless to him." Is this accurate? Is it not rather that his sister's daughter is a matter of indifference to him? This nursling is hardly of interest to him, and he may hold it against her that she is Hamard's child. Later, when he becomes attached to her, when she becomes a conscious, thinking little person, he will be strangely disturbed by the "symbols" on the day of her first communion. Be that as it may, by this forced assimilation, Gustave produces a first aesthetic realization: the *astonishment* that grips him is not that which, according to Plato, is at the origin of philosophy; quite the contrary, it is *aesthetic distancing*, which has the effect of substituting for a rite of ancient origin, but one which will remain living as long as it is kept alive by Catholic communities, a "ceremony of a distant religion, exhumed from the dust." It is Gustave, by his totalizing refusal to comprehend, who transforms the present into a magically resurrected past. From this moment, it is the imagination that perceives. If the ceremony is a resurrection, the group that restores it without comprehending it, in the absolute gravity of religion, must be *possessed* by it. Flaubert refuses to see a gathering of individuals, each of whom intelligently participates in producing a collective result and who are all bound to this and by practical relations, which they produce and sustain; rather, he makes himself see these people as robots, manipulated by a forgotten rite that seeks to be reborn. Teleguided, inhabited by gestures that *force themselves to be made* without then being understood, they are bound to a dusty habitus that vampirizes them. We recognize here one of the derealizing schemes that Gustave will employ all his life—in particular in *Le Château des Cœurs*: subordinating man to his product, whatever it is, but above all to language as commonplace, taking the former as essential and durable, the latter as ephemeral and inessential.[19]

This is not to say, however, that Gustave is not *also* amused to perceive himself, alone among those present, as witness *here and now* to a ceremony in the process of unfolding *in former times*. An excellent de-

19. Obviously, anyone who would want to confront it with the opposite vision (practical free agents becoming objectified by work without immediately being alienated) would also totally fail to grasp reality without even achieving the black humor of the Flaubertian phantasmagoria.

realization of the *contemporary* which becomes at once perception and remembrance, an efficacious event, the unforeseeable and pure object—too familiar, impotent—of reflexive contemplation. The ambiguity of the text, "attending some ceremony of a distant religion, exhumed from the dust," permits us to imagine that he shuttled continuously and at will from one totalizing vision to the other, sometimes dehumanizing *in the present* the people at the baptism by making man the teleguided slave of the thing, sometimes derealizing the present itself and considering the living, who do not yet know that death has long since gathered them to it, in direct contact with the past. A double liquidation: one goes from one to the other since the purpose is the same and a ferocious aestheticism impels Gustave to consider man from the point of view of the inhuman, either to robotize him by seeing him as the means chosen by an inhuman ceremony to maintain itself—inert, absurd, with all the qualities of materiality—or to consider life from the point of view of death. This is what Jules claims to do in the simplest way when he forces himself to hear, through the infant's laughter, the death throes of the old man the child will become. But in that case, death has a future point of view, which implies a less efficacious derealization; here, to the contrary, Gustave utilizes his "estrangement" to turn it into a present view of the present: noncommunication with the human species can be hysterically lived as nonbelonging (this is the first "vision") or as contemplation of the dead species across the unbreachable transparency of noncomprehensive statement.

Whatever use he makes of his astonishment—and it is at this level that it is done, *suffering* a stupor that he himself produces—the malevolent dehumanization of the human is accompanied by no less a perverse humanization of the inhuman: "More intelligent, certainly, were the stones, which once had understood the whole business and had perhaps retained something of this understanding." Taken literally, this line means nothing. It is merely a question of completing the unrealizing totalization. The intelligence of stones is, of course, the beauty of the construction that makes them into its analogue. Rationalized, the "idea" could be expressed in this way: "There was a time when it was beautiful to believe; and in those days that powerful faith produced lofty architectures, which in the freshness of the early years *contained* those pious ceremonies and sublimated them by symbolizing them *through art*. What remains, when faith has changed into mummery, is an inert eternity, the plastic beauty of the lines, which still today retain something of their past meaning." But for Flaubert these banalities are but the tool of a more extreme derealization; in other words, his declarations must be taken *literally*. His eyes wander from one column to the other, from one ogive to the other, from the nave to the windows, while his ears are filled with vulgar, muttered Latin, and he is determined to grasp the nervous elegance of the whole *as intelligence;* or, if you will, he suppresses the builders and makes the stones internalize their subtle sense of proportion, equilibrium, and movement. In a sense, this is easy: the beautiful object, end without finality, witness to a pure praxis, manifests the world as if it were the product of a freedom but does not refer first to the artist; it absorbs and renders its creator's design in anonymity as pure inert exigency. Still, this is merely a first moment: Flaubert's choice is to stick to it. The result fulfills his vows: he contrasts humans to pure materiality and endows the latter with capacities that are properly human, which he denies to humans. The stone sees, hears, and remembers. Consequently, it knows the perverse joy of perpetuating temporalization, of preserving it as a movement while petrifying it. The inert is made guardian of history; matter is memory. Humans, on the other hand, by repeating without comprehension ceremonies that had their meaning in former times, manifest the stereotype of the moment, degradation by repetition: memory is precisely what they are lacking. Thus, through a radical inversion, inertia becomes life *through its very inertia* (for this is what allows the stone to preserve the shape it has been given), and life through its practical temporality becomes inertia (for successive generations do tend to rigidify practices). Flaubert's underlying intentions are well served by these derealizing schemes: if history, for him, is usually nothing more than the inaccessible and imaginary object of meditating on remains and monuments (rather than a rational reconstruction from documents and testimony), it is because he loves to grasp the practical agent insofar as he has become alienated in his objectivization. In these stones with their fixed, heavy gaze, he not only sees the means to dehumanize his contemporaries: he is pleased to lodge in them, in the opaque undifferentiation of matter, their bewitched architects. Whatever the motivation, the impulse is executed for itself and for Art; it is an exercise in derealization that inseparably contains the dehumanization of man and the humanization of the inorganic, and its underlying purpose is to put being between parentheses, to give it the insubstantiality of nonbeing. This objective is attained not through a positive power of *imagining* the intelligence of walls and the inertia of men but, to the contrary, through the art of utilizing the impotence of the imagination.

In other instances Gustave grasps the real directly as the cipher of nothingness. Thus, the signification which creates the synthetic unity of perception must first be experienced *really* as an absence. "At Marseille, I didn't meet the residents of the Hotel Richelieu again. I passed by it, I saw the steps and the door; the shutters were closed, the hotel was abandoned. I could hardly recognize it. Isn't this symbolic? How long it's been since my heart closed its shutters, its steps deserted; in former times a bustling inn, now empty and echoing, like a great, corpseless sepulcher." What matters for him is the *denial* that reality sets against him: all traces of Eulalie Foucault and of their encounter have vanished, but this is what he was seeking: he came less to see her than *not to see her:*

> With a little care and goodwill, I might have succeeded in discovering where "she" is living. But I was given such incomplete information that I was stuck. I am lacking what I am always lacking for everything that is not Art: alacrity. And besides, I feel an extreme distaste for returning to my past.[20]

The unity here comes from a reciprocity of perspective, which enables the subjective and the objective to symbolize each other, reducing them both to mere images of nothingness. There are also, inside the comparison itself, secondary transformations that complete the derealization, for to the extent that the inn represents Flaubert's inner emptiness, this too becomes a "great, corpseless sepulchre."

These examples reveal to us two extreme and contrary techniques of the aesthetic attitude: challenging the real by becoming nonbeing; and discovering in being itself a particular nonbeing (whether it is not or whether it no longer is), which cannot be brought to life or returned to life, even in a mental image, and which denounces the general insufficiency of reality. We must come back to these procedures, the two poles between which Flaubert's imagination will shuttle; we shall find both methods again, later on, in the great works of his maturity.[21]

---

20. *Correspondance*, 1:166. This disgust is itself unrealizing: Flaubert is repulsed not by *evoking* the past while preserving its quasi-unreality as memory, but by rediscovering it *alive*, by encountering Eulalie as a person of flesh and blood and not as a vague reminiscence, porous and unrealizable.

21. Both techniques may coexist in one operation. But they interfere with each other.

To submit the real to the unreal by derealizing it is not to impoverish it, quite the contrary: the guiding scheme is imaginary, but it demands a detailed derealization of the object under consideration, even as it provides the rule for it. *Observation which fuels the imaginary* reveals more qualities in the object than practical observation, but it reveals them in order to integrate them into an imaginary whole. We earlier saw Flaubert, in the role of Don Juan, describe an Italian church in detail, coax out of a primal vagueness the marble, the color of the light, the flesh tint, the dress and finery of the kneeling women, the relationships between the *rose*-colored light and their *brown* necks, etc. An excellent *realist* tableau, except that it is described as it appears to the imaginary eyes of a false Don Juan. In a letter written in the course of the same journey, we find a richer and more meaningful passage:

At the end of April '45, Gustave stops again at Arles. "I saw the Arena again, which I had seen for the first time five years ago. What have I done since?" First derealization: to Gustave, the Temporal Man, who—since his journey with Cloquet—has lived five years of his life, the Arena at Arles represents Eternity (like the apartment of the Collier sisters); he immediately turns it into a *petrified question.* He adds: "I climbed up to the last seats, thinking of all the people who have roared and clapped, and then all that had to be left behind. When you begin to identify with nature or with history, you are suddenly torn away from it." Second derealization: the issue for the young man is to turn the present (disconnected pathways that have yellowed, grass growing between the stones, solitude, the undesirable presence of the Flaubert family) into the unreal, and to *realize* the past (new arena, Gallo-Roman crowds, clamor) on the foundation of *the present moment.* An operation he knows he cannot complete: he will not raise the hallucinatory presence of the past, for this can only manifest itself in two forms: perhaps a series of vague mental images, surging up when he ceases perceiving the amphitheater, or, if he keeps his eyes open, a corrosive acid revealing the insufficiency of being of the present ruin, denouncing its unreality (since the reasons for its being have passed) yet without the enrichment of this degraded perception, floating between being and nonbeing, by phantasms (roaring crowd, etc.). Let us say simply that *this* past, without becoming more explicit, becomes for Gustave the nonbeing of *this* present. I have given above a powerful and still deeper motivation for these derealizing attempts than the artistic desire to exercise the "picture-making faculty of the brain": resentment. It is a matter of drowning the present members of the Flaubert family in nothingness: they are modified in their being in the name of a legion of Gallo-Roman dead. Thus the dead are living but unperceived, and the living, though visible, are dead. A limited operation, as we see, but ambitious since Gustave exclaims: "When you begin to identify with nature or with history . . ." If he is right, the hundreds of thousands of tourists who have since visited the amphitheater and have contemplated it, unsatisfied, trying to recall its memories of *Ben Hur,* can be content: they have identified with history without even knowing it, as Monsieur Jourdain did with prose. I am joking: the sentence is comic, the intention is not. I shall soon come back to it. Nonetheless, the operation has been rather unsuccessful—as are all operations of the kind. Its result is unstable since the unrealization of being as such, that is, with all its richness, is contested by the revelation of its essential poverty, its revealed incapacity to give us access to a vanished reality.

Two days ago I saw Byron's name written on one of the pillars of the dungeon where the prisoner of Chillon was confined. The sight gave me exquisite joy. I kept thinking of the pale man who came there one day, walked up and down, wrote his name on the stone, and left . . . Byron's name is scratched on one side, and it is already black, as though ink had been rubbed into it to make it show up. It does in fact stand out on the gray column, and one sees it the minute one enters. Below the name, the stone is a little eaten away, as though the tremendous hand which rested there had worn it down with its weight. I was sunk in contemplation before those five letters.[22]

What does it mean, "thinking of the pale man who came there"? Not much: there is nothing to think about Byron—at least in this dungeon—except that he came there, wrote his name on the stone, and left. What rings true, by contrast, is: "I was sunk in contemplation before those five letters." Gustave saw the pillar, the name, "from the minute he entered," he drew near and, in his usual way, fell into a sort of daze. Not long ago he regarded Byron as one of the two greatest geniuses of humanity. Now the canvas of Manfred has paled a bit: the two greats have become three, since reading de Sade. Besides, the crisis at Pont-l'Evêque is *also*, as we have seen, a renunciation of Romanticism. Nonetheless, the pale man still inspires immense respect in the young Flaubert. A line from the same letter reveals to us his most secret desire and his repugnance at satisfying it: "One would have to be either very daring or very stupid to go ahead and write one's name after that." Yes indeed, if he had the audacity to write "Gustave Flaubert" beneath the name of the poet, it would be as though he were accepting a literary sponsorship; he would enter the club of great men under the protection of an English lord. One day, perhaps, an adolescent would see those two names dear to his heart and would be sunk in contemplation before them. Gustave dares not. To play at loser wins—for, as we shall see, this is the deepest meaning of his neurosis—he must deny himself even the slightest hope. Thus we have the motive for his daze: the name seems to him a promise, an invitation to dare to believe in his own genius, and almost simultaneously it is a threat, an interdiction; it would be sacrilege for a petit bourgeois with no future, an invalid, to dare to imitate this poet-prince. Gustave worships this man and his gesture; and the man, with his gesture of inimitable insolence, succeeds in destroying him.

22. To Alfred, 26 May '45, *Correspondance*, 1:176–77.

But all this rumination is made in the realm of the unreal: unreal is the brilliant but furiously erased image Gustave makes of himself; and in that light, the pale man's gesture is unreal as well. Unreal but not entirely imaginary: it was, but it no longer is. Imaginary nonetheless: by evoking it, Gustave does not actualize a memory, he forges an image. Does he keep this mental image for long? No: what matters to him is the trace of the gesture, the five letters on the pillar. And precisely because they are a trace, they are derealized by the past. One would not say the same, of course, of an empty jelly jar found in the Bois de Vincennes, although the objective structure is the same: it is a remnant that refers to a past enterprise (a picnic, a game, a siesta on the grass). But this enterprise is so general, so anonymous, we are so sure that it is being repeated at this very moment in a thousand parks in France, that the jelly jar incorporates its past, makes it its present meaning and its practical reality. For an unhappy young writer, the gesture of a prestigious idol is *unique*. There is only one Byron—and who even knows if he took the time to inscribe his name? So the essential thing, a singular event of universal history, is *past*, it no longer is. At the same time, it is forever, since nothing, not even the destruction of the earth, will prevent it from having been; thus the inertia of the letters carved on the stone *symbolizes* the indestructibility of a minute gone by. The name is *derealized:* not only is it just a *trace* of a brilliant past, but it symbolizes the being-in-itself of that past, it *is* that past itself glittering through the present opacity. This is why it fascinates Gustave: glory extinguished, future glory, promise denied, a gesture so near, out of reach, presence, disappearance of the pale man who modifies even the flagstones at Gustave's feet, everything is given in this relic, everything contributes to pull him away from the real, from the present. Yet this is what strikes the eye, what shines in that dungeon; without those letters, *there would be nothing,* Gustave could not even suspect that Byron had ever been there, and if by chance he had known of it, he could not have localized it anywhere, nothing would have helped him, as an analogue, to make it present in its very unreality and to give himself the bitter and fallacious pleasure of enjoying it *in the imaginary.* For this reason he is fascinated by the object: he wants to see it up close, to preserve the smallest details of the memory of this material objectification of a gesture that has traversed time like a lightning flash and was, for a moment, *all* Byron. Therefore he *observes:* the name is inscribed on one side, already blackened but shining on the gray column; beneath it the stone is somewhat eroded. All these determinations of materiality betray its design: for in their inertia they are the *contrary* of the living man they must deliver up to his intuition. And yet they are *he*, all that remains of him, the encasing of a gesture. They perpetuate his glory and mineralize it. This contradiction is immediately unrealized, required not so much to be a trace as to be a metaphor. The name shines because masterpieces have illuminated it; beneath it, the stone has eroded "as if the enormous hand . . . had worn it down with its weight." The metaphor is double. First, the "as if" tries to explain the worn place by the vanished event, to make the significations of the act extend to the being, so that the traces it bears symbolize the vanished person not only in his volition but in his physical presence, in his very weight. And, second, we pass abruptly from the literal to the figurative and the glory of Byron; his genius is translated by the hugeness—entirely imaginery—of his hand. Note that Flaubert focuses on inorganic materiality; he sees and can see only those notches passively supported by a pillar of stone. The contact is with being: the derealization—which turns it into the inessential expression of what no longer is—changes nothing of it, for the opaque plenitude of the in-itself has been reshaped against human temporalization, against history; the perpetual material present seals up the past. Yet the passage to the unreal is accompanied by *observation;* better, it is derealization alone that induces Flaubert to observe; for him to examine objects in detail, they must signify, even in their texture, something other than themselves. Here we have encountered an essential tendency of Gustave's, which gives meaning to the descriptions of objects in *Madame Bovary:* swallowed up by being, he derealizes it by a metaphoric observation that reveals its details but gives them one by one, as parts of a synthetic whole, which can become manifest only beneath perceptible appearances but is defined by its unreality. In short, the real, absorbing but suspended between being and nonbeing by the necessity of signifying the unreal—the human image in person—becomes by itself a surprising and detailed dream, organizing itself according to ideas which belong to Gustave but remain unconscious for him—since they are *"beneath* his life"—and which he contemplates without knowing them as the totalizing and derealizing meaning of his real environment. This is how we should understand the considerations he conveys to Alfred, from Genoa, on the first of May:

> This trip, though very comfortable, has been too crass from the
> poetic point of view for me to want to prolong it. In Naples I
> would have experienced such exquisite sensations that the thought
> of having them spoiled in a thousand ways was terrible. When I

go, I want to get to know that old antiquity to its very marrow. I want to be free, on my own, alone or with you, not with others . . . Then I'll let my thoughts flow without hindrance or reticence until they cool off, giving them all the time they need to simmer at their ease; I'll take on the color of the objective world and I will absorb myself in it utterly and passionately. Travel must be a serious occupation.[23]

This occupation consists of a long and derealizing contemplation in which one *observes* the self by making every detail, joined to all those one has conjured up, express a past totality (which never existed as such), itself merely the objective representation of that other totalized unreality, the phantom-ego of the observer. Gustave *would be absorbed in* the bustling crowd, invisible but sensed in the streets of Pouzzoles; he would *escape into it* through the derealization of the flagstones and cottages that line the embankment—that is, through a minute, totalizing observation. Conversely, this absent whole signifies to him his own absence from himself, his nonbeing as human image; this is what he will express a little later in a passage from the first *Saint Antoine:*

The Devil

Often, apropos of nothing special, a drop of water, a shell, a hair, you were immobilized, pupils dilated, heart open. The object you were contemplating seemed to impinge upon you in the measure that you inclined toward it, and bonds were established. You pressed against each other, touched each other by subtle, innumerable adherences; then, by dint of looking, you no longer saw; listening, you heard nothing, and your mind itself ended by losing the notion of that particularity which kept it alert. It was like a vast harmony that was engulfed in your soul with marvelous shudderings, and in its plenitude you felt an inexpressible understanding of the unrevealed whole. The gap between you and the object, like an abyss bringing its two edges nearer to each other, contracted more and more, so that this difference disappeared in the infinite that bathed you both. You interpenetrated equally, and a subtle current passed from you to matter, while the life of the elements slowly gained on you, like a mounting vitality: one degree more and you became nature, or nature became you.

Thus observation is born in the framework of derealizing contemplation, of which it is one moment; its purpose is less analysis than synthesis, for it presents every detail as the expression of a total-

23. *Correspondance,* 1:167–68.

ization in progress. In other words, it derealizes the plenitude of the in-itself because it totalizes what it apprehends. When it has played its part, it is suppressed; what remains is the inexpressible reciprocity of two imaginary totalities: Nature reflecting the ego, the ego becoming totalized as Nature. Starting with the observation that turns things into the imaginary, the macrocosm passes into the microcosm, and vice versa. By suffering his passivity from the time of his first attack—by renouncing action, which determines, singularizes, and denies—Gustave constitutes pantheistic intention as one of the poles of his imagination; in nothingness he appropriates the plenitude of being as the *image* of its own plenitude, and perceiving as in a dream, he uses "scientific" observation to produce real detail as the structure of an imaginary.

But let us come to the opposite technique. There, the *real* served as analogue to the imaginary totalization of the macrocosm. And then, as we have seen, in these unstable formations that people his dream life there is the *pure unreal,* the imaginary denouncing its insubstantiality. It is not surprising that he constantly vacillates between the two, in view of his permanent temptation from an early age to assimilate totalized being to nothingness. But here is the new twist; what he sensed from the time of *Smarh* he is now certain of: images are not reality proper. They are not reawakened sensations but parasitic nothingnesses; glittering and fleeting when untouched, they turn to ashes if you touch them. Flaubert accedes to being swallowed up because consciousness, that calm lacuna devoid of its inhabitant, becomes a *trap for images:* in love with nothingness, nothingness itself shares their nature. The passions of the dead young man too often revealed the vanity of the illusions they sustained to their own exhaustion: violent and real, those passions wanted to treat the phantasms as realities. In the void, in calm, images grow bold and swiftly populate that pure consciousness which allows itself to be invaded by them without ever using them or verifying their substance; the phantasmagoria will not be *put to the test,* and even while manifesting its own unreality it will never be constrained to reveal its lack of substance. For the reflection of the creator, insubstantiality can become a positive virtue. Jules irritates his sensibility with his imagination but tries to have his mind annul the effects. That is to say, he seeks the image for its ineffectiveness. And because it is still too effective, because his sensibility runs the risk of being troubled by it, he focuses his attention simultaneously on the very richness of the phantasm and on its essential poverty, its nonexistence, in such a way that the illusion of being can provoke merely an illusory emotion. He expresses this idea better in another passage, admirable for its Mallarméan aspect:

> He asks of destroyed palaces with their empty peristyle the sonorous echo of celebrations that resounded beneath those vaults and the luster of candalabras that lit up the walls; he seeks in abandoned sands the trace of the giant waves that cast upon them their vanished monsters and their huge shells of pearl and azure. He thinks of the forgotten loves of those reclining in their coffins, of the future death of those who lean, laughing, over the side of their cradle.

Certainly the banal idea of universal nothingness is familiar to him—he loves to write to Ernest that everything ends in ashes or goes up in smoke, like the tobacco in his pipe. But what is striking here is his method; his mental exercises are the opposite of Loyola's, who set the scene on his interior stage, became absorbed in minutely restoring the details of the crucifixion, sought to *see* in his mind the thieves on their crosses so as finally to evoke Christ on his, a *real* presence—if not in itself, at least in the strength and truth of the sentiments it awakened. Not that he was mistaken about the images or that he saw in them something other than nothingness; he simply made them submit to his enterprise and to the real world; they had to replace it and, since infinite being had produced them in us one way or another, to reconstitute it *in spite of their nonbeing*, with the help of God. It is *for the sake of this nonbeing* that Jules chooses his, as the deliberate use of the double negative indicates in the previously cited passage. Apart from the final example of enumeration, the author multiplies nothingness by itself. He does not ask the few *well-preserved* palaces, the *intact* châteaux, to give him back the echo of vanished celebrations. To stimulate his imagination they must first be destroyed, they cannot by themselves provide the setting and the framework of past events. What is required is the difficulty—if not the impossibility—of reconstituting in one's mind the building itself, so that desire is free to give a content to this irreparably damaged container. In this operation, his shrill pleasure becomes a double surpassing toward an ineffable image, which, no mere ersatz of some ancient presence, denounces itself as a beyond of the impossible, that is, *considered as image*, as a certain form of absence, the inaccessible object of any empty intention. Similarly, the forgotten sands have not preserved the trace of the giant waves of prehistory: there is nothing to see except their settling and their undulations *in the present*. And what Jules asks of them is not even to restore to him those liquid mountains but, through them, the vanished monsters, the huge shells of pearl and azure. A trace, perhaps, would guide his dream. But what is there to say about an absence of trace serving as analogue to an absence of object?[24] Nor can the dead be conceived as presences: the corpse itself is absent, eaten away by the earth. Gustave dreams on their tombs, but not of the deceased, rather of their *forgotten* loves. Forgotten *by whom*? By everyone today, of course. But the word is well placed: it qualifies feelings and not persons; the meaning is clear: we are dealing with former passions, well anterior to death, forgotten by the deceased themselves and *in their lifetimes*. Here again, nothingness is multiplied by itself: it is a matter not only of mentally resurrecting the dead but, through this first moment, of aspiring to a love they have forgotten.

> The pure vase of any potion
> But the inexhaustible widowhood
> Even in death consents not . . .
> To breathe out anything announcing
> A rose amid the darkness.*

Mallarmé is, of course, the writer who carried to its height the science of the negative, of that *nothing* which snowballs, enriching itself with other nothings, and then flexes its joints again and is revealed beyond the abolition of appearances as imaginary nothingness, or as the imaginary quality of Nothingness. But in 1844, Flaubert does not acquit himself too badly in this maze: no one has mapped out the route or has left him an Ariadne's thread. Yet he goes straight to the goal: for him, image used to be a parasite of being; he disqualifies being by treating it as a parasite of image. Sometimes, indeed, he sees the content of his experience as a metaphor, and sometimes he organizes situations which have unity only through the aspired imaginary but which, by their very structure, denounce its nothingness since they evoke the imaging consciousness and offer it no analogue. In this case, the imaginary is even more an illusion: it is the nonbeing of an appearance which even refuses evocation; Jules "*asks*" for it, that is all he can do. But if the sought-after image does not emerge from its nothingness, the real (ruins, sands, etc.) which—by the "asking"—is

---

*"Surgi de la Croupe et du Bond . . . ," from *The Poems of Mallarmé*, translated by Roger Fry (New York: New Directions, 1951).

24. It is this double absence that will tempt him later, as we shall see, when he is planning to write *Salammbô*.

organized to evoke it as its unity, its meaning, and does not succeed in doing so, is aesthetically devalued, appears as a *lesser-being,* struck in its coarse plenitude by a radical impotence: the impotence to evoke the nothingness from which it emerges, into which it falls back, and which at bottom structures it. In this second case, we see the importance that language assumes, surrounding the contours of the necessary and impossible image; indeed, with a little luck, language becomes its analogue, just as in the passage I have been analyzing, in which the words "giant waves" evoke an image within the restrictive framework that is constituted by the words "traces," "sands," and "asking." We shall soon have to ask ourselves if the passive choice to derealize experience is not, in effect, the choice to *make language imaginary.*

We can now understand the difficult passage in which Flaubert, through Jules as intermediary, formulates the first norm of his poetic Art: "*inspiration must depend upon itself alone . . .* External stimulations too often weaken or denature it . . . Thus, one must fast in order to sing of the bottle."

The idea will gain acceptance in the second half of the century. But in this form it may seem obscure or paradoxical, no doubt because Gustave is the first to have expressed it. Negatively, it is the rigorous conclusion of the premises Gustave has posed: if Art is born of distancing and frustration, if in order to depict a feeling one must above all not feel it, and if the Artist is a man in the grip of the unreal, then no *reality* can inspire him. Is it sufficient for inspiration to depend only on itself? Can it manifest itself without the slightest motive? Doesn't Flaubert's norm contain a *petitio principii* (in order to have inspiration, one must be inspired) or amount to suppressing inspiration (since it is impossible and necessary that it be born *ex nihilo,* isn't it true that it does not exist?) and replacing it with the long patience of Buffon?

If readers have agreed to follow all the twists and turns of Gustave's aesthetic thought, they will have understood that beneath its disconcerting appearances his formula proposes an elegant solution to a problem that will long torment his generation. Inspiration originally came from God; in France, after the de-Christianization of the Jacobin bourgeoisie, the question becomes complicated: Hugo, the vatic poet, still claims to write under dictation from on high, but many of the Romantics—especially Musset—uncertain victims of an agnosticism to which they are not resigned, replace the supreme Being at the source of their poems with the pain of having lost him and, more generally, with any sort of suffering insofar as it symbolizes that fundamental calamity. Whence the idea, current in 1830, that intensity of feeling makes the beauty of a poem. Gustave's conception, without returning to the Great Inspirer, has the merit of insisting on the ontological originality of a work of art, that imaginary entity: he refuses to find the source of the Beautiful in the hoarse stammerings of living matter, in other words, accident; if a work is in essence imaginary, the inspiration that produces it must be a free determination of the imagination by itself. This means that a practical agent, even under the dominion of pain, could never effect *here and now* an abrupt passage to images, write a sublime poem, then return to his cares, to his sorrows in love, to his disappointed ambitions, to his real business. In order to produce *only* organized images, the artist must first turn himself into pure image, and the return to the real must be intermittent for him, painful as a bad awakening, and always provoked by external aggression. As a result, for him alone—image manufacturing images, or, if you like, an imaginary unity of the images that haunt him, dreaming his life through the perpetual unrealization of lived experience—the imagination becomes a whole that has no limits[25] but is continually agitated and totalized, whose every singular appearance refers in depth to permanent totalization, on the surface to every other appearance. The organic unity of the images is that of *one* imaginary life, and this in its turn derives its cohesion from the real unity of a life lived in suffered and directed oblivion. Inspiration is neither a mysterious gift nor sudden grace for Flaubert: it is a way of life to which one can accede, like the Sage of Stoa to wisdom, only by an abrupt and definitive break with the past, only by a true inner revolution. It is the imagination deliberately perverted by the suppression of that integrating function, praxis, and producing the imaginary as a permanent conquest of the real, not by labor—which would necessarily be practical—but by *counterlabor,* the only thing suitable to passive activity and which, by the renunciation of the act—constantly renewed but increasingly easier—on the basis of a disinterest suf-

---

25. *L'Education sentimentale*, Charpentier, p. 289. In the paragraph immediately following the one we commented on, Gustave writes of Jules: "*Then* the supreme poetry, *unlimited intelligence*, nature in all its aspects, passion in all its cries, the human heart with all its abysses united in a vast synthesis, each part of which he respected out of love for the whole, without wishing to remove a single human tear or a single leaf from the forests." The *then*, which explicitly refers to "inspiration must arise only from itself," indicates that the totalization is effected in the unreal, and that it marks Gustave's environment with a purely imaginary pantheistic seal. In fact, this synthetic intuition is the intuition of *nothing:* Flaubert's "philosophy" has not progressed.

fered as exis, is identified with the radicalization of passivity insofar as this has as its purpose and necessary result the impossibility of distinguishing the true from the false. So there is no middle ground: either one is *never* inspired, even if one paints or writes, because one has not achieved the initial disconnection, or one cannot stop being inspired, even if one does not write a line. At the end of *L'Education*, Flaubert compares Jules's existence to a desert: it "is serene, like the desert, and rich in golden horizons and unperceived treasures; it contains the echo of all winds, all tempests, all sighs, all cries, all joys, all despairs." Everything has been given to him, after his entrance into the orders, but as reflections, mirages. He is more specific in a letter of 1846 to Maxime: "I know what the void is. But who knows? Perhaps greatness is there, the germ of the future. Be careful only of reverie."[26] The warning contained in this last line is significant: inspiration has nothing to do with lax surrender to a train of mental images, pleasant or melancholy, dangerous because they flatter the passions, which should be forgotten, and because in the best of cases they are a waste of time. The Artist is empty, his inspiration is outside, it pries indefatigably into the real in order to transform it into the possible, that is, into appearance. This is why it is permanent and infinite: its raw material is none other than the world, an inexhaustible reservoir of potential images that will be unrealized without moving and without penetrating the empty consciousness of him who has chosen to be nothing in order *to give himself the all as spectacle*. This is what Gustave tells us in characteristic terms at the end of *L'Education:*

> Arresting the emotion that would trouble him, [Jules] knew how to awaken in himself the sensibility that must create something; existence furnished him with the accidental, he rendered it immutable. What life offered him, he gave to art; everything came to him and everything came from him, the flux of the world, the reflux of himself. His life folded around his idea like a piece of clothing around the body it covers; he enjoyed his power through the consciousness of his power.[27] Extended to all the elements, he connected everything to himself, and himself as a whole, he made concrete in his vocation, in his mission, in the fatality of his genius and his labor, a vast pantheism that passed through him and reappeared in his art.

Once again we have the microcosm internalizing the macrocosm and externalizing it again in Art through an imaginary totalization. In-

---

26. To Maxime, April 1846, *Correspondance*, 1:204.
27. This is what he will later call "alacrity."

deed, the idea lies *beneath* lived experience and conditions it—a good definition of his pithiatism. As for the accident that offers it day-to-day existence, he cannot give it to Art in the form of the immutable without derealizing it by pushing it to the absolute and investing it with a meaning it does not have, or not entirely. We have just given several illustrations of this method. We see how much it differs from that which gave us *Smarh:* rather than gliding above the world, contemplating from above its characteristic particularity, Gustave makes this particularity a mediation between being and image. This center of unrealization is itself unreal: conditioned by his anchorage, he internalizes a certain reality, but by externalizing it again as image, he tends to make that anchorage itself the pure means of imagining. Facticity, reality abolished—or rather forgotten—is no longer anything but this minimal insertion into the world, which allows the poet to be a transformer, capturing being in order to return it in the form of appearance. In other words, he replaces panoramic consciousness with *disconnection,* which gives him the means of remaining inside the world, of deciphering his environment from close up, while keeping the minute distance from his surroundings that allows him to be out of the fray.

Some may see this conquering passivity as an imitation of Alfred's famous "live without living" and of his subsequent aesthetic perceptions. That is possible: the hysteric, fascinated by the other, gladly imitates; nor can we dismiss a priori the hypothesis that Gustave collapsed in the cabriolet in order to justify by illness the aestheticizing immobilism that the Le Poittevin son owed to his father's wealth, or the alternative hypothesis that the symptoms he endured took on the appearance of epilepsy because Gustave had for so long imitated the journalist of Nevers. But what richness he gave to his friend's meager fantasies! In order fully to understand the depth and audacity of his new conception, we must follow it still further and ask ourselves what his absolute foundation is for the systematic derealization of experience.

Jules's passions, when he no longer feels them, are transformed into ideas. Chaste, he no longer experiences lust and so develops a theory of it.[28] This is certainly not a matter of empirical knowledge; the idea is not produced by experience but is born of the tenuousness of lived experience; felt pleasure is resumed and totalized by disap-

28. "Every feeling had melted into an idea. For example, he had drawn theories from pleasure that he no longer felt, and his own theory (*sic*) had been reached as a conclusion to the facts."

pearing into theory, which, as a result, taking it into itself, becomes pleasure-conscious-of-itself. The author proceeds immediately, articulating a very Spinozist theory of error: "If [this idea] was false, it is because it was incomplete; if it was narrow, an attempt should have been made to enlarge it. There was thus a consequence and a sequence in this series of diverse perceptions, it was a problem to which every step taken to resolve it is a partial solution." Error is the arbitrary halt to the totalizing movement of thought. In fact, one always halts: to pass from facts to the idea is to enlarge, certainly, and to transform perceptual knowledge, which is always truncated, into intellectual knowledge. But in this first moment, intellectual knowledge is in its turn limited: it contains, at bottom, only what has been put into it, that is, it totalizes a singular experience. It is therefore a higher degree of totalization, closer to truth than the preceding one, and yet if one takes it outside the movement that surpasses it, it is an error. One will burst its limits, enlarge it *through imagination.* We are a long way, here, from scientific experimentalism. The scientist *never leaves* the terrain of experience: starting from facts, he returns to them in order *to prove* his conjecture, and those facts are what will tell him whether that conjecture is "incomplete" or "narrow." This is the opposite of Gustave's approach: for him, by completing itself, the idea, always larger, always higher, distances itself more and more—in quality and intensity—from the pitiful perceptions which gave birth to it in its elementary form. For when all is said and done, there is only one true idea: that which totalizes the macrocosm and the microcosm. Soon after the passage cited above, Flaubert tells us this expressly: "But since the final word never comes, what good is it to wait for it? Can't one have a presentiment of it? And isn't there in the world some way of arriving at the consciousness of the truth? What if art were this means for him" . . . etc. The *idea* embraces the totality of what is and what is not, of being and the imaginary. If *one could reach it*, it would no longer even be a vision of the all, since—at every step—the content is the same object but idealized and self-conscious; it would be the All in person, the absolute-subject. Yet Flaubert is certain that one never reaches it, however high one goes. The "last word"—become truth—one can only intuit. How? *For Jules,* art will be the means of arriving at the intuition of the truth. But can one imagine others, since Science is excluded? Perhaps, at a certain level of meditation, the philosopher glimpses the Absolute as the limit that he will never reach. Again, what is at issue—for the thinker as well as for the poet—is merely an *empty* and trans-ascendant *intention:* the absolute-subject can be aspired to only as the absent term of an endless ascension. *Present* in every moment of the operation in the form of negativity, as the felt necessity of progression, it can be given "in person" only as *imaginary.* Pure imagination can install itself on the other side of this passage to the infinite and grasp the totalization in progress as a completed totality. From this point of view, the philosopher hasn't the slightest advantage over the artist: for both of them, *truth is imaginary.*[29] Gustave claims to tear himself away from appearances in order to establish the truth, but his real intention is quite different: the imaginary relation to the all has as its function the denunciation of error, in other words, the nonbeing in the heart of every finite truth and, more generally, the derealization of every real particular. From this point of view, the artist has the advantage; the thinker, indeed, has an awkward time imagining totality, he lacks the technique of the imaginary; Art, to the contrary, is manifest as this technique itself *in operation.*

Indeed, let us come back to what Jules tells us about it. He begins by informing us that his agonies have killed his sensibility; this means that he has been purified by them, that he is disengaged from lived experience, from the perceptible, that is, from the *finite.* Here he is, then, established in the idea at the first moment of its evolution: "If every passion is a circle inside which we keep turning, the way to see its circumference and extent is not to remain enclosed in the circle but to put ourselves outside." Jules is outside. This is the moment when, superior to the debauchee "who does not see the magnitude of his debauch," he grasps the "magnitude" of his particularity. What is there to say but that he has put himself above it and contemplates it from the point of view of death? In this he is already superior to the philosopher who, limited by his realist will, carries out real maneuvers and does not leave the realm of becoming except in brief flashes of images. Indeed, the first "artistic" procedure is to consider events and persons *as if* the totalization were already accomplished. Cantor defines the transfinite as the result of an infinite series of operations presumed to have been effected. Hence we may say that the absolute-subject, out of reach but unreally given, is the transfinite substance, and that this substance has two equally transfinite attributes.[30] In fact,

29. Obviously we leave all responsibility for these conceptions to Gustave.
30. In fact, it has three. We shall see the third very soon.

we have seen Flaubert interrogate his particular environment by "identifying with nature and history," that is, he embraces the whole stretch with an infinite gaze and places himself at the end of time. Thus, the absolute-subject is none other than Gustave himself as the imaginary boundary of an infinite series of operations. Or, rather, Gustave positions himself at the point of view of the transfinite substance and of two hypostases (space-time). Transfinite substances are never given directly to the artist except as the abstract aspirations of an absence, but he has the luck to evoke them negatively as the total (and imaginary) truth of any real determination of his experience. Jules has refined a certain method which allows him to treat particularity as a localized and dated expression of the Transfinite. As a result, the transient anecdote is denounced as error, but in bursting its limits it delivers its "true" meaning, which is "immutable"; truth is the accidental, by imagining it Jules forges it—through the destructuring of the perceptions—as the expression of a "vast pantheism." We have seen how a number of manipulations have forced little Caroline's baptism to express the eternal return and the making of the past into the present, in dialectical connection with the making of the present into the past, that is, Eternity—the same Eternity that lets itself be glimpsed through a street organ playing, by an "exquisite affinity," under the Collier sisters' windows. In these two cases—and in all the others—the absolute is manifest as the all, whatever it is, present in its part; this is its content, its material form—and the singular form is merely its negative determination. In this sense, Flaubertian technique consists of neutralizing form in its true singularity and, even while keeping it between parentheses, forcing it to express the transfinite it contains. For example, it is the dated and circumstantial reality of baptism which, emphasized by Flaubert, tends to vanish, thus allowing the emergence of the infinite past through the resurrection of an "exhumed" rite. Every detail of the concrete event is perceived and related to every other, but as imaginary: its function is to express something other than itself, another aspect of the spatiotemporal transfinite.

Gustave presents this idea as a discovery: "Would he have had this idea of art, pure art, without the preparatory anguish he had suffered?" In other words, without the crisis of January '44? We are actually dealing with an intervention. When writing *Smarh* and *Novembre*, the young man hesitated between interior totalization and exterior totalization. But, while the latter corresponded to a mental attitude—to the pride of the "rebound"—the former was still merely a literary solution. At Pont-l'Evêque, his youth is shut down and concluded, he dies: this time he really manages the interior totalization. As a result, he is suddenly constrained to take up a lofty position in order to combat shame: he is ripe to begin a totalization once again, this time through the exterior. He will do it, moreover, several years from now, and that will mean a relapse: the first *Saint Antoine*. But his death to the world has just revealed to him a third way out: engaged in the bonds of the finite, he could take a short leap and regard himself as a panoramic consciousness, embrace the universe with a look, but not *detail* things and men; he grasped only their practical aspect—their coefficient of instrumentality or of adversity. Now that events can no longer help or hinder him, he contemplates them and perceives that each of them—little as one imagines it from the point of view of death—is an *interior* totalization whose moments he can grasp *from the exterior*. *This* baptism reveals itself as a living and melodic unity: it contains the Transfinite, which becomes and is totalized. There is no more need to survey the world, to make exhaustive inventories, to review the vices and virtues of our species, to force together the most heteroclite periods of history, to parade in a directed nightmare the endless cortege of religions and the monsters these have spawned. He who has lived his own life to the end as the tragic and suffered unmasking of the universe has just acquired at his own expense the experience of interior totalization; no need to redo it, each thing in this world redoes it for him. In each singular determination of his environment—the most insignificant or the most fleeting—he will rediscover what he has felt himself, the ubiquity of the All, its total presence in all the parts of its parts, at once as their underlying structure and as the inflexible sequence of their unfolding. In literary terms, Gustave decides at this moment of his thought both that an object is necessary for the macrocosm to become incarnate in it, and that the object is of no importance. In literature this means that one has nothing to tell but the tragic, grandiose emptiness of a Godless universe, but it must be told through a particular adventure, localized and dated. In order to show that the world is Hell, one can of course perch a saint on a summit and have him tortured by a demon; but since a baptism would suffice, today one can just as well take a health official and his adulterous wife: they will do the trick, it is the perspective that is decisive. Without knowing it, Flaubert—still haunted by Faust and the ardent desire to begin *Smarh* once again—has just given himself permission to write *Madame Bovary*.

While working on *L'Education*, he does not yet see all the implications of his discovery. This anxious, bitter soul would like to taste the joys of optimism and convince himself that the anguish he suffered was preparatory. Hence an unconsummated pantheism which masks his pandiabolism.

> Everything that earlier seemed wretched to him was indeed capable of having its beauty and its harmony. By synthesizing it and bringing it back to absolute principles, he perceived a miraculous symmetry . . . The whole world appeared to be reproducing the infinite and reflecting the face of God.

The personal God does not exist, but if *everything* has a purpose, the world has a *teleological unity.*

It immediately becomes apparent, unfortunately, that the totality and its transfinite attributes of "history-nature" have no concrete content. "Alfred has ideas; as for me, I had none." Right, he has none: neither deist nor theist nor atheist nor materialist nor spiritualist, but "rather materialist," this agnostic, who detests philosophy and denies himself the possibility of "concluding," defines himself in his own eyes by his "belief in nothing." Under these conditions, can one consider his pantheism to be a structured vision of the Universe? In '45, he tells us that, all things considered, there is no personal God, yet the world has a teleological unity. But this optimism is a vicious circle: the unity of the macrocosm is its immanent finality, but the only purpose the universe can be assigned is the unification of phenomena. At the moment, dazzled by his discovery, he seriously attempts to paint things white with black ink. He wants his poetic art to be grandiose, he would like to retrieve the cosmic inspiration of Hugo, to whom God speaks without intermediary and who deeply believes that Beauty is the palpable revelation of the True. So he borrows the words and meanings of the period—as de Sade, a half-century earlier, had to borrow the bourgeois idea of Nature; but like the idea of Nature in the hands of de Sade, Hugo's ideas in Flaubert's hands become demented. Hugo is a theist, he believes in Providence; the Beautiful, in his eyes, is not only the expression of the True but also the sign of the Good. Hence he could write, *he* of all people, that "what seemed wretched . . . must have its harmony," for this harmony refers to the eminent wisdom of a Creator. And since God speaks in his ear, there is no need for him to die to the world; quite the opposite, he must live in it and be involved in it; absolute certainties will be communicated to him from above all in good time. For Flaubert, God has disappeared, the absolute is merely the point of view of death; if one has to die to the world, how can one remain faithful to the pantheism that demands, to the contrary, that one mingle, *living*, with the totality of being? The unity of the world appears to the consciousness that has left it; thus beneath the borrowed words, Catharism remains: what reveals itself to the disembodied gaze is the unity of the world *through Evil*, meaning Beauty. And this is indeed the thrust of Gustave's derealizing techniques; it is a matter of negatively totalizing the events that present themselves through appropriate exercises: in one way or another they must be made to appear in their concrete richness as adequate expressions of that Nothingness with which the All is identified. This is not the time to study the part in the light of the All, as he did in *Smarh*, in order to denounce its wretchedness, but to reveal the all in the part through its "vibrating disappearance." The All, of course, is not Being but the equivalence of Being and Nothingness, and finally the triumph of Nothingness over Being; in other words, it is Evil—on this point Gustave has not changed. What is new is that the operation that turns everything into nothingness is never completed: the self-destroying impulse of the real is never pursued to the end; it remains at the moment when reality, by unrealizing itself, unfolds like a fan exhibiting all its rich nuances in order to be annihilated in detail. Thus, neither is annihilation in the all carried to its conclusion, nor does the all as such appear to Gustave in its poverty: there is this suspended sliding in which the invisible transfinite derealizes the qualities of Being and in which Being lends to the Transfinite the infinite irridescence of its multiple details. The real causes itself to be *dreamed* as the inexhaustible and singular concretization of the absolute, and the transfinite—imagined as the meaning of all reality— gives to all visible objects a tragic temporality by presenting itself as their meaning and by producing itself behind them in order to be annulled as it leads them away into Nothingness.

From this point of view, and thanks to the techniques of the *aesthetic attitude*, even a cap, a baptism, a dandelion manifest from the perspective of the absolute-subject the internal time of tragedy, for these object-events bloom only to be annihilated; it is in the name of *the end of history* that Jules, already dead, deciphers today the smiles of a child dead sixty years from now. But death is not given. Jules is in the dismal and vague time of the everyday, or at least he would be if his neurosis were not unrealizing him by projecting him, absolute, beyond the infinite: the gaze he casts on the world is itself an image. In this sense, Gustave has not changed since *Smarh*. Beginning at this period, muddled contingency, disorder, seemed to him to characterize reality and persuaded him that *the real is not on the level of the true*. Truth is not—in '44 as in '39—a trait of the visible universe: it is *what that universe would be* if the hand of a divine artist had remodeled it, transforming that sketch into a unique work of art. And we then observed that this paradoxical confusion of the True with the absolute imaginary could not surprise us, since Flaubert, a passive agent, received the word "Truth" but not the concept associated with it. The author of *Smarh* doubted himself, however, and although he already spoke of Art, he dared not regard himself as an artist. So what is the change that gives Jules this new-found self-assurance? It is quite simply that his techniques are now mature and he has become a "clairvoyant." And by "clairvoyance" I mean the opposite of perception. Let us say that he is now capable *in any circumstance* of grasping the givens of experience as the analogue of an infinite totality. He no longer needs to survey in order to integrate diversities into the rigorous unity of the all; it is sufficient to disengage himself, to take an imperceptible distance. His techniques will do the rest: they will unmask the *strangeness* of the everyday by a subjective *estrangement*, which is the plain refusal to understand it in its banality; they will turn the present into a complete *memory* in the sense that the goddess Mnemosyne, for the Greeks, represented the future as well as the past; and, playing on the three temporal ek-stases with a diabolical adroitness, these techniques will transform the present into a metastable condensation of all temporality—which will allow Flaubert to see in it both time as transfinite and, alternatively, Eternity as the eternal return of the moment. His techniques will be capable of discovering everywhere the "exquisite affinities" that compress connections and bring forth a *meaning* like the melodic unity of temporalization. Across the teleological rigor thus unmasked, Flaubert will grasp the inflexibility of universal *Fatum*. Everything is there: Jules is superior to the young author of *Smarh* because he knows how to effect instantaneous transmutations, because he annexes on the spot the riches of the real for the imaginary. This is his triumph: the mental image is meager; but since by an adroit use of distancing he conditions himself to see without perceiving—that is, he lets himself be invaded by things yet without making them enter by an act into his practical field, without integrating them into his enterprises as real means to a really pursued end—all the nuances of a sky, of a fabric, all the details of a ceremony will serve as raw material to his *exterior* imagination; they will lend their mysterious opacity, their texture, their diversity to several abstract schemes that constitute his Weltanschauung. By this "systematic derangement of all his senses"—far removed from that which Rimbaud intended to practice but quite as profound—Jules lives *in the presence* of the macrocosm. At the beginning, it's true, he isn't yet producing a work of art, but he knows how to manipulate himself in such a way that he perpetually creates the world as a masterpiece by instantaneously remodeling his experience through mental techniques. Now we understand the meaning of this "idea of art, of pure art": it is the imperialism of the imagination. Instead of fleeing from the real, it turns against it, attacks it, and forces it to be devoured by an integrated totality that does not exist, which one can call the world, Hell, or, just as easily, Beauty, and which, by a subtle game, one will offer as the *meaning*, the profound truth of the real that has been swallowed up:

> Jules is penetrated by color, assimilated by substance; he materializes the spirit, spiritualizes matter; he perceives what one does not feel, he feels what one cannot say, tells what one does not express, shows you ideas that have merely been faint suggestions and flashes of thought that surprise you.

Apart from the two last propositions, which relate to written work, all the others concern "clairvoyance," that is, the methodical and immediate transmutation of experience. Art must be a prodigy of equilibrium: derealization, in effect, must preserve all the freshness of the real, must reveal its unperceived aspects. At the same time, making the macrocosm present in the imaginary must never become the object of an explicit aim: if the transmutation were completely lucid, it "would not take,"the imaginary and the real would remain irreconcilable and separate. In truth, nothing must be done deliberately except surprising oneself and searching for the meaning of what one sees. Then the techniques will do their work and meaning will appear—imaginary, for the event has already been transformed into an image, and infinitely obscure since this will be the world itself as mediated through the opacity of the palpable. We realize what adroitness this mixture requires: a little lucidity, a little unconsciousness; a certain way of convincing oneself that one "treats" perception, for love of reality, without completely forgetting that the operation proceeds with a dark passion for nothingness; a manifest and yet discreet presence of the macrocosm, as if it were ready to fly away at the least gesture, a half-clear, half-obscure "meaning," suggested, never explicit, which must appear without anyone appearing to seek it, as if it simply came as part of the process while one is absorbed in contemplating the event and its structure; an attentive flexibility in never forcing anything, in guiding the derealizing invention through the ribs of the real. It is this artisan's skill in mental operations that allows Flaubert to call Jules an artist.

We were asking ourselves, a little earlier, what the absolute foundation of the aesthetic attitude was, for Flaubert. He has given us the answer: it is the totalizing idea, by which we mean the imaginary conviction that the all is present in person in the part, at once for the exaltation of that part and for its abolition, and that this monstrous presence maintains the part to the limits of being and of nonbeing, that is, in the limbo of pure appearance. But the all itself being finally nothingness, the part, by its concrete richness, gives it a deceptive substance precisely to the degree that the all confers on the part a deceptive insubstantiality.

A. The Third Hypostasis

Is the metamorphosis complete? Clairvoyance has made Jules an artist to the first degree; has it allowed him to accede to Art proper? It seems that we have fallen once again into the aporias of 1840. Certainly at the time Gustave was still the Poet—at least partially. Only his ecstasies—which fled the real instead of patiently devouring it— had an incommunicable content, and his unhappiness was simply unable to render them through discourse without impoverishing and denaturing them. Yet, while his attitude has shifted radically since 1840, doesn't the problem remain the same? Namely, how can the intuitions of clairvoyance be transformed into *works*, into real centers of unrealization; how can they be poured into language without being destroyed? If conversion by neurosis is to be a complete success, each transmutation, as a mental operation, must produce by itself the instrument of its externalization and its objectification. But, in a sense, the concrete moment of derealization is like an abstract repetition of the initial crisis; yet how would this repeated death—the passage from real life to the imagination of life, a strictly subjective operation, a choice of subjectivity and of noncommunication taken to the point of autism—how would this contain in itself the promise of being objectified by that great line of communication called talent? Might we not say, quite to the contrary, that there is a contradiction between the choice of the imaginary insofar as it is incommunicable and is the requirement of a *literary* art, that is, the aptitude to overdetermine discourse—which claims to forge bonds between men by communicating meanings? The dreamer, the dehumanized man who dreams his death, is not necessarily an *interlocutor*; indeed, he seems unable to be one. How could the passive agent, suffering his own passivity even unto death—until the moment when radical inactivity reveals to him the Beauty of the world—be transformed into the good *worker* of style whom Flaubert describes in his letters at the time, and who forges his sentence on the anvil, using a hammer, a dazzling symbol that Art is *work, action*?

Flaubert is aware of the problem. In chapter 26 of *L'Education*, Jules, though worn out by exercises in derealization, knows that he lacks *style* and must simply acquire it. His method: reading a great deal, saturating himself in good authors. In short, from the "death of the world," which allows instantaneous access to Art, he returns to the idea of apprenticeship and a "long patience." This is, in fact, a regression: how could eclecticism give him an answer to the question of principle? Can he pour his own incommunicable thoughts into words by studying what—communicable or not—the great minds of the past have communicated? "Jules," writes Flaubert,

> would have liked to reproduce something of the vigor of the Renaissance with the antique flavor one finds beneath its new taste in the limpid and sonorous prose of the seventeenth century; to join with it the analytic clarity of the eighteenth century, its psychological depth and its method, without depriving himself of the acquisitions of modern art; while preserving, of course, the poetry of his own time, which he felt in another way and broadened according to his own needs.

In this text, Gustave confines himself to offering us a potpourri of his preferences: Homer, Rabelais, Molière, Voltaire and Rousseau, Byron; he wants his writing to be a complex dish blending all these elements; the young author himself would merely supply the secret measure of each ingredient. He has lost sight of his profound intuition. For the style *of others* torments him, whatever it is: fascinated, envious, he harbors the hysterical temptation to *imitate* each of the writers he admires; what saves him is their number and the distinctness of their projects. Then he dreams of condensing them all and making his sentence into a kind of cocktail. But how can one enhance Molière with a twist of Byron?

Abruptly, everything changes. Gustave has understood his problem and, without transition, shows us Jules, a little further on, "materializing spirit, spiritualizing matter, perceiving what one does not feel, *feeling what one cannot say, and telling what one does not express."* Between the two last propositions he has deliberately placed an abyss: feeling what one cannot say, Jules places himself as a matter of principle outside of all communication. But the abyss is suddenly breached since he tells what is not expressed, that is, his incommunicable experience itself. The text suggests no mediation between the first procedure and the second; it merely juxtaposes them. Yet, as we know from the letters to Louise, therein lies the entire question: there is the *unsayable* which *must be said,* and if all his life he preserves some affection for *Novembre* it is because he feels he has sometimes managed to suggest it in this work. At the end of *L'Education,* Flaubert reveals his optimism: Jules *has succeeded,* he knows how to handle language. *After* having "disengaged himself from the bonds of the finite," he has perceived that the unsayable, far from being a limitation of literature, constitutes its unique object.

One word enlightens us: he feels what *one* cannot say, he tells what *one* does not express. This Heideggerian *one* represents the common run of men who employ language to serve their trivial ends. And what if style, far from being a better practical use of words, were merely *another* use? From childhood on, Gustave seemed to be in doubt on this question, crushed as he was by the weight of ready-made sentences and commonplaces. Only an obscure intuition can explain the heavy and laborious determination with which he continually engages in puns. "Who are the least generous Spaniards? They are the Navarrese because they live in Navarre [*avare:* avaricious, stingy]. Who are the most bewildered of the Swiss? The Swiss in Uri [*à* Uri = *ahuri:* bewildered, confused]." His letters to his sister and to Ernest are full of such puns. His youth might seem to explain this indulgence. But that is not the case, for from one end of his life to the other he delights in wordplay. He is near his death when he writes to his niece: "Suppose my name is Druche. You would say to me: you are handsome [*beau*], Druche" [*une* baudruche: a fake]." Such continuity of bad taste has only one meaning: Flaubert took pleasure in it because every pun revealed anew the essential ambiguity of language and presented itself, obscurely at first, then more and more clearly, as a coarse symbol of the literary work. Indeed, puns depend on a certain imprecision of codes and of speech in general: the same discourse takes place on two levels—one oral, the other written— which do not precisely correspond. Graphic signs and especially their combinations are more numerous than phonemes—so that for a correctly written communication there are in certain cases several possible ways of *hearing* it. What pleases Flaubert in our old, well-worn languages is that it is still possible to read a certain message in them *with your eyes* and in the belief you are presenting that message to transmit a different one *orally*. The pun flatters his fatalism; he amused himself, like all schoolboys, with Corneille's notorious line on desire, which grows as its effect subsides: once more the human enterprise is ridiculed, since the writer, by the very care he has taken to choose his means, has knowingly been forced to achieve an entirely different aim from the one he had in mind. Thus Laius, in the belief he is doing away with his future murderer, has arranged things himself such that at the appointed place and hour that murderer will be forced to murder him. There is sadism in Flaubert's vulgar pleasantries. And his wordplays present themselves at once as discoveries and as the revelation of the radical failure of the interlocutor, but it is *on this very failure* that he glimpses the possibility of basing a style. What fascinates him is *double meaning*. His wordplays are *written*: yet as the jokes depend on the way one pronounces them, that which is read by the eyes does not contain the *two* divergent meanings. Ernest grasps the question: who are the least generous Spaniards? One claims to give him the answer and its explanation: the Navarrese because . . . But this answer and the explanation—although presented as obvious— seem a piece of *nonsense* as long as we remain in the realm of pure writing. A piece of nonsense or an invitation to find the sense in it? The young joker makes such a show of self-assurance that his correspondent wonders if he has missed something. And something really is there, encapsulated in the written sentence, that designates us as fools or disqualifies it, since it claims to be self-sufficient and isn't. Of course, I am exaggerating, and Flaubert's wordplays are understood at once. Nonetheless, a congenital deaf-mute, had he learned to read, might take from books all the information about the Navarrese save, precisely, the answer to Gustave's question. He would be constitutionally incapable of comprehending a pun, and the explanation "because they live in Navarre" would remain nonsense for him, or an enigma, until the end. Thus, what amuses Flaubert is that the answer is not on the same level as the question: one is posed on the level of writing, the other on that of reading aloud. Ernest and Caroline are swept along: they are transported instantaneously onto the plane of the internal monologue, which is oral. This passage is so easy, so natural, that the visual and sonorous aspect of a sentence or vocable—which are in fact two moments of the Word—appear as its two simultaneous dimensions. As a result, Flaubert's correspondents feel at once pleased and fooled: pleased because the comprehension is quasi immediate, fooled because they sense that language has been metamorphosed in them yet has not been altered, and that it suddenly signifies what it did not signify and, somehow, continues to be incapable of signifying. What is more, this new signification—which seems to be manifest in another language—is in fact the opposite of a signification: it is a piece of nonsense. Or, if you will, it is a pseudo-signification such as is continually produced by free language, that is, language *without people;* the pun is not an intentional production (at least it is not given as such): it is a real determination of heard discourse but only insofar as oral language produces that determination spontaneously, at once in exact relation to written discourse and as the manifestation of its autonomy, of our heteronomy as interlocutors. Words are linked according to rules, and the result is an inhuman signification, an absurdity *for us* but for language a free rapport with the self-to-self. The pun, in sum, forces us to discover language as paradox, and it is precisely on this paradox that Gustave senses one must base the art of writing. Certainly in his wordplays he delights in affirming, in and by the incompleteness of writing, the superiority of the oral over the written—as he will do later, as a stylist, by choosing beautiful vocables "that feel right in the mouth" and joining them according to their affinities of sound.[31] But what especially amuses him—and from his earliest years—is taking revenge on the proverbial locutions that occupy him by haunting his sentences with an absence—which is at once the answer to the question posed and language being determined by its own laws, *against* the people who employ it—and also by uniting significations in an ungraspable supersense, which destroys by affirming itself.

After the metamorphosis of '44, practical language reveals itself to him as a vast pun. A little later, in a passage that we have already cited, he writes to Alfred: "I am sometimes surprised to hear people say the most natural and simple things. It is curious how the most banal utterance sometimes leaves me openmouthed in admiration . . . Have you sometimes listened closely to people speaking a foreign language you didn't understand? That is my situation." We have already

31. It must be remarked, however, that if a pun is communicated orally, the interlocutor can comprehend it only by referring to the image of the written word. What he gets, in effect, is the converse of the statement as it is read. He hears: the Navarrese live in avarice, since the theme is introduced by "the least generous Spaniards," and it is through the visual imaginary that it reestablishes the nonmeaning which is the purpose of the wordplay.

shown certain motives for this stupor (the triumphant common bond and, on the other hand, the conversion, the definitive break with human ends); further, Gustave is clearly taking an aesthetic position here in relation to language. "The most natural and simple things, the most banal utterance . . ." These terms will be repeated on 7 April 1846, when Flaubert will tell Maxime about his niece's baptism and his enterprise of derealization: "It was so simple and so familiar, and yet I could not get over my surprise." It is clear that the goals are the same and the techniques related; but in the first letter it is language that is derealized. Flaubert says so himself, the silliness of certain statements appalls him. But that is not the point: what stupifies him—that is, what he *accuses* of stupifying him—is not that *there is* a language but *that people speak*, that they tear words out of their original silence and turn them into daily babble. Flaubert has eyes only for the part silence plays in any utterance: useless the moment others use it, the word becomes isolated and is posited for its own sake. "The most banal utterance leaves me openmouthed in admiration." "Admiration" is not here a simple variant of "surprise"; the term must be taken in its strongest sense. The most familiar, "banal" expression is revealed as unfamiliar. It shows its singularity as sonorous object to the degree that Flaubert effects a short-circuiting of significations: it is entirely familiar, and yet stupifies because it *no longer means anything*, because Gustave refuses to surpass it toward the signified or the referent. The young man knows quite well that *others* continue to aspire through this material opacity to a certain finite reality, a tool, a practice. But this function no longer concerns him, *for him* it falls into the category of the inessential.

Thus signification falls behind the phoneme; it is an indication of the world of alterity, of praxis and finitude; what is posited for its own sake is an onomastic singularity, or a sentence. And at first these singularities seem like a knot of insoluble problems that throw into question the very possibility of speaking. I don't think it is a betrayal of Gustave to picture him dreaming over these words that occur to him as he looks through an open door: *il fait beau* [it's a nice day]. What is this *il* [it]? And how can one *faire beau* [literally, make beautiful]? And what is "beauty" doing here? What relation does this "beautiful" have with that which is revealed in the pure idea? Of course, he understood the information without even paying attention: warmth, a bit of sunshine, it will not rain—and its practical implications: you don't need your coat. But for Gustave this secondary function merely has the effect of underscoring the strangeness of this verbal joining.

What mystery in these three words, in their relations. How can this turn of phrase—apparently incomprehensible, and referring us to all the structures of our language, to the history of the French and even to that of Rome—how can it in other ears be transformed into that practical advice: leave your coat at home? If people, he thinks, instead of hearing what these words mean were to hear quite simply *what they say*, they too would fall into such a stupor that they would never speak again. The historical depth of the sign, the presence in it of language as totality, throws into question signification itself, which seems overlaid and to have merely a conventional relation to the verbal body that signifies it. But even as it tends to efface itself, the verbal body is affirmed as a strange, autonomous existence that imposes itself on the speaker. Practical man does not speak, he is spoken;[32] discourse produces his determinations in him and through him; thus the speaker becomes the theater of a succession of events which he cannot even observe. Flaubert is the one who contemplates them: he discovers them as another speech; indeed, to one who is disengaged from practical interests and the bonds of the finite, the sentence *Il fait beau still speaks*. But when one is unaware of the origin of this strange impersonal subject, or the way in which *il* can *faire beau* and cannot *faire laid* [make ugly], how can it be understood? At this level, signification—which is transcendence—gives way to a meaning, an immanent and indecipherable unity of three vocables. When Gustave, at home with his family, claims to "listen closely to a foreign language" that he does not understand, he is alluding, of course, to Flaubert family discussions—which are concerned with subjects that do not interest him. But this is not the essential thing. The foreign language is in fact—*as in the pun*—language grasped as something foreign: verbal aggregates appear which are manifestly provided with meaning, as indicated by their rhythm, delivery, cesuras, intonation, but communication stops there. Actually, what is revealed here is language without people; and in order to discover it one need merely reject the activities of the species and stand before it in a state of pure passivity. So, if nothing is understood, everything is suggested: the words reveal their beauty; the sounds, the graphic configuration, allusively

32. This, at least, is Flaubert's opinion. Actually the matter is more complex: people can "be spoken" only to the degree that they speak—and conversely. There is here a dialectical relation which tends today to be forgotten. Language is a sector of the practico-inert. It is eminently suited to the application of dialectical law: people are the mediation between material things to the degree that material things are the mediation between people.

evoke other experiences, other sensations, colors, flavors, many a vague memory. No detail isolates itself, everything is given together in the indecisive unity of a multiplicity of interpenetration: this is what gives the vocable its profound materiality and its opacity.

Here again, with respect to the Word, we find that *estrangement* Gustave experiences in the face of the transfinite conceived as the imaginary texture of every finite object. Indeed, there is a curious ambiguity of language if, taken as a unified totality, it is a being—and not the *expression* of a being—and, if the purpose and essence of each of its particular determinations is *to signify*, it is itself nonsignifying in its organic unity. As if the Word were silence and made itself speech by becoming particularized. The estrangement comes from the fact that the all is present in each one of its parts as the transfinite "history-nature" at every single moment: thus the deepest level of every "locution" *would be silence*, provided one were to consider the semantic whole *as a new transfinite*. But is it so new? Doesn't an identical procedure place Gustave and Jules *face to face* with the macrocosm and with the Word as totality, that is, *outside* both? It is certain, in any case, that the two depths have strict affinities, and that the silence which manifests itself in all speech—as the all is the outstanding meaning of the part—without ever being capable of *signifying* the world, is in a relation of reciprocal symbolization with it. In other words, form and content are revealed together in their indissoluble unity at the cost of *a single conversion*.

If this is so, Gustave's optimism has a legitimate basis: style is not primarily plenitude, a superabundance of verbal resources and inventions, in short, it needn't be seen as a *gift* but as an *attitude toward language* which necessarily follows from the metamorphosis—from the fundamental attitude he took in January '44 toward himself, the world, and life—and which reflects it; style is born of the renunciation of eloquence, just as the "idea of pure Art" is born of the renunciation of the passions and of life. In other words—and whatever the treasures that will later be discovered in it—style begins as *privation*. This was foreseeable. The function of practical language is to establish a type of relationship (through the communication of information, etc.) between members of the same species united by common ends that bring them together but also set them against each other; by renouncing those ends, Gustave puts himself outside of language, which as *practice* is determined as a function of those ends. Hence he discovers the field of the Word at a distance as that which does not belong to him; he acknowledges his past mistake: in wishing to "put poetry into life" through the passions, he used to mistake for *artistic writing* those oratorical flourishes that, far from expressing "human nature" in its universality, still participate in Lived Experience, attempt to make it share the pathetic. Those long tirades interspersed with complaints or violent apostrophes are ruled by whims, by unleashed impulses, and even in "burlesque," in verbal superabundance, *effects* remain, products of affectivity. For lack of "distancing," they aim to convey the experienced feeling but fail to depict it. When the collapse and the rebound tore Gustave from the bonds of the finite, they simultaneously revealed to him the Word in its *totalized infinity*. Artistic style appears as a derealization of language; utilized by finite beings in order to express the concerns of their finitude, words in their practical usage are *finite* instruments, that is, they are limited by their very function. In this resides their *reality*, and while each one refers to language as a whole, that language as a real presence at once gives itself to and hides itself from the finite creatures who use it for determined ends. But for one who has no more reason to use it, it reveals itself unreally[33] as a whole that is of no practical use to him and for this very reason challenges every finite determination with which praxis would affect it.

The ascesis of '44 suddenly forces Gustave to understand that he has approached the problem of style backwards. He had long regretted his inability to render through words the flavor of a plum pudding, that is, naked sensation. But that was because he was still too engaged in the "seriousness" of the world and of language. His mistake, he now thinks, was twofold: on the one hand, he required vocables to express *as signifiers* what on principle escapes the domain of signification, the qualitative structure of the palpable. On the other hand, although from this period his totalizing intention gave him an abstract presentiment of cosmic unity, he had not yet brought *transfinite elements* down into concrete reality as permanent factors of derealization. In other words, he had not yet assimilated the "unsayable" depth of the palpable to the presence of the all in each of its parts; so he kept moving from one abstraction—the synthetic idea of unity—to an infinite diversity of sensations. The reason he regretted having no *style* was not, or not only—contrary to what he believed—that he had no talent: the main problem was that the objects he wanted to speak about—the One without concrete multiplicity, or the diverse

33. We are dealing here with poetic catharsis and not with restitution by the linguist, through the differential, of a language as structured totality.

without transfinite unity—were not susceptible to being treated by "artistic writing." Before he could write, a complete metamorphosis had to be effected, and by becoming entirely imaginary he had to have the total and derealizing experience of the unsayable, that is, to grasp the transfinite in the palpable through methodical exercises. By the same token, it was necessary to grasp the incompetence of practical language—which is not made to render the cosmos in its unity—but also to recognize that it is the only raw material available to a literary work. With this, the *idea of style* reveals itself: it is a particular treatment of the raw material that aspires to win back from praxis the articulations of discourse, not in order to say better—more elegantly, more precisely—what *can* be said by nature, but, to the contrary, to fix by a certain use of words that which by definition escapes them. Style—as he will say later—is the absolute point of view because it composes discourse with a view to suggesting the presence of the transfinite at the heart of finitude and the absolute in the relative. As Flaubert sees it, in practical language—the only *real* language—the relation of the signifier to the signified remains—at least in principle—direct: through the sentence or the vocable I aim expressly at an object, an event, a concept; literature begins with the decision to steal language, to deflect it from its ends, and to make it the means of *making present the inarticulable* without abandoning direct significations. I say *making present* because according to Flaubert one must *render it visible and audible* without showing it. It will be in the discourse—audible if I read, visible if someone reads to me—as the supreme and immanent unity of words and sentences. But it will be capable of emerging—present and indecipherable—only marginally, that is, if the direct significations are preserved and if the reader is absorbed in the practical effort that consists of decoding the message and deriving the maximum number of significations from it. Actually, it is a fake: meaning will appear to the reader from the practical work he will be urged to undertake, which he will pursue from one end of his reading to the other, but *in spite of him* it will collapse before his eyes, demonstrating its own inanity. Of course this trap will be constructed: there will be a selection of significations in such a way that they are the sketch of a story, an anecdote, and for this reason remain permanently on the horizon as the original motivation: we will read *in order* to find out what happens. At the same time, the artist will render them *insignificant* by the distance he has taken and maintained toward the world and language. Thus, as direct and inessential object of the "artistic" reading, the signifying synthesis (expectation, the progressive answer to the question, What happens next?) is effected without passion, and as a result becomes inessential; with this, immanent language, "meaning," becomes realized—almost without the subject's knowledge—as the truth of the Word and its essential purpose.

For quite some time now, as we have seen, Gustave has loved words as things and has made use of their materiality in order to *make present* his dreams. "I shall go to the yellow country they call China . . . I want to see the Malabar's madmen and its dances in which people kill themselves . . . , to die of cholera in Calcutta or of the plague in Constantinople." But until now it was merely a matter of inclination without principle or method, always combated by his tiresome propensity for eloquence. Now he sees clearly: style—*his* style—will be forged by making systematic use of the nonsignifying elements of discourse in order marginally to render the unsayable. As we just said, any practical and particular actualization of language was constituted as a signifying whole, suppressing itself in order to indicate an exterior object, but language taken in its totality is a being, a structured reality that refers only to itself. Flaubert invents his style when he decides to make this being show through these significations as a whole immanent in each of its parts. Hence he makes discourse reveal to us the silent blossoming of the cosmos in each of its finite modes; or if you will, language already totalized as the transfinite, *become the world*, represents the space-time continuum, that other transfinite. Style for Flaubert requires a permanent doubling, that is, a constant dialectic of sense and signification. A simple collection of "beautiful" words would not achieve the desired aim, which is to reveal the flesh of the world *through* its finite manifestations. The object must be the explicit aim, so that one feels the depth of things through the "beautiful" materiality of words; here Flaubert resembles the painters of his time who needed a "subject"—even a simple still life—in order to inflame its colors and make it *something other and more* than colors, but whose principal aim was to reveal through signification (the theme being treated) a plastic and nonsignifying being, a particular thing that is a combination of values and tones.

I spoke elsewhere of a certain yellow rent above Golgotha which was done neither to signify nor to provoke anguish, but which in Veronese's canvas "*is* anguish made yellow, anguish that has turned into a yellow rent in the heavens and, by the same token, is . . . coated with the qualities intrinsic to things, with their impermeability, with their extension, with their blind permanence, etc., and is no longer at all readable." But it must be added that this yellow rent would lose even its *immanent meaning* of anguish if the *chosen signification* (the Crucifixion) did not serve *thematically* and actualize the somber horror of this muted tint. By itself the yellow would remain too ambiguous for anyone to see it as "anguish made concrete"; linked to other colors on a "nonfigurative" tableau, it would take its value from the whole and would be no more than an aesthetic determination of the totality-object.[34] It will take a radical change in attitude, both of the painter and of his public, for painting—at least for a while—to become simplified and to reject as useless or literary the dialectic of being and sign. In Flaubert's time, Delacroix thought no differently in this respect from Veronese. What was entirely new, on the other hand, was Gustave's sudden, blinding clarity: an author can attain *style* if he applies himself to writing the way a painter paints, by pursuing his enterprise on two planes at once without losing sight of either one or of their shifting relations. Of course, he never expressly formulated his thought in this way. But would he so doggedly have persevered in wanting to be an "Artist" if he had not been convinced of the unity of the Fine Arts? The idea was in the air, and around that time in Paris the Goncourts too began to dream of "artistic writing," but they lacked the ponderousness, the obstinacy, and the depth of the Norman workhorse; they confined themselves to stealing the vocabulary of the painters. The real upheaval came from Flaubert. Yet we must be more specific about it and define its extent.

This *being* of the Word is always there, even in the prose of Monsieur Jourdain. Whatever the statement, it presupposes on all levels a system of relations which is nothing less than the totality of possible discourses, that is, a language, a pyramid rising from the phoneme to the lexeme, with each stratum appearing as nonsignifying relative to the stratum immediately above. That had always been known, and no one waited for Flaubert to exploit in "beautiful" prose the extrasignifying elements of language and to draw from them the rhythm and musicality of the line. The rarity of a vocable, its sumptuousness, its historical resonance—what it still retains of its history—as much as motifs, in any period, encourage its adoption by a writer.[35] In short, no one has ever written without making more or less conscious use of the materiality of the Word, that pure being-there which the inten-

34. These brief remarks take no account of tachism, or action-painting, or the works of Ribeyrolle. I have explained my ideas on these elsewhere.

35. There are languages that allow one to go still further: in Japan, Mishima, following many others, also chose his words for their *plastic* beauty.

tional aim surpasses toward the silent opacity of named things. But it must first be observed that the presence of the all in the part, when it is Monsieur Jourdain who speaks, is not *real;* his discourse is differential, and so it totalizes to the same degree that it is totalized. These two aspects of speech, rather than an *accomplished* totality, refer to a double totalization perpetually in progress. For Flaubert, language is a transfinite thing, meaning that Jules holds himself outside an *effectuated* totalization, which implies—we shall come back to this—an imaginary relationship to the linguistic whole. He is highly conscious of this, for when he listens to his neighbors, he delights in scratching at the significations in order to find beneath them and against them language as "foreign," to grasp as oversignifying the stratum of being which, for the speakers, is nonsignifying. This is just what he did at Caroline's baptism, reifying people, revealing the insignificance of their statements and gestures (the priest literally *doesn't know what he is saying*) in order to humanize the stones by finding a fixed meaning in their very materiality. The speaker, literally, whether he is speaking of rain and good weather or of public affairs, does not know what he is saying either. For Gustave, this means staying on the superficial level of language; yet, when his mother and his brother quite unconsciously exchange commonplaces, they are active interlocutors, and their statements stir up the depths of the totality of language. The younger Flaubert son, immobile and passive, pursues his derealizing dream and is pleased to reverse the roles: Madame Flaubert and big brother Achille—like the priest and the spectators—are inanimate puppets; it is language in its materiality that moves them. Doubly so: it imposes its commonplaces on them and *thereby* becomes spoken in its entirety, even in its arcana. Gustave knows very well, however, that the only reality *given* by language is practical; for this reason, the reification of the interlocutors and the living and deep personalization of the Logos can give itself only to a passive agent devoured by the imaginary. And since his attempt—to grasp clear and *un*signifying significations as the means chosen by language to manifest itself in its *non*signifying depth, its total and transfinite *sense*—corresponds term for term to the idea he has developed of style (except that the Artist will be conscious of what he does), we understand that style, born of resentment, is for Flaubert primarily a systematic derealization of speech.

Furthermore, in the great writers of the classical centuries, prose—even in fiction—preserves its practical function: it is a means of communication. Molière's characters communicate with each other, and through their mediation Molière communicates with the public. Certainly they can hide or change the nature of the facts, deceive dotards or fools, but these very lies imply, in both author and spectator, the conviction that the Truth is always "sayable." This is the principle of all classical literature; language is distinct from thought but can express it *adequately:* "That which is well conceived is stated clearly, / And the words to say it come easily" (Boileau, *Art poétique*). From this point of view, the *pleasantness* of a given passage of prose adds nothing to its expressed contents; one would have to say here, parodying Aristotle, that "pleasure is to the [verbal] act as its flower is to youth." We appreciate the musicality of Fénelon, but the harmony of his sentences is not an element of signification; it charms like a melody. Certainly the author works the verbal material: the sentence will be flowing and rhythmical; he will take care to distribute the stressed and unstressed syllables judiciously; he will avoid cacophony and will even search for euphony; he will hunt out repetitions, will make great use of synonyms, that is, vary the form with no advantage to the contents expressed, carefully suppress the alexandrines that cluster inadvertently so as not to provide the reader with "a prose studded with verse." But all this labor remains—at least on the conscious level—a negative preliminary, and in sum a matter of decorum: the point is not to offend the eyes or the ears. And also to please. Writing remains an act of good company. As a result, the polishing is merely the most superficial aspect of the classical style: as it is not a means of surmounting noncommunication, it is produced inside a universal transparency; without entering into details, it is defined by the economy of means. Pascal's witticism "I didn't have time to make it brief," in addition to providing a good example of style, rather well defines the preoccupations of seventeenth-century writers: the sentence must offer a summary of the thought. To express the greatest number of things with the least number of words means to exalt the signification of terms by arranging them in such a fashion, and by choosing their place in the statement with such rigor, that each is *enhanced* and *radicalized* by the others. In centuries of enlightenment that propose in principle that feelings and emotions are always communicable, the writer is convinced that there are a thousand ways of expressing his thought, but that only one is worthy of being written: the most economical. Since the number of words for a definite idea must be as few as possible, however, each word must be worth several others, which is conceivable only if, by rigorous construction, one confers on each a certain power of oversignification. To this purpose, the classical au-

211

thors were inspired, for example, by paradox, a play of ideas which was to their style what wordplay would be to Flaubert's. The pseudo-paradox is offered to the reader with an apparent obscurity that dissolves as it is scrutinized. Many other kinds of abridgments are possible; they all have the effect of providing us, in the midst of universal transparency, with false incommunicables that gradually dissolve in the luminous ether of absolute communication. Why this concern for economy brings us closer to a certain kind of beauty would require too lengthy an explanation here. I am indicating simply the end and the means.

The Flaubertian revolution derives from the fact that this writer, distrustful of language from childhood, begins, in contrast to the classics, by posing the principle of the noncommunicability of lived experience. The reasons for his attitude are at once subjective and historical. We already know what words were for him from early childhood on. But he could not have transformed this negative relation to language into a positive conception of style if the problem had not been endemic to the period and if the preceding generation had not, by celebrating the passions, placed emphasis on subjectivity. Romantic pathos implies a substitution of signifieds: it is no longer a matter of describing the passions insofar as they are *processes* with rigorous articulations and moments capable of conceptualization, but of finding words to render their signification insofar as they are *lived* realities.

To tell the truth, the great Romantics—with a few isolated exceptions—did not make the matter explicit. Even while breaking apart and reworking the style of the eighteenth century, and enriching it with a vocabulary that had been previously "forbidden," they left to their descendants the job of responding to it. Here, then, we have the question as it was posed to the young post-Romantics of the forties: if the objective of fictional prose is no longer to fix in writing the results of analytic psychology,[36] if, in other words, words are no longer employed for the connotation and denotation of concepts, and if, to the contrary, it is proper for the novelist to express lived experience—what is felt—as such, that is, insofar as that experience is not amenable to conceptualization, how can language be appropriated to its new literary purpose? Here, of course, we encounter the noncommunicable: for I can literally name my suffering or my joy, make them

36. As is still the case with Benjamin Constant—although *Adolphe* and *Le Cahier rouge* already bear witness to an underlying contradiction and derive their depth from a constant effort to surpass analysis and, consequently, the concept.

known by their causes, but I cannot transmit their singular flavor. If, however, in the eyes of its successors, Romanticism puts this very flavor in question, and if the palpable in its very idiosyncrasy sustains nonconceptualizable but *objective* structures in the very heart of subjectivity (the taste "of a plum pudding" is at once a lived, nonconceptualizable singularity and a common sensation whose memory can be reawakened in all those who have felt it), this noncommunicable is, despite everything, susceptible of being transmitted somehow or other. One must, so to speak, give up the idea of making language into a means of information, or a means of subordinating the informative function to this new function, which might be called *participation*. In other words, one must not only name the taste of the plum pudding but must make us smell it as well; and the read sentence would fill this new function perfectly if, while *signifying* the conceptual bond that unites the pudding to its consumption, it *were* that taste itself, entering through the eyes and into the mind of the reader.

It will be observed that this change of *literary intention* is manifest at the moment when the ruling class is emphasizing *individualism*. The valorization of the *individual* itself implies the affirmation that "beings are impenetrable." Therefore "natural" language is not made to communicate in depth; yet this would have to be its mission since the incommunicable—that is, idiosyncrasy—is the fundamental value in this ideology. One might say without exaggeration that this contradiction, dimly perceived, is the linguistic basis of the lofty solitude to which so many of the Romantics refer: they declare themselves misunderstood because, beautiful as their writing is, they fail to make felt what they are feeling. And what is for them a negative limit, the young writers of the forties—whether they are called Baudelaire or Flaubert—see as a positive invitation to create an *antiphysis* of language. It is a matter of *reversing* practical discourse and, by full use of the sign, working it in its being as a function of the unsayable to the point that it provides those silent overcommunications that transmit no conceptual signification.

Profoundly individualist, Baudelaire finds *his* solution in the overthrow of poetry. He is not, however, clearly aware of what he is doing, which explains why we find in one of the greatest poets of the century, and in practically all his poems, so many bad lines, which Delille could have written: he keeps oscillating between signification and sense. In Gustave, beginning in '44, the ideas are clearer: style transmits the unsayable by means of the unrealization of language. It is not so surprising that the problem should be formulated in him:

this boy hardly likes himself, he is not an individualist, but he lives in the midst of a bourgeois individualism of which his father—despite his peasant background—is an eminent example. And he has been constrained to internalize a certain original maladaptation under the rubric *anomaly*. This anomaly is not communicable because it is a lesser-being about which there is nothing to say. Yet he *lives* it, in shame and rage, sometimes in pride. And this is what he wants to tell. Not to delight in it—it horrifies him—but rather, as we have seen, in order to infect others with it. Beginning with *Smarh*, he dreams of a corrupting style. At this time, visibly, he hesitates: shall he demoralize by reporting obscene anecdotes, by describing lubricious scenes? Certainly, and here we remain in the realm of significations. But it is on condition that the style is *beautiful*, that the discourse, by its internal quality, by the labor exerted on its being, is in itself troubling. It is not a matter of rewriting *Le Portier des Chartreux* but of injecting perversion as a poison into the minds of readers by the unsayable singularity of the sentence produced. At the time, however, he does not know how to do it; all he knows is the aim—you have made me vile, I will foist that vileness onto you by the beauty of my prose, and you will be worse than I am—and not the means. In '44 he still hesitates sometimes, and we have seen him fall back into eclecticism. But this was merely a transitory lapse, one experienced by all those who *discover* and whose habits of mind make them incapable of remaining constantly at the height of their discovery. To be convinced of it we need merely read the paragraph immediately following the previously cited passage:

> He entered wholeheartedly into this great study of style; he observed the birth of the idea simultaneously with the form in which it is cast, their mysterious developments, parallel and adequate to each other, a divine fusion in which the mind, assimilating matter, makes it eternal like itself. But these secrets are not told, and in order to learn some of them, one must know a great deal already.

Is it the mind that assimilates matter or matter that assimilates the mind by communicating to it its inert eternity? What is certain, in any case, is his project: in the texture of concrete things he must seize the presence of the infinite All—at once matter and nothingness—and transmit it—as the immanent meaning of the discourse—by treating language *in its materiality*. On this level, there are no more rules: everyone must invent his own, the Unique is transmitted by the

Unique. In the same paragraph, Gustave condemns "all poetic Art."[37] How can there be models if everyone's aim is merely to make objective in language his unsayable idiosyncrasy "following the particular character of his talent and in a concrete, unique form, without which the specificity of the work would not exist." Art is difficult because each artist works without rules or recipes, and because for each artist everything must be invented. This contention calmly contradicts the eclectic affirmations we have just examined. Gustave, in order to express his anomalous and yet universal relation to the macrocosm, can have no recourse to rhetoric: such affirmations are all based on the practical function of language and cannot teach him how to realize the linguistic *antiphysis*. A single rule—which is his own and has the aspect of an abstract imperative: write in such a way that everyone, and you yourself, finds himself in his reciprocities of perspective as the silent meaning of the discourse.

We can now understand the true meaning of the readings Jules engages in and Gustave proposes to engage in. He puts us on the track: "By dint of contemplating beautiful works in the good faith of his heart, of being penetrated by the principle that had produced them, and by regarding them abstractly in themselves with respect to their beauty, then relative to the truth they manifest and propound, with respect to their power, he understood the meaning of originality and genius." He reads the great authors in order to catch them in the creative moment: in each of them this moment is singular, therefore inimitable; it can serve him neither as model nor as example. Yet each author, in his originality, puts in question a certain relation between idea and expression: it is this general problem that he grasps through solutions whose particularity is irreducible, before providing his own. Several pages further on, Gustave shows us even more effectively the meaning of this apprenticeship: "In studying his form after that of the masters, and in drawing from within himself the content it had to contain, he found he had achieved naturally a new manner, a true originality." Jules is not *seeking* his form in earlier works: he studies it *after* that of the great masters; what he brings to light *after them* is the complex problem of content and form. But none of the past "manners" can suit him since they correspond to other concerns; it does not occur to him to *adapt* a preexisting form to the "content" that is

---

37. Even as he complacently articulates his own.

himself, that is, his anomaly: it is simply a matter of studying the question and of finding in each case the particular fashion in which they answered it so as to be able to answer it in his turn—not clearly and abstractly but in the obscurity of a concrete decision.

B. Some Remarks on "Loser Wins" Rationalized

Can we say that the style of the first *Education*—or at least of the final chapters—meets Gustave's requirements? Certainly not. It shows that the young author has made a certain progress: less oratorical than the first part of *Novembre,* it is more adapted to the description of facts, the narration of concrete events. Still, it has neither the slightly redundant beauty we encounter at the beginning of the preceding work nor the concise sharpness of its conclusion. To tell the truth, it is rather flat and never offers those semantic overdeterminations that are found in every line of *Madame Bovary* and of which Jules becomes the theoretician. Moreover, Flaubert has never before dealt with these difficult matters, his ideas escape him, he cannot control them; thus he founders in words, in metaphors, and avoids neither obscurities nor mistakes. It is not our place to reproach him for this, quite the contrary; there is something pathetic and admirable about this thought struggling against itself and against the misfortune that threatens it, this poetic Art drawn from his neurosis—an art he is the *first* in his century to discover.

But what about him? How does he judge his work when he rereads it? Quick to be disgusted by what he has just written, to drop everything, his own most pitiless censor, he should roar with fury and curse himself. But he doesn't, he goes on to the end and, most important, indulgently makes us witness to his hero's extraordinary metamorphosis. Up to the very last pages we have been finding in this character the tastes, occupations, troubles of his author: we have seen Gustave choose his readings for him, we have been learning of his literary opinions, and from failure to failure his "sentimental education" has taken place before our eyes; he has gone so far as to mingle in Parisian society in order to verify for himself the vanity of men and their follies. The tone was already surprising: until now, Flaubert has taken pleasure in torturing his heroes before killing them. We find no more of that here; it looks as if he has lost his sadism and his masochism simultaneously: Jules has suffered and still suffers, but it is an ascesis, and the character fully enjoys his author's sympathy. Each of his projects is valued as a step forward on the road to salvation. No more falling back—except at the beginning of the last part, chapter 26, the episode of the "mangy dog in the country." The torturer of Marguerite, Djalioh, and Mazza never amuses himself by playing nasty tricks on his new hero. This is all the more peculiar as in his subsequent work he will set himself mercilessly upon Emma, Mâtho, even Frédéric, and finally on his two autodidacts. Alone, Julien l'Hospitalier—we shall soon see why—benefits from a similar indulgence. Jules can remain a problematic character *to the end.* Gustave certainly cannot make him die since *he is already dead.* At least the author could have left us unsure. As described in the first pages of chapter 27, Jules was largely a foil for Henry. If Gustave had left him there, ending his manuscript with: "perhaps to be continued," that would have been fair play and, all things considered, moderately optimistic.

Yet here, all at once, optimism goes off the deep end and becomes hyperbole. Jules has finished his apprenticeship: he is *no longer anything except in imagination,* and his sentimental education has taught him to feel nothing that is not unreal. At this moment Gustave changes his tone and informs us that his hero has become the equal of Shakespeare. Let us take stock by rereading this previously cited text:

> Existence furnished him with the accidental, he rendered it immutable; everything came to him and everything flowed out of him, flux of the world, reflux of himself . . . Extending to all the elements, he related everything to himself, and all of him was concretized in his vocation, in his mission, in the fatality of his genius and his labor, a vast pantheism which passed through him and reappeared in art . . . He became a serious and great artist . . . It is the concision of his style that makes him so mordant, its variety that constitutes its suppleness; without the correction of language, his passion would not have had such vehemence nor his grace such charm.

Let us recall the hero of *Novembre,* who died of being too small for himself: this suffices to bring out Jules's incredible luck; Gustave, who ordinarily does not bestow gifts, has spoiled him. But didn't he just want to end his novel with a portrait of the Artist according to his lights? Indeed, we observe, not without surprise, that he abruptly concedes to Jules the "fatality of genius"—that destiny-quality which he never dared accord to himself and which is mentioned in the first *Education* only in the concluding pages. It is as if Flaubert, wanting to establish at least once the essential characteristics of the "serious and great artist" as he conceives him, had decided in the course of his enterprise that Jules would do the job nicely, and that he would transform him at the end into a "writer of genius" so that this abstraction should benefit from the concrete traits he had previously given to his character, and so that the singularity of his history should mask the skeletal generality of the portrait—or, better, so that the temporalized narrative of the newly-become artist should hide the theoretical and normative aspect of the final considerations. If he had not warned us that he was recounting the extraordinary adventure of a young provincial touched by grace, we would be tempted to read: "Existence provides us with the accidental, the great Artist must give back the immutable." Or: "In order to be an Artist, one must render to Art what life gives us." The artificial ending of *L'Education* would be a brief ethical-aesthetic treatise on the conditions necessary for "entering literature."

I do not think this hypothesis should be retained. Certainly the normative aspect of this hypothetical description should not be neglected. But the generality of considerations and imperatives cannot hide from us certain highly individuated characteristics that relate only to Jules *as his history has made him.* We are told, for example, that "he hardly remembers his own works, that he is even more indifferent to their destiny once they have been produced than he was anxious, earlier, at their birth." He has almost no concern with fame, "what gives him delight above all being the satisfaction of his mind contemplating its work and finding its measure." His plays are not performed nor his verses printed; he does not care: "When he wants to hear the harmony of his verses, he reads them to himself alone . . . When he wants to see his plays performed, he puts his hand over his eyes and imagines to himself a vast hall, wide and high, filled to the rafters . . . He dreams his actors in the pose of statuary and hears them, with a powerful voice, declaiming his great tirades or sighing his words of love. Then he leaves off, his heart full, his forehead radiant." Gustave cannot believe that he is here describing *the* great writer taken in his generality as *type:* indeed, he is familiar with good authors because they got published and their plays are performed. What we find again here, rather than the imperatives of a literary ethic, are the very particular conceptions of the young Flaubert. Only recently he observed: "I write to please myself"; even more recently he confided to his friends: I don't know if I shall get myself published—or again: it would be splendid to give nothing to the public until the age of fifty and then all at once to give them one's "complete works." We know that his later critique of the first *Education* applies to the character of Henry but, even more, to that of Jules: he reproaches himself, indeed, for showing effects without causes, and for failing to make comprehensible the imperceptible and continuous transformations that will lead Henry to the mundane and bourgeois life, Jules to the solitude of genius. If the conclusion seems artificial, it is not for being added artificially, like the happy ending of *Tartuffe*; but it is simply, and by the author's own admission, that he did not know how to *lead up to it*. Which clearly indicates that Flaubert regards Jules's evolution as necessary. Even if the idea of making him a great artist came to him—which is not in doubt—after January '44, that idea seemed to him the necessary outcome of a rigorous development: it appears gratuitous because he went full speed to the end.

To whom, then, does this "happy ending" apply? To Jules or to Gustave? And whence its necessity? Indeed, we can well imagine that Gustave believed he was permitted to push his character beyond the limits he could not breach himself. There was a time when Flaubert saw himself as a painter or a musician in the imaginary, "without understanding anything of painting or music." Didn't he wish to take his dream to its conclusion in the first *Education*, to dream through writing that he had become a great writer? Compared to mental images, words traced by a pen have that incantatory superiority of being an objectivization; this is something the authors of graffiti know better than anyone. Writing fixes the dream, communicates a dizzying inertia to it, pulls it out of the mind and offers it back again as an alien reality, and this fascinating illusion enlists a quasi-belief. Thus Jules would be the imaginary accomplishment of which the "great man *manqué*" so often dreamed.

This conjecture surely conceals some truth: in other words, Gustave *enjoyed* showing his hero's ascesis and solitary ascension; while he was writing, I imagine, his eyes must often have filled with tears. Is this reason enough to call it wishful thinking? Looked at more closely, an apparent contradiction in Jules's development strikes us at once; here is a man who, at the end of a painful apprenticeship, has found his way: disappointed at once by the real and by action, he has opted radically for the imaginary. Should he not logically *imagine* he writes rather than actually writing? *To be* a writer is to act in the world even if only to derealize it; in short, it is a real enterprise which from the beginning is at odds with linguistic reality and its coefficient of adversity. Recall that Jules "*has failed in all his projects.*" Isn't it a project to create a literary work? Why, then, should he succeed in this enterprise? If he has really understood that the World is Hell, he should not meddle with its machinery: no compromise, his joys will be wholly of the imagination. And it is even clearer that when he wishes for glory it is as a dream: he puts nothing in print, but putting his hand over his eyes he *imagines* a hall filled to the rafters and overcome by the tirades he has put into the mouths of his actors. Why not go all the way? Why *write these speeches*? Why not dream that he has written them? This is the obvious conclusion; Gustave will draw it later apropos another artist, the painter of *La Spirale.* He is to observe that this painter *began* with Art in order to end with pure imagination, that is, with what those around him call madness.[38] Shut up in an asylum, he no longer even paints. Does he dream that he is painting? We have no idea; what we do know is that for him the imaginary constitutes a whole in which he remains enclosed, a whole whose sole link with the real is internal negation. I do not mean to indicate only the ontological difference that separates them but also the concrete opposition that Flaubert underscores, which produces every image in the fantasmagoric totality as a strict antithesis of reality. And this artist is *also* Flaubert, who declares explicitly that he wants to employ his pathological experiences of '44, in particular his "nervous hallucinations," to give a vivid and concrete content to this progressive triumph of the unreal over reality and of nothingness over being. It seems, therefore, that Gustave could provide two endings to the first *Education:* the one radical and logical, which he set aside in order to take it up again in *La Spirale,* and the other, which at first seems a compromise, as if he had been afraid to follow his thought through to the end. In a letter to Louise, when he mentions his project of a "metaphysical novel, with apparitions," he adds: "this is a subject *which frightens me,* speaking in terms of [mental] health."[39] He is too close to the pathological experiences from which he wants to draw inspiration; he must wait. For this reason, and for another reason that will become apparent, he will never write it. Nearly ten years after the attack at Pont-l'Evêque, at a time when he thought he had recovered, he still found himself too close to "those impressions" to give himself over to them "as ideas" and therefore without danger for "him or for the work." So we can easily imagine what his apprehensions must have been in '44, when every day he expected another seizure. Is this perhaps what prevents him from giving *L'Education* its implacable and logical ending, not genius but madness? Jules's experience, in

38. Thus the Garçon, first a poet, becomes the mad keeper of the Practical Joke Hotel.
39. To Louise, 31 March '53, *Correspondance,* 3:146. Flaubert's italics.

this case, would not be communicated to the reader in its real language, it would have to be seen as a coded, desperate message.

I do not think so. Certainly *La Spirale* reflects correctly Flaubert's Manichaeism. If the World is Hell, this Catharist will find in nonbeing merely a salvation which is itself nothingness. But that is a theoretical conclusion, and in any event it is undermined by the fact that great writers have existed, exist, will exist, and that his tragedy until *L'Education* was that he did not believe he could count himself among them. In other words, before '44 he had trouble seeing absolute Hell as an *ordinary place;* he quite often thought it was reserved for great men *manqués*—that is, for himself. In '53 he is much more self-assured: after many attacks—of which we shall speak—he has settled down to writing *Madame Bovary,* and he has the complex feeling of doing an exercise and writing a masterpiece. In any case he has found "his style." He is therefore permitted to dream of a Manichaean and radical experiment which, although he wants to enrich it with his own pathological impressions, does not seem to concern him directly. The asylum, to be sure, is the Hôtel-Dieu and then Croisset; the "apparitions" that are gnawing the writer to the bone will be modeled on his nervous hallucinations. But Flaubert is not mad in '53: and, above all, he is writing. *La Spirale* seems much more like a transposition of *Saint Antoine.* The fabulous opera had to include historical evocations: "The Orient would not be sufficient as a fantastic element—and in the first place it is situated too far away—it would be necessary to go back in time gradually. The Revolution, Louis XV, the Crusades, Feudalism.—From there, the Orient—, then the fabulous Orient."[40] In other words, the failure of *Saint Antoine,* which is too static, too abstract, compels him to dream at times of a modern, dramatic, and concrete fantasy in which madness would replace the Devil, and the hero, individualized and situated in our day, would be the site of a permanent conflict between our daily, dated reality and the derealizing resurrection of history. *La Spirale* remains in the state of a project in part because Gustave is about to find a better formula for *Saint Antoine,* which will allow him, in the third version, to integrate historical evocations into the very heart of the Temptation.

In 1844, it is quite another matter: the debate is centered on *vocation.* And the attack at Pont-l'Evêque appears as an obscure pathological answer to the question he asks himself each day: am I *called* to

40. Gustave's note apropos *La Spirale.*

become a great writer? This is the answer Flaubert transcribes at the end of the first *Education*, and it is a positive one. Hence the hybrid character of the last chapters. On the one hand, Jules's experience is basically pathological, and radical failure implies the wreckage of reason, yet not to the point of madness; on the other hand, in the transubstantiation that turns him into a pure nonbeing and his former passion to live into quietism, a single *activity* is spared—art; a single contact with the real is preserved—the relation to language. This anomaly enlightens us—the terms must be reversed. If Jules does not sink into madness, it is not that the author has held him back out of timidity, but that the original purpose of the final pages (conceived after the January crisis) was precisely to show the conditions necessary for acceding to genius.

Necessary and *sufficient:* such is Flaubert's point of view in 1844. For this reason we are led, like him, to change perspective. He has long said that one must die to the world in order to enter into literature. But until then this ascesis seemed to him a simple condition *sine qua non*, after which one reveals oneself as a genius or a great man *manqué,* according to one's luck. In *L'Education* he goes about it quite differently: provided it is *radical*, the ascesis will produce genius *by itself.* In other words, literary activity is not, in Jules, an inexplicable residue of the previous period; it is clearly the dialectical result of his failures: when one has lost *everything,* one writes. Or, if you will, the reversal of being—and its metamorphosis into nonbeing—cannot be followed to its logical conclusion without producing style as a moment and sign of its radicality. To die to the world *is* to be reborn an artist.

C. The Dialectic of Three Hypostases

Can we even call literature an activity? We have just noted this difficulty: how can this living dead man who is Gustave, who abandons himself to inertia, be a "worker of art"? The answer given in *L'Education* is that Jules *does not need* to be active. Admittedly, in the letters he wrote in 1845–46 Gustave does some boasting about his derealizing techniques and speaks of "analyzing" his troubles "as an artist." In the novel we find nothing of the kind: the great and serious writer is merely a straw man; through him, the imaginary has the task of recuperating the macrocosm and its essential nothingness. It is the possible that *negotiates* the real in order to change it into appearance, to give the finite mode its depth, and to allow us to catch a glimpse through it of the totalitarian unity of Being, whose secret meaning is nothingness. It is the advent of imagination that transforms language into a gratuitous but organized totality—being whose essence is also Nothingness—the moment the impossible man, incapable because of his very impossibility of communicating with those of his contemporaries who refuse to recognize their own impossibility, profoundly conscious of the *inutility* of the Word, sets himself to *dreaming* it. Dreaming the Word or dreaming about words amounts to the same thing since the word, taken as an object of sonorous nonsense, refers on the one hand to imaginary marvels—which one *imagines* while dreaming about the word "China" or the word "Orient," etc.—and, on the other hand, to that transfinite, language, an image of the other transfinite, nature-history. In this case, writing is not an *act*, it is a dream of the pen, and imaginary man does nothing but let words fill the paper like the images of a dream. Style is therefore not originally a quality to be acquired but simply the way in which the elements of the discourse order themselves in the mind or on paper when one loves them for themselves. In *L'Education*, Flaubert is categorical:

> Extended to all the elements, he related everything to himself, and all of himself to everything, he became concretized in his *vocation*, in his mission, in the *fatality of his genius* and his labor, a vast pantheism *which passed through him and reappeared* in Art. Organ of this necessity, *transition of these two terms*, he considered himself henceforth without vanity or complacency. What a small place he felt he occupied *between inspiration and realization!* If he valued his talent, it was in comparing it to that of others, not in admiring it with regard to the beauty of what he must say.

The "great" writer—for Jules is great, as we know—is nothing more than a mediator. Everything is done through him but almost without his concurrence. The essential thing is that he should be an image himself. Then the exterior—the imaginary unity of being and nothingness playing through the "accidental"—is internalized in him in order to be reexternalized in the imaginary unity of language envisaged, through particular words, as a means of noncommunication. More simply, through this medium the world is made speech. This, says Flaubert, is a *necessity*. In other words, the imaginary relationship between the world and language exists before him, will exist after him. An individual need only be determined by his impossibility of being, however, to become an image and a computer of images so that style is actualized through him and *almost* by itself. Between inspiration (the universe-image that is internalized) and realization (the

223

speech-image that reflects it in its being) Jules is conscious of playing a minimal role: "what a small place he occupies!" No *activity.* Beginning with Flaubert, a tendency appears in literature that aspires to empty the work of its author. It is not simply a matter of challenging "literary portraits," à la Sainte-Beuve, in the name of the *Selbstständigkeit* of the accomplished masterpiece, which refers only to itself; indeed, this attitude—which will later lead to "formalism" taken in itself, constitutes a regression toward classical objectivism. The current born of Flaubert (and of his twin, Baudelaire, although the latter, more individualist, makes capricious movements back to subjectivity) is sharply focused, especially in the Symbolist period, by Mallarmé, who in his conception of theater rejects at once characters, action, and dramaturgy so as to preserve only the stage, "majestic overture whose grandeur we come into the world to envisage." He holds, moreover, that the Stage and the Book are "equivalent translations of the work." And the book that he conceives of producing "by an operation called Poetry" relegates (like the Stage) the operating subject to the rank of fortuitous means, necessary but undistinguished, which must become enshrouded in anonymity. For him, as for many an author of his generation, there is a kind of blind *conatus* of Nature which, through human mediation, aspires to flow into language in order to fulfill itself there and become the immanent being of words that express it. On this level a devaluation of the practical subject is effected: action is no more; forgotten subjectivity becomes the pure site where Nature and Language coincide, the one becoming internalized, the other externalized. As a result, despite the futile multiplicity of writings, there is but a single Book, whose pages, still blank, will tell everything for all time, and will reduce the great writers of the past to the rank of scribblers. This is just what Flaubert thinks: there is only one book to write—whether its title is *Saint Antoine* or *Bouvard et Pécuchet.* And everything must be in it, of course. Less subtle than Mallarmé's sylph of chill ceilings, he sometimes envisages this everything in the form of a *summa.* But that is immaterial here—what matters is the lineage. We shall encounter even in the twentieth century, after the First World War, when the partisans of automatic writing base the revelatory metaphysical splendor of language on the provisional annihilation of that bourgeois part of ourselves, the Ego.[41] And certainly the Surrealists would have been infuriated if they had imagined the results of automatic writing as fragments of style: for

41. The *word* they still use. But they give it another meaning: surreality.

them it was the mystery of the Word disengaged by the death of the Subject from its practical functions, bearing witness at once to being and to great desire, and breaking down with the arrogant strangeness of its objectless designations the pitiful barriers of fear that enclose the little ghetto called reality. But Flaubert, whom the ideology of his epoch restrains from daring even to conceive of these audacities, is not saying anything different. What he calls style in '44 is actually language *in person,* not as it is spoken but as it speaks itself, all alone, in the ears of an inspired soul who has only to write at its dictation.

By this suppression of the writer the Surrealists mean to transform the world: there is no act, but one must become alert to the subterranean forces that will change the world. For them, the idea of literature has merged with that of imagination. Mallarmé, more skeptical, believes in imagination. But he sees it as a negative power: he fears that Drama—and, quite as likely, the Book—are merely a dream; how can one abolish chance with that toss of the dice that is, despite everything, the beginning of all discourse—and consequently discourse as a whole? He dies saying: "*It would have been so beautiful,*" but perfectly certain in his wreckage that "nothing has taken place but the place." Whatever the modest and arrogant greatness of Mallarmé, the hero, Flaubert is superior to him as well as to the Surrealists for having begun by a radical *epochē,* or "pause"; put in parenthesis, neither world nor language are real, both are imaginary; the image of things is rendered through word-images. And certainly words are themselves also things, at least as he takes them, but he yokes these things together in such a way as to make them render their mute imaging power; of his conception of style we might say, like Mallarmé speaking of his investigations, that the vocables must reciprocally ignite each other with their fires. But Mallarmé's sentence is willfully paradoxical: those that ignite each other were extinguished, and, since *all* are extinguished, what flame is left for kindling? To this question, Mallarmé gives an excellent answer, which we do not intend to articulate here. Flaubert gives another: *practically,* they are extinguished; all shine and are reflected in each other if the quietist *imagines* them. Imagining a vocable is the opposite of observing it: one is fascinated by it, and without even seeing it clearly one takes it as a springboard of the dream, grasps its form, its taste, its color, its density, its appearance—traits themselves imagined *on the basis* of a real structure—as revelatory of its hidden being, of the immanent presence of the signified in the signifier. This is asking the rich word "Constantinople" somehow to *make present to us* the old Turkish city it designates, its

225

narrow, dirty streets, its populace, its veiled women, all of it with a certain irreducible quality—that special odor belonging to every city—which is doubtless not the *real* quality it offers to travelers but which, for someone who has not gone there, renders it in its idiosyncrasy as irreducible. To dream about words is to derealize them as one has derealized the world, to choose them and match them as a function of the dream—or, rather, within that dream and in order to continue it. Is this a dream about writing? Is it writing? Flaubert's answer will explain his optimism. At the time he was writing *Novembre*, his head was filled with symphonies, but he understood nothing about music. He kept his ruminations distinct from the practical activity of the composer. The composer too, before organizing his sonorous masses, has musical schemes in mind, musical images. But the difference is that the composer imagines harmonic relationships, whereas the young Gustave dreamed that he imagined them: he had no melody in this head but an empty, global intention aspiring to a nonexistent melody—not even as image. For few people *hear sounds* (though all hear noises), and not many more *see colors*. At this time, Gustave also had an activist conception of art. He would always maintain that conception, but *for other people:* work! work! roll up your sleeves, etc. But the comparison of the artist with the "good worker," frequent as it is in his correspondence, must not lead us astray.[42] In '44, literature is not a labor, it is a state of grace. The disaster of January obviously could not engender symphonies in Gustave's head: it is not thus that one changes, one is changed. But words are another matter: there was already a semidictionary in his thought. At Pont-l'Evêque he is conscious of his impossibility of living: this is what disposes him to dream about words, to seek their beauty, made of real but unrealized qualities and of imaginary extensions; useless, language offers him the world, which he is hanging onto by a mere thread. He assembles words according to his taste, according to their affinities, for all the unreality these verbal bouquets suggest to him. This is dreaming, of course. But that is just what one calls writing—provided a movement of one's hand fixes these directed dreams on paper. Thus the great writer is not an activist, and his vocation is inscribed nowhere in the very real convolutions of his brain. He is, rather, someone absent: far from using language, the first condition for having genius is that he should refuse *to make use of it.* Shall we say it uses him? Not even that. This human image, unrealized by the im-

42. We shall return to this in order to make explicit its multiple meanings.

possibility of being, of acting, reveals the imaginary dimension of the linguistic whole. It is on this level that language, in him, will speak itself all alone. Practical people are already *spoken:* the moving sidewalk of commonplaces runs through them. The dead man of Pont-l'Evêque does not escape the rule: language speaks itself in him. But it is wholly gratuitous; the words exert a mutual attraction, ignite each other with reciprocal fires, organize themselves; finally, indistinguishable from the objects they denote, they become the stuff of dreams. He need merely observe them and there he is, like Jules, a great and serious writer.

In other words, *no gift.* The matter is settled. One becomes an Artist by *conversion.* When one has been constrained by a long series of failures to effect a *radical reversal* and, having become an image oneself, to dissolve the real in the heart of the imaginary, there is—since everything is image—no difference between imagining that one is writing and writing what one imagines with imaginary words. The *practical* man, even if he were to devote all his time to reading good authors and to "making" literature, could not—in principle—be a writer. By contrast, you have only to do a somersault and Art is given to you as part of the deal: it is a word to designate the choice of unreality. And style is merely the result and symbol of the effected conversion. Let us not exaggerate, however: imaginary as the Artist may be—and despite the loss of his Ego, which disappeared at the moment of the great shipwreck—it is an *individuated* image; when he receives the accidental and gives us back the immutable, it must be understood that—as a meditor—he is Janus-faced, accident-prone, therefore himself accidental, and yet turned toward the eternal. Accident in him is what remains of his facticity, that is, his memory and the stages of the *particular* Calvary that has made him topple into the impossible. In this sense, his Art—or directed reverie—produces the immutable by coloring it with an accidental nuance, which is certainly unsought and, from one point of view, fixes the limits of the Book, or its determination, insofar as it is negation. From another point of view, however, this almost ineffable coloration, often unperceived by the reader, indicates the necessity—imposed on the real and practical sector as well as on the imaginary—of *incarnation.* The idea, whatever it is, must become incarnate and, hence, singularized in some way, must make itself glimpsed through a particular facticity as both its reason for being and its negation, its beyond. Thus the author's idiosyncrasy appears as the facticity of the work, but in the inside-out world of the imaginary, instead of receiving facticity, as we all do, as contingency, as exteriority at the heart of interiority, the work seems to produce it. In this case, the incarnation becomes an object of worship. This is what Jules calls *originality*. Thus the residue of an individuality which sank at the time of the disaster is taken up again by this eternal and imaginary object, the work, and perpetuates itself as the singularity of the immutable. But of course this idiosyncrasy is not sought for itself; it colors the work in progress while the artist is absorbed in the imaginary capture of the immutable as the substance (the strict equivalence of being and nonbeing) that allows itself to be discovered through accidents. We are far from Romantic individualism here, and this is not what *creates style*; it merely lends it its "originality." Unlike Chateaubriand, Jules does not write to perpetuate his person through the savor of his words, the organization of his sentences and their shape: for him, writing is not meant to delineate his Ego through and in the structures of his discourse. His Ego is dead, along with his passions and his hopes; the purpose is the *Book*, that is, the "vast pantheism which passes through him and reappears in art." Originality is not aspired to for itself: it must never be thought of; that would be to limit the work, to reduce "pantheism" to the wretched viewpoint of a particular subjectivity; rather, it comes of itself, and in a work that must depersonalize the accidental it is what Gide called the Devil's part. Here we encounter for the first time what will later be called Flaubert's "objectivism." It must be recognized that this objectivism is highly nuanced. Yet we cannot doubt that it is a result of the crisis: it is the loss of the Self, a subjective and dated event, which, if it hasn't produced it, has at least completed it.[43] In this sense the absolute-subject, one imaginary matrix of three trans-

43. Various earlier passages from the *Correspondance* indicate that Flaubert found it increasingly repugnant to put himself in his writings. From this point of view, *Novembre* is a farewell to lyricism. But the reasons he gives for this repugnance are not of a literary order: he is afraid, that's all. This gloomy young man, falsely open but actually closed around his anomaly, detests himself and wants to hide his Self, or at the very least cover it up: if the Others perceived it, they would mock him, which his bristly vulnerability could not bear. In the first *Education*, it is otherwise: there is no longer anything to hide since the Ego is suppressed. The objectivism, here, is direct: the goal of literature is to express the imaginary totality of the cosmos through the imaginary totality of language. On this level originality is possible, for it does not express the reality and the passions of a person, or even his anomaly, but merely reflects his insertion in the world and moreover sublimates it, and since the work, detached from the author, reproduces it in the imaginary as the free incarnation of the all—in the way that the Christian God voluntarily made himself man. Flaubert makes us understand, in his way, that the work in its very impersonality must be a "singular universal."

finite hypostases, is none other than the proud replacement, fictive and empty of all singular content—unless, perhaps, the abstraction of a nuance—of an Ego that unhappiness has killed.

Nonetheless, he could be said to have failed to communicate the incommunicable, a task the Romantics left to their successors. But this is not the case. To the realistic reader, of course, he transmits nothing but the fascinating proposal to become unrealized in turn. If this reader, who is in any case Flaubert's direct interlocutor, yields to the temptation, if he turns himself into an *imaginary* reader of the work—which he must if he is to grasp the meaning behind the significations—then all the unsayable, including the task of plum pudding, will be allusively revealed to him.

To understand the signification Flaubert assigns, in full consciousness and quite explicitly in *L'Education*, to the reversal that transforms a negation of negation into affirmation, we must return to his Manichaeism. His gradual conviction, beginning in '38, that he was a washout did not come to him merely from a few literary failures, debatable in any case, but from ideological considerations whose origins, as we have shown, go back to his early childhood. How could he have remained blind to the contradiction that sets the obsessive contents of his first writings against the spontaneous faith he had, at the time, in his genius? Marguerite, Djalioh, Garcia, Mazza are born to suffer; telling of their sufferings, he believes he is making the world see how it is, and he is all the more sincere in that his creatures are, above all, his incarnations. After that, how are we to assume that the author who thus projects himself into these sorrowful martyrs can escape the iron law on his own account? He shows us souls tormented in proportion to the greatness of their desire. And what desire is greater, crazier, more magnanimous than that of being an Artist and producing Beauty in this base world? The conclusion is self-evident: he who writes *Quidquid volueris* must be punished in his literary ambition as much as and more than Djalioh in his love. If he had pushed his conclusions to the limits, the adolescent would have had to tell himself: I am writing the Passion of Man, but since it is true, I am condemned to write badly. At the time, obscure to himself, he allowed himself to be carried away by the pleasure of eloquence, and, with understandable inconsistency, as a writer he felt himself escaping the human condition, which he had been presenting to us as ours and his. After the first defeats, his eyes are open: since we are in the hands of the Great Deceiver, everything is deception. The passion to write, the feeling of being doomed, the tears an adolescent spills over his genius, this world of dark, rich thoughts crowding into him and demanding to be spoken are so many pieces that commit him slowly and surely to the way chosen by Satan. Precisely because he wanted talent and fame in the sincerity of his heart, the adolescent will become a bad writer; when he realizes it, astounded, exhausted, it will be too late: he will never be able to stop writing, any more than he will be able to write well.

It is as if Gustave, between '38 and '44, were questioning himself on the misfortunes of men and his own misery, as if he were wondering whether we victims of the Devil are not his accomplices. Indeed, for this Manichaeist, man and Satan have struck a permanent fool's bargain: we claim to win *in this world below,* which is indeed *his;* he immediately offers us pernicious help, he sends us his auxiliaries, adept at leading us astray while pretending to help us; if we accept his help, we have only ourselves to blame for our defeat. In short, here below, in the real world, he who wants to win is a sure loser. Mazza suffers desire of the flesh for a man of flesh and blood, Garcia maneuvers for honors and power. And the artist? He counts on his talent—a gift that would be *real* if it existed—in order to attain that sumptuous *reality,* Fame, and perhaps that other reality which sometimes flows from it, Opulence. Gustave is well placed to know all about it, he who observed at the age of seventeen: "I am jealous of the life of great artists, the joy of money, the joy of art, the joy of opulence, all those together." Indeed, he is full of Flaubert ambition—which sits so badly with his passivity—and of the familial utilitarianism; his dreams of luxury, of course, give him access to the pure imaginary, but in the daily course of life he knows the value of money. He finds in himself the desire to shine in society, to dominate, to arouse the admiration of some in order to be avenged for the contempt of others. He always wanted Art to raise him above the earth, but looking more closely he finds entirely earthly reasons for his love of Beauty. If beyond the work undertaken he still has mundane motivations—were it only the need to escape his class and his projected profession—does he not contaminate unreality by subordinating it to secular ends? Isn't that precisely what prevents him on principle from writing well, since the preoccupations hidden in his heart suffice to preserve for language—even indirectly conditioned by them—its practical reality, its quotidian weight? Thus, far from being born of the free play of words without men, the sentences he traces have been, despite himself, extracted from daily human discourse, and instead of aiming at simplicity he will be constrained to hide their native vulgarity beneath the false disorders of eloquence or the feeble ruses of rhetoric. And *what* will he speak about if not his own concerns? If he still needs the respect of men, it is because he sees them from below, never from above, contrary to what he claims; how can one understand them if one depends on them? How can one grasp the dreadful and marvelous unity of the microcosm and the macrocosm if—solely from the desire to please— one is bound by the chains of humanity? Captive of his all too human passions—and pride is one of them—the writer will say of men only what they say of themselves among their own; he will tell them the stories they tell each other in the salon, in the smoking room, in a futile effort to tell them better. In short, he will be a *realist:* that is, he will reflect to them the flat image of their interests and their agitations; subjecting fiction to the real, he will not grasp the *qualitative* difference that separates the two and will try to use the imaginary not *for itself* but as the means of suggesting reality. Flaubert felt it is enough to share *one* human goal to share them all. The artist would claim only fame, he *wants to win,* therefore he seeks the Beautiful where he cannot find it: he is condemning himself for nothing. Thus, says the Catharist, no one can achieve salvation living on this earth, for we have only to lift a finger to participate in its endemic evil.

If this is so, what can be done to triumph over Satan? Nothing, since the Evil One is lord of the real and everything "to be done" depends on real means to change reality. But the question is badly formulated. Rather, one must ask if there are limits to his power, and if the course of things, though ruled by him, can sometimes be arrested and produce tornadoes or cyclones in man that the Evil One is powerless to contain. In this case, the answer is clear: if the false vanquisher always loses, one must lose in order to win. Read: to be led by circumstances to lose prematurely, before the date fixed by the Prince of Darkness, to sink to the bottom, to be annihilated while living and, without creating the shipwreck oneself, to consent to it deep down, to adhere to it passively but closely, to make onself seem even heavier in order to hasten the journey to the bottom of the abyss, which is none other than Nonbeing: since the Devil is the all-powerful master of Being, he is powerless over Nothingness. If an accident along the way causes a hitch in the story by way of *realizing* in the case of an otherwise ordinary man the *impossibility* of being, and if that man does not die of it, he will live this failed death, little as he is penetrated by it, as the mundane reverse side of a birth into nonbeing, his own realm, where neither Satan nor his agents will pursue him. In order to trick the Devil, Jules has taken advantage of the circumstances and plunged, like certain insects when they feel threatened, into a false death. No more movement, no more desire, he must hold his breath, agree *in good faith*, insofar as he can, that he has lost everything, even honor, even the transcendence that distinguishes man from things. He lies on his back and has nothing in his head but the consciousness of his impossibility. His body remains in the hands of the Devil, who doesn't hesitate to torture him with a good dose of electric shocks. But the impossibility of being has cast him out of the world and its ends into the infinity of unrealizable possibles (some of which might be—for others—made the object of a realization but appear to the impossible man as pure nonbeings to be contemplated). By the same token, turning back to the real, the impossible man discovers its share of nothingness and grasps nonbeing as an integral part of all human enterprise; better, the real appears to him as the sector of those possibles that might be defined as disguised impossibilities.[44]

What the Devil does not know is that the absolute void belongs to the imaginary, and that the reclining figure he torments feels the work he could not *do* being born and organized in himself. Jules-Flaubert, blank-faced, lets it grow, mute, unreal, almost inattentive, so as not to attract the attention of Satan, but knowing secretly that "Every atom of silence / Is the chance of a ripe fruit" (Paul Valéry, "Palme"). When at last the conjoined influence of three transfinite hypostases will raise his somnambulistic hand to make him transcribe *anything*—images of words aspiring to images of things—the Evil Lord will not be able to stop it.

He can still do harm; the work as a center of derealization escapes him. But ordinarily it has real consequences, and he will not hesitate to act on them: the relation of the author to his book, that of the book to the public. Jules will thwart the Deceiver by refusing to leave the imaginary, where he is ensconced. He knows that he would lose his ataraxia if he were taken with real passion for one of his novels or plays, if he saw it as the fruit of his flesh, if he acknowledged it as his objective reality. So he is careful to detach himself from it; the finished work no longer belongs to him: "He prefers his conceptions,[45] but he can hardly remember his own works, even more indifferent to

44. From the fact that so-called practical successes are actually secret failures.
45. Read: his works, at the moment he conceives their themes and subject.

their destiny once they *are produced*[46] than he was anxious, earlier, at their birth." This curious sentence will trigger memories in the reader: we have already seen that Gustave repeatedly depicted himself as more concerned with his future works than with those in progress. For him it was a psychological trait, and he complained of it: it was because, he said, that dreamed-of Future continually disappointed him. As for the writing he was going to finish or had just completed, he did not feel indifference toward it but, more usually, disgust. A sentiment that was justified, according to him, because the work was good only as a dream—that is, in the future—and because he had no talent. But in the passage we have just cited the tone has changed; what was presented as an emotional trait manifesting the excessive distance between his desires and his means he now gives as the result of the death of the passions: Jules is a great writer precisely because his passions are dead. Hence, we should not expect him to like his works. He allows them to "be produced." And the reason he preserves a certain tenderness for the future work is no longer hope, nor his discontent with the writing in progress; it is just that this work, slowly taking shape, is merely a dream to the first degree, while the other, imprecise, without defined contours but rich in promise, is the dream of a dream, a dream to the second degree. The first, moreover, is *directed:* one trusts in the void, but one knows more or less what one expects of it. The second, insofar as one has put nothing of oneself into it, remains a free play of imagination. It will be observed, however, that Gustave, who previously exulted in the ambitiousness of his projects, depicts for us in Jules a calmer sort of author: he "prefers" his conceptions. No more. This isn't saying much, since completed books merely elicit his indifference. For this reason one perceives that the psychological trait mentioned so often by Gustave between the ages of sixteen and twenty is elevated, in the first *Education,* to the dignity of an *ethical imperative:* "If you really want to write, don't grow enthusiastic about anything, not even what you are writing or will write." To like what one does would be to break the dream and to fall back under Satan's rod. For the same reason his fits of disgust too have disappeared: Gustave abandoned his manuscripts in horror; Jules ends his with just the necessary amount of concern to control the operations.

As far as the public is concerned, the best solution is to eschew it.

---

46. I have italicized this part of the sentence: it signifies clearly that Gustave feels *passive* in relation to the object which produces *itself* in him.

On this ground the Devil could take an easy revenge: he will not prevent Jules from being the means by which masterpieces are written; but if the unhappy man allows his plays to be performed, he can have them hooted down. Shrewdly, the young author writes for no one. Professional critics are dismissed, and readers as well: who, then, should judge the work—or the life contemplated through death—if not the dead man, who views all things and the work itself from the viewpoint of eternity? In this way the Book acquires all its metaphysical importance: it has no need to be read in order to exist: "Is the song of the nightingale less beautiful for not being heard? Is the scent of flowers less fragrant for not being inhaled through nostrils . . . but allowed to evaporate in the air and rise toward the sky?" If men are one day authorized to open one of his books, it will not be to bestow upon it, by their massive approval, a depth and density it still lacked or possessed only potentially. No, they will simply be given permission to admire the finished object; the reading will be like saying a mass, they will add nothing to it. Jules sometimes—rarely—dreams of getting published "so as to penetrate the minds [of men], to become incarnate in their thoughts, in their existence, to see them venerate what he venerates and be animated by what kindles him." In short, the reader is a relative being: he can be determined by the work, imbued with ideas of death and beauty, but he gives nothing in return. For the living-dead, writing is a necessity; publishing is optional, and superfluous besides. It is a matter of his own generosity. And if, weary of solitude, he allows himself to wish for fame, that is no problem: the man-image, without leaving his armchair, will give himself over to it *in the imaginary.* As soon as it is evoked, all of fashionable Paris crowds into the theater: Jules, deliciously moved, listens to the applause. Doesn't he know he deserves it? He has played his hand: his work will not leave the imaginary world. Jules is king of the unreal provided he never leaves it. Sickened, Satan goes off, pretends to forget him. Such is the "Loser wins" of the first *Education:* if I lose on the canvas of the real, I win, as a direct result, on that of unreality. In short, this may well appear to be the underlying meaning that Flaubert, in '45, attributes to his neurosis: it has intentionally brought together the conditions required mathematically to grant him genius. What would he think of this interpretation?

Well, first, that it confirms what we have tried to establish in this chapter. Flaubert's relation to art is the key to his neurosis; conversely, his neurosis has proposed a solution to his problems as a writer: by radicalizing his passivity, it has allowed him to discover the advantage he could derive from it and the literary form that was suited to him—which only a passive agent could produce. There was probably neurotic invention between January '44 and January '45. We can affirm that everything was present from the first attack because, as I have said, the strategies—pathological or not—are temporalized. Moreover, it is clear that the properly neurotic elements in the first *Education* are inseparable from the poetic Art Gustave articulates there. Jules's relations with the public, his fear and his desire to be published, the dreams of glory that arise from autosuggestion and contradict his misanthropy and his sequestration—all these things are incontestably morbid, but at the same time we must recognize them as strict extensions of his aesthetic attitude: if in order to be the *medium* of art one must become a human image, one cannot realize oneself without ceasing to be an artist. In this sense we might say that Flaubert in '45 is a man who *believes he is imaginary* (the negative, pithiatic, and neurotic reverse of metamorphosis) *because* this belief is indispensable to the conception and execution of works of art that suit his passivity (the positive side, an intuition of the fundamental relation of this man to this art, the invention of one through the other, and vice versa).

We should add that Flaubert's testimony, though in many respects contestable, remains that of the interested party and presupposes an underlying connivance with the reported event. In this sense, that strange wager of "Loser wins" must have taken place at Pont-l'Evêque; otherwise, where would the author have found it? Between *Novembre* and *L'Education* there is a gap. As an adolescent and a young man, Flaubert, out of the masochism and sadism of resentment, *was losing in order to lose.* Certainly he took pride in annihilating himself in a perfect shipwreck: unhappiness was a sign of election; only great souls, the victims of great desire, would sink totally. This imaginary dolorism is without any doubt at the origin of "Loser wins." Except that he laid claim to a *total* engulfment; nothing resurfaced, the sea threw up no jetsam: mad, dead, or ruined, the vanquished could neither profit from his supreme dignity, nor express it in a work, nor enjoy it, nor even recognize it. Strictly speaking, only a witness could affirm in the abstract that his failure marked, or even produced, his greatness *by destroying it.* Jules, on the other hand, who is at first mediocre, is made great *during his lifetime* by his failures which "providentially" raise him to the heights. This invention, well enough in accord with his previous pessimism, does not raise him up entirely. It is formulated, it seems, in these terms: radicalize pessimism and it turns back on itself as optimism. Something happens in January '44, an irreducible and intentional transformation that Gustave *felt* (hence his strange calm), meditated on at length, and thought he could explain—something he interpreted in the final pages of *L'Education*. In other words, the appearance of "Loser wins" with the declaration of the neurosis is incontestable. Is *this* the version of "Loser wins" that Gustave offers us? That is the real question.

Rereading the story of Jules, we ascertain that Flaubert dissimulates or deliberately ignores the neurotic *fact*. We have been able to disengage it from his narrative because we know the prior events and because, in the light of those events and the confidences that escape him in his correspondence, the pathological aspect of the end of *L'Education* is immediately manifest. But this happens despite himself. He wanted, to the contrary, to *rationalize* his unsayable experience and, as usual, to universalize it. His reasons are clear: he must reassure himself and give himself proof that the humble optimism shining in the night is not the illusory consequence of the neurosis but can be supported with rational proofs. In short, by assigning to Jules the destiny he dreams of for himself, he seizes the occasion to write for his own use a theoretical and practical treatise on "Loser wins," from which the suspect singularity of his adventure will be excluded. It is a question of showing by a dialectical reversal that the radical failure of man is turned necessarily into the success of the Artist. No mediation, he rejects any help: if Providence counts for anything in this business, it is for heaping on him, *as a man,* misfortunes beyond his hopes. But the subsequent aboutface happens by itself. Later, writing to Louise, he will present his crisis of '44 as the *mathematical* outcome of his unhappy youth; at the time of *L'Education*, he would prefer to say that his genius is merely the mathematical consequence of his false death at Pont-l'Evêque, despair pushed to the extreme. The existence of his illustrious predecessors no longer seems to trouble him: no doubt he has persuaded himself that they were, like him, fabulous failures. He remarks, indeed, in a subsequent letter, that the *person* of Shakespeare entirely eludes him, so much profundity did this author put into the description of contradictory passions that he could not have felt simultaneously. In the light of the first *Education,* we can clarify this difficult text: Shakespeare manages to describe such diverse and intense passions not because they inhabit him at the same time but because, to the contrary, he no longer feels them except through imagination. He can put himself in everyone's place because he is no longer anyone himself: nothing individual is left in this "giant" but a rich memory that will become the very "originality" of his work. The example is a good one: no one knows who Shakespeare was. Gustave can therefore affirm without fear of lying that this author lived twenty or thirty years, like everyone else, in violence and confusion, then died, and subsequently began to write. Gustave himself, moreover, introduces the word "necessity" into his discourse: "A vast pantheism passes through him and reappears in art. [Jules becomes] the *organ* of this necessity, the transition between these two terms." The link of the cosmos to language becomes necessary from the time that the passivity of the artist reveals both of them to him as imaginaries. For this reason the genius of the man-image is fatal. The reversal is thorough: the curse of the Father is turned against itself; by leading the son from failure to failure, to the consciousness of the impossibility of being, he has provoked in him that choice of nonbeing which is genius. And if one should ask why great Artists are so rare in the Hell that is the world, Gustave would probably respond that most people discover too late the implacable denial the world sets against their aspirations, that they deceive themselves, lie to themselves, or else that their shipwreck, as total as his own but more adeptly managed, extends over their whole life, or, still more simply, that they are afraid of losing and deceive themselves to the end. Q.E.D. Neither God nor the Devil nor Father nor neurosis: all is *outside, before.* At a certain moment the world turns and the conversion happens alone, by itself: the freedom of the subject counts for nothing, that's for sure; it doesn't even exist. One can therefore articulate "Loser wins" in the language of the most rigorous determinism.

It is this very rigor that is suspect: we know quite well that it is abstract and that things could not happen this way. Until now, Gustave has adhered to his neurosis; suddenly he disengages from it and constructs, according to his experience, a reassuring but overly perfect model. This is why the difficulties begin, and if we examine his thought a bit more closely, we shall quickly discover the vagueness and imprecision beneath its false exactitude.

Could there not be two versions of "Loser wins" for him, the more recent and superficial of which would find its lucid and rationalized expression in the character of Jules, transformed for the needs of the cause? This version would originate in a vague intuition of the earlier one, which, masked, prelogical, aberrant, appeared in the original crisis or immediately afterward as its fundamental teleological structure. We shall try to establish this thesis by examining Gustave's behavior during the years 1845–47, then in a more general way the relation he establishes in his maturity between inspiration and work, and finally the true meaning of the second and last "happy ending" he ever gave to *one of his narratives:* the *assumption* of *Saint Julien.*

The Real Meaning of "Loser Wins"

A. Gustave Flaubert from 1845 to 1847

Is Jules the incarnation of Gustave? Not entirely. Or perhaps we should say, *not yet*. During the long months of the winter of '44, incapable of writing, he continued to reflect on what had happened to him and tried to refine his *theory* of "Loser wins." He *will be* a great writer, that is no longer in doubt. The spring is coming, he will be allowed to write. Is he going to measure himself from now on against the masterpiece clamoring to be born? No, the second son of the Flauberts is sufficiently prudent: he knows he must first husband his strength and become capable of supporting his difficult mission of unrealizing being, and must put to the service of Art his tiresome habit of living through imagination. He has not written for months; he must now reestablish contact with literature. The simplest way of doing this is to resume the work that was interrupted and complete it. He is modest: he knows he cannot yet infuse it with his genius—that power, still blind, almost unaware of itself, which, if he wanted to use it, would embarrass him with its chaotic violence. No, it is not yet time to spread his wings; he will tell the end of Henry's loves, and what happens to Jules. In the same style—an excellent exercise. And, above all, without forcing the tone. But when speaking of Jules he cannot refrain from announcing the good news. He could not, of course, have written a single line such as those his hero is reputed to jot down just for fun, but he can already fix with assurance the behavior, the habits, and the inner life of a true Artist. He can do so because he has only to depict himself, and also because he already has the faculty of amplifying certain powers that are still embryonic in him but whose development he can foresee. Ordinarily—as every novelist knows—nothing is more difficult than showing the private thoughts of an exceptional character: indeed, the greatest talent scarcely suffices to describe an average man. When it is absolutely necessary to enter a great mind in a fictional framework, one contrives to have it seen obliquely, in eclipse, so as to make it vanish as quickly as possible. But Gustave the apprentice puts his back into it, he installs himself in his hero and reveals his inner life; accordingly, we shall know how a genius lives, how he thinks, and what he feels. For Jules, in Gustave's view, is merely a future self-portrait, or, put another way, a present portrait but exalted by the future. So I am, so I will be, since one cannot be, since one cannot become an Artist without being like this. It is this collision of the future and the present that gives Jules—from chapter 26 on—that curious aspect consisting of real density (he is the Other, the Artist I am not yet become, catapulted over the invalid I am) and, at moments, extreme abstraction. For this man is sometimes merely an *ars poetica*. The enterprise is curious, and to my knowledge no one else has dared to undertake it: to say not what one is, but what one will surely be—what boldness! During the summer and autumn of '44, Gustave is not out of danger, he can work but never for long or without tiring; yet this is the moment he chooses to *have confidence in himself*. For the first time he dares to believe in his lucky star; for the first and penultimate time—he will not return to it before *Saint Julien*—he persuades himself that the worst is the arduous but sure path leading from evil to good.

The manuscript was completed in January '45. It is not difficult to see why Gustave should take time out, so much the more so as his complete cure is slow to come. And then, as I have said above, the constant presence of Doctor Flaubert, quick to see the slightest improvement as a sign of returning health, dissuaded his son from writing too much. Yet if Gustave really saw Jules as the prophetic image of his future, it seems inconceivable that he wouldn't be impatient to throw himself into a new task to take stock of his powers. In any case, if he is not sure of himself or of the themes he wants to treat, if he objects that he is still maturing, one would expect him to throw himself at least into "that great study of style" which helped his character become a "great and serious writer." And he does nothing of the kind. With respect to the essential thing, which is to write, we can verify that, apart from the "scenarios" for his Oriental tale—sketched out, then abandoned—he produces nothing for *thirty-two months*. As for his reading, we shall return to the subject; in any event, from now on it has nothing in common with the vast program Jules imposed on himself. Had Gustave recovered after January '45? Did he immediately stop believing in "Loser wins"? Or did he never believe in it? That hardly seems possible. We shall not understand the meaning of his strange attitude without examining his occupations in detail.

January '45. He completes his novel, reads Shakespeare, does "a lot of Greek and reviews [his] history." On 3 March Caroline marries Hamard, and all the Flauberts, except for Achille and his family, accompany the young couple on their honeymoon. A sad journey: in no time at all everyone is ill; Achille-Cléophas has an eye infection; Caroline is again overcome by kidney pain; Gustave, exasperated by the presence of his brother-in-law, furious at "seeing the Mediterranean for the second time like a grocer," manages to have two nervous attacks. Everyone is bored, except perhaps for the young couple, who, I imagine, would still have preferred solitude. Flaubert, however, has literary projects: he "ruminates" on an Oriental tale, which he reckons on writing during the winter of 1845–46; reading the history of Genoa, he is seized by the "idea for a rather dry drama on an episode during the war with Corsica." Finally: "I saw a painting by Brueghel representing *The Temptation of Saint Anthony*, which made me think of arranging *The Temptation of Saint Anthony* for the theater; but I'm not the fellow for that job." [1] This letter is full of information. First of all, it informs us that Gustave conceived the idea for *Sept Fils du Derviche* right after finishing *L'Education* and perhaps even while working on it; in any case it was not later than March '45, since he expanded on the subject to Alfred when they were in Rouen together ("I'm *still* ruminating on my Oriental tale"). So it is not for lack of subjects that he hesitates to take up the pen: quite the contrary, in this letter, written in May, Gustave announces his decision not to touch his tale for *at least six months*. And since he is thinking primarily of *Derviche*, it is clear that the drama about the war with Corsica and *Saint Antoine* will be spaced out over future years. Thus, 1845, Gustave began to refine that rule of literary life which he would articulate to Louise in December '46: ". . . meditate a great deal . . . write as little as you can." We shall return to this. Meditate, ruminate, it's all the same. The period of gestation must be long, and one must take up the pen only at the last moment, when it can no longer be avoided. But we must also note the return of an old theme in a new guise: Gustave does not say that he reckons on writing his *Saint Antoine;* at the very most he will try, for "I'm not the fellow for that job." What other fellow? Shakespeare, perhaps? Or Goethe? We are no longer dealing with the

1. To Alfred, 13 May 1845, from Milan, *Correspondance*, 1:173.

241

"great man *manqué*," but despair and doubt have given way to an affected modesty. Gustave seems to believe he has grasped his limits: there are literary enterprises in which he can succeed, and the Oriental tale is among them since he does not doubt, in this month of May, that he will complete it the following year; there are other enterprises that demand capacities he doesn't have. Jules had genius; Gustave allows himself talent. Isn't this humility the height of despair? When one has so long dreamed of having genius, is there anything more laughable and more painful than discovering that one will really become second-rate? Isn't this proof, in any case, assuming Gustave believed the preceding winter that he was incarnate in Jules, that he has henceforth abandoned all illusion? Let us continue.

Here he is on his return to Rouen; he proposes to "apply himself as in the past to reading, writing and idling . . . Greek is on the agenda again, and if in two years I cannot read it, I will definitively send it packing; for I've dawdled over it for a long time without knowing anything." These fine plans date from 15 June. On 13 August they persist: "I have taken up Greek again, which I continue with perseverance, and my master Shakespeare." Around the same date he gives Alfred a few specifics: "I keep doing a little Greek.[2] I have finished Herodotus's *Egypt*. Three months from now I hope to be reading him easily; and in a year, with patience, Sophocles. I'm also reading Quintus Curtius. What a fellow, that Alexander! . . . Today I finished Shakespeare's *Timon of Athens*. The more I think about Shakespeare, the more overwhelmed I am . . . Last night in bed I read the first volume of Stendhal's *Le Rouge et le Noir*. A distinguished mind, it seems to me, a mind of great delicacy. The style is French, but is it *style*, true style, as it used to be and is unknown today?"[3] In the same letter he refers to a very different occupation: "I am still dissecting Voltaire's plays. It is tedious but may be useful to me later. One does come across some surprisingly stupid lines." This activity surprised Du Camp: "[Flaubert in '45] applied himself to a task whose utility I never understood. With pen in hand he studied the French theater of the eighteenth century, that is, the tragedies of Voltaire and Marmontel." We do not know how long Gustave persisted in this "task," but the notes he took form an entire file, which figures in the Franklin Groult collection under the title: "A portfolio with the title in

2. With Alfred, Gustave is as sincere as he can be. Note the modesty of that "keep doing a little," which contrasts with the "very much" of January '45, taken from a letter to Ernest.

3. To Alfred, *Correspondance*, 1:189.

Flaubert's hand: 'Dramatic Works of Voltaire.'"[4] In September '45, we find him again, joyously indignant, in the midst of reading Saint-Marc Girardin's *Cours de littérature dramatique:* "It is good to know in order to understand just how far stupidity and impudence can go." After this, information is lacking. Then come the deaths in the family: on 15 January '46, Achille-Cléophas; 21 March, Caroline. On 7 April he writes: I am going to set to work, at last! At last! I want, I hope to slog away enormously and for a long time." In the same letter he declares: "I have the feeling I am quite limited and quite mediocre. I am becoming an artist with difficulty, which makes me miserable. I will end up no longer writing a single line. I believe I could do good things, but I keep asking myself, what's the point?" On *Les Sept Fils du Derviche* he writes: "My Oriental tale has been postponed to next year, perhaps the year after that, perhaps for ever." As if to say that he is not writing and *does not want* to write. As for Greek, he acknowledges that circumstances prevent him from studying it. Curiously, however, he has been kept from it not for six months, as we might believe, but for *six years:* "For the past six years I have wanted to get back to Greek, and circumstances have been such that I still haven't got as far as the verbs." What has he been doing all this time? He daydreams, "enters into the Idea," goes "slightly crazy." In April he rereads Michelet's *Histoire romaine* ("antiquity makes me dizzy"). In June we find him again "working rather reasonably, about eight hours a day." He adds: "I am doing Greek, history; I am reading Latin. I get a little drunk on those worthy ancients, whom I have made into a sort of artistic cult. I endeavor to live in the ancient world; I will get there, with God's help." In another letter he reasserts that *he has lived there.* At the end of July '46, Louise Colet becomes his mistress. He writes to her on 12 September: "This evening I got back to work, but by forcing myself. For the six weeks I have *known* you . . . I have done nothing. I must snap out of this." In fact, he does snap out of it: "I am working quite a lot," he says three days later, "all day doing Greek and Latin, in the evenings, the orient." The Orient, of course, is with a view to his Oriental tale. But all he does is read. He has ordered books from Vasse, and has received them:

> Before the end of October . . . I will have finished these two small
> books. I dabble a little in the Orient for the odd quarter of an
> hour, not with a scientific purpose but a picturesque one. I seek
> color, poetry, sound, heat, beauty. I have read the Bagavad-Gita,

4. Cf. Bruneau, op. cit., pp. 573–74.

the Nala, a great work by Burnouf on Buddhism, the hymns of the Rig-Veda, the laws of Manou, the Koran, and a few Chinese books, that's all. If you can find me some collection of poetry, or of more or less amusing satirical songs composed by Arabs, Indians, Persians, Malays, Japanese, or others, you can send it to me. If you know of some good work [a review of books] on the religions or the philosophies of the Orient, let me know. As you see, the field is vast. But there is much less to be found than you think. You must read a great deal and the result is practically nil. There is a great deal of idle chatter in all this and not much else.

He adds, naturally: "I am still doing a little Greek, and I stuff myself with Latin poets." On 17 September, in a letter to Louise, *those* Latin poets are reduced to a single one, Virgil. Apart from this: "I am still reading my Indian drama, and in the evenings I reread good old Boileau, the legislator of Parnassus." A little later—27 September—we learn that he is going to "start reading my old Shakespeare from one end to the other, and I shall not abandon him this time until all the pages stick to my fingers." For several months he has not even mentioned his occupations; Louise has become irritated, he is trying to calm her; and then he is seeing Bouilhet, Maxime, and throwing himself into great literary discussions with them. On 5 December he confesses that he has done nothing more for a long time: "I am still not working. Monday, however, I will take advantage of my friend Du Camp's sleeping in to do a little Greek in the morning." At the beginning of '47, his reading has scarcely varied: "Today I just finished Byron's *Cain*.[5] What a poet! In about a month I shall have finished Theocrates." He complains of being "entangled in a host of things to read." He hastens to finish them: "I work as much as I can and I'm not making much progress. You would have to live two hundred years to have an idea of any kind." On 23 February: "I am continuing with my Greek, I am reading Theocrates, Lucretius, Byron, Saint Augustine, and the Bible." Not until the summer and his journey with Maxime will he agree to write the "reportage" in collaboration with his friend, which he then entitles *La Bretagne* and which will not be published in his lifetime. In September '47 he gets

5. This is probably a rereading. The Bidault inventory indicates that at Croisset there is a Byron in the Furne edition of 1830 (in six volumes). Certainly Flaubert procured it only after 1837: a letter to Chevalier proves that he did not possess it before this date. But at the time he had such admiration for this poet, it could not have been long before he acquired the volume.

down to work. In what frame of mind the following passage directly informs us: "We are now occupied with writing up our journey, and though this work demands neither great refinement nor previous detailed organization, I am so out of the habit of writing and grow so peevish over it, especially with regard to myself, that it continues to give me quite a lot of worry. It is like a man with perfect pitch playing the violin off key; his fingers refuse to reproduce accurately the sound he has in mind. The tears pour from the poor fiddler's eyes and the bow falls from his hands." We know the strange plan these two men devised: the odd chapters were to be done by Gustave, the even by Maxime. Flaubert quickly becomes disgusted: he reckoned at the end of September that he would finish "in about six weeks." At the end of December he completes the first revision and demands six weeks more "to correct the whole, delete repeated words, and prune a quantity of repetitions." Meanwhile, in letters that are unfortunately undated, he complains of this "exhausting" work. "For three and a half months I've been writing continuously, from morning to night. I am at the very limits of the constant frustration this brings me; I find myself in the constant impossibility of *rendering* it."

The idea of "bringing the Temptation of Saint Anthony" to the theater has run its course. But the first time he writes about it to Louise (he had aready *spoken* of it to her), he announces—just as he had done with the Oriental tale—that he has not yet set to work: "I am going to endeavor this winter to work rather violently. I have to read Swedenborg and Saint Theresa. I am putting off my *Saint Antoine*. Well, too bad. Though I had never counted on making something good out of it, rather write nothing than set about the task half-prepared."

These are the facts. Examining them even superficially, we are struck by one primary piece of information: from January '45 until the summer of '48, Gustave was afraid to write. *La Bretagne* was conceived by the two friends *together*, very likely under the influence of Maxime, who had never reflected on the art of prose; in any case, the decision was made in the exaltation of friendship. Subsequently, neither of the two authors could renounce the common commitment without losing face in the eyes of the other. Flaubert had been thrown into an enterprise he could not consider entirely *his*, since it was born of the *occasion* and not of an inner necessity. Moreover, he was writing only one chapter out of every two, and, curiously, in a letter to Louise he stresses the *impersonality* their method will give to this work. Indeed,

245

this is not the kind of anonymity he ordinarily has in mind: the author, he often says, must never appear but is hidden everywhere. This is not at all the case here: whatever the friendship binding them together, Gustave is in no way present in the chapters done by Maxime. For these reasons he judges himself *less responsible* and, by the same token, does not hide from Louise that he regards *La Bretagne* as a minor work. Thus he can venture to write. But as soon as he has decided to take up the pen, what anguish, what crying! We have cited several sentences which sufficiently testify to his anguish. We shall have occasion to present others still more meaningful: through this travel narrative, Art and the Artist are thrown into question. And the project, conceived in gaiety, becomes a torment as soon as it must be put into execution.[6]

As for his *personal* works—the "Oriental tale" and *Saint Antoine*—matters are still worse: he continually postpones the moment when he will have to set down the first word. Sometimes it is one pretext and sometimes another. Anything will do. Watching him order, then ingest, enormous numbers of works which are necessary, according to him, for his "preparation" but then admittedly have yielded nothing, we begin to wonder if he is not reading simply to delay the time when he will have to put his shoulder to the wheel. Of course, this is not altogether fair: we must also take account of his totalitarian and encyclopedic ambitions. Be that as it may, he has never gone so long without writing, never have his hesitations so clearly revealed his terror. How could he avoid being terrified? He has just declared at the end of *L'Education:* by a strict law, my radical failure has made me the genius I no longer hoped to become. It would be difficult to play a worse trick on yourself. After this conclusion, in effect, he *must* create a masterpiece or never write again. Nothing of what he conceives seems to him sufficiently beautiful: after his initial enthusiasm, he quickly detaches himself for fear of making a mistake and blindly adopting a subject unworthy of him, or one that turns out to be beyond his capacities. And this is nothing: if the subject holds up, he is afraid of the *realization;* from the first chapter or the first lines of dialogue, he will have demonstrated, he thinks, what he is really *worth.* And so he is paralyzed by two opposing forces: hope and the fear of being disappointed.

6. The manuscript completed, he is not so dissatisfied with it after all, since he asks Louise to give it to Gautier to read. More precisely, uncertain of the value of the work, accusing himself, perhaps, of excessive severity, he hopes that the less rigorous Gautier will be enthusiastic enough to persuade him to revise his own judgment.

Works and Readings

The tension here is merely superficial. The real reasons for his sterility lie elsewhere. Let us attempt to return to his occupations from '45 to '47 in order to examine them in the framework of a regressive analysis. He continually speaks of his "work": he "works," "hasn't worked for six weeks," promises "to work rather violently." What does work mean to him? He reads: Byron, Shakespeare, Theocrates, etc. What is reading for him? What importance do books and work have as factors in his neurotic equilibrium?

First of all, work. It is gathering documentation for his tale or for *Saint Antoine*, "doing Greek and Latin," analyzing, pen in hand, the dramas of Voltaire. Thibaudet was the first to signal the intention of failure, which is the common denominator of these diverse occupations.

Why "analyze" the dramas of Voltaire? One of his motives is evident to us in the fact that almost simultaneously he is reading Girardin's *Cours de littérature dramatique*. Around this time, two of his three literary projects are "dramatic." As we have seen, he sets himself the task of writing a play on the war with Corsica and bringing *La Tentation de Saint Antoine* to the stage. Bruneau has rightly observed, "The reason for this work is quite simple: Flaubert was practicing blocking out material, and the admirable composition of Voltaire's plays served him as models for his own scenarios."[7] But this motivation, real and deliberate as it is, does not entirely account for what has been called the work of "cretinizing." First of all, Bruneau's evaluation of the construction of Voltaire's plays seems to me entirely subjective. Is *Zaïre* so well constructed? Better than *Phèdre?*[8] Does the rigor of the plot, if we should really find it "admirable," prevent this play—the least objectionable of Voltaire's dramas—from being a mediocre work? We know Gustave's ambivalence with regard to Voltaire: he admires *Candide* infinitely but discovers some "surprisingly stupid lines" in the tragedies. How can an author so concerned with affirming the unity of form and content study the purely formal structures of a work whose content he finds contemptible—a work that he knows is now spurned by the public? Furthermore, if what he only recently called "thought" demands in each case a literary form that is proper to it and "renders it indirectly," why should Gustave, infused with Romantic

7. Bruneau, op. cit., pp. 573–74.
8. Flaubert liked Shakespeare better than Racine, but he liked Racine better than Voltaire as dramatist.

drama and a lover of Shakespeare, seek in the tragedy of the eighteenth century—which bent but did not abandon the rule of the three unities—a model for constructing his own works? Voltaire's composition is praiseworthy only if one first considers that he had to impose unity of place and time on his intricate plots. As to unity of action, as much can be said: Voltaire does not allow himself several parallel actions in the same play; yet we know that the Elizabethans did. Who is right? This is of little importance: the theater is living and its laws vary. What matters is that Flaubert opted for Shakespeare. He wrote many a scenario in his adolescence in which the plot extends over twenty years, historical plays in several settings, and above all in his dramas, as in his other writings, he wants to put the whole world. Under these conditions, the work he is "ruminating" upon requires another kind of unity in order to be a spatio-temporal totalization.[9] Isn't that why he studies Shakespeare, since he congratulates that writer on having put the whole universe into each of his great plays? Can we say that Shakespearean dramas are not remarkable for the rigor of their composition? This is true only if we take as exemplary the structures of tragedies, meaning a French type of *integration*. Besides, if anyone should declare that great works transcend genres, that the model is of little importance, and that the study of the classics will serve the post-Romantic writer, wherever he situates himself, by revealing to him a thousand tenuous bonds of interiority which can guide his inspiration beyond all the rules of a period, I should respond: then he should have "analyzed" Racine or, still better, Molière, for so many of whose plays he was both director and actor in his childhood, whose "composition" is far more austere and rigorous than that of *Zaïre* or *Oedipe*,[10] and whom, much later, Gustave himself will call a Romantic.[11] Does he really believe that this dissection of Voltaire's plays is a true apprenticeship in dramatic art? All authors are suitable; the only way to learn in this domain is to throw yourself instantly into creating. Gustave certainly understood this when it came to tales and stories. He was not doing an analysis of his favorite writ-

9. It will be noted that *Saint Antoine* somehow respects the unity of place (his hermitage) and of time (the *actual* duration of the temptation). But where is the action? And reality (the presence of Saint Anthony on this particular and specifiable summit) is so inextricably mingled with visions that one finds the *world* before one's very eyes, the dialectical totalization of three transfinitudes and their relations of reciprocity. The unity of the work lies elsewhere, and classical tragedy, with more modest ambitions, could not reveal it to him.

10. In particular because comic effects require skillful preparation and a tight plot.

11. To Léon Hennique, 3 February 1880, *Correspondance*, 8:371.

ers, he was practicing in relation to them what Chenier has curiously called "inventive imitation," that is, without pausing for dissection he moved immediately to synthesis. It was not a matter of borrowings or pastiches.[12] Instead of dissecting the cadaver of a work he infused it with his own life by *making it function* inside an enterprise that appropriated its guiding schemes and style while surpassing them toward original ends. The best example of this procedure remains *L'Anneau du prieur,* which is hardly different from the crib Gustave found in his book of narratives but has an astonishing depth that resides precisely in this minimal difference. The analysis of Voltairean tragedies, far from being a real means of assimilating the rules of dramatic composition, marks on the contrary the timidity of the young author, with his back to the wall, and serves him as an excuse not to write.[13] Isn't this precisely the reason he is so bored when taking notes on *Zaïre?* He carries out a delaying tactic, but his heart isn't in it. When he speaks of it, we find this odd formulation coming from his pen: "This may be useful to me later on." It has been dictated by the same utilitarianism— the detested Flaubert utilitarianism. Gustave uses the words an employee who wants to further his career might use: "I am taking a commercial accounting course twice a week. It is boring but may be useful to me later on." There is something just as crazy about the enterprise as about the justification he offers for it. All the more so as he is perfectly aware of the *uselessness* of his work; all his life he has said repeatedly in one form or another that there is no "craft" in literature. And this is true: since form and content are inseparable, every time an artist wants to implement a new conception, he finds a new task before him, and far from aiding him in his enterprise, the habits he has developed through his previous works become ossifications in his present enterprise, stereotypes that prevent him from adopting an

---

12. Although Gustave, very lucidly, had labeled as "pastiche" a tale—quickly abandoned, moreover—which was vaguely inspired by de Sade. He would have done better, in my opinion, to call it an "exercise in sadism."

13. Love of Flaubert would have to be carried to the point of delirium to claim, as one critic did, that his dissections of Voltaire helped him later, when he was working on the plan for *Madame Bovary.* In the first place, drama and fiction are so different that the author who knows how to "put together" a play is not necessarily capable of composing a work of fiction. The reverse is also true. When writers have tried their hands, successively, at dramatic art and at storytelling, the experience they acquired in the one mode could only hamper them in the other, they had to start afresh. Besides, Flaubert created the modern novel precisely because he never knew how to *put* his books *together:* happily for us, he was unaware of the "rules of composition." The reason *Madame Bovary* has the coherence of a growing plant and the flowing unity of a slow stream, the reason it reveals—despite "made up scenes"—a stammering, *natural* harmony, is that he was perfectly incapable of planning. We shall return to this.

adequate and truly free attitude toward his subject. He should therefore shed such habits as much as he can and renounce the facility
they provide.

We must therefore—as often happens with Gustave—seek the explanation of his conduct in what he says and not in what he means to
say. "This may be useful to me . . . although there are some surprisingly stupid lines in the tragedies." And of Saint-Marc Girardin's
Cours de littérature dramatique: "It is good to know [a bourgeois expression equivalent to "it is useful to know"], so as to understand just
how far stupidity can go." It will be noted that the "because . . . it is
stupid" of the second sentence corresponds exactly to the "although
. . . it is stupid" of the first. Isn't this "although," as Proust says, an
"unacknowledged because"? In this case, he would have chosen to
study Voltaire not *although* his tragedies are execrable but *because* they
are. Flaubert has remained the man of resentment who scours great
works in order to find weaknesses that will allow him to disparage the
author. Jules did not make a mystery of it, he even boasted about it:
"So he was in quest of the courage displayed by cowards; he sought
out the virtue practiced by the old and laughed at the crime committed by the good. This continual equality of man, in spite of himself
and wherever he is, seemed to him a kind of justice that humbled his
pride, consoled him for his inner humiliations, gave him at last his
real human character and put him back in his place." Flaubert will
maintain this attitude all his life, and to it we owe the second part of
Bouvard et Pécuchet, which was recently published.[14] Voltaire, the teller
of tales, is the object of his admiration. *Candide* is an "amazingly
great" work.[15] Perfect! Let us choose to study Voltaire the dramatist,
in short, a great man at his worst. All we shall get from it is a vague
notion of what not to do, and we shall feel a saintly pity for the human weakness of even the best.

Is this the only reason? No. Gustave does not know how to compose, we have seen that well enough in *Novembre;* he is highly aware
of it, and when he thinks about it, he is consumed with anguish. Nor
is he unaware that *L'Education,* with the abrupt hypertrophy of a secondary character at the expense of the protagonist, is not a model of
unity. And he has discovered the same principle of Art in totalization:
everything is subordinated to it; the iron law is that nothing must be
favored; detail, character, setting are there only to disappear by al-

14. An inventory intended to be exhaustive of all the stupidities that have escaped
from a pen.
15. To Louise, 1847, *Correspondance,* 2:67.

lusively announcing the all, which is ineffable and present in all its parts. To acquire techniques of composition therefore seems to him a vital necessity to the artist. He is throwing himself into Voltaire in order to still his anxieties for a moment. But what is the point of this vain enterprise of decomposition, whose vanity he is the first to acknowledge? there is *none* if he stays in the domain of the real. But why assume he has stayed there? What if this endeavor were merely a symbolic resurrection of his past pseudo-activity: from '42 to '44 he *made a show* of reading and analyzing the Civil Code, pen in hand. One might think he wanted to transfer an appearance of labor, from the law to Art. As if he had wanted, at one and the same time, to ridicule action in all its forms, even at the level of literary apprenticeship, and to justify himself by introducing into his artist's life a reminder of the tedium and torment of his life as a student; as if his work, unpleasant and stupid—like that of a monk copying manuscripts—were done not to put him in possession of a method but *to give him merit.* Justification? Merit? In whose eyes? It is too soon to say.

We can say, at least, that he is working when he "prepares" himself for his Oriental tale by ingesting one entire library—and another entire library including Swedenborg and Saint Theresa—to fill out his first *Tentation.* This time he has a positive purpose governing the whole enterprise: *to learn* about specific subjects. Let us look more closely, however. We shall see that this need for documentation, which appeared all at once and will not go away, functions here as an *alibi.* It is to document himself that he continues to put off his Oriental tale from one day to the next, to document himself that he defers *La Tentation* from summer to summer. And although this preparatory "work" might have other aspects, which we shall discern later, it is integrated along with these circumstances into the whole dilatory enterprise that occupies the years 1945–48. Is it work? To begin with, there are two distinct moments of preparation. The first consists of nourishing the dream, of providing certain schemes for the free play of imagination. Here it is less a matter of "local color" than of local music: "I dabble a little in the Orient for the odd quarter of an hour, not with a scientific purpose but a picturesque one: I am looking for color, poetry, sound, heat, beauty." The avowed purpose, in sum, is to *imagine the Oriental,* although directed as it is, this unrealization preserves a certain oneiric character that connects it to the "reveries" against which he warned Maxime to be on guard. But in the same paragraph and without transition, Flaubert indicates the second aspect of this "dabbling." No sooner has he declared, in effect, that his aim is simply to discover the picturesque Orient than he cites among his readings "a great work by Burnouf on Buddhism, and the Koran." Then he adds: "If you know of some good work (a review of books) on the religions or philosophies of the Orient, let me know." This time the preparation is "scientific," a matter of acquiring a body of knowledge. To what end? Is it a question of filling his future work by determining directly or indirectly the behavior and discourse of his characters from this new knowledge, as Zola will do later on? If so, Flaubert's statement would be frankly realist. Or does he simply want to give himself some safeguards, to prevent himself from falling into error pure and simple, or into anachronism? We shall come back to this difficult question in examining Gustave's attitude when faced with realism. What interests us here is that he contests *in advance*, and radically, the "work" he wants to undertake: "You see that the field is vast. But you still find much less than you think; you must read a great deal, and the result is practically nil. There is a great deal of idle chatter in all this and not much else." He is not wrong. All those who have wanted to inform themselves systematically on a subject of general interest know this very well: there are usually one or two basic works, and, for any given period, other books do hardly more than comment on or paraphrase these. Thus, in order to discover an original bit of information in such books, one must accept repetitions, idle comments, what he calls "idle chatter." But if we read attentively what he has written, we establish once again that his pen has betrayed him and that, beyond his clear intentions, it has revealed his underlying idea. One would expect him to say, indeed: "You must read a great deal to arrive at a meager result," and: "A great deal of idle chatter in all this and few new ideas." But if the result is *nil*, if the chatter fills *everything*, why would Flaubert take the trouble to read? The fact that he is thinking and feeling here simultaneously on two levels is confirmed by the structure of the last sentence: "A great deal of idle chatter in all this" implies that there is something else besides chatter. However, Flaubert adds: "and not much else." Thus the two sentences, which seem at a glance simple restrictions, are revealed upon more attentive examination to be radical negations. Considered in this light, they exemplify his attitude toward culture—the very attitude that will later give birth to *Bouvard et Pécuchet*. Why does he read? Why order works that will waste his time? Ah well, primarily, to waste it. And then *theoretically*, despite everything, to acquire a body of knowledge; *in fact*—whether or not it is entirely conscious—to destroy it, that is, so that the claimed knowledge of specialists, internalized, reveals in him its inanity. Last, and more profoundly, to earn by his feelings of disgust the right to write. Here we encounter once again the strange intention that resides in his analysis of Voltairean tragedy: he kills himself to do work that sickens him and *has no point*—which he knows very well; as if this useless effort had the value of a sacrifice or a prayer, as if *labor improbus*, by the constraints it imposes on him, had the function of rendering him acceptable to hidden witnesses. We shall return to this.

Nonetheless, he "does" Greek and Latin. Fine! But how can a young bourgeois of twenty, who has received a classical education, who is an "heir"—to employ the term used by Bourdieu and Passeron—manage "to do Greek several hours a day without even getting to the verbs"? In August 1845, he hoped "with patience [to have a good understanding] of Sophocles in a year's time." *Seven years after* the foreseen term, on 30 September 1853, he writes: "I am also beginning to understand Sophocles a little, which allows me to congratulate myself." On Friday, 31 March 1841, he gave Ernest his schedule for the following day: "I will rise as usual at four o'clock, I will do Homer." On 14 February 1850, from Beni-Souef, on the deck of the boat that follows the course of the Nile, he speaks to his mother of the "good life" he is leading: "We idle, we stroll, we daydream. In the mornings I do Greek, I read some Homer." Must we admire such perseverance or grieve that it is so poorly rewarded? Latin is a different story. And when he tells Louise in '53, "As for Juvenal, it is going rather briskly, except for a misconstrual here and there, which I quickly catch," we believe him. He has a solid foundation in Latin, which he acquired at the *collège;* there was much more emphasis on Latin at that time, not only because it was the direct source of French, but because it was a sacred language (the Church maintained this death-in-life), and because it had served many centuries—and still served to some extent—as a common language. To gain a fairly good understanding of Juvenal, he merely had to extend his knowledge; to understand Sophocles, he had to *learn Greek*, which upon leaving the *collège* he knew hardly at all. How did he study it? No doubt he used translations, since he writes to his niece in '64: "You can well imagine that I have scarcely thought about your Homer. The best translation I know is the one by Bereste. Have a little patience, I will find it for you." He deciphered the Greek words, learned their meaning, then read the French version, and finally returned to the original text, understanding it in the light of the French.[16] This passive activity was maintained until the travels in the Orient, and during several leisure moments in Egypt. It would be resumed intermittently until '53. Subsequently it is no longer even mentioned in his correspondence. What is left? Nothing: he never definitively learned to read Greek, and one day, around 1853 or '54, perceiving the vanity of his efforts, he sent the books and dictionaries packing. To what does this perseverance correspond? There is no doubt that he wanted to perfect his knowledge of antiquity. But if it were merely that, are we to believe that in fifteen years he did not manage it? To understand this surprising failure, we must get to the root of the matter and—since he "reads some Homer"—ask ourselves what *reading* meant to him.

To begin with, it meant rereading. Certainly he keeps abreast of current developments: he has read Stendhal. He "prepares" for his Oriental tale and *La Tentation* by reading specialized works, or else Indian dramas (the *Sakountala*) and sacred texts, pell-mell. But what he calls *reading*, what he considers one of the obligations of his life as an artist, he is careful to specify as rereading. On 23 February '47, he writes to Ernest: "If you were to come back here ten years from now . . . you would no doubt find me at my writing table, in the same positions, leaning over the same books, or toasting my feet in my armchair and smoking a pipe, as always." He adds in the same paragraph: "I am the only one who stays put, who doesn't move, who doesn't change my way of life or my rank."[17] We see how the theme of rereading and that of immutability are bound together.[18] He is hunched over the same books because he is the same man; he is the same man because he is hunched over the same books. On one occasion he manages to make this thought more precise: he has just "finished" Shakespeare; almost immediately he takes him up again from the beginning and announces that he will reread him without stopping until "the pages stick to my fingers." He does this, moreover, with many other authors—Goethe, Petronius, Apuleius, Rabelais, Montaigne. Apropos the latter, he will systematize his rereading ten

16. This is what he does for Shakespeare, at least; he says so expressly in his letters.
17. *Correspondance*, 2:11.
18. The period of reading—when he devoured new books, when he was pursuing his own enthusiastic initiation to Goethe, Byron, Shakespeare—was that of adolescence and youth. He "closed up" in January '44. The surviving old man *rereads* what the young dead man *read*.

years later quite methodically. To Mademoiselle Leroyer de Chantepie, who asked him what books to read:

> Read Montaigne, read him slowly, quietly. *He will calm you.* And pay no attention to people who speak of his egotism . . . But do not read the way children read, in order to amuse yourself, nor the way the ambitious read, for instruction. No, read *to live.* Make in your soul an intellectual atmosphere that will be composed of all the great minds. Study Shakespeare and Goethe in depth . . . But I recommend to you first of all Montaigne. Read him from beginning to end, and when you are done, begin again.[19]

Thus the masterpiece is assimilated to cyclical time, which for Flaubert is a substitute for atemporality. Shakespeare is repeated like the seasons and holidays, family ceremonies, meals, nights and days. His favorite books are part of the repetitive order: Shakespeare, Sade *return;* their mode of eternity is that of the eternal return. It would be better, perhaps, to say that these exquisite cadavers introduce a touch of real eternity—that of death—into the still too temporalized repetition.

Yet Gustave tells us—advising his correspondent to use a method he has refined and which has worked for him—"Read *to live.*" Isn't life a directed process? No doubt. But it is also—still more than inanimate matter—the site of repetition: the same organs satisfy the same needs. And it is under this aspect and under it alone that Gustave considers it. His letter of 1857 is revealing: one must not read for amusement or instruction. In both cases one changes; the "amusing" novel reintroduces vectoral time; we want to know what will happen, we hurry to come to the end, in short, for a few hours we install in ourselves what Gustave wanted to tear out of himself forever: a destiny, another's fatalities. As for instruction, it will produce new knowledge in the self at the risk of transforming one's internal equilibrium. The acquisition of knowledge is a dialectical process, therefore a temporalization. Yet Flaubert enjoins Mademoiselle Leroyer de Chantepie to "study Shakespeare and Goethe in depth." Isn't studying a way of instructing oneself? No: we cannot imagine—whatever the strange slips of the pen that abound in his correspondence—that he would *consciously* contradict himself in the same paragraph. The word should rather be taken in the sense in which an amateur pianist might say, "At this moment I am studying Chopin," which presup-

19. June 1847, *Correspondance*, 5:197. Flaubert's italics.

poses, of course, the acquisition of certain psychophysiological sequences and perhaps a *general* increase in speed, but does not involve
a precise *knowledge* of Chopin's art, his method, or even the enrich-
ments he brought to his favorite instrument. One *learns* more or less
to play, even to decipher, but as far as the composer himself is concerned, one achieves merely a fairly precise but "inexpressible" *comprehension* of his sensibility. If one is not a musician, a musicologist, or
an artist, studying Chopin is a process of establishing in oneself a sensibility that was real for him but for the amateur is merely an imaginary variant of his own feelings. And this is just what Flaubert wants:
"To create in one's soul an intellectual atmosphere that is composed of
all the great minds." Such eclecticism is typical of the period, and
Gustave took it from Cousin while still at the *collège*. Besides, he
might say, as Alain will do later, "The true Hegel is the Hegel who is
true"—an opinion I do not share[20] but which is defensible. The few
"great minds" he admires unreservedly are united, in his mind, when
they reach the heights: for this reason he chooses the image of *intellectual atmosphere*, which roughly evokes a multiplicity of interpenetration and even, under the currents that stir it, a basic homogeneity. It
is important for Gustave to associate himself with imaginary sensibilities; he has all the more need to do so since his own—as he so
often repeated—died at Pont-l'Evêque. These borrowed sensibilities
are naturally *aesthetic*—one must *feel* not only unreally but through an
artist's perception. In short, he adds strings to his instrument:
Rabelaisian laughter, Byronic rebellion and sarcasm, Goethe's demonic pride, de Sade's erotico-epic inventions, Montaigne's irony and
skepticism, Shakespeare's cosmic passions. In essence, this amounts
to *becoming Rabelais through laughter and Byron through rage*, etc. These
geniuses are *roles* that he keeps for himself and plays by turns. To
study them in depth is not, in his eyes, to conduct a critical examination
of their works, or even to enumerate their themes, or, more particularly, to seek—as we are doing here—to restore the unity of an intentional meaning through the diversity of significations. He need only
discover in them occasions for vertigo and install these occasions
"around his soul" as permanent possibilities. For this reason one must
only *reread* so as constantly to revive one's memory of the *role of Rabelais*

---

20. True of *what truth?* In what time, in whose eyes? Isn't one true *also* in error? Does
a crime characterize its author less than an act of heroism? And if, as often happens,
the same agent commits both, what mad optimism would claim to count only the positive action?

or the *role of Montaigne.* To understand this type of activity better, let us catch him in the act—rereading Shakespeare, for example.

August '45: "Today I finished *Timon of Athens* . . . ; the more I think about Shakespeare the more overwhelmed I am. Remind me to speak to you of the scene where Timon uses the dishes from his table to show his contempt for his parasites." [21] To Louise, 27 September:

> When I read Shakespeare, I become greater, more intelligent, purer. When I have reached the summit of one of his works, I feel that I am high up on a mountain: everything disappears, everything appears. I am no longer a man, I am an *eye.* New horizons loom, perspectives extend to infinity . . . I forget . . . that I have been part of the confusion of this anthill. Long ago, in a moment of happy pride (and I should dearly love to recapture it), I wrote a sentence that you will understand. Speaking of the joy experienced in reading the great poets, I said: "I sometimes felt that the rapture they kindled in me made me their equal and raised me to their level." [22]

The passages I have cited, along with many others, make it clear that Gustave reads Shakespeare only in direct and semi-*introverted* liaison with himself. Sometimes he feels *overwhelmed* when he compares his "talent" to Shakespearean "genius," and at other times "exaltation" makes him the equal of the author who aroused it. We recognize here the ambivalence of his abiding feelings toward "great men." He admires them when the impulse of the reading allows him to identify with them; the book closed, the exaltation subsided, he rages in solitude, convinced he will not equal them. An alternation of rising and falling, elevation and collapse, the scheme of high and low—we are quite familiar with it. Flaubert *reads in order to achieve ecstasy:* Shakespeare is the good lord who gives his man the sign to rise up to him. Once again it is the image of a Father, but of a welcoming father, not a surgeon but an artist, who would allow his younger son to identify with him. *After* the reading he falls back into exile, into being overwhelmed. But the book is there to dress the wounds it has made: he need merely open it again. At the same pages—it doesn't

21. The same theme, the same words, *nine years later* apropos *King Lear:* "I was *crushed* for two days by a scene from Shakespeare . . . That fellow will drive me mad"; 29 January '54. *Correspondance,* 4:18.

22. The same theme, the same words, *eight years later* apropos *King Lear:* "His works as a whole give me a feeling of stupefaction and exaltation, like the idea of the sidereal system. I see in it only an immensity in which my gaze is lost in dazzlement." March 1854. *Correspondance,* 4:46.

matter. The letters of 1854 give us a clearer picture of the way Gustave rereads. On 29 January he says that he has been "overwhelmed for two days" by act 3, scene 1, of *King Lear*. The context clearly indicates that he has compared this scene with his own work—he is writing *Madame Bovary*.[23] However, he will take up his reading again, for *in March* he writes: "This week I reread the first act of King Lear." So he began with the third act and finished with the first. The *rereadings* are never done *da capo*; he already knows which passages he wants to find and goes straight to them—never mind whether they are in the middle or at the end of the work. He *communicates* with the author by placing himself *outside of time* before the scene he judges to be sublime, and he already knows enough to foresee the feelings it will stimulate. Subsequently he may retrace his steps, and if the first chosen text was in the middle of the work, he might turn back to the beginning, but that is optional. In other words, these mystical contacts destroy the temporality of the work, its internal development and dialectic. Eternal, Gustave lives in a moment of eternity.

What does Gustave ask of Shakespeare and what does he find in him? Merely by leafing through his correspondence we find the same judgments on this subject repeated year after year. First of all, Shakespeare is *the greatest* because he is cosmic. In 1846: "The greatest [writers] . . . resume humanity . . . , putting aside their personalities in order to become absorbed in those of others, they reproduce the universe . . . Shakespeare is [one of these] . . . He is an awesome colossus, it is hard to believe he was a man." In 1852: "Shakespeare is something formidable in this regard. He was not a man but a continent; there were great men in him, whole crowds, landscapes." In short, Shakespeare succeeded in what Gustave regards as the supreme purpose of Art: totalization. Flaubert especially admires his impersonality: "Who is going tell me that Shakespeare loved, hated, etc.?" He put his passions between parentheses, like Gustave at Pont-l'Evêque, like Jules at the end of *L'Education*. For that very reason he is superhuman; rereading him, "I am no longer a man, I am an *eye*." In sum, Shakespeare's impersonality produces the impersonalization of the reader. We recognize all these themes: Flaubert admires in the Shakespearean canon the success of his own project. This explains how he can unrealize himself in Shakespeare: The role of Shakespeare is Gustave's, playing what he would like to be; the magnifying identi-

23. "When one contemplates those summits, one feels small: born for mediocrity, we are crushed by sublime spirits."

fication is therefore constantly possible. Ultimately, the purpose of re-reading is to make you dream:

> It seems to me that the highest thing in Art (and the most difficult) is not to make us laugh or cry, or to arouse our lust or fury, but to act like nature, that is, to *make us dream*.[24] The finest works have this quality . . . Homer, Rabelais, Michelangelo seem to be *pitiless*. They are bottomless, infinite, manifold. Through small apertures we glimpse abysses whose dark depths make us faint. And yet something singularly gentle hovers over it all.[25]

Flaubert's rereadings involve no attentive deciphering; between the lines they seek whatever can lend itself to his directed oneirism. They are hardly concerned with the text itself, which merely provides pre-texts. Let us look, for example, at the way he describes to Louise the scene from *King Lear* that overwhelmed him for two days.

> In the first scene of act 3 . . . all the characters, wretched beyond endurance and driven quite mad by their sufferings, go off their heads and talk wildly. There are three different kinds of madness howling at once, while the Fool cracks jokes and rain pours down amid thunder and lightning. A young gentleman, whom we have seen rich and handsome at the beginning of the play, says this: "Ah! I have known women, etc. I was ruined by them. Distrust the rustling of their gowns and the creaking of their satin shoes."[26]

This passage calls for a few comments. In the first place, the facts are wrong: the scene in question is not the first but a combination of the second and the fourth. This detail would be unimportant if Gustave had not just reread the play—or in any case the third act. A more serious problem is that one would be hard put to find *three* kinds of madness. I have in vain counted and recounted, and I find only two. For scene 2 takes place between Lear, the fool, and Kent, a man of good sense and a loyal subject who wants to persuade Lear to take shelter. We have here *one* madman: the old vagabond king. Yet we are willing to be indulgent, in part because the mistake was common in the Romantic period. It is true that Lear is a stubborn old idiot whose wretchedness will soon raise him to greatness and who will *subsequently* lose his mind. Then comes an interpolated scene between

---

24. This is precisely, as we have seen above, what Jules in '44 would consider the author's unambiguous (and indirect) relation to the reader: the invitation to dream.

25. To Louise, 26 August '53, *Correspondance*, 3:322. Flaubert's italics.

26. *Correspondance*, 3:18, 29 January 1854.

Gloucester and his son Edmund: an old fogey who has been duped and a traitor—that makes two normal characters. We return to Lear: scene 4 begins, the scene that overwhelms Flaubert with its beauty. Lear, Kent, and the fool are in front of a hut in which Edgar has taken refuge. He immediately emerges: he will be the second madman. Where is the third? Old Gloucester, who appears at the end, has not lost his mind in the meantime, but here is the most curious thing: Edgar's madness is *feigned*. He has earlier declared in a monologue (act 2, scene 3):

> No port is free; no place
> That guard and most unusual vigilance
> Does not attend my taking. Whiles I may scape
> I will preserve myself, and am bethought
> To take the basest and most poorest shape
> That ever penury, in contempt of man,
> Brought near to beast.

We later find him quite reasonable: he *plays* the madman to protect himself—and says so: "Bad is the trade that must play the fool to sorrow."

Critics have recently advanced the idea that Edgar was *doubly feigning*, that the game of madness was hiding an authentic madness. This is admissible for Hamlet but not here, where the feigning is an obvious maneuver and double feigning perfectly useless. The important thing is only that Lear should believe that he is mad. For the central character of the scene is Lear, the king who discovers his nakedness; and what Flaubert did not see—otherwise, would he say "three different kinds of madness howling at once"? (so many words, so many errors)—is that the fool, a professional madman, the image of a certain skeptical Reason, and the feigning Edgar are *necessary* to Lear's development. The characters, far from "howling at once" have a strange conversation, a silent dialogue and sub-talk whose eventual result is Lear's flash of intuition: "Unaccommodated man is no more but such a poor, bare, forked animal as thou art. Off, off, you lendings! Come, unbotton here" [act 3, scene 4] Obviously the dialectical meaning of the scene has escaped Flaubert, although he had felt that "everyone was wretched beyond endurance and driven quite mad by their sufferings." But, even more striking, the very details and secondary meanings were right under his nose and went unnoticed. Edgar does not say: "Ah! I have known women and I was ruined by them"—which would make no sense since this character feigning madness, slandered by his half-brother, has abandoned his wealth and renounced his way of life *in order to flee* prosecution by old Gloucester. The meaning of the long speech in which he cries: "Let not the creaking of shoes nor the rustling of silks betray thy poor heart to woman"[27] is completely different: he recalls his past life, but far from regretting it or complaining of his memories, he judges it pitilessly. In this sense he undergoes the same development as Lear, even more rapidly,[28] and it is Edgar who leads Lear finally to cry out: "Off, off, lendings." Under the cover of feigned madness, the outlaw offers a surprising mixture of nostalgia and self-accusation—of nostalgia defending itself against itself by denigrating the past, self-accusation surging up in each sentence as the judgment of the present on days gone by and intentionally spoiling the charm of memories. And the sentence "Let not the creaking of shoes . . ." must not be completed by "otherwise you will be ruined": it is in itself a categorical imperative defining the norms of life as a function of a rediscovered austerity—which is joined to Christian morality. Indeed, in an earlier line of Edgar's we find a summary of the Ten Commandments: "Take heed o'th' foul fiend. Obey thy parents," etc. The beauty of the scene comes from the fact that it brings a father, swindled by two of his daughters and having misunderstood the third, face to face with a son, misunderstood and hunted by his father at the instigation of his half-brother. As if Lear found himself in the presence of Cordelia who had *become other*, having changed sex, and instinctively attached himself to Edgar as a function of this resemblance.[29]

On this level, the changing partners, the metamorphoses and the correspondences are not meant to lead to philosophical conclusions; they are not *symbols of anything* but give the whole scene an obscure, profound unity full of meaning. *That very thing* should have pleased Flaubert, for it involves an *aesthetic form* indirectly suggesting depth. He failed to sense it because between two rereadings he had forgotten the character of Edgar. Witness the vague way he presents him: "A young Lord whom we have seen rich and handsome at the begin-

27. In the translation by Pierre Leyris and Elizabeth Holland, Pléiade edition, I, ii, pp. 915–16.
28. Let us recall that he resolved to "take the basest and most poorest shape / That ever penury, in contempt of man, / Brought near to beast." In short, the zero degree of humanity. It is from the point of view of penury, with the puritanism of the wretched, that he now denounces the illusions of luxury and the lies of civilized life. He is naked man arrogantly looking up and judging the courtier.
29. Although Edgar only accuses himself, no doubt, *also* with the intention of not accusing his father.

ning . . ." The least one can say is that wealth and good looks are not in question: when Edgar appears for the first time, his half-brother, the bastard Edmund, has already more than half outwitted Glouces-ter; so we *first* see him as a sympathetic and endangered young man who in all innocence is running to his doom.

Around the same time, Flaubert manages to read the works of Bouilhet and Louise attentively and to give them good advice, and a little later he will quite effectively judge and critique the books of his contemporaries. Yet here he claims to be *overwhelmed* by a scene whose general intention and details he is not even capable of render-ing with precision. It is *true* that this is a fine scene, arguably the finest in the play. Thus, paradoxically, he is right to admire it, even if for the wrong reasons. As if his *taste* could locate the rarest beauties but the young man were subsequently incapable of accounting for his choice. To tell the truth, it happens to all of us with a play, a novel, a poem: we are filled with emotion without being able to explain what has moved us. But in Flaubert's case this impotence is pushed to the extreme since he waxes enthusastic, it seems, without understanding what he reads. And how can we allow that he is "*overwhelmed for two days*" yet is not tempted to return to what overwhelms him in order to understand its richness in greater detail, to establish precisely the re-lations between the characters?

The answer is that he is *dreaming*. He has remarked a number of times on the confusion of ideas into which he is plunged while read-ing Shakespeare: "Everything disappears, everything appears . . ." Or else: "This is unfathomable, infinite, manifold . . . there are dark depths, vertigo." It seems that at some moment—perhaps during the first reading—he might have had a complete but "inexpressible" per-ception of the object, of the meaning that emanates from it, and of beauty as the indirect totalization of this meaning through form. Con-sequently, the scene or the chapter is marked. If he then returns to it, assured of having chosen the best, he *is no longer reading, he is dream-ing that he reads;* he makes the language imaginary and takes the words as pretexts, letting his imagination wander. What does he love, then, in this passage from *King Lear?* Not, perhaps, what he *loved* formerly and what he no longer remembers, having failed to refresh his mem-ory by a brief contact with the first act, but, primarily, an audio-visual and utterly superficial totalization which gives him men and nature together: four voices (since he sees *three* madmen and a fool) dis-tracted by unhappiness, each in his way howling the pain of men in the midst of a cosmos which manifests through rain, wind, thunder

262

and lightning its true pantheistic essence and its radical hostility to the human race. And who knows whether deep down he does not find himself again in Edgar when he renounces life, assumes the "basest and most poorest shape," and takes a dive into subhumanity? Of course, Edgar's choice is deliberate, Gustave has suffered his. But it is for this reason, perhaps, that he persists in believing him to be mad, reading his own adventure in the statements made by *that other victim of the paternal curse and of a bastard unjustly preferred.* King Lear, or the fathers punished: Gloucester and the old king will repent too late, and for having misunderstood the love of Edgar and Cordelia, they will die in horror, killed by their Achilles. This eternal story— man is the son of man—which Gustave tells himself in a whisper, is here shouted out to him.[30] Shakespeare's "immensity" gives him a right that Gustave denies himself: the right to go "wild." Underwritten by this "superhuman" genius, the young man can let himself go, secretly unify macrocosm and microcosm—the first devouring the second like an old Saturn—put the curse of Adam at the beginning and end of an oneiric cosmogony, transform the Creator into an unworthy father, and finally, taking himself for Shakespeare, raise himself up to the paroxysm of being, howling, thundering, flashing, shining, blinding, alternately or simultaneously, becoming the quartet of human suffering and the roaring choir of unleashed elements. This is reading through "resonance," of course, but the resonance is so profound, comes from such a distance, that he could easily convince himself of the pithiatic belief that the words awakened by his imaginary reading are rising up from his own "dreadful depths."

In *King Lear* there is much more than this pessimistic profession of faith. Overcome by misery, Lear intuits the human condition by discovering those more miserable than himself; the strangeness of his statements is not the product of a delirium but of a lucidity too new and too powerful to be easily expressed. Hence the "passage to the act," the attempt—immediately aborted by his companions—to tear off the "lendings," the rags that still cover him, to abolish the last vestiges of royalty and appear as the bare animal, the starting point from which a new order may be instituted that is proper to man. As if all

---

30. The rare allusions he makes to the contents of Shakespearean drama show that he finds in it only what he puts into it. *Timon of Athens* excites him because he discovers in it the reflection of his own misanthropy. In Edgar's tirade, he pinpoints a passage that flatters him in his misogyny by distorting it. I wonder whether the fact that greathearted Cordelia—the other *unmentioned* victim of an unjust father—is a woman does not disturb Gustave in his secret femininity.

the effort of centuries had been to hide our needs and veil our bodies, in short, to turn our backs on the truth of the human condition. Instead, true humanism, far from masking our animality, our needs exasperated by penury, should *take these as its starting point* and never deviate from them. Hope, glimpsed too late, vanishes: Lear's authentic greatness will prevent neither his madness nor his death, nor that of Cordelia. Be that as it may, man is possible; curtain. This is precisely what Flaubert cannot accept: the "master" is charged with reflecting to the disciple the radical pessimism that has gradually become one of his own constitutional characteristics. For this reason, the young reader avoids looking too closely at it: he isolates the scene, severs it from its extensions, organizes it in large syncretic masses— storm, madness, etc.—objects of his meditation in which he loses himself dreaming over a word. "The rustling of silk" and "the creaking of shoes" have surely been—since he cites them—the occasion for infinite daydreams. He knows quite well, moreover, that all these hapless characters will find a ghastly death and asks no more than this: what does it matter what might have been? What counts is what *is*, failure. And, in a way, he is not wrong: the glimpsed order is perhaps merely an illusion, all the more cruel as it is revealed to the wretched at the moment that an ineluctable juggernaut is about to roll over them and crush them to death. From this point of view we can say that he stays on the level of the plot, and that the rest, after all, is a matter of interpretation. It would be fair to add that oneiric reading is and remains a reading: unrealizing passivity allowed him more than once to grasp, at the expense of the whole, what might be called imaginary harmonics, inaccessible to critical analysis and refractory to "comprehension" but corresponding, despite everything, to some of the author's underlying intentions; and upon the collapse of objective determinations these harmonics reveal themselves as overdeterminations of the text to the reader who derealizes the sentences and aspires to read between the lines. For beyond what the author has "made happen" on a page, there is what he has dreamed of making happen, which is revealed only to the dream.

But if we ask ourselves what Flaubert retains of these rereadings, the answer is clear: nothing more than what he had *before them*. Life is "a tale told by an idiot, full of sound and fury." This sentence should not pass as Shakespeare's final word. It is Flaubert's. We can be sure that he takes great delight in it, that he sees in it the author's highest thought, and that the page in his *Macbeth* where it appears is dog-eared. He will look it up from time to time, to recover his own phantasms in the objective eternity of print. An Other, a genius, confirms them to him: this is the gospel; at the same time it is *his other*-thought, which he recovers first because he conceived it alone, before knowing Shakespeare, and, more importantly, because he is convinced—as we have noted—that the comprehension of a work is its re-creation.[31] Re-reading, for Gustave, is being vampirized by oneself disguised as Shakespeare or Montaigne. His anthology of great writers of the past is a repertory of incantations.

He goes further: "Poets . . . we inhale existence through the sentence . . . and we find this the most beautiful thing in the world."[32] These words are explicitly concerned with the creative vocation. But their ambiguity, and the fact that they are immediately followed by "And then I was overwhelmed for two days by a scene from Shakespeare," suggest that they apply indiscriminately to writing *and* to reading. The kinship of these two activities derives from the fact that Gustave writes *"to give himself pleasure,"* that is, *to reread himself*. For him, rereading primes creation: it is both at the beginning (the right of great men) and the end (in Flaubert's own prase, "sounded from the throat," for him alone or in public). When he grows wild with Shakespeare or raucous with Rabelais, we might say without exaggeration that he is *rereading in anticipation* (hence those exaltations that are followed, once the book is closed, by a nosedive—he wakes up: *I'm* not the author). Or, if you will, the oneiric aspect of his rereading comes from the fact that the familiarity of the reread passage, as much as its resonances, allows him to seize upon it unreally as his own product. We should therefore take his declarations literally: for him, the *vocation of writer* manifests itself as well—and perhaps primarily—as the *vocation of reader*. That will not surprise us if we recall the importance of reading aloud for Flaubert and the original preeminence of the *uttered word*, the *flatus vocis*. For this unfortunate man whose conception of critical literature provisionally reduces him to impotence, reading great works is an act of ideally restoring that inspiration in which he does not believe: in lieu of God, Shakespeare inspires him. The greatest importance must be attributed to this definition of the artistic relation to the thing written—a relation still undifferentiated: "to inhale existence through a sentence." *What* existence? Real existence?

---

31. A very sound idea. Let us simply note that his conviction is unilateral: if he applied this rule to all reading, he would no longer scorn his public. But he judges it valid only for himself. Moreover, oneiric rereading is indeed the contrary of reading for understanding.
32. *Correspondance*, 4:18.

No, since great works are there to "make us dream." In fact, he is dreaming not even of the imaginary world but of the operation that transforms the world into discourse. In short, of literature. He said one day to Louise, who had asked him for the hundredth time if he loved her: "No, if by loving you mean having an exclusive preoccupation with being loved . . . Yes, if . . . if . . . [and] if you admit that you can love when you feel that a line of Theocritus makes you dream more than your best memories."[33] That he prefers his dreams to his memories of love is not surprising. But what is he dreaming of? Of ancient Greece, of the rustic way of life that inspired Theocritus? Not at all: "The idylls of Theocritus . . . were no doubt inspired by some ignoble Sicilian herdsmen with stinking feet."[34] He dreams of the dream; of herdsmen and shepherds insofar as they are nowhere but in the depths of words; *of words,* insofar as they capture and metamorphose the energies of reality. Rereading submits the reread text to a secondary unrealization.

Beginning in 1845, rereading is presented by Flaubert to his correspondents, perhaps to himself, as the equivalent of the "great study of style" to which Jules dedicated himself "with a sense of urgency" at the end of *L'Education.* Indeed, it *takes its place,* for rereading requires permanent contact with the great authors. But Flaubert's bad faith cannot fool anyone: he *studies* nothing, neither method nor composition; that would require analysis, then recomposition, observation, the conception of hypotheses and their verification, everything he has no concern for and of which we know he is hardly capable. Continually taking up the same chosen passages without bothering to reread the texts from which they are drawn is certainly not an activity but, quite the contrary, a type of passive action. His gaze flits over the lines, and words, transparent through familiarity, passively intertwine; from these inert solicitations are reborn Gustave's familiar phantasms, the sentences that have given birth to them disintegrate in the darkness of inattention. Here is the microcosm, Flaubert playing his role of genius under the assumed name of Shakespeare, or Cervantes; and here is the macrocosm, the sunlit roads of La Mancha or Castille, the thunder and rain of England, ironic echoes of madness and human misery. The conduct of failure is obvious: Flaubert dreams he is the author of a masterpiece. He confesses to enjoying it: "To write nothing and dream of beautiful works (as I do now) is a charm-

33. *Correspondance,* 2:20.
34. To Louise, *Correspondance,* 1:428.

ing thing. But how dearly one pays later for those luxurious ambitions."[35] Yet this sentence designates the naked reverie: Gustave imagines a future Flaubert the way the hero of *Novembre* imagined himself a painter or musician. In the case of rereading, the oneiric structure is more complex, and the work being read serves as analogue to the image of his future writings to the extent that the author—Shakespeare, de Sade or Rabelais—serves as analogue to Gustave himself. Still, this passive action takes the place of literary activity: he reads *so as not to write;* in this masturbatory substitute for the act, he becomes an author *right away* under another name so as not to work to become the writer of genius he wants to be. Now that all the external conditions are fulfilled so that he can finally set to work, his essential objective is to flee the silent demand of his objective freedom. If nothing is beautiful but what is not, if nothing is true but illusion, is it not more worthwhile to live and die in a dream and, rather than write, to vampirize masterpieces so as to give oneself the perfect and constant illusion of being the *Writer of Genius?*

In the light of these observations, we can return to Gustave's strange attitude toward the dead languages; we should now understand it better. Why "do" Greek and Latin? Surely it is in order to read the great authors in the original. Similarly, as we have seen, he nurses the continually disappointed hope of reading Shakespeare in English. Taken in itself, this concern does him credit, but we have seen what it really is: rereading is derealization; even in French, the essential thing escapes him since he forages for the beauties of a work without deigning to begin at the beginning. Actually, why does he need to speak like Homer when, even if he could, he would still go to the *Iliad* only to search out pretexts for reveries? He does so precisely to dream of words from a *dead* language. Not *in spite* of the death but because of it, and for the irreducible residue of impenetrability that remains in each of its vocables. This appears clearly when the issue is Latin, which he understands better. For example, we learn that on 12 August 1846 Gustave *"ruminates"* on Virgil, and on 17 September he explains to Louise the meaning of this singular term: "I am rereading

35. To Louise, 26 August '53, *Correspondance*, 3:321. This comment was made well after the period that concerns us at present, and it must be observed that Flaubert, at the time, was in the midst of working. If he dreamed, it was of what he would do when "la Bovary is completed." Those works, he says, "would be great towering stories, painted from top to bottom." Be that as it may, these daydreams of *refuge*, although they serve him then as an asylum *against* his work in progress, are the same daydreams he nurtured in 1845, the only difference being that the 1845 daydreams exempted him at the time from *all* literary enterprise.

the *Aeneid*, and there are several lines that I say over and over to my-self until I'm quite sated; I won't need any more of it for a long time. My mind is weary of it; there are lines that stay in my head, I am ob-sessed with them, like melodies that keep coming back to haunt you, they sicken you, you love them so much."[36] Is this *reading*? Even less than when he opens *King Lear* at the consecrated pages. At least with Shakespeare he reads the entire scene. But with Virgil he leafs through to find isolated lines—two or three at a time, not more than half a dozen—which he remembers as the most beautiful; he absorbs them by constantly repeating them, and they remain in his conscious-ness through a force of internalized inertia. These verbal clusters *oc-cupy* him. Sometimes they seem to have left empty spaces, and then suddenly they reappear, *like a melody.* They embrace each other with the false spontaneity of an automatism, and these passive syntheses represent the heteronomy of his sensibility. In place of the words, something indecipherable remains for him in their melody, in their very meaning, solely because he is not an ancient Roman and no one is left to speak the language of Virgil and make him feel its singulari-ties *from the inside,* the lived, invented appropriation of the sentence to the idea. *Et ibant obscuri sola sub nocte:* he can go on forever about *this* line and *that* rhetorical formula, but he will never know—having failed in the course of his early history to cut *these* words out of his audio tape himself, having failed to discover the strict necessity and perfect instrumentality in them—the way in which a reader in the age of Augustus heard them. On the other hand, the meaning of Latin words, their very significations, far from growing deeper, tend to be-come effaced to the degree that they are repeated in his head; thus—to use his comparison—a beloved melody, hummed a hundred times over, can begin by "sickening you, you love it so much," but after a time it is transformed into a kind of refrain. Everything is as usual, but the melody, although *reconstituted* as an objective determination of temporality, has disappeared as a subjective determination of our sensibility. We no longer *feel* it.[37] The convergence in Gustave of a cer-tain indecipherability—on the level of style—and the surfacing in him of the automatism tends to emphasize the *materiality* of the Latin

36. *Correspondance,* 1:315.

37. In Gustave, of course, *knowledge* always exists—he knows the meaning of the lines he recites—but after a time this knowledge is no longer actualized: the words re-act by themselves and the meaning is virtual, that is, it is at once present and the object of an operation that is always possible, quick as a flash of lightning, which nonetheless Flaubert *spares himself* precisely because it is available and because, too often begun again, it would no longer *give* him anything.

language. It remains an object of sound whose cyclical return, born of familiarity, has the advantage of *imposing on him from inside* the time of repetition (which he suffers too often, even though he complains about it, as an external constraint and wishes to internalize as living proof of his eternity). He "ruminates": in the face of this inhabited materiality, which resists him yet preserves no "speakable" secret, in the face of this nauseatingly familiar wall, he falls into a quasi-painful stupor—the counterpart of the stupor into which he plunges when he lends his ear to the *practical* language of his intimates. In this last case, the spoken words strike him at once with their ugliness or their material insipidness, and with an oversignification beyond the utilitarian one. Instead, the dazed rumination on a line of Virgil puts him, by the beauty of its sound, into the presence of eternal matter whose secret resistance—a mystery in broad daylight—gives him a sense of the infinite depth of material Being and also of his own exile. An "unnatural animal," as Vercors says, can dream of "being matter," but precisely the abrupt mutation that characterizes the species forever forbids that this vow be realized—except in death. Painful as it is, Gustave wants to *enjoy* his exile. Through the mediation of dead languages he seeks to ground his rapport with Antiquity.

Gustave claims that images of the ancient world sometimes come to him as clearly as memories: "I have lived there!" he then affirms. Other passages from his correspondence between 1845 and 1847, while shedding the metempsychosis vocabulary borrowed from Alfred, are no less affirmative: "I *shall live* there." Meaning: when I read Sophocles in the original and Juvenal without misconstrual, the exercise of dead languages will revive that vanished universe *in the imaginary*. We move here from realistic affirmation, which he doesn't believe in at all (I have seen those ancient crowds with my own eyes), to the solemn recognition—more in conformity with his principles—of the absolute preeminence of illusion. But what matters to us here is not that he *should want to live* in those vanished cities; we must know *how* he wants to live there: as a Roman centurion, as a senator? Is he still dreaming of being Nero? Nothing of the sort. A letter from 1846— Louise has been his mistress for no more than a week[38]—is revealing, articulating his real, unvarnished intentions:

> You want to make me a pagan, oh muse of mine, you with Roman blood in your veins. But *in vain do I work myself up to it through imagination and preference;* in the depths of my soul I have the mists

38. To Louise, 6 August '46, *Correspondance*, 1:218. My italics.

of the North, which I inhaled at my birth. I bear in me the melancholy of barbarous races with their migratory instincts and their
innate disgust with life that made them leave their country in
order to leave themselves. They loved the sun, all those barbar-
ians who came to die in Italy . . . I have always had a tender
sympathy for them, as if for ancestors. Did I not find in their bois-
terous history all my untroubled and unknown history? Alaric's
cries of joy upon entering Rome were paralleled fourteen centuries later by the secret deliriums of a poor child's heart. Alas!
No, I am not a man of antiquity; the men of antiquity had no
nervous ailments like mine.

If Gustave now imagines assimilating the culture of antiquity, it is
as a barbarian, a man of the North. He will never be Nero or even
Petronius: he becomes incarnate as Alaric, a Nordic vagabond dazzled
by the beauties of the conquered city which are given and refused at
the same time. Thus when he claims to return to antiquity—whether
through reminiscence or imagination—he is careful to preserve distance between himself and the pagans he admires: in the Athens of
Sophocles, in the Rome of the emperors, if he can get there he intends
to live as an exile; he seeks not to become integrated with the ancient
city but, present and inactive, to have merely a "glancing acquaintance" with its inhabitants. Glancing—no, that isn't enough: all his
senses will be involved. What he refuses is communication. What he
lacks is a magic ring with the double power to allow him to travel back
in time and render him invisible. In terms of culture, he reckons to
appropriate the "objective spirit" of the ancients but not to assimilate
it. He expresses this with a suspect humility, affirming quite boldly
that the ancients "had no nervous ailments." He himself has one—
"Christianity passed that way." It is therefore possible for him to be
fascinated with the great figures of Plutarch but not to imitate or even
understand them completely. What he admires in the Romans and
the Greeks—especially in the Romans—is a calm adherence to oneself that, personally, he would not want. Nero "makes him dizzy"
certainly because of the sadism he attributes to him but, even more,
because his imperial caprices seem to transform themselves of their
own accord into sentences to be executed without ever being challenged. All those great *soulless* men (they were not infected by Christianity) he sees as manifestations of *pure Being,* of inorganic yet living
matter. He attributes to them feelings of marble and bronze; admittedly, their historians did what had to be done to persuade him. But
he lays it on thick: he makes the most of his opportunities to recon-

struct their culture as the antithesis of ours; and he symbolizes this antithesis in Virgil, in Juvenal, by that inaccessibility which makes their verse—even when repeated a hundred times—words of stone falling from the lips of statues.

For Gustave, the beauty of the ancient world is born of its impermeability: books are steles with words engraved on them. But this impermeability, absolute density of being, is merely another way of designating its perfect nonbeing. Rome no longer exists: that is why it *is*. Gustave is fully aware of this: "In about a month I will have finished Theocritus. As I spell out antiquity, an immeasurable sadness invades me, dreaming of that age of magnificent, enchanting beauty that has gone, never to return, of that world all vibrant, all shining, so colorful, so pure, so simple, and so varied!"[39] The ancient authors attract him because they are in some way separated from us by the advent of Christianity, therefore *more dead* than the great writers of the sixteenth century, with whom he thinks he shares a basic identity of viewpoint despite all the differences. Thus those poems chiseled in dead languages possess what constitutes, according to the first *Education,* the essence of Beauty: absolute consistency as total impalpability, fascinating presence as definitive absence, pure materiality as it escapes the senses in order to make itself imagined through verbal matter, the strict identity of nonbeing and totalized being.[40] In short, antiquity fascinates him because he can view it from the perspective of death. And this is why he does not really want to acquire a perfect knowledge of Greek or even of Latin. To increase one's proficiency, certainly, to avoid misconstruals and false meanings as far as possible; but he takes pleasure in being unable to dissolve a certain opacity that makes a Latin line an essentially unassimilable substance and, above all, a *ruin* that will serve as analogue for the imaginary reconstitution of an absence. It is a matter of keeping his distance from the ancient world, of turning it into another possibility for the human race, realized in earlier times, unrealizable today. In a word, modern man is contested through the man of antiquity, yet this accomplished model is never able to help us: for even if we could fit our conduct to

39. To Louise, Rouen, early 1847, *Correspondance,* 2:5.
40. For the least reading of a Greek or Latin text implies totalization. Shakespeare, of course, is the English seventeenth century at its source. But Flaubert never says so: for him, the power of Shakespeare's genius surpasses any epoch and makes him indeed the contemporary of all the Christian centuries. But the ancient world is a world completed *before* our world; Flaubert, insensitive to the passages and transitions that lead from the Late Empire to the High Middle Ages, sees it all as a self-enclosed totality. As if man had had *two* histories.

his, we would continue to hope, while Flaubert's purpose is to make us despair. When he rereads Shakespeare or "does" Theocritus, he is pursuing different but complementary objectives. In the first case, his purpose is clear: to indicate that the imaginary writer knows unreal pleasures which escape the real genius, that is, in practice. In the second, writing must be discouraged by exhibiting an example in a state of ruin, inimitable and dead, whose stony density contests everything the moderns could, can and will be able to produce. Two modalities of failure that lead to the same preference for silence: the ambitious young man will hold his peace because he cannot be Virgil—a dead man from a dead world which derives its beauty from death—and because there is more pleasure in playing the role of Shakespeare than in actually being Shakespeare. For Flaubert, rereading—Rabelais or Virgil—not only represents the cyclical return of genius, eternity lived as repetition, or even the contestation of all possible writing in the name of the imaginary; rereading is the very destruction of the act of reading and its replacement by dream, or rumination.[41]

Everywhere in these mirages of activity we find the familiar intention of failure. It is so diversified, however, that it seems difficult to locate a single meaning in it: sometimes work and knowledge must be ridiculed even while acquiring an obscure merit through unrewarded effort—as if Gustave were running aground beneath the empty sky to prove that he has taken to heart Taciturnus's formula: It is not necessary to hope in order to undertake, nor to succeed in order to persevere[42]—and sometimes his purpose is manifestly to break his own heart by systematically cultivating exile ("Alas, I will never be a man of antiquity"), and because, according to him, impossible Beauty must "sicken." We must pursue our regressive analysis however. Since failure, beginning in the winter of 1845, has become Flaubert's life style, we must compare his lived experience itself in its most mundane aspect, as he feels it and makes it, to the splendor of the imaginary life he attributes to Jules, his incarnation.

Certainly Jules's life after the conversion is not terribly happy. *On the surface:* in other words, taking account of the subversive reversal, *in reality;* or, if you will, insofar as we might misleadingly reduce that

41. I do not mean that this contact with the dead was useless to him. We shall return later to "the Latin structure of the Flaubertian sentence" at the time of *Madame Bovary*. For the moment, the question is not what classical culture could give him but what he asked of it around 1845.

42. But in fact he adopts only its diabolical and reverse reflection: one must despair in order to undertake and foresee failure in order to persevere.

life to its simple reality, which—though not exhaustive—becomes the object of a truncated, therefore false, idea and is reduced to an appearance: "On the surface sad for others and for himself, [his life] flows in the monotony of the same tasks and the same solitary contemplations." We will have recognized in these few words a feature characteristic of his "constituted nature," subsequently taken up again by the movement of his personalization: sad for others and for himself. The priority of the Other in the designation of subjective facts is once more manifest; it is others who determine the *real*, it is they who declare how sad his life must be.[43] And Jules, in all docility, internalizes their judgment: yes, from their point of view—which always has primacy over mine—this life is sad, it must be; have I not deprived myself of everything? And Gustave hastens to add: "*But* [Jules's life] shone on the inside with magical lights and sensuous flares; it was the azure of an Oriental sky drenched in sunlight." Rereading the final pages of the book, we see that he returns to this theme several times, using different metaphors, which he develops abundantly on each occasion. We may well ask, leafing through the correspondence from '45 to '48, where are the promised lights? Where are the sensuous flares? Jules's celebrations were, of course, exercises of his imagination. Yet "fits of dizziness whirled in his thought, emotions stirred in his heart, lascivious impulses flowed in his flesh." The meaning of his "Loser wins" is here made explicit, an intellectual meaning of an extreme dialectical rigor, as we have seen: the loss of the real automatically gave sovereignty over images. Gustave, after January '45, remained faithful to *one* belief: the imaginary is absolute. Long afterwards he would write to Louise: there is only one absolute truth, Illusion. He has certainly refined the techniques of derealization, grouping them under the rubric "aesthetic attitude." Still, he needed something to derealize: a death "analyzed from an artist's viewpoint," a baptism, an ancient amphitheater, the name of Byron on a column, the misfortunes of Madame Pradier, gourmandizing, in short, the external world—history, society, the passions, ruins, nature. When the opportunity presents itself, he never lets it pass. But between '44 and '46 he is hardly spoiled: a few family ceremonies (marriage, burials, the Mediterranean "revisited like a grocer," short trips to Paris, nothing else). He lives in a conquering dream, yet has nothing to conquer but the Hôtel-Dieu, all too familiar, and then Croisset for a time, the Seine viewed through his

---

43. We seem to hear Maxime talking: the same labors, the same contemplations . . .

window. Apart from that, of course, he waxes enthusiastic with Shakespeare, dreams with Theocritus, rolls Virgil around "in his throat." But we soon notice something: now Gustave *needs written words to dream*. His sequestration prevents him from derealizing the world: he derealizes works of the dead, which have unrealized their time and their universe. In his adolescence, he cradled his phantasms, gratified his desires, satisfied his resentments, his masochism, his sadism: these exercises, to which his pithiatism gave a rare magical power, helped convince him of the surreality of the imaginary. Now, alone in his room, tranquilized rather than troubled by the familiar noises he hears through his door, he forbids himself to revive his inner opera, condemning the daydream because it is still too human and makes him waste his time (even more than the analysis of *Zaïre?*). Is he afraid? Probably: he will confide to Louise that his attacks of hemorrhaging images are essentially caused by excesses of imagination. If he daydreams, he is afraid of irritating his resident demon and multiplying the "fireworks." The "system made for one man alone" involves a rigorous discipline: the words of others are necessary to direct his oneirism and to give him an objective, impersonal framework; if he were to let himself go, God knows what slime would rise to the surface. In short, he holds himself in. Sometimes, however, he abandons himself to reverie—otherwise, how can we explain the warning he addresses to Maxime, hardly susceptible of falling into the same error—but he comes out of it full of disgust and promises himself not to begin again. Does fear explain everything? Surely not: we are still on the surface. Whatever the reasons, the result is clear: except when he reads, it is not Jules's splendid desert he finds within him, inhuman and solitary but peopled by every mirage: it is the void. He says as much to Maxime (April 1846): "I know the void for what it is. But who knows? Perhaps greatness lies there; the future is germinating there." The germination is not perceptible: it is the object of a pious hope. Experienced reality is an immense lacuna. Several months later in a letter to Louise he writes the famous sentence, "The depth of my emptiness is equaled only by the passion I invest in its contemplation." And also: "I have inside me, deep down, a radical, intimate, bitter, incessant *tedium* that prevents me from enjoying anything and fills my soul to bursting." This time it is *fullness* that he takes as his symbol. No matter; in both cases the evil is radical: in emptiness there is *nothing*, not even the promise of an image; and tedium fills *everything* and prevents him from enjoying anything.

Writing again to Alfred, he has two ways of evaluating this system-atic impoverishment. The first is the impress of pride, which gives it the meaning and value of an ascesis: Gustave clears away the under-growth in order to discover himself as he is. In September '45 he writes: "Seek your real nature and be in harmony with it. '*Sibi con-stat*,' says Horace. That's all there is to it." [44] Of course, he recognizes that this fidelity to the self is entirely new for him: "I was not like this before. This change came about naturally. My will had something to do with it as well." The process is not even complete: "It[45] will lead me further, I hope. My only fear is that it may weaken." This is making "good use of the illness"; he just has to make the effort to co-incide completely with his "nature"—which he also calls his race ("happiness for people of our race is in the *idea*") and which generally corresponds to his particular essence. It is noteworthy that this letter is written only a few months after he had finished *L'Education*. Here, his ataraxia is the result of the human creature's total harmony *with his being*, which for him corresponds to *immutability*. Gustave is thwarted in his passivity—just as some people are thwarted in their left-hand-edness. He has been thrown into time, and he has known resent-ments and sufferings that might be called *borrowed* because they arise from an original error and from the character he was obliged to play. Temporalized by mistake, he made use of temporality (Pont-l'Evêque) to destroy time and rejoin the immutable. This is roughly his feeling when when he is carried away with pride. He is not attempting to *cultivate the self* but simply to restore his "nature," that invariable so resistant, by contrast, to all change. So we can see that he is detaching himself imperceptibly from Jules. Jules dissected authors the way Achille-Cléophas dissected cadavers; Gustave took the accidental and rendered it immutable (at least in this instance he had to let the event come to him, if only to corrode it with his acids). He produced master-pieces, which means—despite the monotony of his existence—that he *was changing*.

In August '45, Gustave admits only the single change that allows him to be reborn identical with himself: repetition. The difference be-tween the author and his hero is still more striking if we try to picture their type of "presence in the world." Gustave's great step forward in *L'Education*, the very thing that will one day allow him to write

---

44. To Alfred, September 1845, *Correspondance*, 1:191.
45. His conscious will.

Madame Bovary, is that he invested Jules with the intention of being present in the *circumstantial* world, of recovering the all in the least of its parts and the entire nature of man in the most imperceptible movements of the heart. Certainly he has not forgotten his techniques of derealization and uses them when he leaves his voluntary prison. But when he remains in his room, he returns to his old ecstasies and—as in the time of the negative infinite—forces himself to be present in the all without any intermediary. And when it is not grasped through its particular determinations, as the horizon of the singular, the all is *nothing* or, which amounts to the same thing, it is the abstract idea of the universal. "I am entering more than ever into the the pure idea, into the infinite. I aspire to it; it draws me in: I am turning into a brahman, or rather I am going slightly mad." Clearly, it is not a matter of contemplating the infinite but of *entering into it*, of sinking into it insofar as it is pure and undifferentiated idea. Thus Gustave's "nature," his particular essence, his "race," is immobility grasped as indeterminacy, as a strict absenteeism practice not only in relation to others but also, and more particularly, in relation to the set of subjective facts that constitute the empirical Ego. The effort, here, is deliberate: one must realize and perceive oneself as pure *nonbeing.* Or, if you will, Gustave immobilizes himself by his untenable and ever repeated attempt to give, in himself and in his own existence, *some being to nonbeing.* This is not surprising if we recall that he always assimilated being to nothingness. What strikes us, rather, is the self-destructive aspect of this enterprise. He finds his nature in the negation of all nature, that is, in a conscious annihilation. Or, conversely, he knows the harsh joy of giving, by means of an unbearable tension, ontological status to the radical negation of being that person through whom nothingness—as the devourer of all particular existence—*comes to being* and is substituted for it. One may well ask whether this attitude has any *content.* Or, if you will, whether it is lived as an *experience.* No, for it is quite certain that there is no way to *sustain* it or even, perhaps, to realize it. In other words, he does not really effect it, but he sustains the illusion of effecting it. Which amounts to saying that he radicalizes the enterprise of derealization, which defines itself as artistic in his eyes, when it is worked on external material. Here, the center of unrealization is no longer an external and real object, it is himself, and it is unrealization to the second degree since the identification of being with nothingness (abolition of the real) and nothingness with being (substantiation of appearance) is not given as a result (a poem, a piece of sculpture) but is itself the object of a conscious illusion. He is not the "brahman" he calls being; he is unrealized in it, in other words, he *dreams* that he is entering into the Idea. From this point of view we might say that this *dream* of being the nothingness of being and the being of nothingness represents the zero degree of Imagination, or if you will, the imagination of its perfect nakedness, manifesting itself *without the production of images* by actualizing its simple ontological structure; we know that it is a tearing away from being toward an absence whose being and nothingness it posits simultaneously. Thus for Gustave to be reunited with his nature, he must make himself radically imaginary without producing any image of himself, without designating any role for himself to play (neither Tamberlaine nor Nero, etc.) but that of the slightly mad brahman who coincides with the pure flight of imagination. Taken in its austere and radical simplicity, this return of the imaginary to the self can appear both as the triumph of unrealization—the dream of a dream—and as its intentional failure. What is real here is the return in force of the stupors, along with his disorders. It was on this absence of the *lived* self that Gustave constructed his unreal impressions of "entering into the idea." Yet we might ask what obscure intention continually reproduces them in this dreamer who dreams of nothing. And not without reason, since Gustave's illness—contrary to Maxime's belief—is not conditioned by organic lesions.

Indeed, he insists *on the intention of failure* in the second interpretation he gives of his immobilism. Two letters between June and August 1845 bear witness to it. Pradier has advised him, simplistically, to take a mistress. This advice does have the effect of awakening "strange aspirations to love, although he is sickened by them to his very entrails."[46] In short, he feels the vague temptation *to try*. But he is

---

46. Still another difference between Gustave and Jules. Jules is freed from the "seriousness of sensation." But in exchange he has conquered the mastery of the unreal: "Emotions stir in his heart, lascivious impulses run in his flesh." Lascivious impulses that *are not troubling*, orgies without weariness, since they have the marvelous insubstantiality of the imaginary. Similarly, the wise stoic can tumble down three times, unreal man can offer himself all the sensual pleasures in a state of perfect calm. By total contrast, Gustave's senses are numbed, and love disgusts him. "Serious" disgust, lived "in his very entrails." Do we see him delight, after that, in ethereal debaucheries? Too solitary, he gives in—perhaps—to the temptations of onanism, but *it is need*—an eminently real determination—and he comes away disgusted with himself. If he has recourse, during these solitary pleasures, to images, they are certainly not evoked for their nonbeing but serve as auxiliaries to augment his excitement. The rest of the time, it is tranquillity of the flesh and the inhibitions of disgust. Jules, satisfied with his operatic fantasies, has no desire to masturbate: his sex is dead. And certainly he is not one to be excited by the suggestion that he should sleep with a pretty girl; he would ask: "What for? In dreams I have the most beautiful girls, those who do not exist."

immediately disturbed: "I thought about Pradier's advice; it is good. But how can I follow it? And then where would I stop? . . . A normal, regular, hearty, solid love would take me too much out of myself, would disturb me, I would get back into active life, into physical reality, into common sense, and that is exactly what has been harmful to me every time I've been tempted to try it." In 1843 his abhorrence of "active life" seemed to manifest itself above all in disgust with taking up a career and taking on a bourgeois existence. Now it is life in all its forms that repels him: he has already understood his neurosis and knows that the return to "common sense," that is, to "normal" existence, would be his ruin. Sequestration is no longer a neurotic means of avoiding law school, it has become an end in itself. His only "freedom" is to remain voluntarily in prison. And the letter he writes to Ernest, 13 August 1845, is the echo of this internal debate and of temptation vanquished—not without bitterness: "What I dread being passion, movement, I believe that if happiness is anywhere it is in stagnation; ponds have no tempests." The tone is resigned, the comparison no less so: he wanted to be the ocean, like Shakespeare, but fear reduces him to the size of a pond. His immobilism now has a different function: it reunites Flaubert with his "nature," that is, it detaches him from lived experience and reunites him with the being of nonbeing and absorbs it into the Idea, into the pure imaginary. By comparing himself to a pond, however, Gustave gives another meaning to his mortuary ascesis. From this point of view, stagnation no longer represents the eternity of the unreal, rather it must be pictured as a defensive attitude. Not a gesture, not a word, not a breath: if the unhappy fellow moved, his old shrill and bitter passions, envy, resentment, that negative pride eating at his liver, would all reawaken, there would be an uproar. Let us go still further: if he is not a brahman, if he stretches out his arm to caress a beautiful shoulder, who will say that his collapse at Pont-l'Evêque—easily borne insofar as it cut him off from the world and forbade him all praxis, hence all secular ambition—isn't suddenly going to make him suffer a thousand deaths. Alone, immobile, mute, his collapse constitutes his greatness provided he draws all its consequences and, in particular, considers it an absolute interdiction on leading a "normal life." In-

---

Gustave does not seem to have arrived at this degree of sentimental education: his disgust is real, and Pradier's offer provokes real excitation; he was not thinking of women, someone suggests it to him, and this possibility provokes a desire to make love. In other words, inhibited, twisted, contradictory, an affective life remains in him. And sexuality.

ferior, superior, at Croisset he derides it; the essential thing is that no one can be compared to him. But if he frequents Pradier's salon to angle for pretty women, he reenters the competition; those ladies have other suitors, and comparison will occur naturally: they may find him young and handsome, but he will once more become the second son of the Flauberts, a poor boy who does not know how to do anything, and whose suspect ailment has put an end to his studies; I pity his family, they are well off, yes, the father is chief surgeon, the older son is assured a good position, but it is not a large fortune, if you see what I mean. In short, it is fear that holds him back: fear of suffering and revealing his inferiority to everyone. Thus when Flaubert proudly declares that he "is entering into the idea," we are not surprised by what he admits in another, almost contemporaneous letter or to another correspondent: that his wounded soul is resigned to all frustrations for fear of living. As he will say much later to George Sand: I was cowardly in my youth.

Was he really cowardly? Didn't his refusal to live originate in a deeper, and in a way *positive,* impulse? It is clear, in any case, that in his maturity he considered his reclusiveness and his chastity a form of sacrifice. Anyone who doubts this should recall the letter he writes after the Commanvilles' ruin and the mad rage that accompanies his disarray; he repeats it on every side: *it is too unjust;* he, who has deprived himself of everything, who has led the most austere existence, he *did not deserve* this last blow of fate. *Deserve?* Did he then have rights over Destiny? Had he earned them with his good behavior? This tearful man bears less and less resemblance to Jules. Jules knows no regret; Providence and pride have breathed on his passions and extinguished them, he writes his masterpieces out of that dialectical necessity which we have examined above, and his inspiration, which "depends on itself alone," can in no way *compensate* for a suffered and adroitly exploited destitution that was never the object of a devout ascesis. His heart is dead, therefore he writes, nothing simpler; he does not have the merit of being a hermit in the desert, the desert has come to him in all its imaginary magnificence. The Other, his creator, is dismayed at not receiving the anticipated gratification: he is convinced he practiced asceticism out of virtue; his life seems to him an example of *artistic morality,* and in this time of testing it is no longer sufficient to compare himself to the Christian hermits, he firmly considers himself a saint. As a joke, of course—*at first.* But we know his way, and we know he will not stop until his friends canonize him in his lifetime. Where is the truth? Is he lying when he declares, in '46,

279

that he has just spent the two best years of his life? When in *L'Educa-tion* he alludes indirectly to his alacrity and compares himself to an athlete at rest? When he insists—not always, it is true—on his ataraxia? Is he forcing his memories in '74, and does he depict himself as a martyr to give more power to his reports of bitterness? Neither; in fact, the two versions have always coexisted; sometimes he stresses the one and sometimes the other. But in order to understand this complex attitude, a final point remains for us to clarify: between '45 and '47, how does he envisage his relation to Art? Jules was the Artist; Flaubert therefore had the audacity to claim this title for himself—at least in a near future. But several weeks later, when the finished manuscript is shut in a drawer, it would seem that the quietly sterile young man has lost out to the rages of the "mute who tries to speak." We have seen that his readings and his "labors" serve, among other objectives, to defer, the moment when he will simply have to write. But that doesn't explain why the desire itself seems to have passed. I have said above that his proposed aim was so ambitious, he was afraid he could never achieve it. This simple explanation—which I be-lieve correct on its own terms—is insufficient; he already knew impo-tence and suffered from it, his *Souvenirs* are proof of that. If he were merely afraid of being unworthy of his high aims, what is the source of this new calm? For we cannot emphasize too much, and it is little enough to say, that he saved these aims from the shipwreck: indeed, he ran aground to save them. This certainly emerges from the first *Education*, even if its version of "Loser wins" is overly rationalized. Which means that during the winter of '44, it became radicalized; the personalizing movement has described its last spiral. It is not true that he has freed himself from *all* his passions; if they are quiet now it is because he definitively privileged one, and subordinated the others to that one. Around 1845, Gustave is neither Jules the robot Artist, cre-ated providentially from his heart, nor the paltry nature—anorexic out of a terror of suffering, and so sinking into apathy—that he some-times describes in his letters. In fact, he is the very type of the pas-sionate man. What he has lost are *emotions*—or rather he *exhausts* them in his mad, febrile agitation (crying over a mislaid pen is his way of *not crying* over misery and solitude). But the "system made for one man alone" with its precautions, calculations, avarice, and Ma-chiavellianism, is neurosis and pure passion. Or, rather, it is passion lived neurotically, neurosis in the service of passion. The passionate man, as everyone knows, is rarely moved and shows little warmth but merely an affectaton of cordiality, judging this the best way to keep the curious at a distance. The projects, the undertakings of his entourage leave him cold, but his indifference comes from his evolution into the man of a single project, wholly mobilized, monopolized by an obsession that is at once an impulse, a deeply considered right, a planned action, and a selective vision of the world. When this man is a *practical agent*, he puts his reason and abilities in the service of his undertaking and becomes absorbed in refining complex systems, in combining ways and means with a view to attaining indirectly, at the end of a long patience, the unique objective that has been his obsession. If, like Gustave, he is passive, this entirely relative distinction between fatalities (which sweep him away) and calculating reason (which serves them by exploring the field of possibles) makes no more sense. He *becomes his enterprise.* This can lead him to the point of autism—and we have seen that Gustave *can* push introversion to that point; but even though he might stop himself in midcourse, the passionate man of the passive type internalizes his objective and tries to attain it by the sole action permitted him: passive action, or the manipulation of self by self. It nonetheless remains that he *is* entirely surpassing, project, expectation, and that he has structured himself as *coming toward himself.* Thus we see Gustave scrutinizing *his* emptiness in order to discover in it *his* future in embryo (that organic metamorphosis of the *self,* genius). As a consequence, the hesitations, the weaknesses, the impotence of the years 1845–47, all his conducts of failure cannot be conceived, negatively and from a pluralistic perspective, as the effects of relatively autonomous forces that would halt his principal enterprise, but, to the contrary, must be considered, on the basis of the totalization in progress—constantly totalizing, totalized, detotalized, and retotalizing itself—*as means* that serve the passionate project of writing. In other words, even when he wastes his time and becomes absorbed in stupid tasks *in order not to write,* we can be sure that the stupidity is only apparent and that it is *in order to write* that he is bent on not writing. Not with the *excessively rational* idea that he is not yet mature, that he must acquire the tools, develop a style (which, as we shall see, he is fond of repeating), but with some more obscure and no doubt prelogical intention for which we must cast about in his depths, hoping that in bringing it up the changes of pressure will not explode it before our eyes. And the best way to attain it through analytic regression is to interrogate Flaubert on his relation to Art. Although we can verify in his way of imagining literature during these crucial years a more or less acknowledged defeatism, we must seek the original conduct of failure directly, in the deepest core of his passion. And that will signify *either* that what he demands is not Art but the shipwreck, *or* that he had not lost *everything* in '44, that he knew it and is merely upping the ante, convinced that we win nothing if we do not lose the very thing we hope to win.

In his letters from the time we often encounter sentences or whole paragraphs that denote a curious tendency to devalorize art itself in the moments when he despairs of his talent. A short time after Caroline's death he writes, for example, to Maxime:

> I am going to set to work, at last! at last! I hope to slog away immoderately and at length. Is it from having confronted our own emptiness, the emptiness of our plans, our happiness, beauty, everything? But I strike myself as being quite limited and quite mediocre. I am having difficulty becoming an artist, which dismays me; I will soon be unable to write a single line. I believe I could do good things, but I always ask myself, what's the point? It is all the more curious that I do not feel discouraged; on the contrary, I am entering more than ever into the pure idea, into the infinite. I aspire to it, it draws me in; I am turning into a brahman, or rather I am going slightly mad. I doubt that I will compose anything this summer.[47]

It was easy to understand him when he contrasted Art, the supreme but inaccessible end, to his own mediocrity. It was no more surprising when in *Mémoires d'un fou* he made it his dearest illusion, even while insisting on the inanity of this occupation; in the heat of composition, carried away by his eloquence, he had no time to question himself, or rather he was often sustained by the marginal consciousness of his genius. Hence, two different, if not contradictory, but perfectly logical positions emerge: subjective despair—"Art is great and I am small"; and objective despair, which is much more comfortable—"I may excel in literature, which is no doubt the best of what we find here below but is not, in fact, a big deal." It is perfectly normal that he should shift from one to the other. Less so, on the other hand, is the curious reciprocal questioning of Art and the Artist in his letter to Maxime. The beginning is clear: in the face of death and the pain of the survivors, beauty itself reveals its vanity. This remark contradicts the whole of Flaubert's "system," which, far from reproaching great works for their uselessness, cherishes them because of it: the Beautiful is an absolute *because* it is a vain illusion.[48] We would never have

---

47. To Maxime, 7 April '46, *Correspondance*, 1:203.
48. Perhaps he is thinking especially of the beauty of his sister Caroline, which did not protect her against death. This is not a banality when it is deeply felt during a fu-

expected from him a declaration so little in conformity with his most resolute obstinacies, which could be summed up in these words: "What good is writing since we are going to die?" And it is all the more surprising as literature, for him, is the point of view of death on life, and as these two deaths, moreover, have affected him less than he claims. Let us admit, however, that in the face of Art he might have an ambivalent attitude: to work feverishly at his writing is to create and by the same token to be reborn, but, on the other hand, creation is merely imitation and produces only chimeras. Therefore, and provided we specify that these mood swings take place only in relation to his demiurgic will, we can accept that Flaubert contradicts himself, now wishing he were a God of appearances and now denouncing himself as the Creator's ape. We shall have more trouble allowing that his intuition of the vanity of Art, instead of provisionally stripping Gustave of the will to write, has made him "quite limited and quite mediocre" *as an artist*. If the game isn't worth it, why such dismay at his clumsiness? A strange vicious circle. We might say that in this paragraph there are two opposite conceptions of Beauty, one explicit, the other hidden. The first specifically implicates art in the universal challenge. But the words "limited and mediocre" suggest the second, which is passed over in silence. We should *translate* it as follows: "The vanity of Beauty has so deeply affected me that I am no longer capable of obeying the supreme imperative, which is the Beautiful." Indeed, he immediately adds: "I am having difficulty becoming an artist, which dismays me; I will soon be unable to write a single line." The Beautiful has just sunk into universal nothingness, is this really the moment for it to seem so difficult? Of course, we can repeat here that the strange wager of *L'Education* forces him to become such a severe censor of his own work that he is disgusted with it in advance. Then, in order to reconstitute the movement of his thought, we would have to rewrite this text, beginning with the end: "I am unable to write a single line because I am having such difficulty becoming an artist that everything I can think of seems narrow and mean. But so what? I have

---

neral vigil and pronounced before a ravishing face in the process of decay: all that beauty, a promise of happiness for her and for others, was a swindle. Maxime knew Caroline and thought her beautiful; he could understand the allusion without the need for greater detail. But admitting that Gustave might have had, on the surface, the intention of designating his sister's *natural* beauty, nonetheless this part of the sentence refers more profoundly to the impotence of *all* beauty. He is not thinking here of contrasting Nature and Art: quite the contrary, this materialistic Platonist is highly conscious that Art, like Nature, offers merely an *imaginary* reflection of the *eidos* of the Beautiful.

discovered, on the occasion of my bereavements, that all is vanity, including Beauty."[49] This reconstruction is surely valid. It does not prevent Gustave's "belief in nothing," here reaffirmed, and his "difficulty as an artist," elsewhere called his "taste," from referring us to two different, if not opposed, systems of value. Moreover, the sentence that immediately follows, "I believe I could do good things but I always ask myself, what's the point?" derives its ambiguity from the fact that it can be interpreted according to either system. When related to the beginning of the paragraph, that is, to the vanity of the Beautiful, it means quite simply: since all is dust, what's the point of making works that are good according to the judgment of men but in fact are nothing but fakes? But if we read it in another mode, if we link it to the "difficulty becoming an artist," it must be understood to mean: "I could do good things, yes, like all second-rate artists if they apply themselves. But what's the point? Art demands genius; you must be Shakespeare or nothing."[50] It seems to me very likely that Gustave intentionally maintained this confusion to give rise to two opposite readings, both perfectly valid. In any event, we will surely marvel at a paragraph that begins, "At last I am going to work! To work!" and ends with this profession of quietish faith: "I am turning into a brahman . . . I doubt that I will compose anything this summer." As if he had written the first words in a kind of intoxication and then come up short, gripped by superstitious terror, and replayed his typical theme of universal nothingness in order to ward off the evil eye.[51]

This letter is particularly striking, but it is far from unique; during his years of silence, Flaubert often seeks to minimize the importance of literature. On 4 June '46 he writes to Vasse:

> To live, I don't say happily (that goal is a fatal illusion) but peacefully, one must create another existence for oneself outside the visible, common and general existence, one that is internal and inaccessible to that which enters into the domain of the contingent, as the philosophers say. Happy are those who have spent

49. In other words: they are too innocent and good for a cad.

50. In this case, the "vanity of all" becomes a requirement: so as not to be vain, Beauty owes it to itself to be perfect; this is the misery of man, his bereavements, his future death, which would demand compensation by incontestable masterpieces, and take for its unique subject the "vanity of all," namely the infinite.

51. What he meant by "work," at this time, was studying the tragedies of Voltaire and doing Greek and Latin again. Hence the opposite of "composing," which means, at bottom, to let the work compose itself. But Alfred, described, with faint praise, as the "good worker," is certainly not up on these transformations of meaning.

their days slapping insects on vine leaves, or contemplating with a magnifying glass the rusty medals of Roman emperors. When this is mixed with a little poetry or liveliness, one must thank heaven for making one this way.[52]

The result is literature demoted to the level of coin collecting. In the same letter, indeed, Gustave describes how he spends his time: "I do some Greek, some history, I read Latin, I get a little drunk on those worthy ancients, for whom I've developed a sort of artistic cult. I am striving to live in the world of antiquity, I shall get there, God willing."[53] If it is merely a question of escaping into the ancient world, the medals of emperors will do beautifully, provided one contemplates them until they become unrealized. The texts of Sallust or Virgil, decipherable but resistant, will serve equally well: both medals and texts are, in short, excellent aids to autosuggestion. Art is another, and it hardly matters whether it is contemplative (reading Shakespeare) or creative. Flaubert will define himself in the same terms—or nearly—when he writes several years later to Maxime: I am a bourgeois who lives in the country and occupies himself with literature. The coin collector, after his ten hours of "visible, common, and general" existence, that is, after his hours at the office and before the family dinner, goes upstairs and shuts himself up with his collections; similarly the artist, after fulfilling his social and family duties, retires to his room and rereads Shakespeare or blackens some paper just for himself. It is an *occupation*. What could be more wrenching than this writer who dreams of being a collector in order to practice absenteeism at less cost? I say absenteeism because Gustave has no illusions: when the bourgeoisie at the height of its power will concern itself with *also* having a soul, Estonian readers will take as their most secret *reality* what is in fact, as Flaubert is not unaware, a *derealization*. And if this part of the self is not communicable, he knows the reason for that as well: it is because the imaginary, reduced to the pure moment of disconnection, is an intentional rupture of communication. What has become of his pride? Not so long ago, in *L'Education sentimentale*, he presented derealization as a gift of Providence and as the condition required for acceding to Art; now, if he is to be believed, art is only one means among others—and not the least costly—of achieving derealization. Formerly a sign of election, this now seems to him the most common practice, since to excel at it merely requires a coin

52. *Correspondance*, 1:209–10.
53. Ibid.

minted under Louis XIV. There is no longer any need to be fascinated with the *idea*, to dream that one is dissolved in the infinite, a simple mania will suffice; this resigned confidence is all the more afflicting as it is conveyed to us on a lively note. We shall find it again in various forms throughout the correspondence until his famous avowal to George Sand: all my life is summed up in blackening paper in order to flee anguish and boredom. In those moments, the neurosis—which he calls boredom or anomaly—is always presented as the central thing, and the decision to write as one of its byproducts. He even consents to portray himself to Ernest—to Ernest!—as a chronic invalid, a bit diminished, who is cared for by his family and to pass the time devotes himself to his hobby: "I'm virtually in a rut, I live in a regulated way, calm, regular, occupying myself exclusively with literature and history."[54] A month later, in a letter that we shall soon comment upon, he writes to Alfred: "I swear to you that I am not thinking of fame and hardly of Art." It is as if he needs to conceal his mad ambition from himself, to regard himself in earnest as an old boy beaten by life and indolently conceding, in his retirement, a battle lost in advance and, moreover, without interest.

True, he sometimes takes a different tone. But this is mainly when speaking of other artists: Shakespeare is a continent; one is tempted to believe that Homer, "because of his divine shudderings," had a "more than human nature"; Montaigne's *Essais,* more than any other book, "dispose to serenity." Can one simultaneously denounce the vanity of literature, make it the sad occupation of a shut-in, and give it with such epithets the numinous character of a sacred activity? When he offers advice to Alfred, he forgets all his precautions of modesty for his friend. Alfred confides that he is dying of boredom; when Gustave receives this letter, he is in the same frame of mind: "I was so sad for three days, I thought several times I would die of it . . . I'm beginning to believe that boredom doesn't kill, for I'm alive."[55] Immediately, however, he exhorts his friend: "Have patience, O lion of the desert! I too suffocated for a long time; the walls of my room at rue de l'Est still remember it . . . my lonely cries of distress. I bellowed and yawned there by turns." Has he changed so much, then, he who just the evening before thought he would die of sadness? All of a sudden, however, he elevates his tone: "Teach your chest to consume only a little air; it will open with a vast joy when you are up on great heights

54. 13 August '45.
55. 13 May 1845, at Milan, *Correspondance,* 1:171.

and have to breathe hurricanes. Think, work, write . . . Hew your marble like a good worker . . . The only way not to be unhappy is to enclose yourself in Art and count all the rest for nothing; pride replaces everything when it rests on a broad base." [56] What has prompted such arrogant admonishment? Of course, the close connection between Art and Pride has again been made, that same connection we have observed from his adolescence and which he tries to mask in the letters of 1845–47. This time there is a complete reversal: Pride replaces everything; in other words, there is no salvation but the mad project of rivaling the greatest through his work. And the young writer who gives this magnificent cry claims *at the same moment* to be merely the younger son of a good family, doleful and mean-spirited, who travels with his parents like a grocer. When he once again speaks of himself in this letter, it's as if he were moribund: "I thought . . . I would die [of boredom]; literally. Hard as I tried, I could not stop clenching my teeth." Naturally, these affirmations—effects given without causes—are in fact accusations against Hamard and the Flaubert parents. Gustave knows very well that his friend will not be fooled. Be that as it may, they overlap with so many other allusions to his incurable "obstinacy" that this "agony" does not seem to be an accident provoked by the situation but rather the recrudescence of a chronic state underlying the action of external factors. In short, it is poor Gustave—the wretch—who gives Alfred the advice Jules would give him at the end of his sentimental education, except that this *admonishment* seems to proceed from an activist theory of Art: one must *work*, hew the marble like a good worker. This last image, especially, evokes a violent, even physical labor that simultaneously exhausts and strengthens. Does Gustave preach by example? Certainly not, since he writes subsequently: "I have said an irrevocable farewell to the practical life. Now I ask only for five or six hours of peace in my room, a big fire in winter, and two candles every evening to see by." Nothing more: he does not say what he will do with the solitude he asks for. He barely manages to inform us at the very end of the letter that he will write his "Oriental tale" the following winter. And to wrap it up, this note of humility: in Genoa he had the first idea for *La Tentation*, but "I'm not the fellow for that job."

This letter is striking, less for what it reveals than for what it conceals. It cannot be understood without adding these four words, which are not written anywhere in it but are implicit in his homily:

56. May 1845. Gustave is writing from Milan.

"Do as I do!" Gustave certainly had them in mind, and one detail reveals it: the tense of the verbs for which he is the subject—"I too suffocated . . . I bellowed and yawned"—implies that he has recovered, and that the time is past when boredom was suffocating him. And who, therefore, but the hermit of the Hôtel-Dieu has "taught his chest to consume only a little air"? So he extols this method because he was cured through it; he doesn't say so because he *doesn't want* to. For fear of annoying his friend? He has no such scruples. He seems, rather, to be playing two roles at once, and is afraid of emphasizing the first lest he disclose its contradiction of the second.

Furthermore, the four words that are missing in May '45 are found four months later in another letter, again to Alfred;[57] here we also encounter the metaphor of the good worker, this time applied to Gustave himself. Flaubert has been at Croisset since the beginning of the summer; he enjoys "five or six peaceful hours," which in Milan were the unique object of his desires. Alfred has written him that he admires his success. He answers:

I notice that I scarcely laugh any more and that I am no longer sad. You speak of my serenity, dear fellow, and you envy me for it. True, it can be surprising. Ill, irritable, vulnerable a thousand times a day to moments of atrocious anguish, without women, without life, without any of the diversions here below, I continue my work like the good worker who, with his sleeves rolled up and his hair damp with sweat, strikes his anvil without worrying if it rains, if the wind blows, if it hails or thunders.

What is this slow work? We are in September, he finished *L'Education* in January: that makes seven months without writing a line. He has no intention of taking up the pen again so soon, for he informs us in the same letter that he is going to "busy himself with arranging [his] Oriental tale; but it is crude." Arranging: giving his tale an internal law but not writing it; he is not even involved in its composition, just in "ruminating" on its subject. He will soon acquire books on the Orient in order to immerse himself in "local color." His readings at the time of his letter and in the months that follow can hardly pass for "that great study of style" that seemed to Jules an indispensable apprenticeship. Gustave yawned over a work of Chinest philosophy and closed it, promising himself to take it up again; he relaxes by scouring the *Cours de littérature dramatique* for its silliest bits. In August he "was continually engaged in analyzing the plays of Voltaire." No doubt he

57. September 1845, *Correspondance*, 1:191.

is still doing it. That's all. Where are the hammer blows? Where is the anvil and the burning iron? Is he lying? Does he want to make Alfred believe he has "something in the works"? Not at all: "I swear to you that I am not thinking of fame and hardly of Art. I seek to spend my time in the least boring way, and I have found it." He could hardly be more frank, if not sincere.

In order to understand this new contradiction the passage must be returned to its context. On 23 September 1845, Alfred, who had just written the *Dialogue de Brutus et du Don Quichotte* and "a play in verse, the 'Choeur des Bacchantes,'" says to Flaubert: "I have, my dear fellow, just finished a tale that I hope will amuse you. It is called *La Botte merveilleuse*. I shall tell you nothing of the plot nor of the joke, in my opinion *sublime* (too bad, it's said), with which the play ends. I think it is difficult to do something as agreeably droll. I have postponed the play about Emma Caye, I hardly involve myself now with things that are not immediately publishable." We learn from the same letter that he reads little: Quinault, "an admirable poet," Rollin, Darwin. He is—unusually—in a rather joyful mood, and quite content with himself: "philosophy, poetry . . . , are the two inspirations that God united in your servant." Is he unaware that this good news will exasperate Gustave? How? Because he is *working*? Since April he has written a dialogue, a play in verse, and a comic poem. And he still finds time to read Darwin? Isn't this just what Gustave *ought to be doing*? In his previous letter, dated 15 September, Alfred explained his long silence by saying simply: "I have done a lot of work." Gustave, who has done nothing since January and is not unaware that his readings and rereadings are alibis, could not help *envying* his friend. Moreover, what profoundly irritates him is the nonchalance with which Alfred, so full of himself, announces to him this "*enormous*" thing: "I hardly involve myself now with things that are not immediately publishable." We know that Flaubert at the time often wonders if he will ever publish; among the reasons he advances is the quite honest idea that one should not let one's pen be guided or restrained by considerations alien to art—in particular by the concern with whether or not a work is publishable. This announced preoccupation of Alfred's is enough to suggest that his friend's new works are of mediocre quality. Nor does he delude himself: if Alfred, who is not in the habit of spoiling him, has treated him to two letters in less than a month—sending the second when the first has not yet received an answer—it is because he was happy with his "burlesque" and could not help sharing his satisfaction. Flaubert thinks that Alfred really is in luck and, at the same

289

time, that he is easily satisfied. He is afraid that *La Botte merveilleuse* is insipid and will prompt his contempt for the *Alter Ego,* but he none-theless dreads—without much credence—finding himself in the presence of a masterpiece. In any event, and whatever the result, this literary activism seems worrisome to him: it is too facile. If it pays off so much the worse for Gustave, who has put his money on patience; if it does not pay, so much the worse for Alfred. Flaubert's answer is dictated by spite. Certainly he begins by congratulating the happy author:

> I have a great desire to see your story of *La Botte merveilleuse* and your chorus of Bacchantes and the rest.—Work, work, write, write as long as you can, as long as the muse will carry you. That is the best steed, the best carriage for traveling in life—the weari-ness of existence does not weigh on our shoulders when we com-pose. It is true that the moments of fatigue and weariness that follow are all the more terrible, but so what! Two glasses of vin-egar and one glass of wine are worth more than one glass of colored water. As for me, I no longer feel either the hot transports of youth or that great bitterness of former times. They are mingled together, and make a universal hue.

The opening exhortations refer to a theory of inspiration that Gustave has long since abandoned: Alfred lets himself "be carried by the muse"; this means that he abandons himself to the vulgar impulse of spontaneity—which is precisely what Flaubert did in his adolescence, before the obsession with taste afflicted him with impotence. More-over, this tone of good-natured superiority—which, like the orders he gives him ("work, work, write, write"), is usually taken with refer-ence to decisions that Alfred made spontaneously and without asking for his opinion—is doubled here with an edge of treachery: he inti-mates that Alfred's works do not interest him for their aesthetic value but quite simply for their practical utility: as long as you compose, you are not bored, he is telling him in essence. It is as if he were ordering him to write for the sake of diversion. The effect is to sweep Alfred's production onto the terrain on which Gustave takes refuge when his own works are challenged,[58] as if to reveal to him indirectly what he forecasts for Alfred's. Elsewhere he is careful to add that "the moments of fatigue . . . that follow are all the more terrible for it." Why should this be, unless it is in those moments that the writer re-

---

58. Which will be soon be shown by his reaction when Louise refuses to show *La Bretagne* to Gautier.

reads what he has written and finds apalling what he thought was good? Of course, there is also the fall back into the nauseating contingency of lived experience. For Gustave, both are on a par, and the insipidness of existence becomes all the more sour as one is discontent with the pages he has just written. In short, an idea pierces through Gustave's condescension, which could be articulated as follows: "Write, since it amuses you. When you stop, you will know your pain and the horrible disappointment of having achieved nothing but mediocrity. But what does it matter as long as you've had a good time?"

In the meantime, he shifts quickly to himself, and we learn that he now feels neither enthusiasm nor despair, in short, that he is more *adult* than his elder—for whom art is still a childish pastime. To Alfred, who *is still living,* and for one glass of wine is willing to swallow two of vinegar, Gustave discreetly recalls his superiority *as a dead man.*

Indeed, he has to feel superior to this older friend, whom he once adored and still respects but no longer admires. He will soon write to Maxime: "Send me [your] scenario. Alfred is busy with other things—he is a curious fellow." [59] Anxious, envious, humiliated, bitter, a little scornful, he needs to find a higher perch. But he cannot set his own works against Alfred's since he has done nothing. So he takes it into his head that his friend's previous letter—unanswered (no doubt out of resentment and dignity: it had come too late, after too long a silence)—contained one of the rare expressions of praise that Alfred ever conferred on him: [60] "I admire your serenity. Is it because you are less distracted than I, less assaulted by the *external?* Or is it that you have more strength? You are always happy to save yourself by a means I could choose as well but have not so far wanted to cling to." Since his friend seems to acknowledge Gustave's superiority, Gustave hastens to exalt it; he takes it as a pretext to pester Alfred with literary advice. Curiously, he thinks he is repeating his friend's sentence, while changing its terms and meaning: Alfred said, not without some irony, that he *admired* Gustave's serenity; Gustave's answers him: "You speak of my serenity, dear boy, and you envy it." But envy is Flaubert's perpetual torment; he feels it even now, and cannot help attributing it to Le Poittevin, who is too indifferent, in fact, and too narcissistic to desire what belongs to others. This directed scorn is at

59. April 1846, hence seven months later. *Correspondance,* 1:206. No doubt the issue was already Alfred's marriage, which Flaubert announces to Ernest on the following 4 June.
60. Highly ambiguous: I would write as well as you if I deigned to write.

the source of a dialogue at cross purposes: Gustave is convinced that his friend is asking him the recipe for ataraxia and hastens to provide it: do as I do! Yet Alfred's letter is clear: he is consumed by "the external" (family and social life, whores, drink), knows that he is wasting himself but doesn't give a damn, and specifies that in any case he hasn't the least desire to seek his salvation in literature. Flaubert doesn't want to know; he reproves his suicidal friend as if Alfred too considered Art the supreme value[61] and simply failed to recognize his true calling out of heedlessness or dissipation.

The "slow work" is about to yield its meaning to us. On the surface it is an irritated reaction to the slight works his friend has produced effortlessly and too quickly. Gustave wanted to invest these two words with a whole lesson in literary ethics: you write trifles, you seek publication, you are worldly even when it comes to literature; as for me, I know that genius is a long patience. No sooner summoned, the good worker is charged with representing the *craft* aspect of art and challenging the little martinets of literature who consider writing a form of amusement. The annoying thing is that Alfred is writing and knows that Gustave is not.[62] So it should be the elder exhorting the younger. This is enough to change the role of the hammer blows. In the letter from Milan, they symbolized creation; the worker, moreover, was highly qualified, he was Michelangelo shaping his marble, an inert but precious material. Now the worker has become a blacksmith and hammers on a base piece of iron. It is no longer the finished product that matters, it is the effort, the patience, the indifference to everything that is not the *job*—in short, inferior qualities. More precisely, what interests Flaubert in this laborer is less his labor than his immutability. It is the setting that changes, a storm after fine weather. But the blacksmith Gustave sees does not change; eternity is manifest in him through repetition—the same gestures, the same sounds. This time, he is the statue: his marble arm raises a cold hammer in some garden in Rouen amidst lightning flashes or, if the sun comes out, pigeons. The blacksmith: Gustave commemorated by a statue. Ill, anxious, *I am immutable*, I give myself up to the void and maintain it in myself, using all the stratagems of passive activity. That is my slow work: to condition myself in such a way that I am no more than an

61. "People of *our race* . . ." he tells him. But Alfred is not of the literary race and is well aware of it.
62. In his first letter of September 1845, Alfred asks him if he is still thinking about his Oriental tale and "if its conception is becoming clear"—which suggests that he must have thought it muddy and that he let Gustave know it.

opening onto the unreal—I "send everything packing and myself along with it" in order to recover myself as universal subject in the imaginary. And what will come of it? Is this opening a trap for images? Or doesn't this long, patient gaping, provided it hopes for nothing, *deserve* their visitation?

We shall learn nothing more, at least in this letter. No sooner has the arrogant advisor shot out his "Do as I do" than he is deflated. He has just been speaking clearly, as Jules would have done, and affirming the necessity of an emotional "pause," when in the same paragraph he does an about-face and forswears himself. He has gone so far as to say that "the happiness of people of our kind is in the Idea, nowhere else." And this is what he adds: "I . . . do not think much about Art. I seek to pass my time in the least boring way, and I have found it." What has become of the marble blacksmith? What connection is established between the "slow work" and the "least boring pastime"? Indeed, they amount to the same thing; but in one case, it appears to be an ethico-aesthetic operation, indispensable and sufficient to gain access to art, whereas in the other, having lost its efficacy, it offers the best way of spending his time while waiting for death. We find here once more, and more clearly, the oscillation we have continually encountered in Gustave's letters, two concepts of Art that are contrasting but sufficiently indeterminate for there to be constant shifting from one to the other in the same sentences. On the one hand, Art is a mystery to which one accedes only by a new birth accompanied by a methodical ascesis, *which suffices* provided it is practiced with rigor; on the other hand, it is the hobby of a landowner, a recluse. But even in this second conception, Flaubert preserves his repugnance for literature as a diversion; in any case, one must reread the *great* authors. Thus a passage is forged between the two conceptions: even to the eyes of the bourgeois who occupies himself with literature, the absolute being of nonbeing and of evil, Beauty, is revealed by the masterpieces of the past. Yet *even this*—the dazzled communication with the saints of literature—is often and explicitly presented as the hobby of an invalid.

In the face of these contradictory and simultaneous evaluations— encountered *everywhere*, on *all* occasions in the years 1845–47— should we not assume that Flaubert is concealing his real idea of Art, not only the value he attributes to Beauty but also the nature of his ascesis, his real objectives, and the very meaning of lived experience? This idea appears marginally when he trusts himself enough and speaks naively of Shakespeare, or, as in the letter of September '45, when irritation makes him lose control of what he is saying. When he perceives that he has begun to show his true colors, he abruptly changes direction and palms off his theory of art-as-diversion onto his correspondent or, if he has revealed himself too much, declares that he is incapable of ever being an artist. Furious with Alfred's offhand manner, he retorts by speaking of his *slow work;* but he quickly catches himself—this is saying too much. In any event he extols *detachment;* when he is entirely sincere, he sees it as the only way of achieving the aesthetic representation of the cosmos; and when he distrusts himself, he makes it the shortest road to stagnation, the sole way of being, if not happy, at least calm. However, when he instructs his correspondents on the merits of ponds, smooth and calm, hiding their slime in their depths, and when he writes that his serenity is in the depths of his soul, hidden beneath continual exasperation, illness, moments of atrocious anguish that torment him "a thousand times a day," he is not really speaking of the same thing. In one case the calm is superficial and the passions are underground, lurking, ready to surge up if he moves; in the other, the violence, the rages, the anguished moments are immediate experience, serenity is the underlying exis and can be obtained only by an emotional pause, which consists of putting these superficial tumults between parentheses, of living them as non-experience, as worthless small change, and, through the negation of the subjective, of slyly and indirectly designating the immutable tranquillity of the Parmenidean One. Even the outcome is different. In one case, the immediate given of consciousness is ataraxia. In the other there are acrimonious rages, mental disorders that Maxime has not failed to observe; and Gustave's work—which escapes Du Camp's simplistic gaze—aims at rendering them harmless in order to reduce them to merely what they are: sounds and tremors that don't engage him in the least. Yet he defines himself now by one attitude and now by the other. And as soon as he senses he is overemphasizing serenity—the fruit of an ethical tension—he reverts to stagnation, an attitude of withdrawal born of the fear of living, and seeks to give the impression that both states are equivalent. There is thus one road to Art, and Flaubert has set out upon it: I have not quite finished my *Education sentimentale* but I am almost there. Yet he says nothing about it—or as little as possible. Why? Why so many obscure pages of his correspondence, in 1845–47, in which he contradicts himself from one line to the next? Why is Jules the Arrogant—always present, always loved—passed over in silence? Why does he want to deceive the reader? What is he afraid of?

B. "Loser Wins" as Hope for a Miracle

"Loser wins": Gustave dimly perceived it in the decisive moment when he collapsed at his brother's feet, or perhaps later between referential attacks when, bedridden and pondering his illness, he was attempting to find its meaning. If someone else were involved, we might see in it a theme of compensation: an accident transforms a young man "with a future" into an invalid. If he decides to regard the misfortune that shatters his life as a providential gift that has forced him to withdraw from the world so as to bring him to himself or to God, he is perhaps determined, after the fact, to change the meaning of a fortuitous, unforeseen, unforeseeable humiliation that pounced on him from the outside yet must be internalized. But we know that accident counts for little in the crisis of January '44, that Gustave's illness, prepared for since childhood, prophesied many times by the victim, is indistinguishable from life, and that it is at once suffered and intentional. In short, he *immediately* discovered the basic meaning of his fall, the intention to deny man in order to acquire the gifts of the artist, and on the basis of this intuition he constructed the end of *L'Education*. But this empiricist who, while loving the Idea, detests *ideas* and, even more, systems, has for once systematized too much. He has logically reconstructed a magical operation—and there, we discover, if not the compensation, at least the deception. By injecting necessity into it after the fact, he sought to *take out insurance* and, even if Providence should not exist, to define the rules of the game—from what he calls his knowledge of the world—in such a way that losses are automatically translated by proportionate but always superior gains. He has even invented a negative dialectic, the best example of which—and at the same time the verbal expression of the fundamental scheme that presides over the last pages of *L'Education*—is provided by this sentence: "Jules was enriched by all the illusions he lost." [63]

But if we reflect on it, the intention that precipitated him to the bottom of the carriage, arms and legs gone limp, seems at once more

---

63. The illusion he is speaking about here has nothing in common with the grand, plenary Illusion which he will tell Louise is the absolute truth. At issue here are beliefs bound to passions: the fidelity of a friend, the constancy of a mistress would be, in this sense, illusions since the imaginary is enslaved by it to the real, to the practical. Thus to lose an illusion is to lose a determination. And Flaubert, in the statement that follows those earlier words, explains rather well that the loss of an illusion is the negation of a negation: "As the barriers that had surrounded him fell away, his sight discovered new horizons."

humble and more madly audacious. He has certainly not yet refined his system; when he flees from Paris and Hamard's pain, he still believes that the worst is certain and that the best man loses out. Thus the obscure wager that sinking into abjection will win genius is not wagered *on anything*. It is not even a matter of calculating one's chances: one must rely on higher authorities, one must trust, in the face of and despite everything. Stripped of all the artifices that masked it in the subsequent reconstruction, "Loser wins" appears to be the sudden capitulation of an embattled swimmer who stops struggling against the currents and the waves and lets himself go: there, I give myself up to you, bear witness that I struggled to the end. If I die, it is because I was not made to live; if I survive, it is because you will have saved me in all gratuitousness, or for reasons known only to yourself. Thus the fall is a speech addressed to silent powers that watch him go under without making a sign, and when he opens his eyes again, he is unaware of their final decision. These semisymbolic characters are, as I have said, the two faces of Achille-Cléophas, both sides of the coin, God and the Devil, exalted and sublimated.

The Devil cannot be softened. He must be neutralized *by consenting to him all the way along*. Who is the Prince of Darkness but the personification of the paternal—and bourgeois—ideology, namely *determinism?* Lived by Flaubert in despair, this conception of scientism suppresses morality as well as art: the law of exteriority *does not compose;* the real, always exterior to itself, can never offer anything but an illusion of unity. Thus genius, the power of superintegration, has no real existence: how could a heap of colliding atoms ever produce it? With regard to existing as a determination of the imaginary, this is excluded: the laws of nature *know* only reality; *homo sapiens* and *homo faber do not acknowledge* imagination except to subject it to their practical projects. Knowledge—as the philosophical practitioner always thought—is theoretical and practical action on being, so it tends toward the Absolute, whereas art, the filigree of nonbeing, is merely idle gossip. When he wrote *L'Education,* impassioned by his discovery, Gustave had not yet understood the extent of his commitment: it was not only a question of losing everything *as a man,* or even *as an artist;* this disaster had to be proclaimed the logical consequence of his stupid ambition: a new Icarus, he wanted to fly, unaware that the malicious Demon has decided to subject us to the laws of gravity so we should crawl on the crust of the globe and be condemned to mediocrity. Today he recognizes his mistake: genius is not compatible with the laws of nature; for wanting the impossible he has at last deserved

296

the memorable plunge that broke his back; tormented by "dreadful anguish," this convulsionary manages to demolish the mental structures that might have allowed him to plead honorably: "Well done; my father was right, why didn't I listen to him?" When Maxime writes, "Flaubert was a novelist of great talent; without his illness, he might have been a genius," it is not out of pure malice: Gustave wanted to play that role for him, he wanted to make him witness to a proclaimed collapse. His pride, of course, often compels him to act out of character, especially when others take him too seriously. That is when he speaks of his "slow work." But he immediately takes fright—the Devil is within earshot—and begins again to play the bourgeois whose infirmities keep him in the country and who, incapable of writing, rereads the works of others.

For there have been men massive as a continent; even today there is Hugo. In short, genius exists, it has existed, it will exist tomorrow. But since it is established that it contradicts the laws of the universe, an all-powerful will has suspended those laws in every particular case. A great writer is always something of a Lazarus: he suffers the common fate, dies, and begins to stink; at this moment, someone intervenes by snapping his fingers, time reverses itself like an hourglass, he rises up again, a genius. If Gustave merely wanted to trick the Devil, there is no need for him to believe in his character: let him hide his projects from others, let him avoid mulling them over in solitude, let him pursue them with a silent determination, that is enough. But as soon as God is involved, the unhappy young man is compelled to despair. Indeed, if He exists—and nothing is less certain—He has abandoned the earth to the Devil. In any case, it is as if He had. There is not a single proof of His presence, not even a presumption of it, apart from the religious instinct, a splendid aspiration found incarnate only in foolish practices. If the world is Hell, it is obvious that any figuration of the sacred is necessarily its infernal simulacrum. On one point, in any case, the Almighty is in agreement with Satan: life must be a long Calvary; as an adolescent, Gustave observed in his notebook: humanity has only one purpose, that is to suffer. In other words: this, at least, is my purpose. Now he is going to use his dolorism to acquire merit by conforming to the will of God. And so we have his daring wager on the night that almost broke him: to suffer *in the presence* of the absent God. I would say that the wager is a double one: agnostic because his diabolical father killed faith in him, Gustave makes the Pascalian wager—*without losing his agnosticism*. In order to save not his soul but his last chances in this world: God exists because

He alone makes genius possible. By the total acceptance of suffering in January '44 and in the years that follow, he makes a second wager out of resignation. Since God wants this suffering, the invalid, by the good use he makes of it, acquires merit in His eyes. But merit is not always rewarded, Gustave has paid dearly for this knowledge, he who always thinks he deserves the successes of others. Likewise *he wagers* that God will choose him *on this earth,* and that at the end of a sad and monotonous life He will give him genius and glory.

But for this double wager to allow him to win, it must be thrust down to the very bottom of his consciousness and never spoken. It's the rule of the game. God witholds Himself, that is the fact of the matter. Therefore one must reject all religions, that is what He wants. Here agnosticism serves Gustave: this impossibility of faith must be lived thoroughly, one must refuse the temptations of faith, proclaim to the end that man is alone on the earth, abandoned to the Devil, that is, to mechanism. To be in complete accord with divine will, there is no need even to seek it, groaning, as Pascal put it; one needs to have the certainty that will not be found on earth. But *one must continually suffer because of it.* We see the trickery and the most basic intention of failure: Gustave will suffer divine absence all his life precisely because he thinks that his suffering is agreeable to God. If he contests His existence by despairing of it, it is because he wagered, wordlessly in January '44, that He existed. This attitude is all the easier for him to adopt as it is merely the organization and radicalization in bad faith of his disbelief and the frustration resulting from it. The intentional structure is reversed, however: he suffered from not believing; now he affirms his disbelief *in order* to suffer from it. The moment of agnosticism remains intact: it is quite true that he cannot have faith; but through the pain that results from it—which has become *good* pain— he affirms the God he denies. Formerly the pain was merely a straying, now it is *meritorious,* and through this merit its status has changed, it becomes a mute affectation of Transcendence. Gustave enters into the role: he will be the one whom the entire universe discourages from believing—in conformity with the views of the eternal Being—and who, convinced of His nonexistence by reason, by science, by higher authorities, does not cease, despite his disbelief, to affirm that He exists through a simple and profound refusal to resign himself.

Beginning in 1845, Gustave understood that his illness was a conversion in the religious sense of the term. But in his Manichaean universe, this conversion cannot in any case manifest itself as a direct communication with the Divine since the devil reigns over minds themselves. A single change: formerly, he could not believe; now he keeps himself from believing because he does believe. Is this to say that his bad faith is constant? Certainly not: nothing is so concerted in Flaubert; besides, his silence with respect to this operation, even within himself, makes his bad faith unstable. There is no doubt that he often falls back into a naive agnosticism—which characterized him before the crisis—and, more rarely, is on the verge of believing, as happened to him during his adolescence. Yet I shall try to show that the emphasis henceforth is on trickery.

If they know how to avoid the Devil's crude tricks, the Almighty should be able to recognize His own and save them in this world. On one condition, however: that they keep themselves from all hope, that they persist in despairing of their worldly ambitions. For Gustave, nothing is clearer: since he *must* not believe in God, how should he believe in Providence? Jules profited from it, which sufficiently demonstrates Flaubert's secret vow. But Flaubert, as we know, never reveals himself except in fictions. With the manuscript complete, the oyster closes up again: one must be determined to lose, that is the command. In *L'Education* Gustave revealed to us the *technical* meaning of his project: systematically to disqualify all received impressions and, putting lived experience between parentheses, to realize himself deep down as pure serenity, as the absolute equivalence of Being and Nonbeing. At the end of the ascesis, he will be so completely empty of self that his own existence can be achieved only in the imaginary and through the detachment proper to the imagination; then he will become Lord of images. This is the meaning of the *slow work*. But of course this is what he must carefully avoid saying or even thinking. As long as he works fervently on himself, Gustave will abstain from thinking about Art and, more particularly, about making it the purpose of his enterprise. With the same insincerity the good Christian does good out of obedience or charity but not to deserve Heaven. If Gustave "enters into the Idea" for glory or to free his genius, he remains prisoner of his terrestrial interests. It is proper, *on the contrary*, during the ascesis to insist firmly on the vanity of the Beautiful, to indicate some disdain for literature, that minor occupation, and simultaneously to lament his own impotence. The contestation of Beauty is part of these mental exercises: as long as our mystique is not utterly despoiled, as long as its particular essence is not defined as the identity of the quintessential real and the imaginary, the Beauty he will encounter along the way—whether in a line of Virgil or in a scene from *King Lear*—will not be true Beauty. Or, at least, Gustave will not yet be prepared to grasp it in its plenitude: if he laid claim to it when so many ties still bind him to the earth, he would be lost. But neither should he decide to deny it in the name of some certainty, as if he intuited that he would grasp its meaning better at a later stage; that would suggest that he has been given a sign, a guideline, which is not even conceivable in the dark night he must endure. One does not *find* Beauty: one day it will impose itself like a providential requirement. Consequently, Flaubert is determined to doubt; he writes to Louise: "I love Art and I hardly believe in it,"[64] or, "You believe that I love study and art so much because I busy myself with it. If I were to probe my real feelings, perhaps I would discover that it is nothing more than habit. I believe in the eternity of only one thing, *Illusion*, which is the real truth. All other things are merely relative."[65] And when he speaks of writing, it is as an organic function: "I write for myself, for myself alone, as I smoke and as I sleep. It is almost an animal function, it is so personal and intimate."[66] The slow work is presented to God as pure, hopeless fidelity to a religious ideal.

For it is all the same, isn't it, to believe in God and in his own genius, since there is proof that the latter is a grace bestowed by the former. The gallant young man rejects human ends, just like a saint, but since Heaven is silent and grace is denied him, he remains on the level of the negative Infinite, contesting everything and "beginning with oneself"; he does everything in his power so that genius may come to him: he enters into the Idea and becomes a Brahman, that is, slightly mad. Let us understand that the evocation of Hinduism (undoubtedly by mistake: this "Brahman" looks to me very much like a bonze, a Buddhist monk), immediately followed by an allusion to his mental state, shows that Flaubert means to signal the two aspects of his absenteeism: to "enter into the Idea" is to put himself in permanent contact with the sacred *if* God exists; if He does not exist, it is to sink into madness. Nothing of all that is wished (or almost nothing: "My will also had something to do with it"); things happened because they had to happen; Gustave did not need to succeed in order to persevere. The "nature" of this "great man *manqué*" is such that he has maintained his postulations against all evidence, becoming a demand addressed to no one and perpetuating itself without the least hope in an inhuman solitude beneath the empty sky: God ought to exist to

64. *Correspondance*, 2:13.
65. Ibid., p. 51.
66. Ibid., p. 40.

give me the genius I lack, I will not give this up; refusing worldly goods and the company of men, I will remain empty, in a state of permanent receptivity, determined to deserve the grace that will never be accorded me. Let God make the next move.

The general meaning of the *slow work* is rather close to that which Jules gave to his evolution. For him, the void, lived as a detachment from being, was the necessary and sufficient condition for writing a masterpiece. At issue was an internal connection between two notions—annihilation, genius—in which one engendered the other without mediation. Now detachment, the necessary condition of genius—on this point Gustave has not wavered—ceases to be sufficient. The void is a kind of precondition that *can* provoke the intervention of a force at once intimate and alien (which the *other* has always been for Flaubert). It is tempting God, that's all. The relation of vacuity to Art is no longer a strict one: the mediation of a third party is necessary for it to be established. In a way the order of the notions remains unchanged, since the third party, or mediator, is none other than the All. But the All has doubled itself: officially it remains the pantheistic universe of transfinites; but secretly, and through humility alone, Gustave conceives it as the continuous Creation of a personal God, the rigorous and reflective unity of the Cosmos, which alone has the possibility of opening to its creatures the infinitely infinite world of possibles. Flaubert does not pray—with a few exceptions, one of which we shall be discussing—for his Passion compels him to incarnate the agnostic-in-spite-of-himself. But his brahmanization is equivalent to a prayer: hidden God, in whom I must not believe and whom I would love with all my soul if I had permission to do so, look; I have rid myself of all that men have given me, and here I am, alone and naked, virgin wax as on the day of my birth, because I want to receive my life only from You.

Gustave gives Buffon's saying, which he so eagerly repeats, a new meaning. How can he preserve the classic meaning—"Go over your work twenty times"—when he doesn't even work? When he portrays himself as a modest craftsman, it is out of prudence, to proclaim insincerely the mediocrity of his talent. But when he writes: if genius is a long patience, who *would deserve* it more than I, when he has just spent two and half years musing without touching his desk, it is clear that patience has nothing more in common with the *labor improbus* to which it was first related. It is quite simply a humble expectation without indication of duration. Gustave thereby reveals a conception of Art more adapted to his constituted character: it is a passive activity.

One must do nothing, want nothing, solicit nothing, be unaware even of this expectation, then it can happen—with the concurrence of this God who does not exist—that the point of view of death, of the immutable, of Nothingness may become that of Art; in this case the infinite totalization of the imaginary appears suspended in Nonbeing as the clamorous and variegated expression of that mortuary lacuna. And the Idea, the intentional and sympathetic relation of this Nothingness to the agitation of unreal phantasms and of the unrealized real, asks for and produces words that will fix this tumult forever. A letter to Louise Colet dated 13 December 1846 gives an accurate rendering of what might easily be considered the first manifestation of that "choice of impotence" which characterizes the writers and poets of the second half of the nineteenth century:

> Work every day patiently an equal number of hours. Become accustomed to a studious and calm life; you will find in it, first of all, great charm and you will draw strength from it. I also have a mania for staying up all night; that leads to nothing but exhaustion. You must mistrust everything that resembles inspiration and which is often merely preconception and a self-generated facticious exaltation that has not come of its own accord. Besides, one does not live in inspiration. Pegasus more often walks than gallops. The whole trick is in knowing how to get him to change gaits according to your will. But for this, we musn't strain him, as they say in equestrian terms. One must read, meditate a great deal, always think about style, and write as little as one can, solely to calm the irritation of the Idea, which insists on taking some form and will revolve inside us until we have found one for it that is exact, precise, adequate to itself. Note that one succeeds in doing things by dint of patience and sustained energy. Buffon's saying is blasphemous, but it has too often been denied.

Work patiently (Latin, Greek, English): these pseudo-occupations are destined to sustain the emptiness of the soul and one's anorexia. Think of style: habituate yourself to taking language for an imaginary (and not, as Jules thought he could do, assimilate the direction and dealings of others). Above all, do not write: challenge Romantic inspiration, which is passionate, hence factitious and too real at the same time (one *generates it oneself* because one has not taken renunciation, namely patience, far enough); meditate: put yourself in a state of openness to unreality. But you will take up the pen only out of necessity: here, inspiration is replaced by exigency; the idea "revolves inside us until we have found its form." But this exigency itself is a grace: it guides, produces, and rejects words, and we know truly that it has found its adequate expression when its "irritation" subsides and we again find peace. Nothing smacking of activity in the writer: the Idea is the Infinite that devours him and chooses its form by elimination, it is the heteronomy of language. Indeed, its "irritations" give birth to small works that make him *have patience*, sometimes simple sentences that flow, unrecognized and unknown, from his pen. If God manifests Himself and gives plenary grace to the writer, the exigency of the Idea will be total. It will demand expression in a whole book. From here on in, the cause will be won.

Romantic inspiration is rejected: Flaubert recalls the enthusiasms of his adolescence, his fits of eloquence and his impulsive writings; he judges them severely: it was insincerity itself, this provoked exaltation in which he beat his sides to find something to say. However, in another form he retains the idea of the inspired writer: God is there, invisible. But the Romantic conception is positive: God whispers in our ear, it is the brimming over of a soul suddenly inhabited, spilling onto the paper. Flaubert's conception is negative and based on the absence of the divine; be that as it may, through a certain but unknown grace, which must be merited by patient humility, the moment comes when the absolute negative—that is, the perfect lacuna of the soul—*demands* that one set fire to the whole of language in order to seal it before the world as its pure negation through the realization of the unreal and the unrealization of the real. At issue is a sacred imperative that cannot impose itself without simultaneously bestowing the means to obey it. This means that the Idea cannot claim its form before having unrealized all of language. That is God's role: the writer's is merely obedience; he has sacrificed himself so that from his own unreality may spring a normative relation of Nothingness—the Idea as undifferentiated Imagination (without any particular image)—to language taken as a reservoir of verbal images. That comes when it will. And meditation on style does not aim at the progressive amelioration of the latter: it is a mental exercise; one dreams of words, and as a result one accustoms oneself to regarding them as dreams. Nothing more: a beautiful line pondered—when it is written by another, of course—reveals its derealizing function in relation to practical language. The ideal is to arrive, through frequent rereadings, at the moment when its meaning, still present but too familiar to impose itself, becomes its pretext and when its sonorous density presents itself as a disturbing materiality utterly consumed by the imaginary. These ponderings can teach nothing and are not meant to do so; their function is

303

to elevate the mind, to put it in contact with the sacred—through the intervention of *sacred texts*—and to *confer merit on it*. Think unceasingly of style, says Flaubert, in the tone a Christian would use to say: think unceasingly of God. Indeed, between the believer who thinks of God without ever encountering Him and the mystic who, in rare moments, encounters Him with such intensity that he does not know whether he possesses Him or is possessed by Him, the difference is *qualitative*. The frequency and application of meditations by the first have no chance of gaining him access to the status of the second, unless God wills it. Similarly, the man who is *always thinking of style*, whatever his ambition, will nonetheless fail to become that mystic, the writer. He will simply maintain within himself, by the constant use of language as silent transfinite, the religious tension that makes him agreeable to the Almighty.

This is just what Gustave did quite intentionally from January '45 until the writing of the first *Saint Antoine:* he waited. We understand the meaning of his strategies of failure: like the referential attacks, but in their own way, they renewed the fundamental failure of January '44. Far from aiming at some practical progress, Flaubert's occupations can properly be understood only if we see in them the imitation and negation of all real action, even writing. They *have* to be absurd and like caricatures: in that way they indicate to Flaubert *from inside* that he is not made to act, that action, whatever it may be, is decomposed in him and exposes its futility. The rereadings have a deeper purpose: to suppress the difference between the author and the reader in such a way that the latter, receiving the read text as a series of passive syntheses, feels expanded to the point of believing that he produced it and by the same token grasps creation itself as a passive activity and is prepared some day to produce inert syntheses controlled by the Idea. In any event, we are dealing with a pastime which, while furthering the self-destruction of the artist, his passage to the imaginary, manifests his goodwill to the two witnesses of his life: I have lost, I know it, and see, I am completing my own ruin. Which means, on the one hand: I am not leaving your Hell; on the contrary, I am burying myself in it, assuming my defeat by exploiting it in minor and degrading failures. And on the other: I suffer and I leave myself in Your hands, by myself I want to be only nothingness, and I wait for being to come to me from You. Now we can better understand why Gustave's total literary sterility did not compromise his tranquillity of soul. In 1840, the mute *wanted* to speak and did not succeed: despair, tears of rage. In '45 he wants to keep silent, and it is this underlying intention which is at the source of his ataraxia. 1845, '46, '47: three mystic years, deliberately infertile; a passive but adroit diplomat, Gustave shifts for himself between the Devil and the Good Lord, trying to please the latter without displeasing the former.

C. "Art Terrifies Me"

We have seen Gustave's distress when, at the end of *L'Education,* he attempts to answer for the work of art as he understands it—vampirization of being by nonbeing, center of unrealization, triumph of appearance as such, concrete identification of Evil and Beauty—sometimes by the Evil One and sometimes by the Almighty, which leads him to invert their roles, or rather to radicalize the inversion we encounter in his work, beginning with *Le Voyage en enfer.* This is what led us to assume the existence of a cruder and more profound "Loser wins," which regressive analysis allowed us to establish. In this version, it seems at first that the principle of Evil and the principle of Good are in place and correctly exercise their powers: Satan does only harm, so nothing is asked of him, he is made a fool of, that's all; it is God one implores, it is God that one seeks, groaning, it is from Him that one awaits grace. But if we reflect on it, don't we rediscover the same confusion in this terribly crude wager as in its rational elaboration? Not entirely the same, since the Devil is practically eliminated; but the Almighty multiplies his functions: all by Himself He plays the God of Light and the Prince of Darkness. Is it indeed the *good* Lord that Gustave invokes and seeks to tempt by his stoically borne sufferings?

Let Him hide himself, well and good. We have known since the sixteenth century that He has moved out: the laicization of all sectors of human activity left Him—from the beginning of merchant capitalism—no more place in space or time. Let Him take pleasure in torturing his creatures, well and good. After all, it is rather in keeping with the ways of the Christian God. And Gustave did not invent salutary trials or preach that pain should be put to good use. But he asks Him to guarantee the nonbeing of being, and it is not rightly His business: man can have access to appearance by virtue of his own nothingness, but the absolute Being is excluded from it by his very plenitude. How can Flaubert want the Creator of all *reality* to introduce it into the dark universe of succubas and incubas, which is the realm of Satan? And if the greatest geniuses are those "who laughed in the face of Humanity," if the Artist's purpose is to demoralize, if

Gustave's desire is to write like an angel to turn his readers into beasts—even into beasts in heat—in short, if Beauty is Evil, is he quite certain of knocking at the right door? Has he changed since *Smarh?* Everything suggests the opposite: in the first *Saint Antoine,* as in the "Mystery Play" of 1839, the Devil and the Author totalize the world through evil. Our young convert smells the sulphur: it is against Satan that he must play the game. Yet he would lose everything with no reward. Therefore, he must address himself to God: to a demonic God who would not be a bad Devil. Is there such confusion in this tormented soul?

Let us acknowledge, to begin with, that Flaubert has a penchant for black masses and has even taken himself for Satan on occasion. The legend seized him belatedly, making him a benevolent boor, but his contemporaries were not all fooled by it. Everywhere he announced his misanthropy; Jules himself, after several suspect enthusiasms, proudly confesses his hatred of men. Is this a reason not to invoke God? The churches are full of worshipers ardently imploring Him to chastize their fellow men. If wishing for Good were all that was needed to enter a church, churches would be empty. You retort that at least by all this black magic, by these *ante mortem* and *post mortem* sanctions demanded out of goodness of heart, it is the Good that one claims to serve, and the believer, thank God, has a good conscience. Thus logic is saved if not morality: of the just God one asks only just interventions, which reward the pure and punish the wicked. Whereas Gustave, it must be confessed, demands that the Creator commit genocide. And later? If he judges the whole human race corrupt—without even excepting himself—between the desire that is savage but conscious of its own futility and the homicidal prayers of pious souls, there is merely a difference of degree. God serves Evil as well as Good, since man created Him. He even has the properly satanic job of making Evil seem like Good and Good like Evil, if only it is asked of Him.

This is not the issue, however. At the moment in the pitch-black night of Pont-l'Evêque when Flaubert resolved to endure the worst, he felt distantly, deep within him, the obscure need for the worst not always to be certain. In Gustave's mad stubbornness as he runs toward his doom, there is the somber conviction that the Devil gives nothing away, that his atrocious and definitive debasement will not even give him the chance to write. Consequently, gripped by the flashing terror that the truth of this world really is atrocious (he *believed* it until this point, that is, he played at believing it), he revives his dead God and puts himself entirely in His hands. There is no time for this resigned intention to be made explicit: in that "fatal moment," Gustave is concerned not with inventing new structures for himself but with recovering those of his childhood—which have always persisted beneath the black feudalism. Gustave calls the Father to his aid. We have discovered, on the tactical level, that the original attack involved an intention of love: the unloved boy tried to find paternal tenderness in it once again. We understand now that on another level this regression had a strategic meaning, more obscure but fundamental: it was a matter of falling back again forever into the golden age, that beneficent time when the world was good, when the all-powerful Father and the gracious God sustained each other and indeed were one. In that golden age, paternal feudalism was the symbol of religious feudalism, and vice versa; for the little vassal it was the moment of innocence, of accord with the self. Beyond his present conflicts, beyond his resentment of the dark Lord, what the convert of Pont-l'Evêque attempts to recover is this identification of the Father with God, which guaranteed his personal identity. Then, pain was *merit:* one suffered *in order to be consoled;* wasn't this the underlying meaning of Flaubertian dolorism? Already passive, little Gustave had merely to display his wounds: they would certainly confer *no right* upon him since the generous love that enveloped him gave *more* than anything one could expect of it. But the merit was a humble appeal, and the child put trust in his Lord: he would be heard. All he had to do was to *abandon himself* to him, to follow the inclinations of his constitutional passivity, certain of being fulfilled. The future was already a destiny since it came to him through another, but it was a happy destiny. And here is Flaubert in January '44, at once one of the damned, sinking toward his doom, and a passive agent *abandoning himself* (simply because he will attain the worst only by *letting himself go*). But the meaning of the abandon—not only in the case we are describing but in general and as it appears to eidetic intuition—is *never* despair, that bristling, horrified, abstract tetanus, neither is it the calculated hope of the practical agent, but rather a hope without qualities, an act of faith in the future. Something is going to happen; the Other, in whatever way, will take charge of this life that one refuses to assume. Such is the meaning of the "Loser wins" of Pont-l'Evêque: "Father, I am sick, take me in your arms and comfort me!" As if this fierce, total shipwreck had the effect and purpose of causing hope to be reborn, as if this desolate proof that Evil triumphs, whatever you do, could not be lived as a Passion without prompting the rebirth of a childish belief in the Good.

The real "Loser wins" appears as the inevitable counterpart of the determination to lose. Just when Gustave, drunk with resentment and unhappiness, topples over in protest against the black Father, against Satan—"Here is what you have made me"—he transforms this disaster into a human sacrifice of which he becomes both author and victim in order to attract to himself the divine benediction; or, if you will, it is homage that restores *good* feudalism. But obviously the awaited Gift cannot be *just anything*. God the Father is solicited by a pious boy of twenty-two, who has lived, whom a painful childhood has formed, who formed himself from it; when he asks that his sufferings be rewarded, he has long decided on the only fitting compensation—genius—and has long conceived of Art as a black mass. If God exists, if He is the All-Good, He *will give* what is asked of Him: His infinite and gratuitous generosity, the magnificence of the awaited gift that involves nothing less than the provisional suspension of natural laws, everything conspires to hide from Gustave the fact that he intends to make the Lord play the role of the Evil One and that he solicits from Him the disqualification of His Creation to the advantage of its diabolical image. Actually, he hopes for a boon from the Other. A boon for himself alone, a mark of love that comes to reward his merit: the contents of the boon, perfectly defined, are not put in question. Only one thing is certain: if Gustave's wishes are fulfilled, it can be only by a good Lord. As for the ordeals, the sadistic absenteeism of this high personage, that can hardly surprise him: indeed, his relation to the symbolic Father has been lived too long in ambivalence; behind the "eternal silence of the divinity" he will assume—*without telling himself so*, of course—the infinite love of which he is perhaps the object, just as after the fall, around the age of seven, he tried for some time to imagine that Achille-Cléophas's irritated indifference was only a crust that hid an infinite tenderness for his younger son.

Thus Gustave finds himself engaged by his entire history in a contradictory process which consists of earning through his painful agnosticism the Almighty's gift of the keys to Nonbeing, the Good Lord's bestowal upon him of the right to Evil, the Father of Man's authorization to demoralize the human race. Has he understood this? The end of *L'Education* would seem in this case to be an attempt—hardly conscious but systematic—to resolve the contradiction: if "Loser wins" is a strict succession of events, God is eliminated by

Himself, His mediation is useless, and the reversal occurs automatically. In other words, we do not leave Hell, since failure issues in nonbeing, or, if you like, since the impossibility of being represents the deepest essence of Beauty. Beauty, indeed, is not a plenitude but its contrary: it appears to the public as frustration; better still, even made manifest through a work, it *finds no public*. Jules doesn't even need to refuse publication—out of purity, out of fidelity to nonbeing; *the fact is* that no one ever offers to publish his works: were he to show them, they would be too beautiful to give pleasure. In *L'Education*, Art is not a reward for failure, it is failure itself totalized in depth with all its consequences: Jules, one of the living dead, takes death's point of view on life, all the while knowing, since he persists in living—at a minimum, it is true—that this point of view itself is an Illusion. In a sense, failure has *given* nothing at all except those famous coins that turn into dead leaves if you try to use them. But it is precisely the afterglow of the *idea* of the coin in the dead leaves that manifests the absolute contestation (derealization of metal by its metamorphosis, derealization of leaves by their past essence, surpassed, unrealizable, yet sustained by the reminiscence of that unforgettable entity, gold) and defines itself as a sorcery worked by Beauty. Jules owes nothing. To anyone.

But *can he*, without external concurrence, surpass despair? That, I believe, is the chief weakness of *L'Education*. Since the most serious failure for one who wants to write is the impotence of the "great man *manqué*," is it sufficient to live it for the lack to transform itself into genius? Gustave is never clear on this point, and *L'Education* asserts more than it demonstrates. The moment of radical failure is conjured away, since, as we have seen, the Artist is born of the failure of the man, whereas it ought to be shown that *he is born of the failure of the artist*.[67] The man denied, strictly speaking and through a pure play of concepts, can become the Artist affirmed: it is the negation of a negation which is dialectically possible since the second concept differs in nature from the first. Indeed the Artist, for Flaubert, is above our species and shares neither its ambitions nor its ends: if we were to accept these premises, it should be theoretically conceivable that he is born from the man like the butterfly from the chrysalis. But the Artist denied (the failed great man conscious of his inadequacies) cannot by

67. At the end of the book, Gustave cannot prevent himself from having recourse allusively to God, thus mingling with the logical and diabolical conception of "Loser wins" that original and disturbing conception which refers to divine goodness.

his shipwreck alone transform himself *into the Artist* since this is the same concept that the negation should, at the same time and in the same connection, restore in its plenitude. Therefore a mediation is necessary which, *from another point of view,* restores to the man in despair what has been lost. This is why we earlier evoked Kierkegaardian repetition.

Gustave has more profoundly—if not more explicitly—outlined here and there what might be called a theodicy of failure. Although the unreality of the Beautiful is so strongly emphasized in *L'Education,* we recall that Gustave rather mutes its satanic aspect, even going so far, in certain passages, as to make Art a hymn to the glory of God. Let us not believe that he simply wants to dissimulate his thought: we have noticed his oscillations and his distress from the time he began to write; he extolled lyricism, outpourings, the sweet tears of the soul even as he was writing *Smarh.* Fundamentally Flaubert is a *black* writer, and he knows it. But he has retained a certain conception of the vatic poet from his first contact with the Romantics, chiefly with Hugo. He has no doubt that Art has a metaphysical mission—since it totalizes man in the cosmos and the cosmos in man: isn't that what tempted Goethe in *Faust?* For the author of *Smarh* and *La Tentation,* the revelation of the real is one with its negation, but this is because reality, unmasked, falls by itself into dust. Gustave still hesitates between two phraseologies: the Romantic ("the poet looks at the stars and shows the way") and the other, which will gain increasing currency (the poet is cursed, his works are flowers of evil, he is jinxed) and which Gustave is indeed the first to take up. Yet, whether it is a white mass or a black mass, Art, in Gustave's view, is certainly a mass. Its sacred character is not in doubt, therefore it must contain positive elements for which the Spirit That Always Denies cannot be responsible: it is, if you will, the strict totalization of appearances, the density of the unreal that makes great works, whatever the subject, and is related to order, to the Good, therefore to Being, since Evil left to itself would sink into disorder. Thus, even in *Les Infortunes de la vertu* God is present, though elusive: He is that which guarantees its *composition.* Hence that strange paradox: Good, by preventing Evil from *decomposing* in conformity with its essence, sustains and penetrates it with its lofty demand, but as a result it gains in virulence: when Evil can harm *with efficacy* and demoralize, it is because it is no longer entirely Evil. Admittedly, we are only a step away from wondering if the very extent to which Evil is radicalized does not indicate

310

that it is in the service of Good. This is hardly surprising: there are plenty of theologians who try to clear God's name by proving that the evils that come to men with His concurrence and His permission are the necessary conditions of more general goods, such as the maintenance of universal order. Gustave's theodicy is more somber, however, it is better suited to his Manichaeism; it allows him, at least momentarily, to do without the Devil: the Almighty in His bounty is concerned to increase our merit by crushing us with it without respite. As if Art, an exquisite crime born of despair, were charged with perpetuating our unhappiness. As if God said to the Artist, "You will be born and will die in despair, cursed. You will persist in denying My existence, and I will not undeceive you. You will have My invisible assistance only that you may produce works which will the better dishearten your species. Your merit in My eyes will be twofold, for your unhappiness will be extreme and you will infect others with it. Such is the will of the infinite love I bear you." The eternal Father, who, the better to rob us of being and in order to augment our merits by crushing us even more, would thus favor sorcerers, artists, Lords of Sleight-of-Hand; and these, thinking to sell their soul to the Devil, would make themselves the aids of Providence. To tell the truth, this theodicy is never developed to its conclusion, since Gustave *must* remain agnostic. And the poor fellow often goes astray. It is at the end of one of these strayings, surely, that he writes to Louise: "Art terrifies me." Certainly he puts at the top of his list of preoccupations the *technical* enigmas of creation and composition, but he cannot help seeing them as the expression of an impenetrable and sacred mystery, which refers back to *the ontology of the Beautiful*, the difficult dialectic of Being and Nonbeing. For a work to be beautiful, he tells himself, it must have such a density of the imaginary that Being—Beauty revealing itself as *superappearance* or absolute appearance—seems to come to masterpieces through nonbeing, allusive, ungraspable. If, at first glance, Nothingness appears to vampirize Being, one can, upon reflection, wonder whether it is not Being that vampirizes Nothingness. Thus, beyond the contestation of the real by the unreal, the transfinite totality of possibles, the Beautiful would appear as the cipher of true Being, which, coinciding neither with the imaginary nor with reality, would necessitate and first produce Illusion in order to proclaim itself in Illusion at once as an absence and through a *gift* (the internal cohesion *given* to Evil). Thus we find once again in the original "Loser wins" an *exploited* "presentiment" that we encountered very early in

311

Flaubert: the image, by its very nothingness, is the sole line of communication with God, who is present in it as he who must escape forever from this life and from this world. Hence the vicious circle that "terrifies" Gustave: through the unrealization of "beings,"[68] Being manifests itself in its absence as that which authorizes the very possibility of this unrealization.

D. ". . . GOD OF SOULS! GIVE ME STRENGTH AND HOPE!"

After January 1845, Flaubert lived permanently on two levels: absolute pessimism, and hidden optimism feeding on the pessimism. This can be demonstrated by scores of passages taken at random—or nearly—from his correspondence or his private notes. For example, in the light of what was just said, the reader will give a more complete interpretation of the visit to the holy places of Jerusalem. But since the issue here is the relationship Gustave establishes *while living it* between Art and Religion, I prefer to skip a few years ahead and compare two crucial texts, both of which deal with the composition of *Salammbô*. The first occurs in a letter addressed to Mademoiselle Leroyer de Chantepie, dated 4 November 1857; the second is a jotting in a notebook during the night of 12 or 13 June 1858.

In September '57 he sat down to write *Salammbô;* two months later he wrote to his correspondent:

> I must have a Herculean temperament to resist the ghastly tortures to which my work condemns me. Let them be happy, those who do not dream the impossible! One believes oneself wise because one has renounced the active passions. What vanity! It is easier to become a millionaire . . . than to write a good page and be content with yourself. Two months ago I began a novel set in the ancient world, and I have just finished the first chapter; but I find *nothing good* in it and I am in despair over it day and night without finding a solution. The more experience I have in my art, the more this art becomes a torment for me: imagination stands still and taste grows. That is my misfortune. Few men, I think, will have suffered as much as I through literature . . . Have you noticed how we love our sufferings? You cling to your religious ideas, which make you suffer so, and I to my chimera of style, which consumes me body and soul. But we are perhaps worth something only through our sufferings, for they are all aspira-

68. I take the word in the sense of the Heideggerian *Seiendes*.

tions. There are so many people whose joy is so vile and whose ideal is so limited that we should bless our unhappiness if it makes us more worthy.

Flaubert is really discontent with his first chapter. A little earlier, in October, he wrote to the editor of *La Presse* and begged him "to say no more about this novel than you would if it had never existed (to spare me ridicule) if I abandon this work because of the impossibility of executing it, which is quite possible." Yet this discontent cannot be as profound as all that, for three weeks after the letter to Mademoiselle de Chantepie he writes to Feydeau: "I finished my first chapter for good or ill . . . I have undertaken a proud thing, my friend, a proud thing, and I'll bust a gut over it yet before getting to the end. Don't worry, I won't give up. Gloomy, grim, despairing, but not a dimwit." Was it enough for him to take up his chapter again and revise it a little to transform his laments of 4 November into this victory song? That is hardly believable. So he was exaggerating a little when he unburdened himself to the heart of his "dear correspondent": this old lady was the public he dreamed of so as to play the despair of a man who has placed a desperate bet. All the themes are in place, and we find them again one by one. First, although he speaks of *work*, he makes writing a passive action by posing as a man who has "renounced the active passions." And then he defines Art as a quest for the *impossible*. The beautiful is not simply that which does not exist but that which cannot exist. That which in itself has such a power of nonbeing that its evocation—even imaginary—is forbidden. He specifies that impossibility, moreover, in his letter to Feydeau: "Think a little . . . of what I have undertaken: to resurrect a whole civilization we know nothing about." Here we find Jules's double negations: at the time, Gustave would not bother to resurrect even a moment of Greco-Roman civilization, although he has abundant documents and testimonies at his disposal, so that the difficulty would not be overwhelming. But the difficulty becomes impossibility when a society must be pulled out of the nothingness that swallowed it up, along with all its monuments. It existed, however, therefore it is *imaginable;* this is what tempts Flaubert: to reveal the true nature of the imaginary which as nothingness itself becomes manifests in its purity when, starting with nothingness, he takes on the impossible task of making present a being that has been annihilated.

At the same time, of course, beneath the surface there is the prelogical and optimistic idea that imagination, provided one knows how to use it, is the real reckoner of being, that it renders the essence of "beings" *before* one meets them or *when one can no longer meet them*. In any event, Gustave's "value" and the source of his martyrdom are but one: *he desires the impossible* by knowing it; he seeks to give being to what is principally nonbeing. In other words, he agrees in advance to lose; in fact, he *wants* to lose, he is set on losing, it constitutes his merit. With a stubbornness whose result he knows in advance, he raises himself above the *ontic* realm and challenges it all in the name of what *ought to be* and never will be. And here we have once more the "You must, therefore you cannot," which at the time of *Smarh* characterized the satanic imperative represented by the work of art as reality. But this time it is the Artist himself who becomes the mediator between the possibles of this world and the impossible *"being-as-it-should-be,"* the *ontological* structure of the Beautiful. He defines himself by this obligation, which is unrealizable and for that very reason assumed. The site of suffering and damnation is himself: he is "consumed," body and soul, by the "ghastly torments to which [his] work condemns him." However, he "acquires experience"; but even that can only augment his unhappiness; here, indeed, Flaubert reintroduces a very old theme: the opposition between imagination and taste. Imagination, as we know, was arrested in him—at least that is what he claims—at the age of fifteen. Experience, on the other hand, enhances the growth of taste, the naked demand for the impossible. The gap increases with time, since the power to imagine stagnates. In other words, in the void, *taste* throws into relief the indefinable schemata that neither images nor words can fill. He will be specific about this later—again apropos *Salammbô*—in a letter to Feydeau: "At every line, at every word I am at a loss for language and I am frequently forced to alter details." In this case the verbal scheme is a definite demand, required by a concrete fact. But the *verbal image* is missing. *Language*—as derealized language—does not provide the word; therefore "detail" must be renounced and replaced by something less "unsayable." This is to fall from the impossible—the avowed goal of the work undertaken—to the choice of the *optimum* possible at the price of an abandonment. The compromise is in itself a defeat: the meaning of the work is changed by it, for by dint of concessions the work, far from being the advent of the unrealizable, risks becoming for the author merely a synthetic determination of the possibilities of writing and his own possibilities. As a result, these concessions are made in despair: with each of them Flaubert measures the infinite distance that separates what he does from what he wants to do. For him, art is a refined, elaborate "torment"; the Idea, a rigorous and precise demand but without determinate contours (since it is by definition out of reach, and no invented content can fill this container and thus mark its limits), has the constant effect of disqualifying words and images, insofar as they come to him from his own mind, by signaling their fundamental inadequacy—hence "despondency, irritation, boredom." What can be done? Drop the manuscript altogether? He thinks about it but does not allow himself to do it. As he began the work in full awareness, as he desired the impossible for its very impossibility and in order to challenge by a futile negation—which is proud of being futile—the totality of the real and of the possibilities attached to it, he must maintain to the end this dissenting conduct of failure. To the end: to the moment when, from concession to concession, from torment to torment, he will have produced a mean work that will ratify his defeat without losing sight of an inaccessible constellation. No doubt he wanted the Beautiful. But the Beautiful *beyond his reach.* The intention was not to conquer it and make it come down to earth but to become its witness here below by suffering *by and for Beauty* as one of the damned. Hence the fundamental purpose is conjured away, another takes its place: "We are worthy . . . only through our sufferings, for they are all aspirations." At this moment it is religious penitence that surpasses everything, and Art is demoted to the rank of pretext.[69] He goes further. We have already surprised him comparing the artist to a numismatist. The theme resurfaces, linked to dolorism: "my chimera of style." The ambiguity of 1845–47 recurs here: is it the very idea of total derealization of language that is chimerical? Or is this unrealization, possible for others, in other times, in other places, impossible for Gustave *here and now?* Art is vanity, I am too "mediocre and limited" to be an artist. Uncertainty is adroitly maintained: the worst must be certain.

But who knows what is worst: the radical impotence of a damned species to which Flaubert belongs, or a diabolical Providence that has given him the ambitions of genius while paralyzing his imagination in order to keep him in the realm of mediocrity? In truth, both points of view are defensible, and as each challenges the other, the best thing is to make one pass into the other indefinitely and replace the contradiction—thanks to the vagueness of the terms—by a vicious circle. The

---

69. The reader will have recognized the procedure: Flaubert, as he did apropos *La Botte merveilleuse* and *La Bretagne*—suddenly substitutes morality for art. Art being impossible, the effort of the Artist, by its very futility, confers on him an ethical value.

worst is finally the magical interpenetration of these two contradictory worsts. This ambiguity seems a bit artificial: it is maintained by
sleight of hand in front of the old lady's easily deceived eyes. The
prisoner of *banal being* has to show the dizzy height of *aspiration:* here
we have come back to the old leitmotif of Great Desire and dissatisfaction. It is not by accident that Gustave compares his own misfortunes
to the religious sufferings of his correspondent. In Hell, the greatest
torment is still to be deprived of God. Indeed, Gustave does not refrain from having his say: "We are worth . . . something only by our
sufferings . . . We should bless our unhappiness if it makes us more
worthy." The point is *to acquire value* by a constant and deliberate conduct of failure. Suffering makes us *more worthy.* But who determines
this *worthiness?* An absolute is necessary to guarantee the ethical value
of dolorism. It cannot be Satan, *against whom* the operation is launched
and who, to perfect his work, must compel his victims to realize their
supreme unhappiness in abjection. For the relation unhappiness-
merit to become objective, it must have reference to God. But as He is
not named in the passage we are considering, the relation remains
subjective. Only an adroitly placed "perhaps" ("We are perhaps
worth something") suggests that the immanent bond—without any
acceptable basis—is hypothetically susceptible of receiving a transcendent authorization. It is as if Flaubert were saying: "Consensual
suffering contains the humble prayer that a transcendent being may
exist who considers it meritorious." This is not a proof but a presumption of the existence of God; in being constituted by itself as postulated merit, suffering generates an alternative: either God exists and
dolorism is objectively *valid*—or else He is not, and the subjective
necessity of the process proves the existence of Hell because the most
spontaneous development of lived experience is in itself a deception,
and we are tricked to the marrow of our bones. It is naturally toward
these black conclusions that Flaubert's exposition is directed: "Have
you noticed how we love our sufferings. You cling . . . ," etc. To love,
to cling: the emphasis is on the subjective. He plays the game: since
he is in Hell, he is losing every step of the way; the humble leavening
he believed he found in his suffering he now knows was a lie to the
self, an absurd and degrading overcompensation. His sole pride will
be to assume that illusion itself vis-à-vis the Devil, and to suffer in
order to *deserve* everything while aware of one's mystification. In
short, one loses in order to lose, in the pride of despair.

The piquancy of these declarations is that they come not from an
unlucky writer but from a man whom glory struck like lightning.

After Madame Bovary, Gustave repeats in the same terms what he was saying between '45 and '47. Does this mean he is lying? No; unless it is to himself. He explains to Mademoiselle de Chantepie what he must believe if he wants to lose in order to win; he tells her this in order to convince himself of it, the way he wrote to Eulalie to convince himself that he was in love; it is flagrant autosuggestion. In the religious "Loser wins," he has the chance to win only if he loses *absolutely*—if he is unaware of the rules of the game. Therefore, he practices being unaware of them: literature is a torment that does not pay, perhaps a chimera; in any case, it is his misfortune not to believe in miracles; his lot is thankless labor forever unrewarded. If he constantly laments—I am wearing myself out, I am torturing myself, I am killing myself in harness, etc.—it is because work, for him, is not a real praxis: can one be so unhappy when exercising a freely chosen activity? He works not to *find* the apt expression, the "smooth and flowing" style, the musical phrase, but to *deserve* finding them. He makes drafts, copies them, recopies them as many as fourteen times, inflicting on himself the stupid labor of retracing vocables that have already been retraced—and from one draft to another hardly a word is changed. He is *waiting.* He is waiting for the miracle that will let itself be caught in the trap of his despair and give birth to a flower through his sullen pen. He is really a copier, like Bouvard, like Pécuchet. A copier of himself. His work is a necessary charade and strongly resembles the one he played when faced with the Code in 1842–43—except that his role of student conferred no merit on him other than the merit of obeying his father by doing violence to himself, while since January '45 the *labor improbus,* the martyr's zealous submission to a command he is not even sure he has been given, is designed to make him *deserve the miracle*—and even the existence of the eternal Father. When he knocks himself out tracing his penstrokes, we can almost hear him murmur that prayer of Simone de Beauvoir's heroine: "My God, make it so that you exist."

Is this *all* that work *is,* for Gustave? It is too soon to decide. We shall study in detail the plans, the drafts, the erasures, the deletions that have come down to us, and we shall have to ask ourselves if this feverish way of working does not have two quite distinct functions, one of which, at least, is *practical.* For the moment it is enough for us to have shown that—at a particular level of signification—intellectual work is *playacted,* and that it has the specific function of representing failure as a concrete determination of lived experience. Thus Gustave reverses the terms when he claims that his sufferings give birth to

317

work: in fact, he works in order to suffer; for this passive agent, labor is fundamentally an *affliction*, it is the internalization of the curse of Adam: "You shall earn your bread by the sweat of your brow." But affliction—degrading if it really is a matter of earning bread—becomes a noble torment if sweat drenches the brow of the "good worker" *for nothing*, if he is tortured in order to produce a work which he knows in advance will serve nothing and will be a failure besides. From the time—around 1840—that he stopped writing in a state of possession, in trances of lyricism and eloquence, Flaubert ran up against a strange paradox, which disconcerted him for a long time: if taste is master, and if literature must be critical, the enterprise of writing is practical.

Gustave concurs with the "legislator of Parnassus, good old Boileau," when he orders the writer to go over his work twenty times. But as a passive agent, a pessimist and misanthrope, Gustave condemns all human activities—even those of the professional writer—and wants the "discoveries" of genius to be the unfathomable inertia of matter and to constitute themselves in him as passive syntheses without *any manufacturer's label*. He admires great works because the author has withdrawn from them and they have taken on the opaque and solitary being of natural objects. For this very reason, however, they must have given themselves to their creator, when he wrote them, with the inhuman generosity of things, like a landscape suddenly revealed when you go over a mountain pass, which, in its unjustifiable gratuitousness, may seem like a gift.

This second exigency is older and more profound: it suits the passivity of his constitution and the feudal structure of his universe. But the other, more thought out, more constructed, better adapted to the great choices of the post-Romantic generation and to Flaubert's condition of average man, the son of a "professional," must have imposed itself on him when a kind of verification of impotence led him to adopt, not without repugnance, Buffon's "blasphemy." The work-penance, a *subsequent* invention of January '45, is an effort to surpass the contradiction. Flaubert *inflicts it on himself*, primarily to obey Bouileau but also, since true Artists are never satisfied with their work, to give himself at least a chance to equal them by sharing their dissatisfaction. But as soon as he makes his work in progress into an enterprise, he considers that he is dooming it to failure, for he situates it *in the field of possibles* when the essence of the Beautiful resides in its impossibility. He is condemning himself to suffer, therefore to deserve. The impossible *must not be desacralized*, that is, it must never be the designated end of a human enterprise that would "make it a possibility," unless that enterprise had the fundamental intention of failing and of signaling in advance the radical heterogeneity of the profane and the sacred. Through work, Gustave renews original sin and its punishment; consequently, the supreme end leaps up to heaven, inconceivable, inaccessible, and becomes once again the unknown object of a pure "aspiration." But while his pen runs over the paper, the words it traces, too familiar to arouse direct attention, exercise an "auxiliary fascination" on Gustave. The pseudo-activity of the copier absorbs him sufficiently to prevent his mind from forming precise thoughts; not enough to take away from him a sort of marginal attention to the passive syntheses of lived experience. While working, Gustave maintains himself in a state of "gaping," he opens himself up in advance to the Gift; his false activity protects a kind of imageless oneirism, the dream of an expectation. In any event, panting, moaning, realizing through the charade of work our human condition in its abandonment, he remains perpetually available to the chance miracle, the particular happy detail of style, the discovery of a word or phrase, impenetrable passive syntheses which he need only transcribe and whose strangeness, quite as much as inertia, would allow him to *imagine* that they had just been created in him, expressly for him, by a divine grace merited at last.

Thus Gustave thinks he has resolved his problem: the work is at once the product of labor and manna in the desert, a random determination of discourse, an indecipherable and providential bestowal. But when he writes to Mademoiselle de Chantepie, he cheats, specifying that the expectation is without hope, indeed, that it is the most acute form of despair. With admirable yet insincere lucidity, he gives the real explanation of his youthful torments and, quite specifically, of his nervous illness: "Ruthless with myself, I uprooted man with all my might, with both of my hands full of strength and pride. I sought to turn this tree of verdant foliage into a naked column and to set atop it, as if on an altar, some celestial flame . . . This is why I find myself at thirty-six years of age so empty and sometimes so fatigued!" It's all here: the ruthlessness toward the self, or rather toward the human condition, the effort to deny needs, pushed to the point of hysterical impotence, the rejection of passion and of human ends, the attempt to transform life into inorganic matter, eternal and smooth, preserving from the original tree only its verticality, in short, the frenzied choice of inhumanity even at the price of a fall into the subhuman. And all these preparations, all these stubborn negations have no other purpose than to *doom Gustave* in order to ignite "some celestial flame" at the top of the *dead* column that replaces him. These words clearly indicate that the flame, indeterminate by nature, or rather situated beyond any ontic determination, was not conceived as the final term of a positive and practical enterprise, but that—as object of an aspiration that understood itself without knowing itself—it had *to reward* the systematic self-destruction of existence to the profit of Being. Literary work is the daily repetition of self-destruction and the symbolic equivalent, later the substitute, of those dehumanizations that are intermittent but more radical than the referential attacks. The words "altar" and "celestial flame" are there to remind us of the "*sacrificial*" character of the refusal to live, and that Art is a religious rite whose purpose is to produce its own myth in sacred texts.

We recognize this torchbearer: it is Jules. Or, rather, what remains of Jules after his ultimate metamorphosis. And the evocation of this character suffices to unmask Gustave's bad faith: the positive hero is presented here as pure negativity; the verb tenses, the choice of words, the context—all concur in denouncing the radical failure of his enterprise and condemning it. "Little by little I have worn myself out, shriveled up, withered. Ah! I blame no one but myself . . . I enjoyed fighting my senses, torturing my heart . . . Ruthless with myself . . . ," etc. The meaning of the paragraph, therefore, is: I had a "*quite beautiful* youth" and I destroyed myself; what's left of me at thirty-six is a withered old man. The comparison chosen is of the sort to circumvent the judgment of the dear correspondent: who would not think *at first*—it is a naturalistic convention—that it is a crime to uproot "a tree with verdant foliage" in order to make a column out of it? The enterprise is thus mad and sacrilegious. Was it a success, at least? No: the two uses of the imperfect [*déracinais, voulais,* "was uprooting, was wanting"] discreetly let us know that the failure is radical: the column has not been fashioned; the tree, half uprooted, has neither the splendor of dead wood nor the fecundity of living plants; it is *worn out*, and when the forest around it is covered with an impenetrable foliage, hardly more than a few sick leaves appear on its stumps, yellow without greening, and fall before autumn comes. In short, Jules was a madman's dream, I was doomed through my own fault; *I should have chosen life,* the passions, love, spontaneity, and literary fecundity. I am no longer a man and I shall never become an artist; it might even be concluded without too much exaggeration that the only way to be a great writer is fully to accept the human condition.

Does Flaubert really push humility so far as to think *that?* Don't we know that he has always hated—and will continue to hate—life, needs, agitation, men? And how can he eulogize his lost youth *in the same letter*—"a great confidence in myself, superb leaps of the soul, something impetuous in all one's person . . ."—by systematically skewing the facts, and by basing his system of values on frustration and suffering? He must go to the end of his "dark night": to lose on every front it is not sufficient to show he is a laborer without genius who wants the impossible and knows that no miracle will happen to him. Gustave must confess—in a distraught but *meritorious* misunderstanding of all his "slow work"—that he has taken the wrong turn, that the true road to art was the natural and the spontaneous, that under these conditions, far from meriting the miracle that God persists in denying him, he has actually *merited blame:* the hellish road on which he has gone astray (strictly through his own fault) leads to nothing; it is a dead end: he will be left there alone. The apparent contradiction between this passage and the preceding one rests on the fact that Flaubert's dolorism makes his purpose rather too obvious: even if merit is a subjective illusion, he still takes too much pride in it to maintain, solely by virtue of his despair, that this illusion at least *ought to be* reality. In short, we are dealing with a solitary challenge— waged by pain—that imagination makes to the real. This optimism does not sufficiently conceal its strategy. The black pessimism of the second passage aims at the same goal but proceeds masked: if misfortune produces merit, not even a possibility of hope must remain. In this passage we recognize the model that Gustave had in mind: the moment he takes self-denial to the point of considering himself the *guilty one,* deprived, damned, forsaken, giving way beneath the weight of his self-accusations, the Saint finally achieves sainthood. He achieves it but does not even suspect it: if Gustave plays at saintliness, he must also play at ignorance and regard himself as damned through his own fault just when he is saved.[70] In other words, his laments can attract divine grace to himself provided he does not know it and is determined to underestimate what he does. When will he know it, then? That is not certain; perhaps never, perhaps on the other side of death, perhaps in a flash, in the midst of thunderous applause. What is certain is that the reward is offstage,

70. The difference is that the Saint never consciously doubts the existence or the goodness of God. He regrets his faults but refrains from committing the inexpiable sin of despair.

and its possibility, in the heart of the dark night, is assiduously ignored.

And what if it really *were* despair? If he could never emerge from that night? To these questions I shall give only one answer, which is Flaubert's own. This second text also relates to the preparation of *Salammbô*, but this time Gustave is writing only for himself. He had left Paris, gone to Tunis, spent several days at Carthage, then by way of Constantinople has reached Philippeville and from there Marseille, Paris, and Croisset. Returning on 9 June, he slept forty-eight hours straight through; then, after rereading and correcting his travel notes, he wrote these words in his notebook: "Let all the energies of nature I have breathed penetrate me and let them be exhaled in my book! Come to me, power of plastic emotion! Resurrection of the past, come to me! Come to me! It must be done through the Beautiful, living and real as it is. Have pity on my will, God of souls! Give me strength and hope! (Night of Saturday, the 12th, to Sunday, the 13th of June, midnight.)" René Dumesnil is certainly not wrong to call this scrap of eloquence an invocation. I believe, however, that it would be more correct to view it as an invocation followed by a prayer.

To begin with, Flaubert summons chthonic powers; it is almost a magical conjuring: even more than invoked, the "energies of nature" are imperiously convoked. We see his pantheism once again, what might be called the declared aspect of his sense of the religious. In Tunisia he had the impression that the macrocosm was swallowed up in him or—what amounts to the same thing in his case—that the human microcosm in his person became cosmic. Through all his pores he absorbed great natural forces, the sun and heat, the air heavy with odors, the blinding light, the sea spray. But this identification with the world is an intentional process: he left the world below in order to *become nature once again* and to join the splendid universe of paganism. Indeed, in his eyes, pagans are defined less by their polytheism than by pantheistic naturalism: they *are* Nature, they have its simplicity, its elemental strength, and its impenetrable grandeur. Here he is, then, an imaginary pagan: the penetrating heat, the hurling wind, the dazzling sunlight serve him as analogues to *imagine* the pagan soul. When he returned to Croisset, he assigned himself the task he gave to Jules: having received the accidental, he will render the immutable. The accidental: whatever can offer him a quick, highly particularized journey (date, season, etc.) in which everything presented itself as "something that will never be seen twice." The immutable: *Antiquity*, such as Eternity—Death and absence—has changed it into itself.

However, he knows very well that the moment of pantheistic ecstasy is *past*; assuming that Gustave once felt himself to be a block of light and earth fissured by the fires of Africa, the telluric energies that passed through him then—and already existed for him as such only on the basis of an unrealization of perceptions—need merely be recalled. But *precisely*, as we have seen, that is enough for him. Master of his memory, he gathers his recollections in order to construct from them an imaginary antiquity: he has reread and refined his notes, he has remembered landscapes, events, and, above all, states of the soul; sure of it, he sends out a call to the forces he has at hand and invites them to sacrifice themselves so that radical unreality may be born of their death: come to me, docile and faithful memory; recollections of my great cosmic effusion, come to me. Come obediently to perish in my hands so that the supreme truth may be born from you, my continued creation, Illusion. Taken in this abstract and, all things considered, rational form, the invocation implies a profound optimism. In this domain, there will be no obstacle. Indeed, what worried him before the journey was the "psychological side of [his] history." He still felt like an Alaric dazzled by ancient Rome but haunted by the mists of the North that cannot penetrate beyond the appearances of this sunlit pantheism. In order to *think antique*—to grasp at the root the mineral feelings Gustave attributes to the Ancients—one must make oneself into *all of antiquity*. And how can this be achieved in the absence of any monument? The answer is simple: by incorporating African nature, the most total monument since it is *ancient in itself*. Mission accomplished: he has turned himself down there into *alma mater, natura naturans*, engendering and thinking a society swallowed up *beginning* with the sands, rocks, and sea that formerly created it under the action of the sun; he has realized his dream of being matter. Now, this mineralization of his soul, disappearing as concrete reality and remaining as mental disposition, is going to serve him as the operational scheme for the creation of antique characters with their passions, their mores, their vision of the world. What he went to look for in Carthage was the Carthaginian "psychology." He found it, or rather became that transfinite himself, the *antique world*; he knows how to produce his heroes as the diverse incarnations of an identical Antiquity.[71] In short, this captain mobilizes his forces—"Resurrection

71. This means that he knows he can, when he wants to, condense the mass of his singular memories into a structured totality whose general determinations will serve as the internal rule to his creation or exploit them as singular details so as to make each of them the raw material of an invented anecdote.

of the past, come to me!"—for a battle he is sure to win. Is this really the man who was sniveling in November to a troubled old spinster? His imagination has broken away from the stagnation he was then inveighing against: it is a forge, a crucible; it has resumed the function he has been assigning it since '44, which is not to produce images *ex nihilo* but to transmute the real into the imaginary by means of rigorous techniques; in short, he puts his trust in it. But the invocation goes still further and consequently reveals the extent of Flaubert's real ambition. Great masterpieces, he has told us, are like natural products: they have the mysterious beauty of a cliff, of the ocean. And we know that he ordinarily claims to be "crushed" by the genius of those who have created them; they are beacons, he, at best, will be merely a torch. Yet the invocation shows quite well that this humility is part of the devilish game he is playing. Alone at his desk, impassioned by what he feels capable of doing—through the rereading of his notes—he agrees to reveal his intention to himself: the energies of nature must be exhaled in his book. In other words, like *King Lear, Salammbô* will be a slice of nature; all the elements will be united to produce it: it will be sky, sea, savage desert, sands blown by the wind. With this book, in a word, Flaubert will equal the greatest. His ambition is to restore Antiquity as Nature and Nature as eternal Antiquity. Obviously such a task is inconceivable without some resource to mysticism. Flaubert surrenders himself to the belief that he is a transformer of energy: this suits his constitution as passive agent, his profound belief that Art is a passive activity. At this moment he dreams that he has really amassed natural forces and that they will be reexternalized through his pen as a masterpiece. What confidence he must need to leave it up to *the world* and to entrust blind chthonic powers with the task of producing a work of art whose materiality will come from them and whose unity will come from him. Has the world become good? Quite the contrary: *Salammbô* is perhaps Flaubert's most sadistic work; in it, man is afflicted with a double impossibility of being by Nature within (*homo homini lupus*) and without (radical hostility of the universe); the agony of the mercenaries in the procession of the sacred Ax resumes these two aspects of the curse of Adam. All the elemental forces Gustave thinks he has absorbed are "exhaled" in his book in the form of genocide; inhuman in his vows, he summons the inhumanity of Nature to realize the Beautiful through radical Evil. An optimist for himself—he has ceased to be man—he asks the implacable macrocosm to manifest that allergy to our species which has delighted his misanthropy since adolescence.

324

In this sense, the invocation shows the self-criticism of September '57 in its true light: when he claims to regret having uprooted the man he was, he pushes insincerity to the limit. If he blamed himself, it would be rather for remaining too human, for he asks of his journey to realize a plenary inhumanity within him. *Antiquity,* rediscovered in the desert, is the animosity of materiality against man; man "resurrected" as antique is a statue, superbly inorganic matter haunted by the illusion of living. Note the significant line, "One must create through the Beautiful, living and true nevertheless." Living and true *nevertheless;* we are not going to say that the Beautiful is the antithesis of truth and life, that would be stretching the text too much, but rather that Beauty *resists* when the artist tries to represent life in its truth "through it": supreme Beauty is absolute Illusion, and Art the point of view of death. Why, then, does Flaubert claim to give his work these extra-aesthetic qualities? Because they already figure in his initial project as requirements: this black magician wants to "resurrect the past"—that says it all. For the past to remain as absent as possible and as dead, he must give it the maximum presence. In other words, just as the fantastic is fully felt only if the author makes it appear in the flat, realistic life of everyday banality, so Beauty will appear as irremediable separation only if the phantoms raised manifest themselves in the work with all the violence (colors, movements, passions) they *used to have.* At this moment, life and archaeological truth become *aesthetic* requirements, and the Beautiful can assign two tasks to the Artist: if he recounts contemporary events, he must slip the unity of future annihilation, like a subtle poison, into the confused exuberance of the present, as if later death had a retroactive effect; if he speaks of a past time, he must present to us what is irreducibly and notoriously annihilated with all the dynamic characteristics that were manifest in it. In both cases the goal is the same: to disqualify temporalization by Eternity. In the first, however, life and truth, in the most banal sense, are givens, and the artist's concern is to manage things so that Death—as Cocteau said of a road accident—"takes its characters alive." This task corresponds to the rendering of the dialogues that so tormented Gustave when he was writing *Madame Bovary.* Daily life furnished him raw material in abundance; here, life and truth pose no problem. But how is one to "take" practical language "alive," to introduce it in the rough and without modifying its realistic structures into a work where all the other words are reciprocally bound together by the subtle ties of unrealization? In the second case, to the contrary, Death is the primary given and, indeed, where *Salammbô* is concerned, the almost total annihilation of that which could inform us about a vanished civilization; the Artist's concern must then be to inscribe life into it insofar as it was disqualified in advance in its own time and was ridiculed by that abolition, *then* future, *now* past, but forever eternal. Thus for Flaubert, to "resurrect the past" is wicked work, and in his hands "life and truth" become demonic instruments. We now understand the *nevertheless:* with Antiquity—twice defunct—the Beautiful is furnished in advance. Does Gustave love anything about the Romans, then, but their metamorphosis into Being, namely their Nonbeing? If it is merely a question of becoming unrealized, it will be enough to dream of Rome, of Carthage: this is the aesthetic attitude. But one must work creatively, the artist tears himself away from the pondered dream that feeds on itself in order to compose the written dream by asking history[72] for the raw material indispensable to constituting a real, permanent center of derealization through a book. We can conclude: Flaubert *remains* Jules, he has abandoned none of the conceptions articulated in the first *Education,* and the invocation itself represents a reaffirmation of the "Loser wins" dialectic, that is, the rationalization of the original "Loser wins." But he hides that arrogant loyalty from himself as long as he can out of superstitious fear of the Devil, and, save in rare and brief moments of escape, confines himself to a studied *Miserabilism.*

Suddenly the tone changes, the other "Loser wins" appears, and we move without transition from the dialectical rationalization buttressed by sorcery to the humble wager of faith, to prayer. "Have pity on my will, God of souls! Give me strength and hope!" How are we to understand this curiously restrictive formula: God of souls? At first glance it contrasts with that "God of bodies" implicitly contained in the invocation: he prays that a providential grace will accord him the *moral* virtues he needs to complete his work well. But this opposition shows *in relation to what* this Divinity is determined, not what it is in itself. For the word "soul," in Flaubert, is never taken in its Christian sense. We shall be enlightened, on the other hand, if we recall that for all his quasi-materialism, the "soul" does not correspond to consciousness, at all, not even to the "psyche" as a totality of the "monologue" and the "dreadful depths." We have noted in a preceding chapter that he gives this name to a lacuna, or rather to a major priva-

72. Flaubert, in this particular case, has little difficulty conceiving of it as a *transfinite,* for the ancient world seems to him, as it would to Spengler later on, one complete story with a beginning and an end.

tion, that is, to the religious instinct. "God of souls" must therefore be understood as the hidden or nonexistent principle that corresponds or ought to correspond to our "aspirations." But Gustave departs here from his intentional agnosticism, addressing himself directly to the eternal Being as a *personal* God. Chthonic forces are *convoked:* one feels that he has the advantage over them. By contrast, he begs the Almighty—a little cavalierly, I admit—for His pity. Yet the Spinozist substance would be as incapable of pity as an earthquake. At the very least, pity assumes consciousness and, in a way, love, since it always goes *beyond* justice. Of course one can claim that Flaubert's prayer contains an implicit "if you exist." But nothing supports the assumption that this mental restriction was really in effect at the time Flaubert was writing. He has just reread his notes and revised them; he is content: through them he already imagines an admirable work that will be *his.* He is seized by enthusiasm; dazzled, he still has one worry: the subject is splendid but will he be capable of treating it? Yes, with God's help. In an impulse of naive passion, he unmasks himself and *shows* the foundations of the negative theology he needed so badly and which he invented *alone* because no one was in a position to teach it to him. God of souls means, very specifically, God of love whose existence is proved by Your intolerable absence, God Whom I must possess for having suffered so much because of never finding You. The negation of negation is changed into affirmation: the revolt of instinct against agnosticism is here presented as the equivalent of an impossible affirmation. God *is* because He does not exist. All these tricks seem dated today, when negative theology is a hundred years old. At the time, they were new: it was a matter of reducing immanence to being merely itself—that is, pure despair—in order to turn this suffered and denied abandonment into an inflexible right to the transcendent.

What Flaubert asks of God is efficacious grace. That strange formula "Have pity on my will" becomes clearer to us when we recall that Flaubert *has no will*—being of passive constitution—and he knows it. He knows and repeats from the time of *Quidquid volueris* that he can have no passion. He has said a hundred times that he is always dreaming of the book he is going to write and disgusted with the one he is writing. This time he is sure of his business: *Salammbô* stands up to scrutiny; it is himself he doubts, he distrusts his instability. What does he need, then? Strength: a steady, continuous vision, fidelity to himself, hence to his enterprise. But where is he to find this strength, having constructed himself entirely from a verification of absence, that is, the impossibility of affirming? He must therefore have recourse to divine aid. And how, we may well ask, can he doubt his perseverance after staring at *Madame Bovary* for so long? Precisely: he hates *Madame Bovary*, it was an *ordeal;* he had to *endure* it to merit writing *Salammbô*.

In the name of accumulated merit, he also asks for hope. He understands, therefore, that his despair and his passivity reciprocally condition each other. His instability makes him abruptly *despair* of the project which, a moment before, made him exult; conversely, it is the silent consciousness of his practical incapacity that compels him to tumble down each time: if there is not even a beginning of action, one can hope for nothing, one dreams that one hopes. This was the case with Gustave before 1847: passive, he conceived a vague and entirely imaginary project; in those moments his hope remained oneiric—he dreamed *it would be* a masterpiece. The real desire to write returned to him but, at the same time, ran up against the paradox we have indicated: art is an act, Gustave is merely passion; he would lose confidence and let everything go. However, deep down in him was that other belief: art is passive activity. But he could not find the thread through that labyrinth. Now, at least, he knows his Ariadne: it is God. If he *hopes*, the work will be woven by itself; faith will be the leavening of his passive activity. Hope, belief in the miracle, in the exceptional possibility of the impossible, is itself a miraculous gift; it is grace that will be visited upon him, perhaps, if he has indeed applied himself to realizing within himself the wretchedness of man without God. The operation does not unfold, we well understand, without manipulation. Be that as it may, it produces in him a belief all the stronger in that it is most often masked, the belief that is revealed in the night of 12–13 June. Superficially it preserves a certain uncertainty: he doesn't say that he hopes; he just asks for hope. But isn't there already an ardent hope in this appeal to the goodness of the Almighty? The following day Flaubert will fall back into his gloom. Not quickly enough to mask from us that the proclaimed despair of November '57 and the enthusiasm of June '58 are complementary: the discourse of despair would become tedious in the long run if from time to time the clouds did not part. Conversely, the author would lose all merit if his exultation were prolonged: Flaubert must be at once the man who seeks, groaning, knowing that there is nothing to seek, and the one summoned on occasion by an inaudible, mute voice: "You would not be seeking me if you had not found me."

328

E. ". . . Our Lord Jesus, Who Carried Him up to Heaven"

"An abundance of delights, a superhuman joy *descended* like a flood in the *swooning* soul of Julien . . . And Julien *rose* toward the blue spaces, face to face with Our Lord Jesus, who *carried* him up to heaven." These are the last words of *La Légende*. The permanence of themes and words is notable: we find them again at thirty years distance as they were offered to us in the *Mémoires d'un fou*. First of all, the absolute vertical: joy *descends* (curiously, "like a flood," which—at least as far as its cause is concerned—is in fact the *rising* of the water level); Julien *rises*. Then passivity: the saint has swooned—like the student Flaubert when he was *drowning* at the edge of created worlds. Finally the assumption: Julien is carried up to heaven. This consistency can only underscore the astonishing transformation of the guiding idea and the accompanying change of signs: what descends is celestial joy; the saint himself rises without intending to return, he will remain up there forever. It is no longer Satan who carries him off and compels him to make a vertiginous ascent into the eternal void: Christ has taken him in his arms, the "spaces" are blue. Was the author trying to depict the naive faith of the late Middle Ages? Obviously; nonetheless he used his own schemes—the oldest, the deepest—and only these. One could object that these schemes are also imposed on him by the subject. Precisely: he chose the subject *because he recognized them in it* and because he wanted an objective law to impose them from the outside. We must return to this tale.

In 1845 or '46, he confides to Maxime his desire to recount the life of Julien as depicted in the stained glass window of the cathedral. In 1875 he decides to set to work. In short, the conception goes back to the first years of his illness—the hardest ones; the writing begins at the moment of his ruin. Thirty years lay between; yet without saying much about it to his friends, save for Bouilhet, and rarely to him, Flaubert never abandoned his project. Why did he choose to recount this story? Why did he provisionally abandon it for *La Tentation*? Why did *La Légende* remain inside him so long, undying, like a task he had promised himself to perform? Why did he decide to write it when he was wandering at Concarneau, "deploring [his] ruined life"? If we can answer these questions, we may be able to understand how Flaubert *lived* his primitive "Loser wins" and simultaneously the mode of existence it assigned to him.

But we must first reread *Saint Julien*. What is saintly about this murderer of men and beasts, a parricide into the bargain? His charity? He hardly has any; his anomaly has excluded him from the society of his fellowmen: "In a spirit of humility he told his story; then everyone fled . . . , they closed their doors, they shouted threats at him, they threw stones . . . Repulsed everywhere, he avoided men." Is it credible that he would not hate them after such blows and insults? Chased out of cities, the parricide sometimes sighs deeply when he looks at closed doors and windows. But he truly has love only for nature, and by spilling his father's blood he could be said to have calmed the ardent, raging thirst he had for the blood of beasts: he contemplates the colts in their meadows, the birds in their nests, even the insects, "with transports of love." But the animals themselves have forgotten nothing and flee, unappeased. He has saved children, but without warmth: the author is careful to tell us that it was *at the risk of his life;* Julien is less concerned with restoring these scamps to their disconsolate parents than with committing a useful suicide. We see how true this is when our generous savior, after verifying that "the abyss rejects him and the flames spare him," resolves to kill himself with his own hands and, unable to manage it, indifferently lets those around him shift for themselves in danger. Are there no longer any children at the edge of cliffs, in burning houses? If there are, Julien doesn't want to know about it. He sets himself on a riverbank, and "the idea comes to him to devote his existence to the service of others." This existence is less than nothing, filth in the eyes of men and, first and foremost, in Julien's own eyes. But since even death does not want him, his life may just as well be of some use. Therefore, he will be a ferryman. Gustave has only a few words to describe the travelers who use Julien's services, but enough to shoot them down. Some of them (the least bad) reward his pains with the remains of food or belongings they no longer want. Others, brutal, shout insults and blasphemies—we do not not know why. Julien treats them with gentleness, they insult him. With the glacial detachment of his humility, he gives them his blessing: let them go hang themselves, God will take charge of them. In short, contact with the human race is reduced to the *minimum.*

Will he at least be saved by faith? He seems irreproachable on this score: he has believed like a peasant, from childhood on, without ever questioning that belief: "He did not rebel against God, who had inflicted this parricide on him, and yet he was in despair because he had been capable of committing it." But this unshakable belief hardly lends itself to mystic ecstasies, to delicious swoons in which one loses oneself in the bosom of the Lord. This Christian is so filled with God that he never thinks of his faith and doesn't even dare to pray. He is so distracted he even forgets to call on the vast goodness of the Almighty to beg his forgiveness. We note that he enjoys recounting his story—"out of humility"—to everyone and anyone, but *never* to a priest. Not surprising if we recall Gustave's view of parish priests. We are puzzled, however, at his readiness to leave a great sinner of the Middle Ages alone beneath the mute heavens *without intercession:* this is the most egregious anachronism in a tale that was intended to be the faithful restoration of an epoch in which the Church reigned.

Julien, then, does not shine by the transports of his faith or by his hope or his charity. As far as hope is concerned, he is so deficient that after the murder he commits the inexpiable sin of despair. So where does his merit lie? It must be a great merit to allow this criminal to achieve not only salvation but canonization too. Yet it is none other than his horror of self. The basic characteristic of sainthood will be one of the earliest constituted structures of Flaubertian affectivity taken to its extreme.

Julien is bad from childhood on. One fine day, while killing a mouse, he discovers in himself an inextinguishable need to murder. Soon afterward he begins the systematic massacre of the surrounding fauna. This strange frenzy has all the characteristics of Flaubertian sadism. The future saint is still a child when, finding in a ditch a pigeon that he has just felled but that is not quite dead, he "is irritated" by this persistent life: "He set about strangling it, and the bird's convulsions made his heart beat, filled him with a wild and tumultous pleasure. At the final stiffening, he felt faint." Later, "he does not tire of killing." Seeing stags "filling a little valley . . . and pressing against each other," he "chokes with pleasure at the hope of such carnage." A desire to murder that has visibly sexual origins, as indicated by the swoons and choking that precede and follow it. But what is especially striking is the contrast between the violently *active* aspect of the "carnages" the hero gives himself up to and the *passivity* of the pleasures the hunt brings him, which resemble swoons. It must be added that Gustave emphasized the oneiric aspects of these massacres. "Julien did not tire of killing . . . and thought of nothing, had no memory of it whatsoever. He had been out hunting in some other country for an indeterminate length of time, and by the very fact of his own existence, things happened *with the facility experienced in dreams.*"[73] The rhythm of the narrative itself preserves something nightmarish: things

---

73. My italics.

appear and disappear abruptly, in the nick of time. If we replace these beasts with human beings, we shall have the masturbatory truth of this legend: the massacres are dreams; as an adolescent, Gustave indulges in onanism while imagining tortures, his orgasms accompanied by a happy abandonment to his native passivity: each time he comes closer to losing consciousness. This is how he sees himself around 1840: bad but passive, dreaming of extraordinary sufferings, incapable of *inflicting them*. The death of Achille-Cléophas will be natural, but the young man will be afraid he provoked it by his homicidal tendencies, magically, as if that murderous hatred he harbors for the human race were merely a screen for the hatred he feels for his parents. The truth, as we know, is different. But having discovered in himself this proud malice—proudly confessed in his stories, too often appeased by masturbatory fantasies—Gustave cannot help generalizing, out of habit, and making malice the immediate consequence of original sin *in everyone*. He conceives the curse of Adam in this ultra-Jansenist form: all are damned, all vicious to the core, all haunted sexually by the imperious desire to kill. In short, the species is rotten from the start: to live is not only an interminable and insipid misfortune, it is a permanent crime. No one tears himself away from it while he lives; thus we divine that Sainthood will not be characterized by accession to a superior state or by an effective grace that would allow one to combat base instincts: the saint is an earthly creature unless countermanded from above, fair game for Hell. The stag's prophecy, however, so similar to that of the prophetess in *La Peste à Florence*[74] many years before, causes an insight to dawn in Julien. He does not discover his wickedness directly, but he grasps the horror of homicidal desire by its magical consequence, parricide. The desire to hunt constantly plagues him, but now it arouses in him a dread of himself: he no longer knows whether the awakening of his hunting lust and the pleasure with which he thinks of it indicate only that he prefers the hunt to his parents, or whether, to the contrary, he desires to kill the wildfowl only *in order* to be led, without having wished it, to commit the murder of the father. Whatever it is, Julien's wickedness is mediated. Denounced by others, familiar, at once assumed and denied, it is consciously experienced *in the only suitable way:* in horror. For Gustave, this attitude is still not meritorious, it is simply *true;* human nature is such that it can be lived *authentically* only in disgust.

74. And to those prophecies that mark the calvary of Emma Bovary.

The parricide takes place through a concurrence of *providential* circumstances (that will lead Julien to sainthood the way Jules's providential frustrations push him to genius): it could not be otherwise, it is Destiny. Julien acknowledges his role in it, however: there is no fatality in this affair but his own nature. That nature, moreover, has just *realized* itself: this imaginary bad man has gone to the limit of himself, he has become a real criminal. Formerly he thought he could escape himself. Now the exits are blocked, a blinding light illuminates his act: until then, Julien understood himself as the unhappy product of radical Evil; now, radical Evil is his product. The virtual is actualized irreversibly, and Julien becomes irreparable. His wickedness, formerly dreamed and provoking a dream of disgust, is inscribed in the world; he is a man through whom human nature is objectified. Impelled by vice to the paroxysm of being, he is no longer anything but his essence, and yet he has his essence outside the self since it is affirmed by an action torn by time from his grasp: he *must* destroy it, but it is indestructible; his being is behind him, a past surpassed, unsurpassable. At the beginning, Julien struggles against his act, as if he could still separate himself from it, as if, denouncing *his* parricide publicly, he could cease to be *the* parricide. In vain: this self-criticism merely has the effect of universalizing his crime by calling down upon him universal reprobation; in fact—though he does not know it—it achieves for him the abandonment necessary for the horrible work he must perform on himself. On this point the author's intentions are not in doubt; in the legend that inspired Flaubert, Julien goes begging on the roads *accompanied by his wife:* that is the true medieval conception; not only does the crime fail to break the sacred bonds of marriage but the wife even participates in it, despite her innocence, by a reversal of crimes which is the satanic equivalent of the reversal of merits. Gustave suppressed this faithful companion in order to give Julien the lofty solitude he himself suffered and enjoyed so much. In any event, this penitent begging appears to be a first step, still quite easy, on the most uncomfortable of paths. The parricide, having taken refuge in nature, quickly perceives that his humility will never allow him to compensate for his crime. He is then persuaded that his only recourse is systematic self-destruction: since he *is* his own fault, he hopes to abolish it by annihilating himself. Without success: neither his pious feats nor his mortifications will resurrect the two old people nor efface the thrusts of his dagger. But death does not want him: he is condemned to remain on earth, the horrified contemplator of his own past. Impossible not to think here of the dichotomy of *Novembre*, which prophesied that of January '45: a child was dying in a storm of passions, transports, and unhappiness so that an old man should be born who had no other function than to delve into the memory of the first. And Julien's parricide is like a death; this turbulent and passionate man has lost even his vices, he is merely a horrified gaze, steadily contemplating the last recollection of his dead memory. When he has understood that abysses reject him and conflagrations spare him, he discovers despair. That is, he sees clearly that he wants the *impossible:* what has been cannot be effaced. His failed suicide—the last of the suicides that punctuate Flaubert's works, the most startling of which is recounted in *Novembre*—appears as the premature and entirely subjective conclusion to this despair: Julien dreams of suppressing the unbearable repetition of an inexpiable sin. It will be observed that he is no more concerned with Hell now than he was with Heaven. This member of medieval Christianity believes only in nothingness. Not for an instant does he imagine he will be made to pay in another world for his triple crime—parricide, suicide, despair. For Julien as for Gustave, Hell is on earth. He gives up the idea of killing himself, however: bending over his own reflection, he believes he sees his father. An episode with multiple meanings. We shall retain only one of them: when he sees this face bathed in tears, it seems to him that his resurfaced parricide is blocking his way to suicide. In other words, death settles nothing. No doubt it suppresses Julien's subjectivity, that nest of vipers and torments, but the unhappy man understands that his subjectivity has no more than an inessential reality; annihilated, it would leave untouched the statue of iniquity his crime has permanently sculpted for him in the minerality of the past. In short, suicide is a useless act. Since death does not want Julien, and since he renounces the idea of taking it for himself—as if, when all is said and done, it was worthier for a subjectivity to remain so as to assume the infamous past and *to suffer from it*, as if he were afraid in dying to leave that gloomy solitary face in the hands of others, in its inexplicable objectivity—the life he must lead appears to him a slow rotting, which in itself *is not sufficient* to reach its goal. It is prolonged, that is all one can say, because it has lost its death. He can no longer even *live* his crime, as he did at first when he seemed to extend it unceasingly; he hardly thinks of it now, and from time to time the hallucinatory image of two bloody bodies, suddenly appearing, crushes him with its horror. But this ever increasing remoteness of the cursed night, far from attenuating his despair, deepens it from day to day. For his objective essence gradually escapes him, yet never ceases fundamentally to determine his subjectivity, which receives no new qualification from the present, having become merely the unbearable and increasingly vague recollection of a crime. On this level, the sin of despair is total: it is no longer even a question of living in order to hate himself; Julien lives and hates himself, that is all. What should he do with his still vigorous body? "The idea came to him," Flaubert tells us, "to devote his existence to the service of others." We need only slight familiarity with Gustave to see the absurdity of this decision. Remember how he used to rail against philanthropists? And how he and Alfred swore to each other never to employ their talents as lawyers "to defend widows and orphans"? Nor have we forgotten the hatred Jules declares for his fellowmen, or the rejection of human aims and the contempt for action that appear on every page of the correspondence. Besides, who are these people—brutal and ungrateful—whom Julien, in a patched-up old boat, takes from one side of the river to the other? Merchants making the crossing to sell to the neighboring town; a few pilgrims going from abbey to abbey. To serve merchants is to bind his workpower to those *material interests* which Gustave never ceased to scorn—essentially, Julien is making himself the mechanism of a utilitarian enterprise whose ignominiousness reverts to him. As for the pilgrims, they are making an effort to assure their salvation; but painful as their road is, how gentle are the pains they inflict on themselves, pains that will gain them the goodwill of God, compared with the atrocious destitution, moral torments, and physical pain that Julien imposes on himself, knowing he will never be saved. In short, he knowingly pursues his self-destruction, brutalized by pain and degradation, not in order to expiate the inexpiable but to hurt himself, to slip to the depths of abjection. He seeks to chastise his mortal remains not in order to come closer to God but, to the contrary, to move away from him. Gradually horror becomes familiar, wretchedness becomes ordinary: thwarted, sullen, degraded, living the hateful disgust of being himself but no longer thinking of it, Julien as he bends over his oars becomes like Gustave, a man of repetition. He goes back and forth from one bank to the other, his mind darkened by the fatigue of a thankless task; in the evenings he collapses, exhausted, just to begin again the following day. Let us pay our respects in passing to that apparent calm in unhappiness produced by the eternal return—a calm that is worse than a storm.

Suddenly the leper appears, so heavy that the boat can barely leave the shore. Julien's first feeling is one of considerable compulsion, stronger than any exigency engendered by his hatred: "Understanding that it involved a command that must not be disobeyed, he took up his oars." Haven't we already seen that the Beautiful, if it is to visit Gustave, can take no other form than that of an obligation to be fulfilled, alien, frightening, irresistible? But that isn't the issue for Julien: he will have to take the leper to the other shore, feed him and refresh him, and then at last, "naked as the day he was born," "stretch out" on that rotting body covered with ulcers and "scabs of scaly pustules." He clasps him, chest against chest, and glues his mouth to "bluish lips that exhale a breath thick as fog and nauseating." And why, we might ask, does he do this? Out of love? Surely not: this diseased person has nothing lovable about him, though the author has observed that there is "in his attitude something of a kings's majesty." Certainly Julien is charitable—without warmth, as we know. But if he lies naked on the leper, it is not *primarily* to warm him: it is because those wounds, that running pus, fill him with a disgust never before experienced. Here is a chance to conquer the distraught resistance of all his organism and to inflict upon himself the most exquisite discomfort, its intensity measured by the repugnance he must overcome. In short, it is a hideous chance he must not miss. And then, beyond this immediate objective, there is another, more distant and more important: he seeks the contagion in order to contract leprosy, to become that ravaged body which revolts him. Note the verb the author uses: Julien "*stretches out*" on the leper. A passive activity: he extends himself to his full length on the living bed of the leper, he *weighs* on the decaying body of the traveler, we might say he sinks into it. This horizontal "stretching out" is like the beginning of a fall—broken by the purulent mass into which he sinks, that is, by the leper, as if the descent into Hell were halted by finally hitting bottom. Julien exhibits a kind of hysterical vertigo when faced with the corruption of a living body, as Gustave previously exhibited a fascination with the journalist of Nevers. *Contagion* here recalls *imitation.* The impulse is the same, since Gustave, on his father's faith, thought that madness was earned and saw it as the utmost abjection. Logically, the story of Julien should finish the next day with this vast disgust carefully sought as vile ecstasy: the leper should depart at the first rays of the sun, having infected him with his leprosy. The parricide should abandon even his work as boatman—proof that he cared little for helping men but only for self-mortification. Leprosy is the body taking responsibility for the original taints of the soul and the curse of Adam. Is it believable, at least, that this somatization would have cleansed Julien of his stain? He, in any case, when holding the leper in his arms, has no thought for his own salvation. He wants to touch the depths of abjection and, since he cannot die, to suffer an indefinitely prolonged, squalid agony. Angry with himself, he wants to be damned. At this instant, Jesus reveals himself and carries him up to Heaven: in flagrant contradiction to the principles of the Catholic religion, it is for having despaired of God that Julien will be saved.

The Lord in his extreme goodness had expressly willed all that happened. He did not make man in His image: He sought, rather, to realize in each of us the very depths of vice, baseness, and suffering, and then He created in all souls a vast need of Him to frustrate them by His absence. In this theology, Cartharist evasion is itself rejected: we are in the world and will not escape from it, even by breaking our solidarity with human ends; should we try to perch above ourselves, our intention will be tainted from the outset since our nature is evil, and the result can only be sinful: the characteristic of Evil, if it is radical, is that it cannot be escaped. The creature has only one recourse, which is to attack himself, to practice systematic self-destruction in hatred of himself and the world. Ordinarily, men hide their terrible mandate from themselves, they deceive themselves, they lie to themselves: such men are damned in advance. But he who, having recognized himself in his Truth, tears out his heart with both hands, is chosen of God, and his sufferings are pleasing to Him. Julien is canonized in advance, an old man predicted it at his birth: his inexpiable fault will allow him to break the matrix of inauthenticity and to hate himself without hope; thus does he realize the essence of human nature, which is nothing but self-denial. God created him brutal and bloodthirsty. He led him by the hand to parricide—the author says clearly that He "inflicted" it on Julien—then, when the chips were down, He left him to his atrocious sorrow. In this *other* will, which decides and prophesies a Destiny, then compels its victim to realize it in such a way that the victim feels led with an irresistible sweetness by that docile complicity of things found only in dreams, yet also feels responsible for his crime or, at least, extremely guilty and without the slightest mitigating circumstance, we shall readily recognize an old idea of irresistible *Fatum*, the curse of the Father and the savage will the progenitor exerts to realize his design.

In *La Légende* we may say that, man, like the child Gustave, is a monster put on earth to suffer. What has changed since *La Peste à Florence?* Only that in 1875 the reconciliation with the father is confirmed. The late Achille-Cléophas does not figure in *La Légende* merely in the

337

form of a benevolent country squire who adores his only son; he is also God the Father, a hidden but beneficent God. Julien, prisoner of himself, can only endure the atrocious destiny He has reserved for him, discovering in it nothing but a calamity. But the author keeps himself at a distance; he sees the event from the outside, objectively, in all its dimensions, and can declare with pious ardor: if Julien has suffered, I bear witness that it was for his own good. Gustave has of course stolen the ideas of the ordeal and of efficacious suffering. But he has transformed them for his own use: the Catholic does not remain without help in misfortune; there is the Church, which bears witness to him that God wants his eternal happiness; there are the intercessors—Jesus, Mary, the saints; and God can always send him His grace. Suffering purifies him, certainly, but first of all he knows it, and then there are other purifications such as confession and communion; the Council of Trent long ago decided that man was weak but certainly not naturally inclined to do evil. Flaubert plays fast and loose with the Council and radicalizes everything: man is rotten, damned; that's the way God wanted it. The gentle rosary of trials told by a Christian existence does not exist: there is only life, that nauseating squalor which the human monster must live from beginning to end. God has pulled man out of nothingness so that hatred should exist in the universe. Here, by two different paths, Gustave and the Christian are joined: since the Lord is good, He has not engendered Evil solely for His pleasure; He sees human suffering merely as a means. To what end? On this point, Gustave is not informative. But we know him well enough to divine his reasons; already in *Agonies* he confided in us: all the unhappiness of man comes from his *determination*. The *real* is an impoverishment of infinite possibles, it is therefore finitude and nothingness. But—another change that occurred after 1844—the Creation is no longer an irreparable fault: it has become a necessary evil. The real must exist in order to negate itself in hatred, in order vainly to attempt to transcend itself through that religious appeal to the infinite which can be born only in finitude, and in order to let itself be devoured by the imaginary, the ambiguous cipher of God. For Flaubert, the moment of reality—that is, of facticity and of abandonment—is not the purpose of Creation but quite the contrary, the first degree of an ascension toward Being. Thus when God leans over Julien's despair, He laments his suffering but He values, in this frantic negation of the self, the contesting of all *"beings"* in the name of an ontological truth that remains out of reach; in the parricide's determination to destroy his inexpiable fault, God can discover and love the bitter and disappointing search for the impossible, the sole greatness, in His eyes, of the prisoners of the human race. In other words, Julien is chosen because he has the obscure intuition that man *is* his own impossibility since that creature denies his finite determination in the name of an infinite he cannot even conceive. This said, the *heautontimoroumenos* can do nothing more *by himself:* an impossibility conscious of itself does not abolish itself for all that (contrary to what is said in *Novembre*) and continues to vegetate in the mire of time. When he has actualized his essence by being perfectly bad, and perfectly in despair at being bad, the Almighty must intervene by a miracle to make possible the impossible. Julien's crime is indelible, but the Lord, by carrying the parricide up to Heaven without tampering with the annulled crime, without suppressing a single detail of it, turns it by a logical and miraculous metamorphosis into the means He has chosen in His wisdom to engage Julien on the path to sainthood. With this tour de force, Gustave has succeeded in preserving intact the black, cursed world of his adolescence and integrating it into a calm religious universe.

All this of course is what we find in *La Légende* of 1875, the only one we can consult. But we are sure that the story, had he written it in 1845, would have been the same: the themes, the values, the twists of plot existed even before he was aware of them; he found them in the stained glass window itself, which was inspired by a German medieval romance, and in a "Historic and Descriptive Essay on Glass Painting" written by his drawing teacher. The saint's adventures had to be told as they had taken place and *in order*—hunts, parricide, despair, salvation—or not told at all. The myth of the cursed hunter could tempt Flaubert only by its objective structures, those restored in the work; and the meaning he then discovered in it, to the degree that it articulated through those structures what he was or believed he was, could not differ much from the meaning he gave it in '75. We can therefore affirm that, at the age of twenty-three, the young invalid had chosen to preserve his pessimism and to illuminate it by the invisible light of the Good. What is striking, however, is that Julien succeeds Jules and will provisionally be abandoned for Antoine. As if Gustave could embody himself only in three characters at a time. The trinitarian character of his self-representation is confirmed by numerous letters in which he envisages his work as a triptych: Antiquity, the Middle Ages, the Modern World. Antoine, Julien, and Jules.

Antoine, Julien, Madame Bovary.[75] Antoine, Julien, Bouvard and Pécuchet. Herodias, Julien, A Simple Heart.

Around 1845, Flaubert incarnates and objectifies himself in two quite different characters, Jules and Julien; both live in him and feed on him. At this period, however, Jules's story is the one he tells, and Julien, dearer to his author perhaps, remains in shadow. Why? Because Jules is the son of pride; his apotheosis is born of a prodigious rebound; one can write of him without much preparation, in a transport of glory: his genius crowns an ascesis facilitated at the outset by "providential" circumstances but later pursued consciously and deliberately. He manages to be reborn without owing anything to anyone. *Feeling* himself to be Jules arouses an almost unbearable joy, the terrible gaiety and dizzying freedom of the Nietzschean superman: it is like dancing. Thus, Gustave rarely feels the strength to play *for himself* and in the intimacy of lived experience this blazing satanic role; he prefers to fix it on paper, so that his ink, scarcely dry, should reflect it back to him as his permanent possibility, his highest truth, and also so that it should remain at a distance, fascinating but quite simply *presented*. Jules, or the death of the heart: a cry of triumph that must be voiced on the spot, a dizzying character depicted in haste so that this *self*, projected outside the self, should become as quickly as possible *the other that one is.*

Julien is a child of darkness. There is shame and fear in objectifying him. He is Gustave's most intimate role, his *essential* drama, the original "Loser wins." No sooner is he conceived, however, than Gustave abandons him: in Genoa he betrays him for *Saint Antoine.* It is too soon to bring him before the footlights. He must return to the hell of doubt; antiquity will represent skepticism. But Antoine cuts a pale figure between Jules and Julien: he has neither the triumphant strength of the one nor the desperate violence of the other. In 1856, when Gustave returns to the cursed hunter, he is—provisionally—too late: he has finished *Madame Bovary,* whose heroine is an anti-Jules, despair without genius, and who dies damned. Gustave prepares to do battle with the *Revue de Paris,* with the Parisian publishers. The "exercise," after all, does not seem so bad to him. Will luck perhaps smile upon him?

75. This is what he writes to Bouilhet in 1856: *Madame Bovary* is completed, he is correcting fragments of *Saint Antoine;* he wants to write *La Légende* so as to present, at almost the same time, an evocation of antiquity, another of the Middle Ages, and a modern novel. The idea is taken up again in '75, almost word for word, except that he writes *La Légende* first and then decides, in the course of editing, to follow it with two other tales.

He has ceased to understand the *lyrical* meaning of *La Légende*. It would be timely, however: the damnation of Emma, set against the world and against herself, would take on quite another meaning in the light of Faith. She must go to her doom and destroy herself, horribly. But who knows whether she is not saved by her "aspirations"? Flaubert *feels* it; he also feels that a dry "alacrity" strips him of any possibility of self-indulgence: we see from his letters that he is preparing to restore the vanished Middle Ages in a glacial Parnassian work; as if his underlying impulse had swerved and turned away from its object as it traversed more superficial strata to reach the periphery. He searches for proud, sonorous words in works of venery, divines that he is indulging his pleasures too much, gives up; he will keep the story for some other time, when circumstances are more propitious.

1875. Overwhelmed by his nephew's ruin, he flees to Concarneau. He is in torment: the fall of the Empire has already undermined him, this new blow of fate finishes the job. He has fits of rage followed by choking; alone in his room and sometimes in public he is shaken by bouts of sobbing and weeping, then sinks into a torpor verging on imbecility: "From time to time I am overtaken by prostrations in which I feel so annihilated that it seems to me I am going to die." Sometimes he cannot even write a note to his niece, his hands are trembling so. Stomach cramps, bouts of nerves, everything returns. The worst is that he senses and believes he is doomed. I am old, he says for the thousandth time since his adolescence. But this time it is true: "When the mind no longer naturally turns toward the future, one has become an old person, that's where I am." He has no more "resources": he is finished, they have killed him, he has nothing more to say: "As for literature, *I no longer believe in myself*, I find I am empty, which is hardly a consoling discovery." He has so little energy that it seems to him he is letting himself die. "If ruins on the outside are added to internal ruin, which one already feels intensely, one is quite simply crushed." I shall not recover from it, he says, and indeed, although bankruptcy is avoided and Croisset preserved, he never will recover. This means that the great work will never be finished, that the Commanville bankruptcy will lead to Flaubert's artistic bankruptcy. Always discontent with his past works, he had hope only in the work still to come—that is the one that will equal the Masters. But the future is broken; never were Sade and Satan so obviously right: *Virtue must be punished, it is the law of this world.* He is so convinced of this that he writes to Madame de Loynes: "I had sacrificed everything in my life to my peace of mind. That wisdom was vain. That is above all

what pains me." His wisdom, his sacrifice, consisted of his long medi-
tative retreat at Croisset: precisely for that reason it is in Croisset that
he feels threatened. His generosity, his tenderness, his paternal attentions were aimed at Caroline: therefore misfortune will come to him—
it is only justice—through Caroline's husband. After his mother's
death, Gustave resumes in the person of his niece his entire family—
that family first dominant and terrible, then divided, without which
the old bachelor could not have lived. It is the family that will conse-
crate the ruin and finally the destitution of this family man. What a
chapter to add to the *Infortunes de la vertu*. On 11 July, he writes tear-
fully, unguardedly: "Flavie's devotion touches me. Nor did I doubt it.
Provided she is not punished for it." There we have his pessimism
confirmed. I would say as much of his misanthropy; he is irritated
with his niece and the unseemly advice she offers him; no doubt also
with her ingratitude. As for his "poor nephew," of whom he will say
some time later that he was not born to make his happiness, he holds
him responsible for everything and is secretly determined to despise
him. Never were the gloomy intuitions of his adolescence so fully veri-
fied, never did life so fully give cause to that "complete presentiment"
which almost half a century earlier had foreseen its hideousness and
disgust. In short, the knot is tied; Uncle Gustave's life has justified the
presentiment of his adolescence: Hell is the world, and the damned
suffer in proportion to the ambitions they have nourished.

From the time of his arrival at Concarneau, however, he begins to
dream of Julien, and a few days later, on 25 September, he informs his
niece: "I have written (in three days) half a page *of* the outline *of* the
legend *of* Saint Julien l'Hospitalier." In his letters, complaints alter-
nate with news of his work: *La Légende* progresses slowly at first, later
at a good pace. It's merely a matter of thirty pages, he keeps saying.
Yes, but if one takes into consideration the time he put into writing
thirty pages of *Salammbô* or *Madame Bovary,* we shall find it reasonable
that *Saint Julien*—begun on 22 September, continued in Croisset, then
in Paris, in the midst of financial turmoil and changes of residence—
was finished on 18 February 1876, testifying to sustained and success-
ful labor. How does he explain that he has undertaken in the greatest
despair the most optimistic of his works, and that he has gotten it off
in one go? For circumstantial reasons, which are not false but which,
taken alone, are hardly convincing: he was foundering a little with
Bouvard et Pécuchet, and then the financial disaster hit, which rendered him incapable of, or, at least, disgusted with, writing. He abandons his great projects and decides to undertake a tale, a "brief little

thing," so as not to let himself be overwhelmed by grief—for the sake of mental hygiene—and also to find out "whether he is still capable of turning a phrase." Even without external cares, there is no doubt that he would have put aside his great work for a while: he needed to take his distance. His misfortunes are one more reason to suspend his work: he would need notes; a whole library; there is nothing of the kind in Concarneau. This does not explain, however, why he chooses to exercise his pen on, of all things, a subject he has pondered for thirty years.

He must be aware of this, for he adopts a slightly disdainful tone when speaking of his "little work": it is a trifle, he says, an amusement, a stylistic exercise, "a bit of nonsense a mother will be free to let her daughter read." This is how he spoke of *Smarh* when he was disgusted with it. Another phrase will surge up from the past: "As for me, I feel uprooted and rolling about at random, like a dead leaf. But I *want* to force myself to write *Saint Julien.* I will do this as an exercise, to see what the result will be." This voluntarism is so odd, coming from him, that he is surprised by it himself, and, fearing his niece's skepticism, italicizes the verb *to want.* But it is not accidental: if he means to minimize the importance that the theme of the parricidal Saint has long assumed in his eyes, he is compelled to claim that the story is in itself ordinary, the contents taken at random, and that he is forcing himself to write it despite his inner resistance: it bores him, this edifying nonsense, it is a *pensum,* a school exercise. Yes—like *Madame Bovary.* This term, which has not been found in his correspondence for many years, suddenly awakens our suspicions: around 1855 it signaled the disgust Flaubert felt for the "petty folk" he was writing about, for the "wretched" milieu in which he was obliged to situate his story. What is that term doing here? The subject is noble; he has always dreamed of reviving the Middle Ages, its great primitives and their humble faith; and then he dreams of forging a new style to render the period. He knows that this style will have to charm through a calculated obsolescence, through a naïveté more apparent than real, he already hears the resonance of the dazzling, moribund words that must be revived in all their splendor to designate the things and customs of a vanished time. History becoming unrealized as Legend, the Legend, a pure means of reviving a historical epoch and rendering with "scientific" seriousness the feelings of vanished men; the tumult of life reproduced from the point of view of death; and this macrocosm, the medieval world, closed upon itself and rigorous, totalized through the adventures of an extravagant hero: isn't this the work of art Flaubert is dreaming of in all its purity? Is this really a "trifle," this richly textured tale that speaks of God, Man, and Fate? Could he regard it as such? Did he ever write "trifles"? Circumstantial works? Doesn't he despise books that do not tell *all?* If it were necessary to prove his bad faith, I would recall that Gustave in 1856 wanted to make *Saint Julien* the third wing of a triptych, with *Saint Antoine* and *Madame Bovary* as the other two. So it is inconceivable that he should have decided at that moment that *Saint Julien* was unworthy of the others. We are forced to conclude that Flaubert is concealing his hand, that he is being insincere to the point of lying. It doesn't ring true that Gustave, struck with agraphia by unhappiness, should write just anything, despite his grief, solely to retrain his pen. Quite to the contrary, he throws himself into *"La Légende" because of his grief,* as if he recognized in his reversals the occasion, so long awaited, to write it. We are now able to explain this paradox.

In 1845, in the chiaroscuro of the cathedral, in the colored light falling from a stained glass window, Gustave discovered what might be called the technique of the two-tiered narrative. His truth, as we know, has long been manifest to him as his otherness; he is first of all an object, his essence lies outside the self, in the hands of others who reduce his subjectivity to a series of insubstantial epiphenomena; the subject itself, in him, is put in question; it is a simple decoy whose claimed apperceptions are contested a priori by the gaze of others. Hence the ethical and consequently aesthetic problem: How can one recuperate this gaze? Literally: How can one show subjectivity at once lived in its penumbra and deciphered, objectified by one who knows its Truth? *La Légende* brings him the solution. It is only readable on two levels at the same time. Julien *is* a saint, we have always known it; even before looking at the images of his life, we are forewarned: they will show us the life of a saint. Thus every event is presented with a double meaning. *Lived,* it is a link in a chain of crimes and catastrophes that lead Julien to terminal collapse; therefore he has a terrestrial future that cannot be separated from him. *Told,* it represents *inexplicably* but surely a step on the sacred way that leads to canonization. In other words, he has a celestial future that we know in advance because it is *already realized.* In this sense, the two-tiered narrative offers nothing new to Flaubert: there is Lived Experience, an implacable succession of events to be lived—the reader or spectator, too, must await the outcome—there is the gaze trained on Lived Experience, a gaze that this same spectator shares with the Artist, the gaze of history and death that compresses a detemporalized temporality into a moment of eternity and breaks duration by putting the final term of the adventure *before* the initial term as its meaning and purpose. What is new, on the other hand, is that the point of view of the Artist coincides with that of God. Also, although Jesus does not intervene before the final pages, His appearance, much awaited, has nothing in common with that of the *deus ex machina* in ancient tragedy. The Almighty is at the beginning as at the end of this story, we are *with Him,* we regard Julien from above without very well understanding His impenetrable designs but assured by the Church that all will end well: yes, yes, he kills his father and his mother, but have no fear, good people, that was predestined; all precautions are taken, *for you are told that he is a Saint!*

This is the way Gustave as prophetic understands it. God's point of view doesn't need to be rendered in words. The title is sufficient. And if there is any need to spell it out, the reader will have recourse to three oracles, two placed at the very birth of the cursed hunter—"He will build empires"; "He will be a Saint"—the third rendered at the end of the first third of his life: "You will be a parricide." These fore-warnings authorize us to read between the lines; indeed, they force us to do so, and subsequently Gustave can restrict his narrative to the terrestrial misadventures of his hero, emphasizing his savage violence, his sadism, for we are already in heaven and our blessed souls marvel at the knowledge—*formal and empty* intuition—that Evil is made to serve Good and to give forth an odor of sanctity from the darkest of crimes. *La Légende,* as Flaubert tells it, renders admirably the ambivalence of the sacred: terrible here below, beneficent on high. But the author pretends to concern himself—at least until the conclusion—only with the *black* aspect, while compelling us, the readers, to decipher the events from the point of view of the white sacred; the upper level is all the more present for being carefully hidden since he has perched his readers on it. Hence our growing sympathy for Julien, that monster in the eyes of the world: when honest folk shut their doors against him or throw stones at him—which, according to Gustave, we would do in their place—we blame them, from the height of our perch, cherishing him with the divine love Our Lord bears him and with which Flaubert has secretly touched us. Below there is merely a bad man who has turned his wickedness against himself and abhors himself; from above, we contemplate a martyr whose very faults single him out for the greatest suffering, that is, for the greatest "aspiration," and our love for him comes from the darkness in which he lives, from the deep humility that makes him misunderstand that very aspiration, the best of himself, and to see merely crime, hatred, and vain penitence in the divine dissatisfaction that never ceases to stir him, never allowing him to sit back and say: I have done enough.

Flaubert is writing for the Christian West. And we are all still Christians today; the most radical unbelief is Christian atheism, an atheism that despite its destructive power preserves guiding schemes—very few for thought, more for the imagination, most for the sensibility—whose source lies in the centuries of Christianity to which we are heirs, like it or not. Thus, even though we might like to change the world and deliver it from the great rotting body that encumbers it, even though we would refuse to poison souls with a morality of salvation and redemption, when a somewhat bizarre writer shows us a saint who is unaware of his own saintliness and dies in desolation, there is no doubt that we are moved in the most childlike recesses of our mind: Christians in the imaginary, we go along. We did this when Bernanos published his admirable *Curé de campagne,* in which—since Flaubert, techniques have advanced—the upper half of the tableau is merely an absence,[76] with the work ending on this earth it never left, and we the unbelievers are compelled in all sincerity to effect the assumption ourselves. For this young priest is good, he is pure—even in the eyes of an atheist. And if God is dead, his acts are futile and his sufferings too real; unhappiness has the last word. And we love this child in agony so much that we resurrect God to save him.

Comparing the work of Bernanos and Flaubert, however, we discover the latter's craftiness, his unrelieved blackness. Taken by himself, Julien is not in the least likable, there is no trace of love in this lost soul; we find in him first the passion to destroy life everywhere, and then self-destruction pushed to the limits: hatred of the world converted into hatred of self. On this point, the author is not faking: he declared he was bad and disgusted with himself at the age of fourteen (and probably much earlier); he proclaims himself such at the end of his life, in this tale that he regarded for a moment as his literary testament. In order to save a character we love, Bernanos compels us to revive old beliefs in the imaginary. Stronger than he, Flaubert forces us to reestablish the supernatural and the upper level *so that we can love his Julien.* With no particular sympathy for his destructive frenzy but won over in advance to the author's point of view by our

76. The priest speaks in the first person. Let us imagine Julien recounting his own story under the title *Diary of a Parricide.* The art of Bernanos is to make us feel the "Transcendent" allusively, without leaving the realm of immanence.

Christian education, we love him because he is loved *without knowing it* with an absolute love. Thus his self-hatred dissolves and becomes pure merit without our ceasing to witness the havoc it wreaks in our world. In short, Gustave uses a very Catholic schema in order to astonish us by a sleight-of-hand. We sense it, we let ourselves be moved, and as a result we are affected by an imaginary belief in what is not believable in order to love him who is unlovable, a bad man who has turned his wickedness against himself. We recall the ambiguity of Garcia, of Mazza, even of Marguerite, those unloved characters whose unhappiness made them antipathetic, of Emma herself, festering with hatred and resentment. Julien is no more worthy than they, and in a sense he resumes them, for they too were disgusted with themselves insofar as they disgusted the author who embodied himself in them.[77] What is different about him? Only one thing: Gustave convinces us, peremptorily but not without art, that his parricide is the object of an infinite love; we are therefore constrained to impose silence on our antipathy so as not to look bad and because the Catholic schemes are formally maintained: we feel within us and in the story the presence of an ineffable, dark unreason, which is not the least charm of this astonishing work.

Victim of the Other, Gustave dares to defend himself by opposing *to others* the absolute Other who can only be God; the unloved man dares to believe: *God loves me infinitely.* Abandoning a sad *Cogito* that offers him little protection, he agrees to be illusory beneath the eternal gaze of absolute knowledge: he feels "seen" and "known" from birth to death—death both future and forever past; he happily agrees to be providentially guided by the hand that pulled him out of the mud and maintains his existence by a continuous creation. Finally, discharged of all responsibility, he knows the happiness of being acted upon. What a happy ending! Is it entirely believable? Certainly not, that would be too good to be true! Of course when he falls, breathless, in the night of January '44, the fall is a surrender to God; his underlying intention is to invent the invisible love that his Creator bears him: he will live henceforth *beneath a Gaze*. But *it is on condition that he know nothing about it:* not a single ray must illuminate Julien-Gustave's benighted soul. Perhaps this is an attempt to square the circle? No: the solution to the problem must be sought in Art. His encounter in '45 with the Saint of the stained glass window allows him to recognize himself in the cursed Hunter, but not directly: it provides

77. He hasn't even the excuse of being unloved in his childhood.

him, as I have said, with a technique and makes him feel a kind of *aesthetic* evidence. It should be understood that he grasps *an object*, a story told in comic strips, dense and rich, which seems to totalize a whole vanished world, and proposes to him a complete and satisfying vision of life; the two-tiered narrative, a procedure that is both familiar and marvelously new, seems convincing to him in its formal beauty. But this perfect ensemble remains imaginary and the facts reported have never taken place. Here the evidence is not the hard encounter with an obstacle that derails an enterprise and imposes itself in its irreducible nature, with its sharp outlines; it is the total contemplative adhesion to a pure image that exists nowhere and is nonetheless inscribed in *this* window in *this* wall. And the conviction it prompts in Flaubert is *also* of an aesthetic order; it is a commandment: write this legend, translate into words the gentle impact of this stained glass; extract *your* masterpiece from the charming work of an anonymous deceased craftsman. What attracts Gustave is the apparent gratuitousness of the subject: it is not a matter of *concluding*, of constructing a plot to prove a thesis, but of making the Idea the very technique of the narrative and its condition of readability. Indeed, the story is already told. The theme, the technique, the dialectic of the impossible and the miracle, of pessimism and optimism, all is given to him in advance, he can do no more than change the details. Did he understand that he was being offered the way to express his expressible wager? In any case, he *recognized* these images without really knowing that he recognized himself in them, and his recognition took the form of a contemplative enchantment and a task. "I will write this legend," can have only one meaning: I must make it mine, attach my name to it because it already belongs to me, and has from all eternity. Nowhere will he say: it is my truth. This would be to betray himself, and Flaubert does not live in the world of truth. But taking it as his task, as a permanent possibility of his art, he does more than envisage the transmutation of a plastic imaginary into a verbal imaginary, he inscribes it inside himself as a permanent wrinkle of his thought. Well before beginning the work, he finds in the calm reality of this unreal tale the objectivization he has been seeking. *On condition* that he appropriate it for himself as his future work, he can establish it inside himself as a matrix of images and at the same time as his *quasi-real* determination, which has come down to him through the years, reserved *for him alone* despite sieges, pillages, and conflagrations, by a majestic natural inertia. This consistency of the ancient imaginary delights him more than anything; he sees in it a kind of unreal equivalent to reality. Hence he is *affected* by it: we can be sure that he is not in a hurry to work on it. Quite the contrary: he knows only too well that completed works disgust him; he is open with Maxime about his projects, one trusting day, but his letters of the period breathe no word of them: he shares only his short-term, moderate objectives. As for *La Légende,* he caresses it, thinks of it lazily; it becomes what he wished it might be: a category of his thought and sensibility. This means that he can hide, and hide from himself, his religious "Loser wins": if he wishes to assure himself that his fine despair will be rewarded, he takes the story of Julien and tells it to himself on the pretext of working at it. And indeed he is comforted by it. Certainly the real has no need of a legendary confirmation, but no one can say that the extravagant wager he made at the time of his fall is concerned with realities. Gustave has suffered enough from realities; by falling, he alleviates his pain and turns it into a role: on the basis of his old and all-too-justified moroseness, which as we know was not always sincerely felt even then, he throws himself into playing for God the role of the Man-without-Hope. This new character and his *Great Spectator* are both unreal. That doesn't matter, however, for in this farcical tragedy one must never mention the public or look as if one knows it might be there. Be that as it may, *Saint Julien,* a work in progress, serves as security for the representation Flaubert gives himself: this antique product of the social imagination guarantees, as a singular universal, the almost disturbing singularity of the neurotic "Loser wins." This role establishes a reciprocity of mirrored reflections between the legend, with its objectivity as *legend,* its demand to be told—therefore reobjectified—the *real* structuring of its original contents (it is imaginary *in what* it expresses, and of course neither Julien nor the talking stag seem to Gustave other than images, but the structure of the story is real in the sense that it imposes itself: it must be told *this way* or not at all), and, on the other hand, the role Gustave is determined, deep down, to play before God and which *is lived* as an *imperative savor* of lived experience structured by mute intentions. Nothing out of the ordinary: these are two homogeneous determinations, two commandments both aspiring not to praxis but to the *production of the imaginary through Gustave,* and construing the present from the future, that is, from the task to be fulfilled. In this task, in both cases, the purpose proposed is the same: to make the religious "Loser wins" the ultimate secret of the terrestrial world. Flaubert, an atheist in spite of himself, and Julien, a believer—he is a product of his time—but incapable of imagining for an instant that God can be good and incapable even of begging His forgiveness, communicate with each other across the centuries. Moreover, the mediator of these tasks is Gustave, not by accident but because he is the man to whom both these imperatives address themselves. Thus when, alone in his study, he plays the role of a man in despair motivated by the disgust aroused in him by what he has just written, the command to lose even more, and to gamble prodigally, may well reveal its wholly singular function in the particular system Gustave has made for himself if the aesthetic imperative to recount his role as though it were the story of another were not reflected from *above*, in the mute attempt to make him despair, and did not communicate to him its perenniality, its social character, and its inflexible objectivity (or if you will, the inevitable and real structures of the objectivization it demands). So that the solitary writer, in his self-loathing, no longer knows if he is playing his own character or getting accustomed to Julien's. Conversely, when he envisages the legend in his clearest consciousness as artist, he senses in the legend, and in the character of the Saint, something infinitely close and familiar, a kind of ubiquitous Grace, an anonymous encouragement that comes from the late Middle Ages and is nonetheless addressed to him alone but does not *tell* him anything; and if he feels a divine designation in the mute solicitude of the aesthetic imperative, if he feels deliciously moved by the window, it is because Julien's story, insofar as he has decided to assume it by telling it again, has somehow been charged by him with representing his own, a chalice that must be drunk to the dregs. The dialectic of reflections again becomes complicated: he knows in advance that he will write *Julien*, for he has ordered himself to do it, disgusted with himself and with each word his pen will trace out; but he will not doubt its perfect success since the legend has designated him, from such a distance, as its unique narrator, since the German writer and the painter on glass have attempted to live and have each set their hand to this charming sketch only to submit themselves, as good servants, to him who was predestined, in a distant future, to make it a jewel worthy of God.

Thanks to the stained glass window, the religious "Loser wins" remains a stifled language, unspoken: when Gustave wants to encourage himself it is Julien's objectivity he looks to, enchanted *not to have invented* but *to have received from the outside* this hero after his own heart. A current runs permanently between his Dionysiac determination to go to the limits of dolorism in order to become meritorious through it, and the Apollonian representation of that determination by a bouquet of painted, impersonal images. In 1845, however, Flaubert is not in a hurry to write: he will occupy himself with *his* Julien later, much later, perhaps at the end of his life; this would be logical since divine reward becomes manifest at the end of an existence. In that strange *empty* temporality which he has reserved for himself—and which often has the ignoble taste of boredom—he knows that a long road separates him from death. In other words, *he has time* to take up and transform into masterpieces the works of his adolescence in which everything is set, even the themes and sometimes even the particular subjects, and which are already nontemporal statements since the past has fixed them. A single novelty: hope, God. It is plain that he has no desire to start work on *La Légende;* it is his talisman. If he prematurely obeys the imperative that commands him to make it his work, it will lie behind him, *accomplished, finished,* stripped of its former powers by its very objectivization. This is the moment, on the other hand, to carry out the work of despair that the parricidal Saint performed on himself. Gustave's mystic and surreal optimism gives a new meaning to the literary expression of his pessimism: Evil reigns on earth, an unsurpassable truth here below *which must be told,* a meritorious error in Heaven, since he believes he divines at certain moments that God demands of him the radical and enraged contention of His Creation as a sacrifice. He will treat gloomy subjects, he will make himself sadistic and masochistic, condemning his creatures to Hell and living their sufferings like a passion. And then, one fine day, quite late, he will write *Saint Julien* to tell the inside story before taking his leave. Thus *La Légende,* the always future task, allows Gustave to produce *Saint Antoine* and *Madame Bovary.*

In 1856, as we have seen, he feels like shouting in triumph: he decides to take up the task. But in fact he has never been farther from Julien, for Jules is the one who should celebrate victory; he rather quickly abandons the project. In '75, on the other hand, he doesn't hesitate for a moment, throws himself into writing, and never goes back on his decision. He feels he is in mortal danger, convinced that he will not survive financial ruin—and, indeed, although his situation is less precarious than he believes, he will barely survive it. At Concarneau, alone and naked, defenseless, threatened with the loss of Croisset, his protective shell, he experiences *his reality* to the point of nausea. The Commanville disaster makes him a gift of an unbearable future—penury and dishonor—and, by the same token, like menopause, resurrects and totalizes the past. The imaginary is crushed: no art without "freedom from care"; for five months Gustave lives with his niece "in the condition of people awaiting trial, in mortal and incessant anguish. Each day is a long torment."[78] He is afraid of judiciary liquidation. When it is avoided, the bourgeois dormant in Gustave finds the urgency of this future of unbearable "shame" replaced by the wretched, nauseating future of worries: selling, borrowing, reducing one's style of life. He has little understanding of the alternating hope and disappointment that are now the lot of the Commanvilles, nor is he informed about it; but the ignorance in which he is kept only makes *more real* to him the vague threats he feels hanging over the family. In a word, before the ruin, the future was the lived eternity of Art, scarcely disturbed from time to time by the appearance of a book; now Gustave is without recourse; a fall back into his neurosis might save him, but he will not save his income by plunging into subhumanity. In '44, the vigorous patient had "his whole life before him"; his life: the birth of Art based on the premeditated murder of the real. In '75, it is reality—the most inexorable bourgeois reality, Money—that murders the Artist. As a result, he turns upon that "enclosed" life of his in order to flee from the future into the past, last refuge of the imaginary, but especially because his present adversity is a *conclusion;* he knows quite well that the chips are down, that he is worn out, finished, that nothing now separates him from death but a narrow bed of care. Now real, he contemplates the dream he was *from the point of view of reality.* His entire existence appears to him, *accomplished,* in its poverty—what life is not *poor* for one who turns back to it? That's *all it is,* and it will never be anything else. Indeed, he is fond of writing at this time that he has no more "intellectual future," and in the same letters he calls up his memories with melancholy: "I think of the past, of my childhood, of my youth, of all that will no longer return. I wallow in unbounded melancholy."[79] Reading him, however, we might believe that he is trying to revive former moments of happiness to set against the unlivable present. In a sense, that is not untrue: in 1875, childhood—which he so often cursed—seems to him like a golden age by comparison with his current misfortunes: it was ease, the period of Flaubert honor. In the name of reality he denounces his old, dissipated fits of anger, he discerns their histrionic aspect: no, nothing was that serious. In this sense, if the plunge of January '44 was—among other things—a parricide, the financial ruin, by bringing the whole of his wool-gathering existence into focus,

78. *Correspondance,* 3 (1872–77), Supplement, p. 211.
79. To Turgenev, 3 October 1875, *Correspondance,* 3, Supplément, p. 213.

effects what analysts call the "reconciliation with the father." But when he is being more sincere, with George Sand, for example, he does not conceal the fact that the rare moments of happiness he rediscovers or invents are not the purpose of his search: the goal is to retotalize *completed* existence from the point of view of reality, and this operation endlessly begun anew is not accomplished without profound bitterness. "I walk along the seashore, reflecting on my memories and my sorrows, deploring my ruined life. Then the next day it's the same thing over again."[80] His memories are not cheerful, far from it: he is struck not by the contents of moments gone by but by their character of no-return, which makes this life, which he had wanted to be an *eternal return*, a directed vector, a *real* process of degradation. Above all, whatever his former afflictions, he is struck by the discovery of their futility. A wretched, angry adolescence, a haggard youth half-way between submission and protest, then the great sacrifice and these thirty years of monastic life, all pleasures denied, the monotony of implacable labor, chosen destitution borne without weakness—all that will have been in vain. Something was supposed to come of it that never materialized. And since the intrusion of the real exploded this oneiric existence, Gustave is no longer certain that, even had his austerity produced masterpieces, it was all worth the trouble. He returns to his former doubts: Art is merely an illusion. As long as his private income gave him the option of writing, he counted on his future writings to justify his permanent holocaust. Since external ruin and the ruin within unite to pension him off, one must draw the line, conclude, and there is nothing to conclude but that the worst is certain and that the Devil always wins.

This conclusion overwhelms him, arrests his bitter self-disgust, and substitutes a flood of tears: he weeps for himself because he has no other recourse against the fixed, abstract dryness of despair. I have worked so hard, he keeps saying to himself, I have imposed *such* sacrifices on myself, I have rejected *so many* happy opportunities—for nothing. At this moment, every day, he is choked by pity. Yes, in his room or on the beach at Concarneau, Gustave takes pity on his life: in the light of his misfortunes he discovers in it great merit patiently accumulated in good faith, in the most candid zeal; and he finds unequaled beauty in this noble, truly human enterprise which is swallowed up *without reward*, torpedoed by the bankruptcy of a fool. To succeed, in his eyes, is scarcely meaningful: Maxime succeeds, Gustave does not

---

80. *Correspondance*, 3, Supplément, p. 215.

deign to do so. Failure alone, always foreseen, always aspired to—at least on a certain level—casts its mysterious light on this whole existence for a man who believes he had already left it. An *unmerited* failure whose thundering negation sets in relief the humble, tenacious faith of a man who has lived only to acquire merit even in his awareness that Heaven is empty, that the Devil punishes the deserving, and that the goods of this world are always undeserved. Doesn't such zeal—and such knowledge of its futility—refer, beyond agnosticism and the black pantheism based on Nature's sadism, to a humble, childish piety whose naïveté has resisted nihilism and is justified even as it is snuffed out and pessimism triumphs? This unexpected tenderness in him is nothing other than an awkward attempt *to be loved*. And, because nothing is more difficult for him, he immediately evokes the Other, the Saint who is unaware of himself and is penetrated by divine love; in this figure, through the mediation of God, he has some chance of feeling lovable and of enjoying his hidden being at last. Spontaneously, without hesitation and without the slightest doubt, he sets to work on *La Légende* and keeps at it until it is done. In it, he recounts *his life* as it was lived in the past by a lord of the Middle Ages, and as it always appeared to the supreme Being. He recounts it without omitting his death, because indeed he believes he is about to die. And the kiss of the leper is the supreme test: for the worst is not waging a battle against language in solitude, it is the real, so long held at bay, jumping the Artist like a thief and taking hold of him, depriving him of the power to write; it is the improvidence of a businessman reducing Gustave to having lived fifty years for nothing. Passing the test will be proof that he is "still capable of writing a sentence," that Art is still possible for him when reality triumphs, and that taking this triumph as the chance reason for his ultimate message, he can affirm the preeminence of the imaginary even as he is being engulfed.

When Flaubert sets himself to the task, finally obeying an imperative he gave himself more than thirty years before, he is assured of playing his final card: by executing the order, he suppresses it and, as a result, loses his talisman; in its place will be a book like so many others, the realization of a center of unreality. Then the author will be empty, without security. But these considerations do not stop him: at the precise moment when the game of "Loser wins" becomes impossible, it is fitting to fix it forever in a work that will decree its rule and, even while transforming ludic gratuitousness into aesthetic unreality, will give it the surreality of Art. It is as if, in a single stroke, Flaubert had abandoned his role—on the verge of death or senility, misfortunes he foresees by turns—and projected it outside himself through an act, as though offering up to everyone, beneath a mask, the meaning of his life and affirming—he who is so ill suited to deliver an assertoric judgment—what the truth of this world, and of the other world, *should be*. He divests himself of "Loser wins" by objectifying it: externalized, this game becomes a center of unrealization. After the death of its author, unjustly cast down, it will continue to propose its rule to all its readers. Gustave allows himself to be convinced, one more time, by the fascinating ambiguity of the artistic work as he sees it: it exists, that is certain, with its internal laws and the strict principle of its totalization; hence, what it says *imposes itself* and in a certain way is a determination of being; yet, on the other hand, it is wholly unreal and its fundamental project is to derealize the reader. But who knows, Gustave wonders, if this derealization is not the only sign the supreme Being makes to us in the closed universe of realities? Thus, as he writes *Saint Julien,* he seems both to eternalize a beautiful dream and to deliver, by negating *"beings,"* the great ontological law, the law of love that governs us all. We must chance it and trust to God: *Saint Julien* is the deepest secret of an imaginary soul who tears it from himself suddenly and throws it at random into the stream of life, like a bottle into the sea.

Can it be said that in the years following this realizing divestment Gustave entirely renounces the game of "Loser wins," lacking the means that allowed him to play it? Such a contention would err on two counts: first of all, *Saint Julien* was conceived as a swan song, the cry for help of a poet destined to be swallowed up by the mire of reality. But Flaubert survives, and things turn out tolerably well: he is not deprived of Croisset, he will be able to continue to live his anchorite's life there. Tranquillity—if not alacrity—is restored to him, as well as the possibility of writing: he must *live* this unexpected surcease, and how should he do it, being Flaubert, without reintegrating the *persona* that has become his nature? Just because the author survives, *Saint Julien,* despite its excellence, is no longer that ultimate masterpiece, his testament. It will be followed by other tales, and Gustave will again take up *Bouvard et Pécuchet;* in short, he must write. But how can he write without being an imposter? So he will pursue the game to the end, and we shall find in his correspondence the same complaints, the same doubts, the same terrors as in the period of *Salammbô.* Yet he is less convincing, seems less convinced; obviously, the game bores him. First of all, he has lost the fine, Apollonian omen, *La Légende,* that allowed him to marvel at his destiny by way of the personage—

355

the only named one—of his incarnation. Now he must play in darkness an all-too-familiar role, which worries him. Besides, he is broken by the events of '75: he will not recover from them; the fragile equilibrium between the unreal and reality will never again be recovered. The real has won: Saint Polycarp is merely an old bachelor horribly alone and financially ruined. He knows it; he also thinks this is not a test but the common condition, there is nothing in it that marks his election. He is scarcely enchanted by his glory: it has been sullied, then endlessly contested; "I am embarrassing . . . ," he says. It might be said that the game languishes because there is no longer anything at stake: Gustave is done; if his last book were better than all the others, it would add nothing essential to his glory. Now Flaubert is worth *what he is worth:* he feels that this value, detotalized by the scattering of consciousness, is *unrealizable* but nonetheless assigns him a definitive place in history and reduces him to never being more than that stranger he is for himself. In these final years he knows he must draw the line; he plunges into the past, trying to collect and hold in his hands this life of austerities, *profitable* in spite of everything, neither a success nor a waste. He works, he knocks himself out reading thick, monotonous books he cannot always understand; the dryness of his enterprise repels him. He has been dreaming of it, however, in various forms, from the time of his youth; but after 1875 he is no longer at the peak of his hatred: even misanthropy needs alacrity. Prematurely aged, abandoned by his niece, he needs tenderness and accepts it with gratitude if only it is offered; this is why he loves the gentle Laporte. Despite his obstinacy, he no longer sufficiently believes in what he is doing to go to the trouble of despairing of it in any profound way. "Loser wins" is perpetuated in him discreetly, by force of habit, and because it is necessary to him in his work. But he has no more despair because he has no more hope. There remain a few loves: Laporte, Maupassant, Madame Brainne; and a modest, excruciating sadness. He is cured of the neurosis that held him in its grip for more than thirty years, but at the same time he has lost his character—that is, *his* character, for he was the "actor of himself"—and finds again, after a whole falsified life, the painful defenseless estrangements of his childhood.

At this time we can offer merely provisional conclusions concerning the strategy of this neurosis. It seems clear, in any case, that the rationalized "Loser wins," born of a rather profound intuition of the meaning of the fall at Pont-l'Evêque, was developed to the extreme by

Gustave in a moment of alacrity that I place between June 1844, when the illness subsides, and January 1845, when the first *Education* is being completed. Consequently, as I believe I have shown, he rarely alludes to it, and it is the underlying and original "Loser wins" that explains most of his procedures as an artist. Julien is his man—much more than Jules, about whom we shall speak no further. Let us not imagine, however, that this rationalization was useless: as we have seen, it allowed him for the first time to understand *his* art. Moreover, it is not unthinkable that it remained inside him on a certain level, and that he did not speak of it for fear of the Devil.

At this point we lack two dimensions for understanding Flaubert's illness completely, and we shall now examine them in turn. First, the neurosis is historical and social: it constitutes an objective, dated fact in which the characteristics of a certain society—bourgeois France under Louis-Philippe—are brought together and totalized. In the next volume we shall try to compare it as such with other neuroses to see whether it might not belong to a family of ailments that appeared for the first time in that period. This study will allow us to approach the *artistic movement* around 1850. Second, Gustave's malady expresses in its plenitude what must indeed be called his freedom: what this means we shall understand only at the conclusion of this work, after we have reread *Madame Bovary*.